BREATHLESS DAYS, 1959–1960

SERGE GUILBAUT AND
JOHN O'BRIAN, EDITORS

BREATHLESS DAYS, 1959–1960

Duke University Press Durham and London 2017

Designed by Heather Hensley
Typeset in Garamond Premier Pro by Westchester Publishing Services

Library of Congress Cataloging-in-Publication Data
Names: Guilbaut, Serge, editor. | O'Brian, John, [date–] editor.
Title: Breathless days, 1959–1960 / Serge Guilbaut and John O'Brian, eds.
Description: Durham : Duke University Press, 2017.
Includes bibliographical references and index.
Identifiers: LCCN 2016033436
ISBN 9780822360230 (hardcover)
ISBN 9780822360414 (pbk.)
Subjects: LCSH: Art, Modern—20th century—History and criticism. | Arts,
Modern—20th century. | Arts and society—History—20th century.
Classification: LCC N6493 1959.B74 2017 | DDC 709.04— dc23
LC record availablea th ttps://lccn.loc.gov/2016033436

Cover art: Still from *Breathless* (1960). Courtesy of Photofest. Background:
© Michael Ransburg/Shutterstock.com.

Duke University Press gratefully acknowledges the Social Sciences and
Humanities Research Council of Canada and the Terra Foundation for
American Art, both of which provided funds toward the publication of this
book.

Chapter 1 reproduced from *Cahiers du Cinema*. Published by Cahiers du
Cinema © Cahiers du Cinema SARL.

CONTENTS

ACKNOWLEDGMENTS

Following a productive graduate seminar at the University of British Columbia called "Breathless Days: Art in Europe and Las Americas, 1959–1960," we decided to probe deeper into the pivotal postwar years of 1959 and 1960. Visual artists, filmmakers, writers, and musicians at the time found themselves grappling with a rapidly accelerating world in which the old political orders were fracturing and the threat of nuclear confrontation was rising. The intersecting cultures of Western Europe and the Americas were on the boil.

We are grateful to the Fondation Hartung Bergman, Antibes, for offering to host a three-day symposium on the theme of "breathlessness." "À Bout de Souffle" brought together scholars from Argentina, Canada, Colombia, Cuba, France, and the United States to discuss what was at stake in the transformations under way in 1959–60. The atmosphere at the Fondation was congenial, but the discussions were sometimes tense. We would like to thank Éric de Chassey, Andrea Giunta, Juan A. Gaitán, Jonathan Katz, Hadrien Laroche, Richard Leeman, Régis Michel, Antonio Eligio (Tonel), and Cecile Whiting for their generative insights on the subject. We would also like to thank the staff of the Fondation, in particular François Hers, director at the time, and Bernard Derderian, curator of collections, as well as Hervé Coste de Champeron, Marcelle Driesen, Marianne Le Galliard, and Jean-Luc Uro. They not only provided us with access to the Fondation's remarkable archives but also encouraged a critical approach to art history.

After the Antibes symposium and its attempt to make sense of the two-year period, we realized that more work had to be done. We decided to organize a public forum at the University of British Columbia, Vancouver, which took the shape of a conference accompanied by an online component (and later a web archive) to facilitate the exchange of ideas. We are indebted to all those who participated in the forum, in person or online, and especially those who presented papers that opened up the field of investigation: Bruce Barber, Carla Benzan, Clint Burnham, Jill Carrick, Allison E. Collins, Marcia Crosby, Tom Crow, Blair Davis, Éric de Chassey, Mari Dumett, Aldona Dziedziejko, Steven Harris, Mona Huerta, Hadrien Laroche, Susan Lord, Tom McDonough, Régis Michel, Ann Reynolds, Kjetil Rødje, Tyler Stovall, and Angela Zhang. The conference and its digital extensions received financial support from the university, notably the Department of Art History, Visual Art & Theory and the Faculty of Arts. We also received support from the Social Sciences and Humanities Research Council of Canada (Aid to Research Workshops and Conferences), the Consulat général de France à Vancouver, and Pacific Cinémathèque.

The Morris and Helen Belkin Art Gallery mounted an exhibition during the forum called *Breathless Days 1959–1960: A Chronotropic Experiment*, which explored artistic exchanges between British Columbia and California. Organized by graduate students enrolled in art history and curatorial programs— Carla Benzan, Allison E. Collins, Shaun Dacey, Aldona Dziedziejko, Darrin Martens, and Sarah Todd—it functioned as a case study on the theme. We extend thanks to Scott Watson, director of the Belkin, and to Shelly Rosenblum, curator of academic programs, for their enthusiastic participation in the venture.

Graduate students have been involved in all aspects of the "Breathless" project, including the book. Those in the seminar assisted in the organization of the Vancouver conference and the website. Thanks to Abram Dickerson, Aldona Dziedziejko, Karl Fousek, Asato Ikeda, Matt Lewis, Rebecca Lesser, Fan-Ling Suen, and Angela Zhang, as well as to Bill Matthews for his design expertise. Our greatest thanks are owed to Carla Benzan, who assumed responsibility for countless aspects of the project. She was its star, as it were, its Jean Seberg. We are also grateful to Molleen Shilliday for translating the French contributions to the book into English with elegance and skill, to Eva Tweedie for securing copyright permissions, and to Christopher Pavsek at Simon Fraser University for discussing early Godard with us. Jeff O'Brien was involved in the preparation of all aspects of the book manuscript leading up to its presentation to the publisher. He was Benzan's costar, Belmondo to her Seberg. (If Godard could turn the gangster film inside out in *À bout de souffle*, we can also turn his actors inside out.)

The book benefited from the advice of two anonymous readers of the manuscript. They approved of the book's premise and offered cogent suggestions for making the contents better. Finally, we wish to extend our deep appreciation to those institutions and funding bodies that supported our research: the Art Gallery of Ontario, Toronto; the Brenda and David McLean Chair in Canadian Studies at the University of British Columbia, Vancouver; the Clark Art Institute, Williamstown; the Getty Research Institute, Los Angeles; the Fondation des Etats-Unis, Paris; the Fondation Hartung Bergman, Antibes; the Hampton Research Grant UBC, Vancouver; the Institut national d'histoire de l'art, Paris; the Social Sciences and Humanities Research Council of Canada, Ottawa; and the Terra Foundation for American Art, Chicago.

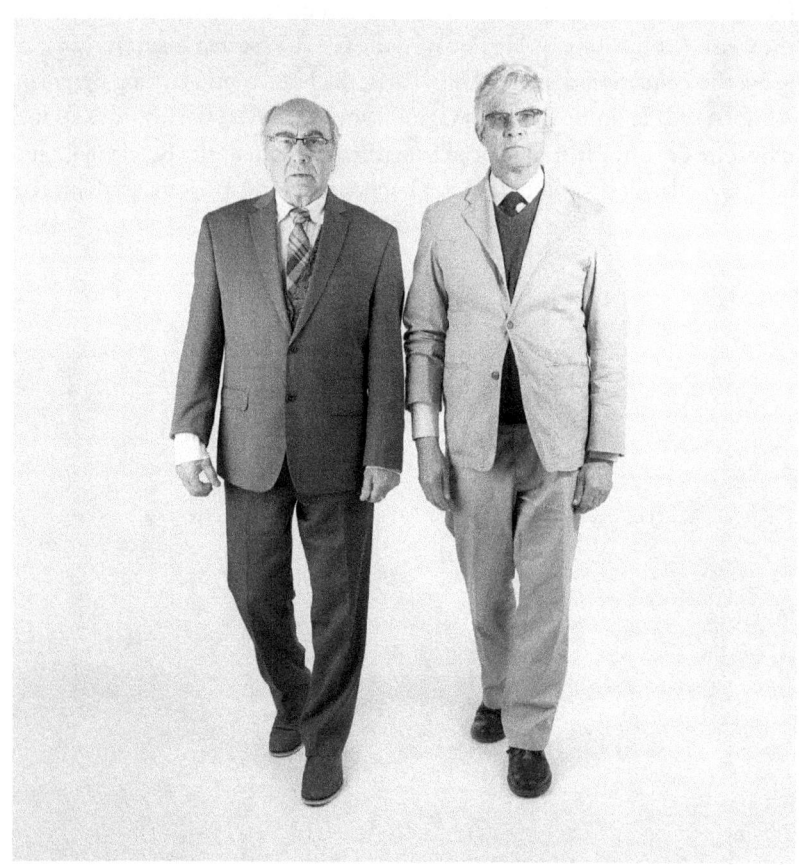

FIGURE I.1 Robert Bos, *Homage to Yves Klein (Coming In)*, 2015. Gelatin silver print. Courtesy of the artist.

Serge Guilbaut and John O'Brian

INTRODUCTION

Patricia to Michel: "I want to know what's behind that mask of yours."
—Jean-Luc Godard, *À bout de souffle*, 1960

If Patricia wanted to know what was behind Michel's mask, *Cahiers du Ci-néma* wanted to know what was behind Godard's *À bout de souffle*. The maga-zine asked Godard during an interview why the critical attitudes expressed in his writings were at odds with his insistence on improvisation in the film. Godard admitted he had improvised while shooting *À bout de souffle* in the late summer of 1959—it "was the sort of film where anything goes," he said—but he also emphasized that he had started with a plan and had stuck to it.[1] Jean-Paul Belmondo and Jean Seberg's dialogue was written, not made up as the film went along. Locations were scouted ahead of time. "What I wanted was to take a conventional story and remake, but differently, everything cin-ema had done. I also wanted to give the feeling that the techniques of film-making had just been discovered or experienced for the first time."[2] The use of a handheld camera as well as sharp jump cuts in the editing contributed to the film's critical success and notoriety. Along with François Truffaut's *The 400 Blows* and Alain Resnais's *Hiroshima mon amour*, Godard's *À bout de souffle* was a message from the present to the future. A general reorganization of art and politics was under way in 1959 and 1960. This book focuses on precisely these years and is written, with the exception of the *Cahiers du Cinéma* interview, from the vantage point of the present moment. "The past is the fiction of the present," Michel de Certeau observed, by which he meant that historians

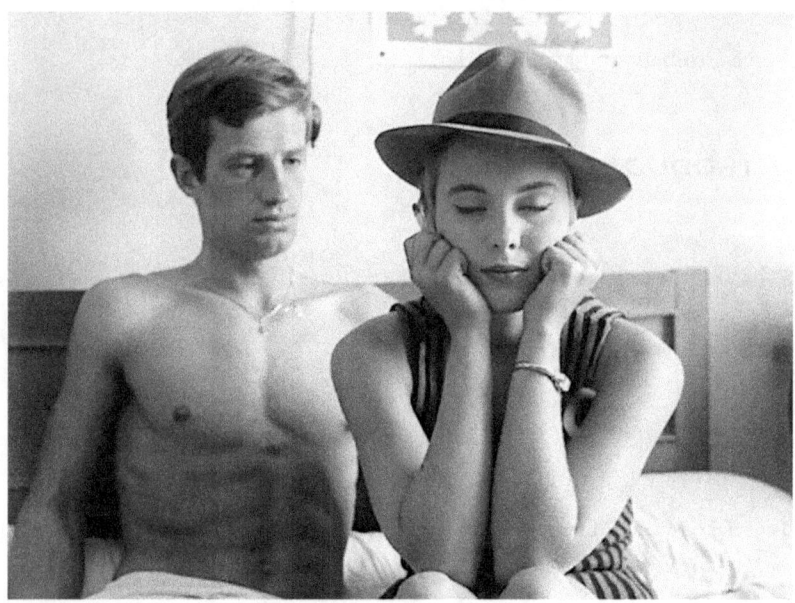

FIGURE I.2 Jean-Luc Godard, *Breathless*, 1960. Publicity still.

turn to earlier epochs to address what they cannot always say about their own time.[3]

À bout de souffle took the gangster film and turned it inside out, making the genre count in new ways. As Godard was preparing to make the film, Buddy Holly died in a plane crash near Clear Lake, Iowa, while on tour in the American Midwest. Fans propelled the song "It Doesn't Matter Anymore" to the top of the pop charts, reversing the message conveyed by the title. His death did matter, and the public response to it reflected the temper of the times. The mood in most Western countries was far more somber than it was nonchalant. After a period of postwar reconstruction, the Cold War had entered a zone of intensifying fear and anxiety. Even President Dwight D. Eisenhower, a five-star general in the United States army during World War II, felt it necessary to warn against the threat of the military-industrial complex to which he was connected.[4]

Fred Kaplan characterized 1959, in a book that took the date for its title, as "the year everything changed."[5] The *Wall Street Journal* called 1959 "an authentic *annus mirabilis*" in a review of the book, but it could just as easily have called it an *annus horribilis*.[6] The invention of the birth-control pill and the microchip, along with cultural developments such as Pop Art and Nouveau

Réalisme, were only half the story; the other half involved the rising threat of nuclear confrontation and the first American casualties in Vietnam. In addition, old political orders were crumbling. Fidel Castro took power in Cuba, and Charles de Gaulle took power in France. Political realignments were the talk of the moment, and cultural redefinition was occurring around the globe, while the hands on the clock of postwar modernity moved faster and faster. During the years 1959 and 1960, visual artists, filmmakers, writers, musicians, and thinkers found themselves grappling with a rapidly accelerating world. The changes left them gasping for air—"breathless."[7]

Looking behind the mask of contemporary scholarship, this book explores how the history of postwar Western art is constructed and written.[8] Writing does more than record history by putting events into words; it *produces* history. The grand narratives of aesthetic and cultural development, from modernism through postmodernism, have lost much of their exegetic power in recent years. The same can be said of national narratives, including Kaplan's monograph on 1959, which concentrates primarily on the United States. Grand narratives and geo-egocentric histories lack the explanatory force of histories that are multipronged. We are therefore interested in providing a heterogeneous account of how culture was produced in different locations under the sign of escalating globalization and of the militarization of everyday life.[9] In *Strange Rebels*, Christian Carryl examines key political events in 1979 and argues the year was more significant than 1989 and the fall of the Berlin Wall that defined it.[10] We are also arguing for the significance of 1959 and 1960, though we stop short of claiming the years eclipsed 1968 in their importance, and for a better understanding of the ideological alliances and frictions between countries and artistic movements.

The chapters collected here excavate a brief period of historical time. They provide thick descriptions of the years 1959 and 1960, in Clifford Geertz's sense of "thick," by drilling down into layers of artistic activity in Western Europe and the Americas.[11] The results resemble those of an archaeological dig—"archaeology of the present" was a catchphrase at the time—sometimes revealing gold and sometimes rubbish, what Clement Greenberg identified as *kitsch* in his 1939 article on the subject.[12] The chapters examine both the gold and the kitsch, what shines and what does not. By focusing on the crucial years of 1959 and 1960, the writers bring to light lateral and often surprising connections between divergent artistic milieus. In the exploration of cross-disciplinary topics on art produced in Western Europe (primarily France and Italy) and the Americas (primarily the United States, Brazil, and Cuba), the goal is to remap the cultural and geopolitical commonalities and differences that define each region and national situation. We want to produce a new critical cartography, a multilayered understanding of a pivotal cultural and political moment during the Cold War.

Another reason for providing a series of focused studies on specific events and works is to unravel the complex layers of signification involved in their production. Marcel Duchamp's *With My Tongue in My Cheek* does not look the same after reading Hadrien Laroche's account of it. Not only are *With My Tongue in My Cheek* and other works analyzed in dialogue with their own period problems, but they are also analyzed as landmarks in the chaos of everyday life. As we see it, the works crystallize historical issues at the same time they address the culture that produced them. In 1959–60, art in Paris, New York, Havana, Milan, and São Paulo was being produced in a proliferation of styles, all of which were jockeying for position with one another. The variety of styles makes sense only if they are understood as having emerged from a cauldron of disagreement that was on high boil. Works of art are always submerged in the antagonisms of their time. They speak it and are spoken by it in a process of becoming. Art not only gives us something to look at but also something to read (perhaps especially something to read).

Cold War scholarship on the decades following World War II has tended to focus on the immediate postwar period from the mid-1940s to the early 1950s and on the revolutionary years of the 1960s. By comparison, studies of 1959 and 1960 are few in number and seem unsure whether they should be looking backward to the 1950s or forward to the 1960s, as if mesmerized by an arbitrary dividing line between the two decades. Instead of marking an end or a beginning, we see the historically decisive period as representing a pivotal moment that speaks to our own times. By engaging in a collaborative examination of political, social, cultural, and aesthetic phenomena, the book shows how new ways of thinking and acting materialized during the timeframe. Eleanor Flexner's 1959 feminist call to arms, *Century of Struggle*—a history of the suffrage movement in the United States—was followed a year later by the Food and Drug Administration's approval of "the pill."[13] At the same time, and not by coincidence, skepticism about binary classifications—straight/ gay, white/black, male/female, colonized/colonizer—and about modernist claims to absolute truth intensified. Changes that occurred during the period anticipated developments in subsequent decades.

January 1, 1959, began with a Cuban bang, and soon after the United States and the international community recognized the newly formed Castro govern-

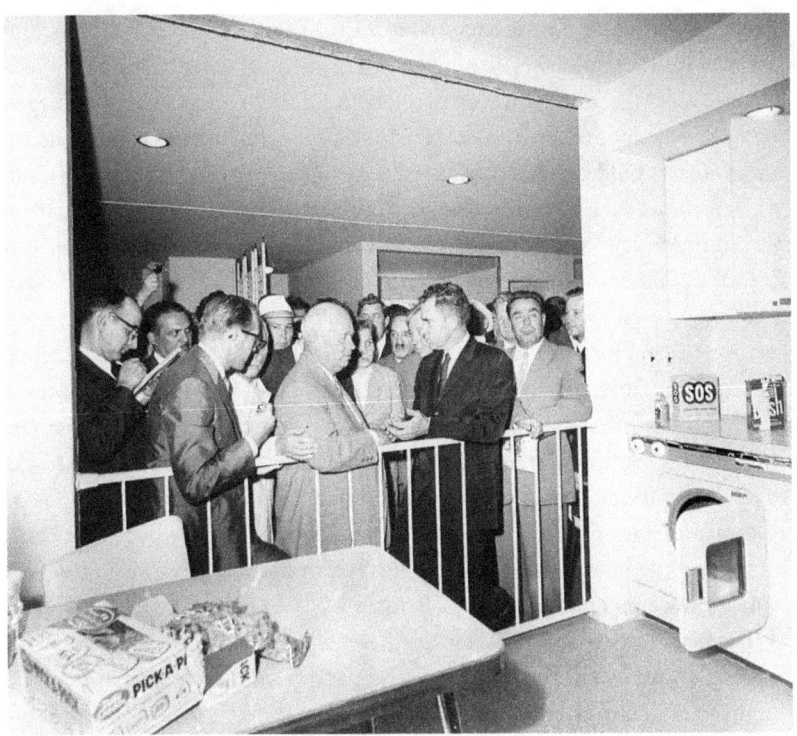

FIGURE I.3 U.S. Vice President Richard Nixon (*center*) and Soviet Premier Nikita Khrushchev (*left center*) are engaged in a discussion as they stand in front of a kitchen display at the United States exhibit at Moscow's Sokolniki Park, July 24, 1959. While touring the exhibit, both men kept up a running debate on the merits of their respective countries. Standing on the right is Khrushchev's deputy, Leonid Brezhnev. AP photo, © 1959 the Associated Press.

ment in Havana. The Cuban revolution had succeeded, and another transformation occurred a week later when Charles de Gaulle was proclaimed president of the new Fifth Republic in France on January 8, thereby replacing a parliamentary government with a presidential system. In Moscow, the famous Kitchen Debate of July 24 between American Vice President Richard Nixon and Soviet Premier Nikita Khrushchev appeared to announce a more relaxed and humorous relationship between the two superpowers, but on September 19 Khrushchev was denied entry to Disneyland, the American dream machine, when security forces declared the Magic Kingdom out of bounds to him. The premier was furious and asked if the United States was keeping "rocket-launching pads there."[14]

Although Western economies continued to expand, Cold War pressures and new political alliances were upsetting traditional ways of seeing and understanding. With the formation of the Fifth Republic, artists in France began to create new models of cultural activity that redefined what cinema, literature, and art could be. They addressed the exigencies of everyday life in Cold War consumer society with a formal inventiveness that challenged traditional procedures. "New" was the operative adjective: *la Nouvelle Vague, le Nouveau Roman, la Nouvelle Génération, le Nouveau Réalisme*. The emergence of *Nouvelle Vague* or New Wave cinema, which was indebted to Italian Neorealism and American cinema, soon became a powerful example for Third Cinema, the anticolonialist and anticapitalist Latin American film movement. Meanwhile, in the United States, while the ethos of Abstract Expressionism and its emphasis on individual freedom was being vigorously exported, Pop Art was starting to critique it. The revival of the American folk movement as a major cultural and political force also dates to the period—the Newport Folk Festival was founded in 1959—and along with jazz opened up new possibilities for reimagining an increasingly complex society.

The new models of art and culture helped to inject Western culture with utopian ideals. Jazz was pivotal in France, and played a key role in how the country set about refashioning its postwar image. As Ludovic Tournès explains in his chapter, jazz was also pivotal in the reconfiguration of boundaries between high and low culture. After being banned by the Nazis during the war, jazz was associated with resistance and subversion and widely celebrated following liberation. Although jazz remained politically and artistically significant, it also ignited a fierce debate. The French felt they had to choose between two types of jazz, traditional New Orleans jazz or the more transient Bebop, and the choice became a major symbolic issue. The practice of New Orleans jazz, considered by many as the "authentic" form, was aesthetically opposed to fast tempo Bebop and Cool jazz, with their intellectual leanings.

The debates around jazz were complicated by France's ambivalence toward the United States. The critics Hughes Panassié, Boris Vian, and Charles Delaunay often characterized the birthplace of jazz as racist and reactionary, pointing to events such as the 1959 beating of Miles Davis by New York City police between sets at the jazz club Birdland. Vian, a major voice in the debate, insisted early on that the French were better able to understand American culture than the Americans because of the supposedly progressive political views and open-mindedness of the French. African American writers such as Richard Wright and James Baldwin were invited to Paris by the

French government, and Duke Ellington and Miles Davis were also accorded official recognition. Public discussion of Miles Davis's interracial affair with the Saint-Germain-des-Prés singer and poet Juliette Gréco revolved around a supposed lack of prejudice exhibited by Parisians. During this period of the Cold War, Paris wished to be seen not only as free-spirited and innovative but also as a center for the appreciation and international distribution of an American art form often discriminated against at home. In the years leading up to his death in France in 1959, the American jazz saxophonist Sidney Bechet became as well known on the French Riviera as Picasso. Bechet's celebrity status reflected not only the significance of jazz in France but also the symbolic battle being fought around it.

John Coltrane's desire to be photographed at the Guggenheim Museum, New York, in front of a painting by the French abstract artist Pierre Soulages was not by chance. Coltrane's selection went against the grain of the American avant-garde who were not only suspicious of "classical" tendencies in contemporary French art but also critical of Frank Lloyd Wright for designing exhibition spaces in the museum that they considered to be dysfunctional. Soulages's *paintings*, Wright's *museum*, and Coltrane's *music* were all engaged in the expression of an intellectual modernity that rejected notions of violence and existential angst. Coltrane wanted nothing to do with the clichés surrounding black jazz as instinctual, archaistic, and close to nature. His music, exemplified by the album *Giant Steps* from 1960, was a fierce manifestation of intellectual freedom in an urban environment that paralleled the controlled rage of the Civil Rights movement. Coltrane's appearance at the Guggenheim in front of a Soulages painting was a clear message that the times were changing.

At first glance, Alex Katz's work of 1959–60 does not appear to have caught the message that the times were shifting. But first appearances are sometimes deceiving. Éric de Chassey argues that while Katz is often designated as proto-Pop given his associations with the world of fashion and consumerism, his work refuses such easy pigeonholing. It is not "proto" anything. To grasp what is distinctive about Katz's work, it is necessary to recognize that his use of photography and cinema paradoxically freed his paintings from considerations of reproduction. Rather than tying the image to the referent, photography and cinema provided Katz with the kind of autonomy he needed to introduce into his work a different kind of reality.

During the race for global hegemony between the United States and the Soviet Union, France succeeded in forging close ties to Latin America in the backyard of the United States. France used its state institutions to reestablish

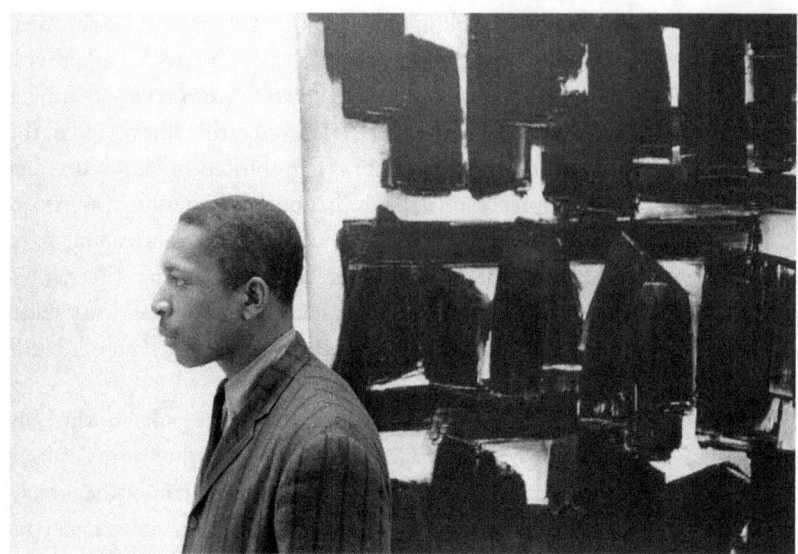

William Claxton, *John Coltrane at the Guggenheim, New York City (in Front of a Painting by Pierre Soulages)*, 1960. Gelatin silver print. Photograph by William Claxton/ Courtesy of Demont Photo Management.

the cultural influence it had wielded in Latin America before the war. Modern art was a particular point of friction between France and the United States in the postwar period. In 1947 the wealthy Brazilian collector Francisco Matarazzo Sobrinho spurned offers from the United States to collaborate on the creation of the São Paulo Museum of Modern Art and chose instead to work mostly with France. At the time, Matarazzo was on the International Council Committee of the Museum of Modern Art, chaired by David Rockefeller. Instead of buying American art for the new museum, Matarazzo purchased French art. The art critic Léon Degand was given responsibility for selecting and transporting across the Atlantic several crates stuffed with modern paintings made in Paris, mainly works of geometric abstraction. At the same time, the future art dealer Leo Castelli was asked to select abstract American paintings for the opening show but after a series of missteps the United States section was canceled and New York artists such as Jackson Pollock and Theodore Stamos were not represented in Brazil.

Degand's emphasis on geometric abstraction helped to introduce a new visual language into a country that was rapidly modernizing, as discussed by Aleca Le Blanc in her chapter on Brasília and the invitation to the International Association of Art Critics to visit the country. As a measure of its influence, the Neoconcrete group in Rio de Janeiro, which included Lygia Clark and Lygia Pape, split in 1959 from the Concrete group in São Paolo, which had developed a distinctive form of geometrically based painting and sculpture. Neoconcrete, which was also indebted to the example of geometric abstraction, wanted to introduce more sensuality into its work. Paris continued its strong relationship with Latin American artists after 1959–60, including those artists who moved to the city to escape authoritarian regimes, and who were involved in transforming geometric abstraction into entertaining Op Art.

In the context of political change in Latin America it is vital to look at Cuba and evaluate the revolutionary euphoria that swept the country in 1959–60. It was a fragile moment. The chapter by Antonio Eligio (Tonel) underscores the diversity of the art that defined revolutionary change while also insisting upon the inextricability of the weave between aesthetics and politics. The first few years of postrevolutionary culture in Cuba are less well known than they ought to be. From the start of the new regime, the art community questioned the socialist dream being offered up for collective consumption. In popularly accessible media such as film, graphic satire, and cartoons, artists addressed the existential difficulties that troubled individual lives in Cuba, while at the same time remaining attuned to international discourses in art, including those of contemporary art. The work of the graphic artist and cartoonist Chago, who had joined the rebels in March 1958, is instructive. His comic strip *Salomón*, which features a confused intellectual, provides a compelling image of the uncertainty that characterized Cuban everyday life immediately after the revolution. When Chago decided to produce a book of satirical drawings a few years later—"humor that makes people think"—it was censored by authorities.[15]

Two major technological developments of the late 1950s and early 1960s, satellite communication and the microchip, became pivotal in the acceleration of transnational flows of information and capital. Following the launch of Sputnik in 1957, and later of the robotically guided missions of the Luna program that began in January 1959, new Soviet space-age technologies produced intense anxiety in the Western world. Developments in culture must be understood in the light of these phenomena, as cultural producers of all kinds had to deal with the repercussions. Several contributors to this book observe that beneath the surface of Western consumerist bliss lay the haunting specter of nuclear confrontation. In 1959–60, fears of atomic annihilation kept families awake. The situation became even more tense when France became a member of the "nuclear club" with the explosion of its first atomic

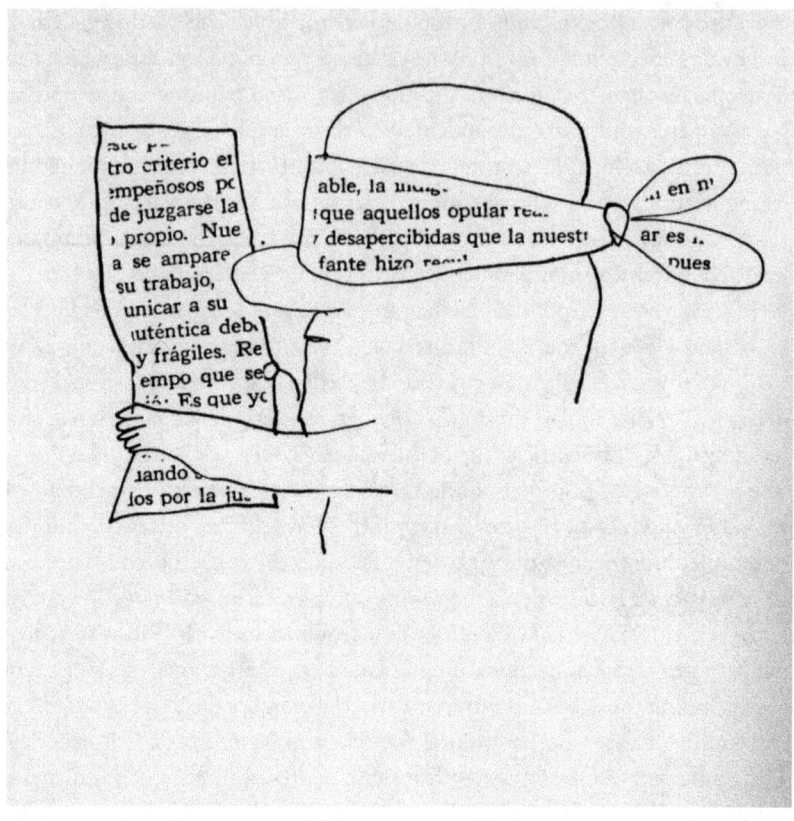

FIGURE 1.5 Chago (Santiago Armada), from the series *El humor otro*. Drawing/collage. Cuban art collection, Museo Nacional de Bellas Artes, Havana, Cuba.

bomb in the Sahara on February 13, 1960, during test Gerboise Bleue (Blue Desert Rat). The use of the Algerian Sahara for the atomic test while the Algerian war was still in progress was, one might say, a bellicose signal from the de Gaulle regime.

"The possibility of doomsday," Hannah Arendt observed in her book *On Violence*, was the sixties generation's "first decisive experience in the world."[16] It was also the first decisive experience of the fifties generation, who practiced Duck and Cover drills in the United States and Canada, watched the film *On the Beach* (1959) at drive-in movie theaters, and participated in antinuclear peace demonstrations. Doomsday scenarios were not unique to the sixties generation. Kjetil Rødje demonstrates how doomsday fears fueled the horror genre in ways tinged with irony and humor in his text on Hollywood

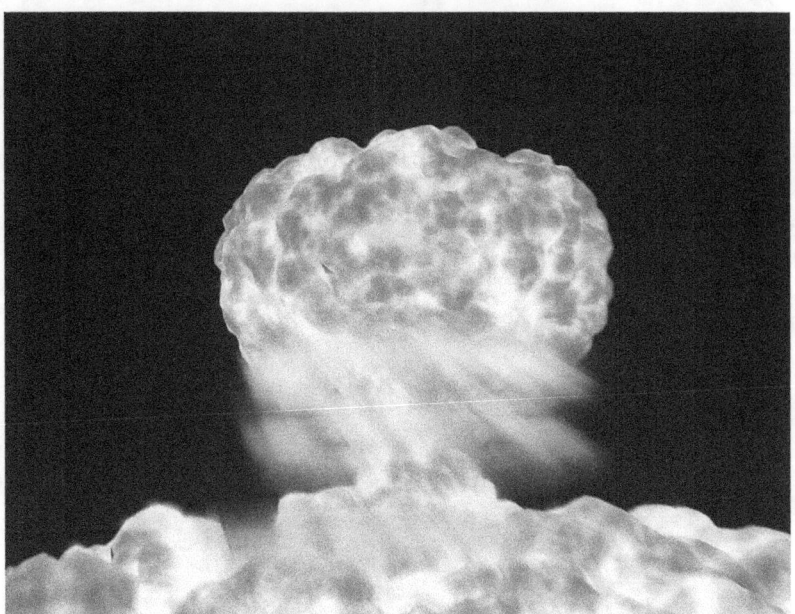

FIGURE I.6 Michael Ransburg, *Gerboise Bleue (French Atomic Explosion in the Sahara)*, 1960. Courtesy of Fotolia.

exploitation films. Taking William Castle's cult thriller *The Tingler* (1959) as a case study, Rødje discusses not only transformations in American filmmaking at the time but also how Hollywood became a mise-en-scène for the unstable American unconscious. In concert with other films by Castle, Vincent Price plays the role of a mad scientist. Price is researching the "physiology of fear" when he finds a parasite in human beings that feeds on the emotion of fear. *The Tingler* is rife with gimmicks, including electric vibrating devices inserted into the seats of theaters where it was screened designed to produce a shivering sensation in the body. Viewers were instructed to scream for their lives when they experienced the vibrations—to violently wake up, as it were, from the American Dream. Although some artists of the time were representing the atomic age with subtlety and sophistication—the film *Hiroshima mon amour* by Alain Resnais, the Auto-Destructive art of Gustav Metzger, and the book *A Canticle for Leibowitz* by Walter M. Miller Jr. all appeared in 1959—Castle deployed crude techniques to agitate spectators accustomed to the passivity of television. The film literally propelled viewers out of their seats and forced them to respond to their fears. At the end of the movie, as

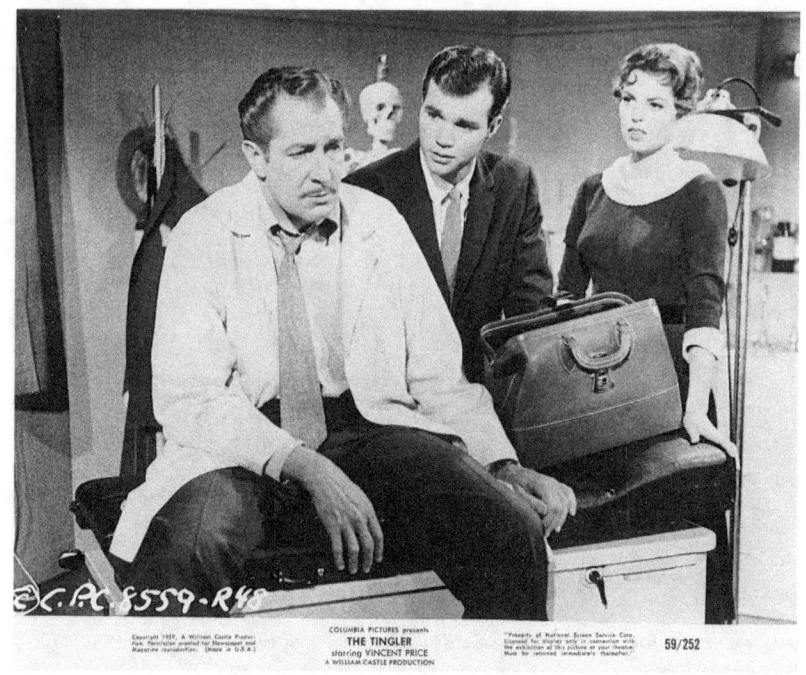

FIGURE 1.7 William Castle, *The Tingler*, 1959. Publicity still.

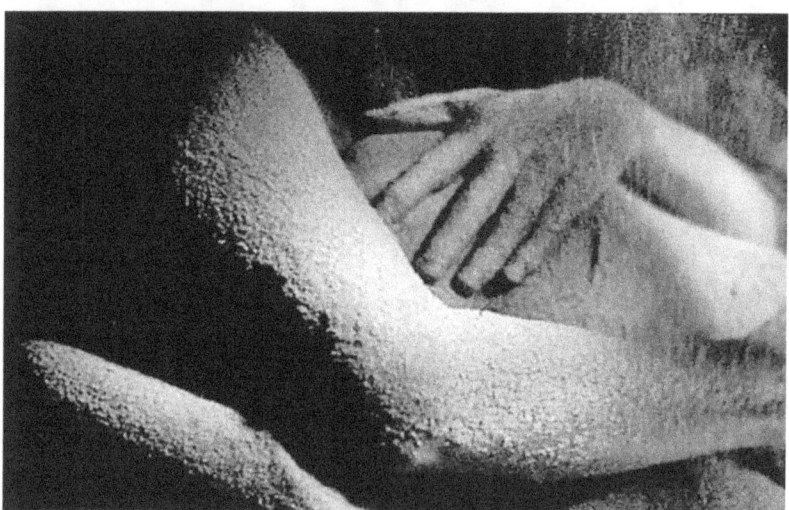

FIGURE 1.8 Alain Resnais, *Hiroshima mon amour*, 1959. Publicity still.

audiences were getting ready to leave, a strange cloud invaded the space of the theater. The cloud was a primal reminder that a miasma of radioactivity could arrive in their midst at any time. From high to low, from Resnais to Castle, the mushroom cloud was inescapable.

Gustav Metzger and other visual artists rendered doomsday symbolically. In 1959 Metzger began producing Auto-Destructive art in London by spraying acid on stretched nylon surfaces while audiences were invited to watch the action paintings consume themselves. The work relates to the slashed paintings of Lucio Fontana, the fire paintings and "Anthropometries" of Yves Klein, the shooting paintings by Niki de Saint Phalle, and the self-destroying machines of Jean Tinguely. Metzger feared the possibility of nuclear war; Auto-Destructive art, he argued, was a political weapon against the social systems that made atomic weapons thinkable.

Allen Ginsberg's poems "Howl" and "America," which were written in the midfifties, struck a particular chord with young socially conscious American audiences in the period under discussion. These audiences were no longer prepared to smile and leave it to Beaver. They wanted to hear Ginsberg read in person and to listen to his refusals of nuclear insanities as well as to his frank presentation of homosexuality. "Listening to the crack of doom on the hydrogen jukebox," they identified with the anxiety and anger in the poems.[17] Along with Jack Kerouac's *On the Road* (1957) and William S. Burroughs's *Naked Lunch* (1959), "Howl" and "America" are defining works of the Beat movement. In his chapter for this volume, Clint Burnham discusses *Naked Lunch*, which was published in Paris while the author was living at the Beat Hotel in the Latin Quarter, in relationship to *Seminar VII*, which was delivered a few kilometers away by Jacques Lacan over the course of several months in 1959–60. Like the authors themselves, both of whom had a penchant for scandal, the book and the seminar were sharply at odds with conventional wisdom and mores, including the admonition to love one's neighbor. "The neighbor remains an inert, impenetrable, enigmatic presence that hystericizes me," declared Lacan.[18] Burroughs was no more inclined to normalize the concept of the neighbor than Lacan, whether it was in the form of the family next door or of Cold War nations facing off against one another. What is horrible in our neighbor, Lacan and Burroughs concluded in their separate ways, is also horrible in us.

The Beat movement was quickly transformed by the mass media into a trendy avant-garde. It was analyzed, dissected, and criticized in magazine articles such as "The Beat Mystique" in *Playboy* (February 1958), by Herbert

Gold; "The Philosophy of the Beat Generation" in *Esquire* (March 1958), by Jack Kerouac; and books such as *The Holy Barbarians* (1959), by Lawrence Lipton. It even became fashionable to rent a Beatnik to attend select parties for a fee of forty dollars a night, according to a report in *Life* magazine.[19] Fred McDarragh, a photographer who specialized in the Beat scene, came up with the idea, and *Mad* magazine countered with a proposal to rent a "Square" for Beatnik parties, complete with polka dot bow tie, white-on-white shirt, blue serge suit, and saddle shoes.[20] Meanwhile, *The Subterraneans* (1960), a movie based loosely on the novella of the same name by Kerouac, trivialized both the book and Beatnik life. Beatniks were becoming last week's news and being supplanted by a different type of cultural formation, fueled by consumerist desires and demands. The 1958 film *Les tricheurs* by Marcel Carné represents a heroine, Pascale Petit, who desires a Jaguar sports car so much that she is prepared to sacrifice what she loves for it. The film is a parable of logo culture, in which the automobile as the ultimate sign of postwar modernity kills the person who wants it most. *Les tricheurs* became a symbol of freedom and sexual liberation for a generation of French adolescents attracted not only to fast cars but also to the jazz sound track featuring Roy Eldridge, Stan Getz, Dizzy Gillespie, Coleman Hawkins, and Buddy Rich. A decade earlier, Simone de Beauvoir had published *The Second Sex*, an analysis of the oppression of women that anticipated the theatricalization of female sexual freedom in films starring Pascale Petit, Françoise Sagan, and Brigitte Bardot.

During the long period of reconstruction following World War II, Paris worked hard to restore its image as the universal art city. The problem, as discussed by Richard Leeman in his chapter, was that the French art establishment improperly evaluated the cultural changes occurring in the Western world. Paris tried to reconstruct its image based on prewar values, on the reputations of contemporary old masters such as Pablo Picasso and Henri Matisse, without exhibiting younger artists in its museums and without understanding the challenge posed by New York. The French were stubborn when confronting the United States, as stubborn as the comic-book hero Asterix in his confrontations with Roman power. The first episode of *Asterix* was published in the magazine *Pilote* in October 1959 and rapidly became the humorously self-critical symbol of France—a new France, but still a France unable to shake off some of its old clichés.

After the American Mark Tobey won the International Grand Prize at the Venice Biennale in 1958, Will Grohmann wrote in *Der Tagesspiegel* that "the unwavering fortress of the French school was shaken."[21] Two years later, how-

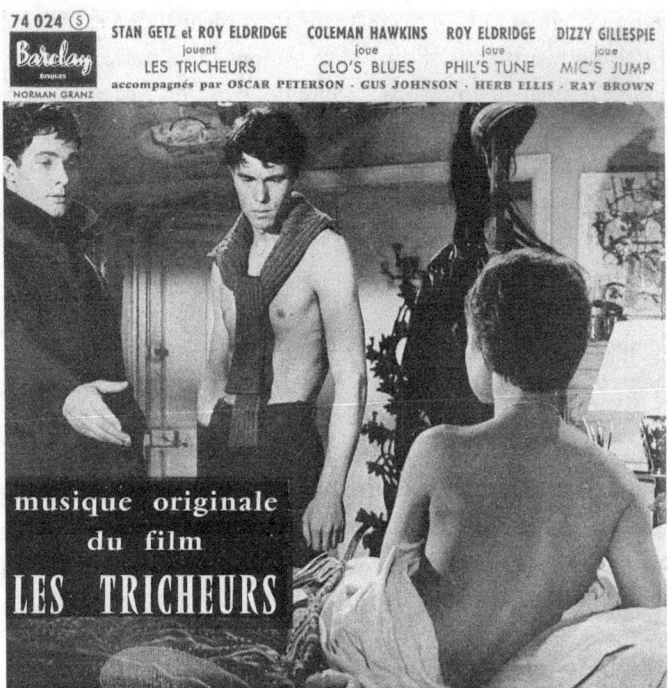

FIGURE 1.9 Jazz at the Philharmonic, *Les tricheurs* (sound track from the film), Barclay, 1958–59.

ever, the Venice prize was divided between Jean Fautrier and Hans Hartung, who was working in France. This permitted the French to believe that they were still running the show. They failed to see how rapidly the world and international communications were changing. While contemporary American art had been shown in Paris during the fifties—Jackson Pollock's black-and-white paintings had been exhibited, for example, at Studio Paul Facchetti in 1952—it was not until the end of the decade that American art flooded into Europe. The second iteration of Documenta in Kassel, organized by Arnold Bode and Werner Haftmann in 1959, was devoted exclusively to American abstract painting, and in the same year two exhibitions, *Jackson Pollock* and *The New American Painting* organized by the Museum of Modern Art, New York, in conjunction with the U.S. State Department, toured Europe. Leeman describes the exhibitions as a "war machine" in the battle for cultural ascendancy.

In an effort to counteract the weakness of the French art establishment, André Malraux, the French Minister of Culture, joined with the writer and curator Raymond Cogniat in 1959 to create the Paris Biennale, an exhibition restricted to artists under the age of thirty-five. Among the American participants was Robert Rauschenberg, whose "combine" painting *Talisman* made such a strong impression on the writer Alain Jouffroy that Jouffroy concluded traditional painting had become "anachronistic, paltry and pathetically out of touch."[22] Pierre Restany, who coined the term *Nouveau Réalisme* in response to American Pop Art and Neo-Dada, half-jokingly titled an article in *Cimaise* "U.S. Go Home and Come Back Later."[23]

Notwithstanding ongoing reservations in France about American influence, Rauschenberg and Jasper Johns, Leo Castelli's "enfants terribles," helped to forge better connections between Paris and New York by befriending Jean Tinguely and Niki de Saint Phalle. Mari Dumett discusses the relationship of the artists in her chapter. She observes that Peter Selz, then curator of painting and sculpture at the Museum of Modern Art, was the American commissioner of the Paris Biennale, where he met Tinguely and saw his gas-powered drawing machine *Meta-matic No. 17* in action. Like Rauschenberg's combine, Tinguely's machine dispensed with the strict boundaries of medium being insisted upon by Greenberg, whose version of modernism was represented at the biennale by the paintings of Helen Frankenthaler. *Meta-matic No. 17* was also humorous, attracting large crowds. Selz invited Tinguely to make a work, which the artist subsequently titled *Homage to New York*. It was a motorized sculpture fashioned from junkyard detritus that performed its own annihilation in front of a surprised audience in the sculpture garden at the Museum of Modern Art in March 1960. Rauschenberg participated in the project at the invitation of Tinguely by inserting a small money-throwing machine into the sculpture that derisively fired silver dollars at the onlookers.

Tinguely and Rauschenberg were both engaged in redefining notions of art by putting audience participation at the heart of the production. Hollywood films also promoted audience participation and, in a related but different way, so did the *nouveau roman*. The nouveau roman provided readers with a new type of freedom in literature, a way to use the text as a form of self-examination, as a detonator of change. Luc Lang points to the novels *La jalousie* (*Jealousy*) by Alain Robbe-Grillet and *La modification* (*A Change of Heart*) by Michel Butor as proposing a literature not only open to interpretation but also capable of activating an interrogation of the reader's life. In *La modification,* Butor recounts a seemingly banal story of a man traveling by train from Paris to Rome in search of change in his personal life, and in the process makes the reader a participant in the protagonist's transformation.

The reader is invited to think through the issues, not just read about them. Along with the protagonist, the reader is asked to reevaluate his or her life during the course of the twenty-two-hour train trip and the series of mini-events that occur along the way. According to Butor, the mini-events function like atomic bombs that liberate energy to reveal startling viewpoints previously hidden from view. By actively participating in the discoveries, the reader—like the protagonist of the novel—engages in a *prise de conscience*, a raising of consciousness. Reading and looking would never be quite the same again. From erudite novels to visual art to popular films like *The Tingler*, readers and viewers were being destabilized and transformed by means of self-critical astonishment.

Tom McDonough explains the renewed importance of Francis Picabia for advanced art in Paris, Milan, and New York during 1959–60. Younger artists searching for models of social and aesthetic subversion were attracted to Picabia's Dadaist and Surrealist legacy. They saw his work as part of a larger critique of consumerist culture, an attack avant la lettre on the *société du spectacle*, the term coined by Guy Debord in 1957 to describe the rapidly changing circumstances of postwar capitalism. The effects of an accelerating consumer culture were being more and more discussed by the press, which often blamed the United States for the new developments. Debord's films, including *On the Passage of a Few Persons through a Rather Brief Unity of Time* (1959), are instances of cinematic *détournement*. The strategy of subverting an image by placing it in a different context from that of the original, from which different context it draws meaning, was first articulated during the midfifties in Brussels by Debord's colleague, the poet Marcel Marien.[24] Debord's films are Situationist critiques of spectacular society. Although his achievement rests primarily in theoretical and political writing, the filmmaker and the artist cannot be separated out from the writer.[25]

In 1959–60 Cold War anxieties were bound up with a desire for extrication from ideology. They were also bound up with a stage in the development of mass consumption in which the ideal citizen had become conflated with the ideal purchaser.[26] At the core of every sustained critique of Western consumerism were concerns about the pacification of everyday life and its consequences. As was also the case with Pop Art, Jill Carrick observes, most contemporary commentators on the Nouveaux Réalistes interpreted their work as an engagement with the allure and abundance of commodity culture. The French art critic Pierre Restany publicized the Nouveaux Réalistes by mounting exhibitions and writing manifestoes, commenting on their presentation of objects drawn from the everyday, and in the process helped to inject new vitality into the Paris art world. He also helped to unite a group of artistic personalities as different as Arman, Yves Klein, Martial Raysse, Daniel Spoerri, and Jean Tinguely. Restany was hunting for symbols—some would say hunting for logos—of a new society. He described the work of the Nouveaux Réalistes as "transparent" and optimistic.[27] In contrast to this strangely upbeat interpretation of an avant-garde movement functioning within bourgeois society, Carrick observes that many of the accumulations of objects displayed by Arman and others were taken from stockpiles of outmoded goods, suggesting loss and melancholy. Her reevaluation connects the work of the Nouveaux Réalistes to issues such as the Holocaust that were still difficult to address in 1960.[28] Régis Michel's chapter, which begins with Klein's leap into the void and Godard's obsession with it, moves in a different direction from Carrick's analysis. Acutely aware of the corruption of the art market and of the exploitation of images addressed by Debord, Michel identifies an iconoclastic trend in European art that was theatrical. "Klein's heritage passes through the *theater*," he observes. The leap made by Klein in Fontenay-aux-Roses parallels the rupturing of conventional cinematic syntax—*À bout de souffle*. Godard's jump-cut editing forces the narrative of the film to explode and gasp for breath. The leap and the film are the opposite of spectacle in their refusal of a society dominated by consumerism and the marketplace. Against accumulation, Klein and Godard opt for erasure.

The questions raised by Picabia, Tinguely, Klein, and Godard about consumer culture and the reification of the art object are, of course, present in works by other artists engaged in reframing art as a philosophical activity central to everyday life. Carla Benzan discusses Piero Manzoni's "meta-artistic commodity critique" following his break in 1959 from the *arte nucleare* movement founded earlier in the decade by Enrico Baj and Sergio Dangelo. At this transitional moment, Manzoni wanted to escape being boxed in and was looking for larger intellectual space in which to work. He wanted to be able to mediate the complexity of the times with irreverence, humor, and any other strategy that seemed productive. His attacks on visual convention and the commodity, as described by Benzan, walked a fine line between utopic and dystopic positions.

The line drawn by Marcel Duchamp, Hadrien Laroche observes, was between Paris and New York. By the time he produced his three-dimensional play on words titled *With My Tongue in My Cheek* (1959), which is the primary focus of Laroche's chapter, Duchamp's work was undergoing critical reappraisal on both sides of the Atlantic for the way it had transformed the art object and ideas about art. Duchamp recognized the significance of the audience's share in a work of art, the spectator's participatory role in its completion. "The creative act is not performed by the artist alone," Duchamp stated in 1957. "The spectator brings the work in contact with the external world by deciphering and interpreting its inner qualifications and thus adds his contribution to the creative act."[29] Duchamp deployed deconstructive humor and irony to engage the spectator in his work, which is evident in *With My Tongue in My Cheek* on several levels while also revealing the workings of the art market.

The reorganization of art and politics that was under way in 1959–60, and the speed with which it was occurring, caused Duchamp to put his tongue in his cheek. It is still there. That is one reason why the period we are addressing in this book still seems contemporary. In our present time of permanent war and democratic decay, of financial crisis and the spectacularization of art, of successful tax revolts and not-so-successful spring revolutions, we find ourselves, once again, breathless.

Notes

Finding neither the introduction to this volume nor the chapter on Yves Klein by Régis Michel to his taste, the owner of the Klein archives denied permission to reproduce the artist's work. We have replaced two of the censored images with photographs taken by Robert Bos. They are intended as a homage, with a nod to Gilbert and George, to the in/out/ying/yang qualities of Klein's *In the Void Room*. Another replacement image was pulled from our own archives. It was made at the Tourcoing lycée by a student in 1959, a year before Klein's leap, and flies in the face of copyright oppression.

1. Jean-Luc Godard, "Interview with Jean-Luc Godard," *Cahiers du Cinéma* 138 (December 1962), trans. and ed. Jean Narboni and Tom Milne, in *Godard on Godard: Critical Writings by Jean-Luc Godard* (London: Secker and Warburg, 1972), 173. Reprinted in part in the current book as chapter 1. Page numbers refer to the 1972 version.

2. Godard, "Interview with Jean-Luc Godard," 173.

3. Michel de Certeau, *The Writing of History*, trans. T. Conley (New York: Columbia University Press, 1988), 10.

4. Eisenhower's "Farewell Address to the Nation" was written in 1960 and delivered on January 17, 1961. See Charles Griffin, "New Light on Eisenhower's Farewell Address," *President Studies Quarterly* 22 (summer 1992): 469–79.

5. Fred Kaplan used the phrase as the subtitle for *1959: The Year Everything Changed* (Hoboken, NJ: Wiley, 2009).

6. Edward Kosner, "When the World Tilted—Again," *Wall Street Journal*, June 15, 2009.

7. Kristin Ross also uses the word *breathless* to describe the period. French postwar modernization, she states, was "headlong, dramatic, and breathless." Kristin Ross, *Fast Cars, Clean Bodies: Decolonization and the Reordering of French Culture* (Cambridge, MA: MIT Press, 1995), 4.

8. This book emerged from focused workshops that took place in France and Canada. The first workshop occurred at La Fondation Bergman Hartung in Antibes in 2009, and the second at the University of British Columbia in Vancouver in 2010, with scholars from Europe, North America, Cuba, and Argentina.

9. Laura McEnany, *Civil Defense Begins at Home: Militarization Meets Everyday Life in the Fifties* (Princeton, NJ: Princeton University Press, 2000).

10. Christian Carryl, *Strange Rebels: 1979 and the Birth of the 21st Century* (New York: Basic, 2013).

11. Clifford Geertz, "Thick Description: Towards an Interpretive Theory of Culture," in *The Interpretation of Culture: Selected Essays* (New York: Basic, 1973), 3–30, used "thick description" to explain not only human behavior but also the context for it.

12. "Memory is not an instrument for surveying the past, but its theater," observed Walter Benjamin, "just as the earth is the medium in which dead cities lie buried. He who seeks to approach his own buried past must conduct himself like a man digging." Walter Benjamin, *Berlin Childhood around 1900* (Cambridge, MA: Harvard University Press, 1996), xii. See also Clement Greenberg, "Avant-Garde and Kitsch" (1939), reprinted in *The Collected Essays and Criticism*, vol. 1, *Perceptions and Judgments, 1939–1944*, ed. John O'Brian (Chicago: University of Chicago Press, 1986), 5–22.

13. Eleanor Flexner, *Century of Struggle: The Woman's Rights Movement in the United States* (Cambridge, MA: Harvard University Press, 1959).

14. Matthew Farish, *The Contours of America's Cold War* (Minneapolis: University of Minnesota Press, 2010), xi.

15. Lisandro Otero, foreword to *El humor otro*, by Chago (Havana: Revolución, 1963), 6–7. Unless otherwise noted, all translations are ours.

16. Hannah Arendt, *On Violence* (San Diego: Harcourt Brace, 1970), 17.

17. Allen Ginsberg, "Howl," in *Collected Poems, 1947–1997* (New York: HarperCollins, 2006).

18. Jacques Lacan, *The Seminar of Jacques Lacan*, book VII, *The Ethics of Psychoanalysis, 1959–1960*, trans. Dennis Porter (New York: W. W. Norton, 1997), 141.

19. "Beats: Sad but Noisy Rebels," *Life* magazine, November 30, 1959.

20. *Village Voice*, June 16, 1960.

21. Will Grohmann, *Der Tagesspiegel*, September 7, 1958.

22. Alain Jouffroy, *Une révolution du regard: À propos de quelques peintres et sculpteurs contemporains* (Paris: Gallimard, 1964), 193.

23. Pierre Restany, "U.S. Go Home and Come Back Later," *Cimaise*, series 6, no. 3 (January–February–March 1959): 36–37.

24. See *Les Lèvres Nues*, the magazine edited by Marcel Marien from April 1954 to September 1958.

25. Bruce Barber, "The Artist Manqué: The Case of Guy Debord," unpublished essay provided by the author.

26. Lizabeth Cohen, *A Consumer's Republic: The Politics of Mass Consumption in Postwar America* (New York: Vintage, 2004).

27. Pierre Restany, "À 40° au-dessus de Dada," in *1960: Les Nouveaux Réalistes* (Paris: MAM/Musée d'Art Moderne de la Ville de Paris, 1986), 267.

28. Benjamin Buchloh discusses the "collective disavowal of the immediate historical past" at this time in "Plenty or Nothing: From Yves Klein's *Le Vide* to Arman's *Le Plein*," in *Premises: Invested Spaces in Visual Arts, Architecture, and Design from France, 1958–1998* (New York: Guggenheim Museum, 1998), 88.

29. Marcel Duchamp, "The Creative Act" (1957), reprinted in *Theories and Documents of Contemporary Art*, ed. Kristine Stiles and Peter Selz (Berkeley: University of California Press, 1996), 819.

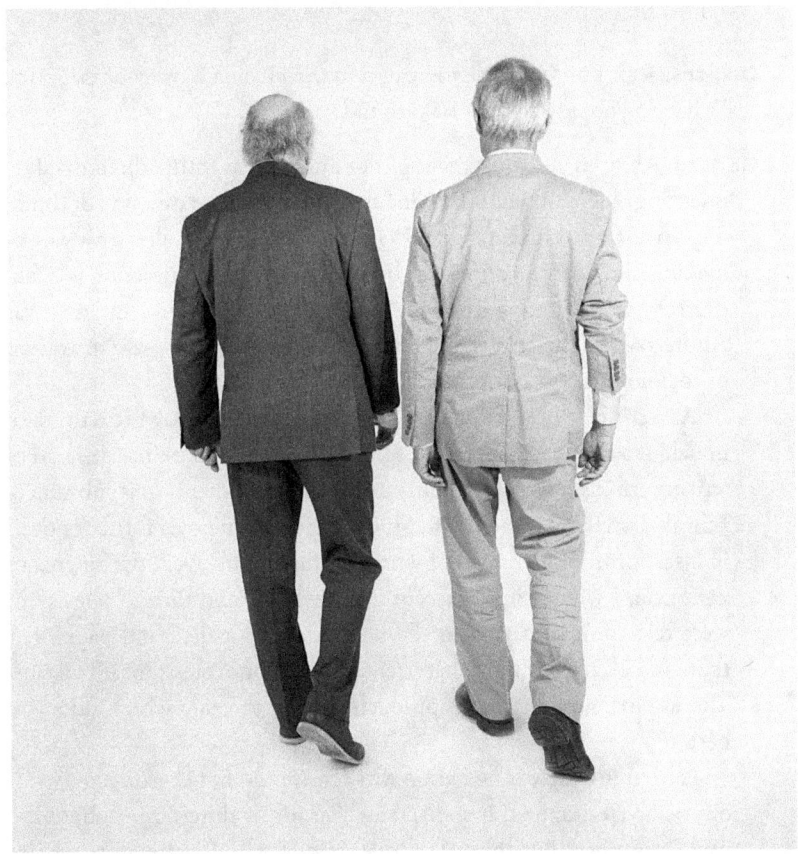

FIGURE I.10 Robert Bos, *Homage to Yves Klein (Leaving)*, 2015. Gelatin silver print. Courtesy of the artist.

CAHIERS DU CINÉMA INTERVIEW

Cahiers: Jean-Luc Godard, you came to the cinema by way of criticism. What do you owe to this background?

Godard: All of us at *Cahiers* thought of ourselves as future directors. Frequenting ciné-clubs and the Cinémathèque was already a way of thinking cinema and thinking about cinema. Writing was already a way of making films, for the difference between writing and directing is quantitative not qualitative. The only complete hundred-per-cent critic was André Bazin. The others—Sadoul, Balasz or Pasinetti—are historians or sociologists, not critics.

As a critic, I thought of myself as a film-maker. Today I still think of myself as a critic, and in a sense I am, more than ever before. Instead of writing criticism, I make a film, but the critical dimension is subsumed. I think of myself as an essayist, producing essays in novel form or novels in essay form: only instead of writing, I film them. Were the cinema to disappear, I would simply accept the inevitable and turn to television; were television to disappear, I would revert to pencil and paper. For there is a clear continuity between all forms of expression. It's all one. The important thing is to approach it from the side which suits you best.

I also think there is no reason why one should not be a director without being a critic first. It so happens that for us things came about the way I described, but this isn't a rule. In any case, Rivette and Rohmer made 16mm films. But if criticism was a first rung on the ladder, it was not simply a means. People say we made use of criticism. No. We were thinking cinema and at a certain moment we felt the need to extend that thought.

Criticism taught us to admire both Rouch and Eisenstein. From it we learned not to deny one aspect of the cinema in favour of another. From it we also learned to make films from a certain perspective, and to know that if something has already been done there is no point in doing it again. A young author writing today knows that Molière and Shakespeare exist. We were the first directors to know that Griffith exists. Even Carné, Delluc and René Clair, when they made their first films, had no real critical or historical background. Even Renoir had very little; but then of course *he* had genius.

Cahiers: Only a fraction of the Nouvelle Vague have this sort of cultural equipment.

Godard: Yes, the *Cahiers* group, but for me this fraction is the whole thing. There's the *Cahiers* group (along with Uncle Astruc, Kast and—a little apart—Leenhardt), to which should be added what one might call the Left Bank group:[1] Resnais, Varda, Marker. And there is Demy. They had their own cultural background. But that's about the lot. The *Cahiers* group were the nucleus.

People say we can no longer write about our colleagues. Obviously it becomes difficult having a coffee with someone if that afternoon you have to write that he's made a silly film. But the thing that has always distinguished *Cahiers* from the rest is our principle of laudatory criticism: if you like a film, you write about it; if you don't like it, don't bother with tearing it to pieces. One need only stick to this principle. So, even if one makes films oneself, one can still say that so-and-so's film is brilliant— *Adieu Philippine*,[2] for instance. Personally I prefer to say so elsewhere than in *Cahiers*, because the important thing is to lead the profession round to a new way of thinking about the cinema. If I have the money, I prefer to pay for a page in a trade paper to talk about *Adieu Philippine*. There are people better qualified than me to talk about it in *Cahiers*.

Cahiers: Your critical attitude seems to contradict the idea of improvisation which is attached to your name.

Godard: I improvise, certainly, but with material which goes a long way back. Over the years you accumulate things and then suddenly you use

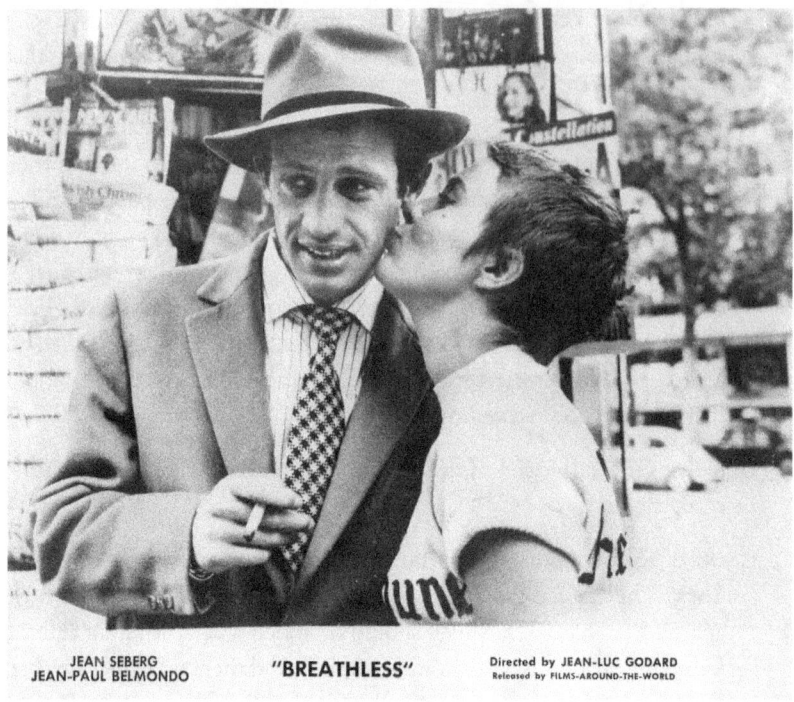

JEAN SEBERG
JEAN-PAUL BELMONDO   **"BREATHLESS"**   Directed by JEAN-LUC GODARD
Released by FILMS-AROUND-THE-WORLD

FIGURE 1.1 Jean-Luc Godard, *Breathless*, 1960. Publicity still.

them in what you're doing. My first shorts were prepared very carefully and shot very quickly. *À bout de souffle* began this way. I had written the first scene (Jean Seberg on the Champs-Elysées), and for the rest I had a pile of notes for each scene. I said to myself, this is terrible. I stopped everything. Then I thought: in a single day, if one knows how to go about it, one should be able to complete a dozen takes. Only instead of planning ahead, I shall invent at the last minute. If you know where you're going it ought to be possible. This isn't improvisation but last-minute focusing. Obviously, you must have an over-all plan and stick to it; you can modify up to a point, but when shooting begins it should change as little as possible, otherwise it's catastrophic.

I read in *Sight and Sound* that I improvised Actors' Studio fashion, with actors to whom one says "You are so-and-so; take it from there." But Belmondo never invented his own dialogue. It was written. But the actors didn't learn it: the film was shot silent, and I cued the lines.

Cahiers: When you began the film, what did it mean to you?

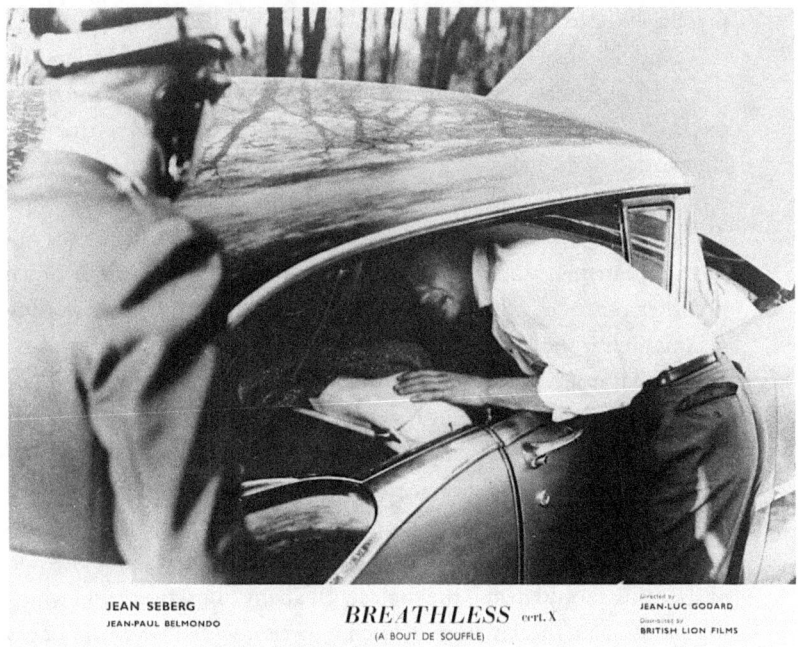

JEAN SEBERG
JEAN-PAUL BELMONDO

BREATHLESS cert. X
(A BOUT DE SOUFFLE)

Directed by
JEAN-LUC GODARD
Distributed by
BRITISH LION FILMS

FIGURE 1.2 Jean-Luc Godard, *Breathless*, 1960. Publicity still.

Godard: Our first films were all *films de cinéphile*—the work of film enthusiasts. One can make use of what one has already seen in the cinema to make deliberate references. This was true of me in particular. I
thought in terms of purely cinematographic attitudes. For some shots I
referred to scenes I remembered from Preminger, Cukor, etc. And the
character played by Jean Seberg was a continuation of her role in *Bon-
jour Tristesse*. I could have taken the last shot of Preminger's film and
started after dissolving to a title, "Three Years Later." This is much the
same sort of thing as my taste for quotation, which I still retain. Why
should we be reproached for it? People in life quote as they please, so
we have the right to quote as we please. Therefore I show people quoting, merely making sure that they quote what pleases me. In the notes I
make of anything that might not be of use for a film, I will add a quote
from Dostoyevsky if I like it. Why not? If you want to say something,
there is only one solution: say it.

Moreover, *À bout de souffle* was the sort of film where anything goes:
that was what it was all about. Anything people did could be integrated
in the film. As a matter of fact, this was my starting-point. I said to

myself: we have already had Bresson, we have just had *Hiroshima*, a certain kind of cinema has just drawn to a close, maybe ended, so let's add the finishing touch, let's show that anything goes. What I wanted was to take a conventional story and remake, but differently, everything the cinema had done. I also wanted to give the feeling that the techniques of film-making had just been discovered or experienced for the first time. The iris-in showed that one could return to the cinema's sources; the dissolve appeared, just once, as though it had just been invented. If I used no other processes, this was in reaction against a certain kind of film-making; but it should not be made a rule. There are films in which they are necessary; and sometimes they should be used more frequently. There is a story about Decoin[3] going to see his editor at Billancourt and saying: "I have just seen *À bout de souffle*; from now on, continuity shots are out."

If we used a hand-held camera, it was simply for speed. I couldn't afford to use the actual equipment, which would have added three weeks to the schedule. But this shouldn't be made a rule either: the method of shooting should match the subject. Of all my films, the one in which the shooting method is most justified is *Le petit soldat*. Seven out of ten directors waste four hours over a shot which should take five minutes of actual shooting: I prefer to have five minutes work for the crew—and keep the three hours to myself for thought.

What caused me a lot of trouble was the end. Should the hero die? To start with, I intended to do the opposite of, say, *The Killing*: the gangster would win and leave for Italy with his money. But as an anticonvention it was too conventional—like having Nana win out in *Vivre sa vie* and drive away in the car. Finally, I decided that as my avowed ambition was to make an ordinary gangster film, I had no business deliberately contradicting the genre: he must die. If the House of Atreus no longer kill each other, they are no longer the House of Atreus.

But improvisation is tiring. I have always told myself: this is the last time, I can't do it again. It is too exhausting going to bed in the evening and wondering, what am I going to do tomorrow? It's like writing an article in a café at twenty to twelve when the deadline is midday. The curious thing is that you always do manage to write it, but working like that for months on end is killing. At the same time it is to a certain extent deliberate. One feels that if one is sincere and honest and one is driven into a corner over doing something, the result will necessarily be sincere and honest.

The only thing is, one never does exactly what one intended. Sometimes one even does the opposite. At least this is true of me; but at the same time I am responsible for everything I do. After a certain time, for instance, I realized that *À bout de souffle* was not at all what I thought. I thought I had made a realistic film like Richard Quine's *Pushover*, but it wasn't that at all. In the first place I didn't have enough technical skill, so I made mistakes; then I discovered I wasn't made for this kind of film. There were also a lot of things I wanted to do but which I can't bring off. For instance, those shots of cars looming through the night in *La tête contre les murs*. I would also like to compose shots that are magnificent in themselves like Fritz Lang, but I can't. So I do other things. Although I felt ashamed of it at one time, I do like *À bout de souffle* very much, but I now see where it belongs—along with *Alice in Wonderland*. I thought it was *Scarface*.

À bout de souffle is a story, not a thesis. A theme is something simple and vast which can be summed up in twenty seconds: vengeance, pleasure. A story takes twenty minutes to sum up. *Le petit soldat* has a theme: a young man is mixed up, realizes this, and tries to find clarity. In *Une femme est une femme*, a girl wants a baby right away. In *À bout de souffle* I was looking for the theme right through the shooting, and finally became interested in Belmondo. I saw him as a sort of block to be filmed to discover what lay inside. Seberg, on the other hand, was an actress whom I wanted to see doing little things which amused me: this was the *cinéphile* side of me, which no longer exists.

Notes

Portions of the original interview published in *Cahiers du Cinéma* 138 (December 1962); republished in English in *Godard on Godard: Critical Writings by Jean-Luc Godard*, ed. Jean Narboni and Tom Milne (London: Secker and Warburg, 1972), 171–76. Notes are reproduced from the translation.

1. "The Left Bank group": So-called not only because they lived on the Left Bank in Paris, but because their cultural background (literature, politics and the plastic arts) was very different from that of the film-oriented *Cahiers du Cinéma* group, comprising Godard, Truffaut, Chabrol, Rivette, Rohmer, and Doniol-Valcroze.

2. "*Adieu Philippine*": Jacques Rozier's first feature.

3. "Decoin": The veteran director Henri Decoin, whose films—e.g., *Les Inconnus dans la maison* (with Raimu, 1942), *La Vérité sur Bébé Donge* (with Gabin, 1951)—are competently made but reveal no individual personality.

PART I

CHEEK TO CHEEK IN PARIS AND NEW YORK

MARCEL DUCHAMP
The Signature Machine—Identity, Authority, Dispossession

Changer de nom, tout simplement.
—Marcel Duchamp

It could start like this: 1958. The end of May 1958. Almost sixty years ago. Teeny and Marcel got off the train at Orly. In Marcel's words: "I've been married to Teeny Matisse since January 16, 1954; no kids yet except for three ready-mades."[1] They would spend the summer in Europe; in June, Marcel would decide to show Teeny the house where he was born in Normandy. They would then travel to Blainville-Crevon (in the lower Seine), where Marcel was born on July 28, 1887. There, they would meet the new owner, Maître Le Bertre, who bought the notary's office from the artist's father, Eugène Duchamp (born Justin Isidore Duchamp). Then they would go all the way to Massiac (Cantal) to see his father's birthplace. They would rent a car, follow the sun, and arrive on the Côte d'Azur on July 17. The couple would stay at Sainte Maxime (in villa Kermoune) and would go to Vence to see the Rosary Chapel designed by Henri Matisse.[2]

The man of whom I speak was seventy-one years old. So, once again, I find myself drawing the portrait of an elderly man, so lucid, so chaste, capable of becoming a man, rather than himself, that is to say, taking hold of "the anthropomorphosis of maturing and aging,"[3] according to another MD, Michel Deguy. In other words, and more simply put, this is a man capable of *Tongue in Cheek*. To sum it up quickly, here is an artist whose uniqueness stems from "elegance at its most fatal, more than elegance, an ease that is truly supreme"

(André Breton[4]), along with his sense of humour, irony, and derision, a man capable of maintaining distance from himself and laughter that comes from within. I could have given this work the same title I once gave to a work on Jean Genet: *The Last Duchamp*.[5] In any case, the time period whose impact interests me here consists of a sequence of events marked by a new breath, a gleam of light (his happiness with Teeny), a mixed joy (his return to his place of birth) that started with the couple's visit to Blainville-Crevon (June/July 1958) and ended with a letter, signed and dated July 28, 1964.

The sequence of events began with a trip to New York/Paris, a reminder of another Paris/New York trip—the first trip—on June 6, 1915 (departure from Bordeaux at Rochambeau, arrival in New York on June 15). In *Comment New York vola l'idée d'art moderne* (*How New York Stole the Idea of Modern Art*), Serge Guilbaut showed how after World War II there was a market shift in the art world from Paris to New York due to an offensive led by American critics and institutions. This happens to be a good starting point for another story. Could one not argue that rather than a theft perpetrated by the Americans on French soil, Marcel Duchamp, a Frenchman, had invented contemporary (rather than modern) art *between* Paris and New York: a simple snow shovel, January 15, 1916 (the first *readymade made in the United States*), a comb . . . this would set off a shift in everything from chronology to mood. Another story would be that of a man who readily set off for New York, invented the readymade on the spot, and thereby changed the course of things—geographically, historically, and aesthetically—in regard to art history and its divergences as they are most often analyzed and studied. The story of *how* remains valid, in particular the question of this shift toward the United States in the market. Within the sequence of events, we must take into account the singularity of Duchamp, who did the roundtrip more than once. On his way back he touched down in Blainville-Crevon, Cadaquès, and then, finally, Milan. Duchamp single-handedly complicated the relationship between the United States and Europe (rather than New York and Paris): "I am not going to New York, I am leaving Paris." He complicated this relationship on at least two levels: the aesthetic and the economic; and, I will add, on the historico-political level. He transformed the object, perceptions, and meaning of the art market. He authorized another reading, shifting concepts and offering new ones. This shift does not imply talent, or know-how, or work. To grasp it, we must closely study the readymade in terms of the signature. The readymade constitutes an object, a sibylline phrase, and a signature. A signature requires a name, an alphabet, and a hand. Work from the

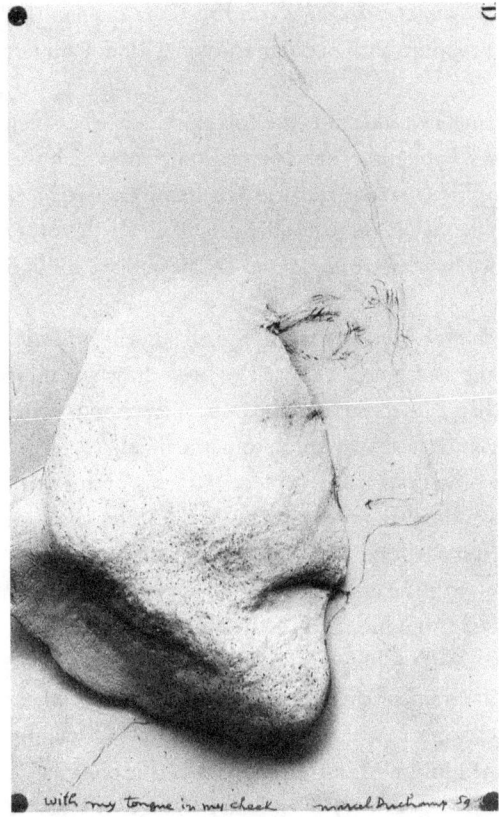

FIGURE 2.1 Marcel Duchamp, *With My Tongue in My Cheek*, 1959. Plaster, pencil on paper mounted on wood. Collection of Centre Georges Pompidou, Musée National d'Art Moderne. © Estate of Marcel Duchamp/ SODRAC (2015).

years 1913–21 can be read in a mirror of the sixties, a mirror that would break in 1964. It is about a return, about repetitions and replicas. It is what I call the *signature machine*.

Inscribed in ink, I read: "*With my tongue in my cheek Marcel Duchamp 59.*" A FACE AND A SIGNATURE. A three-dimensional play on words heightened by the literal exploration of the molding process. Note the attention brought to the model, to the mold, to the template, to the expression "*to break the mold*," meaning to break with tradition. We could interpret *Tongue in Cheek* in this way. In the same light, there is already a tradition here—plaster cast, model, artisan work—and the deconstruction of the tradition, which is one of the paradoxes of the signature. We could evoke malic molds, waffle molds, cake molds, and other molds of the artist or of his models. It seems to me that this three-dimensional work belongs to, or constitutes a separate piece of, what was left over from the work in progress:

Etant donnés: Maria, la chute d'eau et le gaz d'éclairage (1944–66). This erotic machinery must have a rapport with our signature machine: I am not yet sure of its nature.

What's more: if I had the time, I would study the correspondence between *Etant donnés* and James Joyce's *Finnegans Wake*, the existence of which was kept secret until the end of his life (1922–39), as was Duchamp's masterpiece (1944–66). One finished his work on the eve of World War II; the other started in its wake. These two works are separated by twenty-six million deaths.

Jean Suquet said of *Etant donnés*: "What disturbs me, if you will [in *Etant donnés*], what disturbs me is the two holes, it's that I've been drawn to these two holes so I can be shown that."[6] I believe that one must see, without being embarrassed, what's going on with these two holes: to name them.

Tongue in Cheek could be a prosthesis, a relic, a piece or a scrap of this work that began on the road between the Jura and Paris: "point of escape, the road will be where the hole to infinity is found." This slow process started with attempts at plastering breasts (with the anatomic complicity of his lover), at rubber breasts (the purchase of a thousand fake breasts for the surrealist catalogue *Prière de toucher*); the various molds previously cited; "L'Objet-Dard," and so on; even the model or mold of the woman "*au chat ouvert*" made from a metal framework and other materials on which Marcel Duchamp was to apply leather to give the illusion of skin. "In any case, this plaster cast is made to resemble the skin that goes over it and that changes the whole conception." He used pigskin.

Let's get back to the subject at hand. As Bernard Marcadé, the French biographer, said, by way of metonymy and many quotation marks: "In the year 1964, Marcel Duchamp's activities are essentially focused on the artistic 'management' of his readymades." Marcadé also describes "the 'grandeur-nature' edition of the thirteen 'historic' readymades that the Milanese dealer [named Arturo Schwarz] would carry out in the second half of 1964 and which he said were Duchamp's idea." The proliferation of quotation marks, the childishness "which he said were Duchamp's idea," along similar lines to "he's the one who says who he is," and the vague expression "artistic management" do not measure up to what the author says, no doubt while pinching his nose, which is less appropriate than tongue-in-cheek. It is not yet the time to question this description of Marcel Duchamp's activities; what we are concerned with now is the denial.

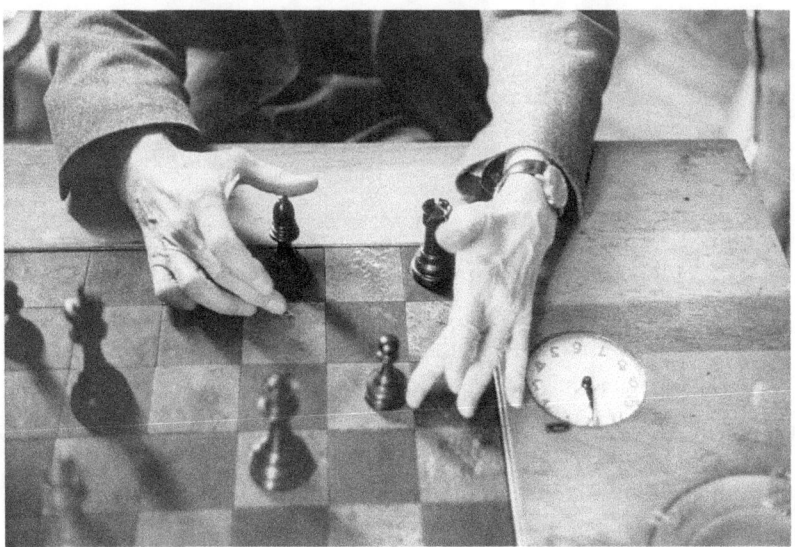

FIGURE 2.2 Alexander Liberman, *Marcel Duchamp*, 1960. Gelatin silver print. Courtesy of the Getty Research Institute, Los Angeles (2000.R.19). © J. Paul Getty Trust.

"This edition definitely puts an end to the anarchist politics of signatures," said Marcadé. The proof was a letter, written, dated, signed, and sent by Marcel Duchamp on July 28, 1964. It was addressed to a certain Douglas Gorsline, who asked Duchamp to sign a bottle rack and who would receive by way of this letter a flat-out refusal. The recipient of this letter matters little: it addresses much more than a single person. Duchamp wrote, and in my opinion this little piece of epistolary history is of capital importance: "I just signed a contract with Schwarz in Milan, authorizing him to produce an edition (eight replicas) of all of my readymades. I have therefore agreed in writing to no longer sign any readymades in order to protect this edition." He added, to console Gorsline, the poor fool: "Your finding has the same metaphysical value as any other readymade; it even has the advantage of not having any commercial value." *Tongue in cheek.*

"My hand became my enemy in 1912," stated Duchamp. With the other, he would do artisan work, would keep signing not only readymades but just about everything that was handed to him, all the while declaring, I repeat: "I have therefore agreed in writing to no longer sign."

This period of five years (1958–64)—as many years as a hand has fingers—overlaps with another period, of life and then of work: the visit to the house where he was born, evoking birth; the July 28, 1964, letter foreshadowing the artist's death, in Paris on October 2, 1968. With *Tongue in Cheek* in mind (Cadaqués, 1959), he was now steering away from the return (Schwarz edition) of the readymades in 1913–21, in view of the signature.

1

To date is to sign. And inversely. One's signature is comparable to a monument because it contains a memory and it holds the trace of a life. The letter in which the artist states, "I have therefore agreed in writing to no longer sign" is signed and dated July 28, 1964. This constitutes an event and the event is the signature itself. Marcel Duchamp signed his poetic art that is also his artistic testament on the anniversary of his birth.

If this scene were to be represented by a painting then we must imagine a table around which a group of men have gathered, in similar fashion to the group of doctors from Amsterdam gathered around a deceased man in Rembrandt's *The Anatomy Lesson of Dr. Tulp* or Cézanne's *Card Players*: hands, above all else, hands. Otherwise, it could be a more modern work, something like Francis Picabia's *Cacodylic Eye* (1921)—a work of signatures—if this scene hadn't already been represented by Duchamp's friend through the geometric line of *Machine without a Name* (1915). Indeed, if the signature machine should be a readymade, we must imagine an object from the signature book or stamp family, a curious device, descendant of a Braille machine or of a piano organ. A heavy, cumbersome, strange instrument. All in all, a comical object.

This scene calls for a notary, Duchamp's father, his son, who signs his name Marcel Duchamp, as well as Arturo Schwarz, the ringmaster of the circus of names. Serge Guilbaut would be present and by his side and nearby would be Arturo Schwarz, the pair of them laughing. There are witnesses present: Thierry de Duve, Gilbert Lascault, Jean Clair, and even Élie Faure. In the background are Max Ernst, Robert Lebel, John Cage, or even Daniel Buren, who are making faces. Cézanne is there. And in the library are Jacques Derrida, Alain Robbe-Grillet, Francis Ponge, Raymond Roussel, Claude Simon, and many more.

Then we will enter the notary's office and therein see a notary scene. Why a notary scene? What does one do there? One signs. Generally at the bottom of a contract.

In one sense, the scene brings together the painter and the notary: in other words, father and son. How did the signature appear in painting? I am not going to recount this history. From the byzantine icon on which weighed the impossibility of the signature because of its function as a sacred image; to the signature right on the canvas—superimposed, even—without any relation whatsoever to the scene represented that underlines the pellicular space of the painting and highlights the painted surface; by way of the signature from the end of the thirteenth century onward, on the lower edge of the frame around the canvas; then on the parapet, a false frame or zone of silence that attests to the compromise between the impossibility of signing, the refusal of the signature, and the desire of the painter to intrude on the image by inscribing his name.

What interests me is when signatures first appear in painting, toward the twelfth and thirteenth centuries: "Painters and notaries seem to have met the same difficulty in finding ways to make the presentation of the name compatible with the logic of their art."[7] As the signature historian Béatrice Fraenkel states in her book on signatures, by choosing the base of the document as the place where they inscribe their name, the notaries agree with the solution adopted by painters. By appropriating this custom, notaries seem to claim the status of artist. They sign their agreements as the painter signs his retable. The juridical act is therefore both a "work" and a text. The signed agreement echoes this duality. Each of them, the notary and the painter, sign outside of the text, at the bottom of the page. Here, the father and son exchange places, which is the very least of the paradoxes I am underlining here.

We begin to see to what extent this matter of the signature relates to the relationship between father and son, and how this relationship brings transmission into question. Because the notary and the painter are both the first ones to sign, they share this archaeology and this invention of signing the deed, both as text and object and as the invention of signing a painting; because Duchamp the father was a notary and Duchamp the son was initially a painter; because Duchamp the father's craft was to sign and because Duchamp the son in abandoning painting did not abandon his name and never ceased to sign; and finally because the cessation of the signature—in addition to breaking from this routine that lasted fifty years—was initiated on the anniversary of Duchamp's date of birth, the same day that his father gave him his name. And yet, when I sign, it is always a matter of exchange with myself that maintains an infinite inquietude right until death. Signing my name is also always a birth certificate. In signing I am handing myself over to myself, my name each time for the first and last time. "I mess up the act of birth and violate a tomb," writes Jacques Derrida in *Signéponge*.[8] That is why the dated and signed affirmation of the cessation of the signature on the anniversary of Duchamp's birth is an act of a radical nature, the signing of which is abyssal.

The action of the last Duchamp evokes for me the heraldic custom that consists of "*briser ses armes*." A *brisure* is a modification made to a coat of arms by an individual who, being neither the eldest son nor the leader, cannot wear it as it is. It is a game with the name of the father. But not just that. And not always with the same father. There is always more than one father.

This is not the first time I have made such a discovery. In fact, I was quite interested in the relationship between the painter Paul Cézanne and his banker father, Louis-Auguste Cézanne. Another matter of debts and dates. Delving into his *Correspondance*, I uncovered the father of modern painting's famous sentence: "I owe you the truth in painting and I will tell it to you," which was addressed to a critic and signed by Paul Cézanne on the day of the anniversary of his father's death, October 23, 1905, as if the painter were pronouncing these words over his father's tomb. Paul Cézanne died the next year, ten years to the day of the banker's death, who was also his creditor for many years. The anniversary of his father's death was, in an anticipatory, untimely way, then also of his own death. The power of Cézanne's promise to his father to commit to telling the truth is such that it includes an agreement with death, as if Cézanne had sent the letter, date stamped, to the ghost within himself or to his own death. There is the tomb, the crypt, an exorbitant contract.

We could compare *les arts poétiques* of Cézanne and Duchamp in view of the date of their signatures. Compared to his father, the notary, or to Cézanne, Marcel Duchamp's emancipation was complete. Cézanne was committed to telling the truth; Duchamp was bound to no longer sign. Cézanne's gesture hung in the solitude of a painter's life who didn't sign his paintings; Duchamp's was secured to a commercial contract that authorized the production of replicas in series. Cézanne committed himself in the name of his father to a certain degree; Duchamp, as a son (which is the same, of course).

2

So, what was his intention? We must look at what friends, contemporaries, and even art historians have to say before turning our attention back to this decisive gesture. Because what's been given here precisely is access to history, to a past that had been hidden, repressed, neutralized by tradition.

Back to it: Milan, July 28, 1964. The contract with Arturo Schwarz allows the creation of a new edition of the thirteen readymades. According to Schwarz (quoted by Marcadé), it was Duchamp's idea—he was upset that the originals had been lost and that they could not be gathered in one place. It was a naïve and simple hope. According to others, Duchamp's main motivation was to make a little profit. Seeing as he had given away the majority of his works, his reputation had not translated into economic gain. Duchamp's official, conscious arguments are mediocre. All painters have made copies, he said; no sculptor in the history of art is unique; it is rarity (not uniqueness) that gives a work its price (its "artistic certificate"). His friends were dumbfounded by the role upheld by this model of artistic integrity. The scene with the notary triggered a series of smaller scenes: a jealousy scene, a self-delusion scene, a breakup scene. If the readymades deconstruct the modern notion of originality, the replica deconstructs this critical potentiality, they say. In other words, Duchamp became a manufacturer, the manager of a small business that sold his signed products rather than a genius who authenticated his creations by signing them. Robert Lebel refused to include these replicas in expositions. John Cage wondered why these replicas, which were more akin to trade goods than to art, had been authorized. Max Ernst thought that this transaction would scorn the public. Daniel Buren maintained that Duchamp had betrayed himself in permitting Schwarz to make these replicas (the same Buren who decorated the head office of the bank BSI Ifabanque recently in Lugano). The exposition was called "*Ils sont peintres*" (They are painters) in reference to "*Nous ne sommes pas peintres*" (We are not painters), proclaimed by BMPT (Buren, Mosset, Parmentier, and Toroni) in Paris in 1967. "They don't make paintings, they make cheques," Duchamp used to say.

In short, this gesture left witnesses and minds perplexed, admirers disappointed, and imitators encouraged. So, if we believe the "friends," by accepting the contract with Arturo Schwarz and the edition in series of his readymades, *in fine*, Duchamp played against his own team. Or against his own name, his proper name, the proper of his name. In any case, no one was ready to follow Marcel Duchamp in his ultimate deconstruction of painting, of the signature and therefore of the subject.

The art historian remained blind to this gesture. In fact, it was never seen at all. Like a readymade, this turning point remained invisible. The event was hidden by common questions linked to tradition and to the abandonment of tradition, being two reciprocal and apparently contradictory contracts, each concealing the other and masking the event.

In his book on abandonment titled *Pictorial Nominalism* (1984), Thierry de Duve describes these two contracts well:

The most fundamental thing that industrialization had suppressed was the contract of initiation that linked the master to the apprentice. The education of the painter no longer happened by means of the ritual transmission of a technical knowledge, which the masters alone possessed.... The transmission of studio secrets was a gift that the elders gave to the young only if they judged the latter worthy of it; thus, it had the symbolic value of a true rite of passage. The thorough knowledge of the technical qualities of pigment had to make the painting last; it also had to make tradition itself last. This would no longer be the case now that the availability of the tube of paint rendered this knowledge exoteric, now that painters could try to enter into the craft independently of one another, now that tradition itself could no longer hope to last, but would take on the seasonal rhythm of the industry.[9]

De Duve further explains:

The readymade was an offspring of the abandonment of painting, which broke a filial line, but also, paradoxically, picked up its heritage. It was even the act by which the abandonment would have been no more than a cessation of activity that history would never have bothered to register.... But it is equally, we might say, a notarized act that acknowledged receipt of the history that preceded it and that was the history of painting. If there was a "death of painting," the readymade was the codicil at the bottom of its last will and testament. Whoever says "testament" also means heritage, transmission, the passing of powers, and the passage of tradition to the living.[10]

Two parts of a whole: a contract between the master and the apprentice that spans the history of painting; at the bottom of this contract of tradition, the codicil, that is to say a deed subsequent to a testament, modifying, completing, or voiding it. The codicil voids the tradition by maintaining it, since there is a testament, a heritage. Thierry de Duve—who dedicated his book to his parents—is not really at ease with what pertains to transmission, to heritage, and, therefore, to the signature. Or, more so, he is terribly traditional on the subject.

His focus is tradition, he says: wanting to revive at all costs "that particular tradition that has been called modern art, modernity, or modernism, which has all the appearances of an antitradition and which is to be 'photographed' in the privileged instant when it reveals what it transmits: a name, the name *painting*"; wanting to make abandoning painting into "the passage by which its name is detached from the specific craft that legitimized it." De Duve further declares that "the readymade is the transition by which the name *painting*, having lost its specific legitimacy, nonetheless connects with the generic name *art*,"[11] through his efforts to turn readymades into objects of painting and not only of art (which seems to be quite farfetched or at least a bit audacious and perhaps pointless[12]). His incapacity to escape tradition or the break with tradition—which overlap with each other and both obscure the event taking place—connects with the abandonment of the hand, which is also the abandonment of retinal painting and therefore of "the traditional idea of the painter, with his brush, his palette, his turpentine," in order to save the word *painting*. In other words, Thierry de Duve throws the baby out with the bathwater (or the brush with the pail water); he throws out the signature with the hand.

The art historian has forgotten the war and the signature: the war specific to the signature of a man in conflict with himself. The only time he names it is when he revisits the traditional definition of art historians. Never for a moment does he see the abyss of heritage or of the signature. He rejects this question, abandoning it to his peers: "For art historians, in fact, the author is but a signature, a seal of authenticity, a self that is always coherent and transparent to the self, who evolves according to traced lines of influence, of divergence, of maturity."[13] On the strange structure of the signature, the art historian does not pose a single question. We ask ourselves if this work is indeed attributable to such an author, this painting to such a painter, but according to Derrida in *Signéponge*, "as regards the event of the signature, the abyssal machinery of this operation, the commerce between said author and his proper name, in other words, *whether he signs when he signs, whether his proper name is truly his name and truly proper*, before or after the signature, and how all this is affected by the logic of name and reference, of nomination and description, the links between common and proper names, names of things and personal names, the proper and the non-proper, no question is ever posed."[14]

If I do not ask these questions about Marcel Duchamp, son of a notary obsessed with hands—his friend and foe—who signed all of his readymades and did so with more than one name; who bore a proper name, which was also a common name; who signed a contract stipulating the cessation of the signature: who will do so in my place? If we do not take into consideration the effects of the signature, we cannot interpret Marcel Duchamp's gesture in 1964: the cessation of the signature. The risk then is to miss the point of the radical political, aesthetic, and economic nature of this gesture made by the last Duchamp.

3

Let us now look more closely at Duchamp's very hand. "My hand became my enemy in 1912," declared the artist. It is not until 1964 that Marcel Duchamp definitively settles the score. In the meantime, he remains ambiguous for fifty years. At the moment when this little scene takes place, an array of contradictions had in fact been looming for a half century. This tension is proper to Marcel Duchamp's hand and the work of history. With his gesture, he is going to put an end to several decades of doubt in regard to the place assigned to his proper hand. Between the abandonment of retinal painting and the abandonment of the signature—an abandonment that was both a radicalization of the signature and also a hyper signature—there is a life. Now we can say that things have been achieved.

It was under the master of repetition that Duchamp first wished to finish with the hand. "For me, the idea of repetition is a form of masturbation for the artist. It is very natural, it is olfactory masturbation, dare I say, in other words, every morning the painter wakes up and needs, apart from breakfast, a little whiff of turpentine," said Marcel Duchamp to George Charbonnier in 1961.

Francis Ponge made a similar comment when he evoked his profession by way of a painter's, therefore making a link between writing and painting: "Everything happens for us just as it happens for painters who wouldn't have anything in which to soak their brushes but an immense pail that they've all used to water down their colors since the dawn of time. . . . It is not a matter of cleaning the Augean stables but of painting a fresco by using their own manure."

Finally, Jean Clair saw the contradiction that still reigned at that time:

The moment Duchamp decides in fact to abandon the fragrant magma that is painting with turpentine, when he claims to carry out an "art of precision" and to create a "beauty of indifference," *therefore to completely let go of the hand*, Duchamp finds himself in the place of a handyman who is absolutely unable to forge the tools of his ambition, because he is obligated to invent from nothing the techniques that will allow him to avoid appealing to his hand; yet, these techniques do not exist. . . . With him, there is ambiguity. There is a certain conflict: I won't touch it, I won't put my hand on it, *"please do not touch,"* but since the technique is nonexistent, and he is almost obligated to also reinvent the perspective—he is obligated to *disguise himself* as a handyman and an artisan. Hence the hours spent in his studio every day, in utter silence, in utter secret, where he doesn't tolerate that we come disrupt him while he's in the midst of working.[15]

And yet, with writing or with painting, according to Ponge, it is a matter of leaving behind the filth to write cleanly, to "write something proper, something neat and clean. This, is it not, is often the reason, maybe one of the principal reasons for writing," he said.[16] One of the main reasons to write or to paint is precisely to write one's name properly, indeed one's proper name. The contract with Schwarz was going to clear things up properly, once and for all.

We must understand Duchamp's 1964 gesture first as a subjective gesture—it was an event for himself. This gesture should not be immediately covered by an onslaught of interrogations on origin, tradition, economics, money, or commerce but more so as a founding subjective gesture. It must be approached, freed, grasped on its own in order to give access to the history with Duchamp as its subject. This gesture must first be understood in terms of the Duchamp name, his life and then his work. Here, Duchamp first settles a question that is proper to him: the question of his name, of the transmission of his name, of the work that transmits this name. It is a relationship to oneself as father and as son. Son of his father and father of his works, but also the son of his works. The relationship with these objects, his readymades—which are in a sense orphan objects—is complex to say the least: they do not rightly belong to anyone but are signed. The paternity of these works remains open if not infinitely problematic: I will revisit the telltale story of the *Fontaine* (1917), signed with the male pseudonym Mutt, which means bastard; Marcel wrote to his sister that he or she had been sent to the salon by a friend of his and under a male name.

At the same time as he signs the contract authorizing the duplication of the readymades, he allows for the replication of his signature, that is to say an infinite distribution of his signature. But, by the same token, he puts an end to the autographed signature.

At that time, in the sixties, Marcel Duchamp was signing everything that was given to him, everything that he was handed: So whereas the witnesses, friends, and historians see only the expansion of Duchamp's property, the commercial enterprise, the mass production, a little or a big profit, we must understand that with this gesture the contract also limits Duchamp's actions, restrains his capacities, and to a certain extent constrains him; he can no longer sign. To my mind this limitation is also liberation. It is in the moment when Duchamp is, in a way, incapacitated: he can no longer sign. In this moment, he removes himself from (voluntary) servitude. Therein resides the truth of his gesture. Marcel Duchamp accepts the law and becomes free. The contract with Arturo Schwarz—which obliged Marcel Duchamp to relinquish his signature and, by the same gesture, duplicated, replicated, and complicated that signature infinitely or nearly—was signed and countersigned, which implies an imprint of Duchamp's signature that could be deposited at the bank. This imprint of the same sort or out of the same mold used by Duchamp at Cadaqués to form the mold of his cheek (*Tongue in Cheek*) replays and outplays the life and then the works of Marcel Duchamp by imposing the signature of a subject that is multiple, divided, and split.

4

If the era is a list of names, here it is a matter of the same name that transforms over fifty years. I will now list Duchamp's names (that should be read and compared with those from the readymades, further down):

Marcel Duchamp
Mutt
Rrose Sélavy
Marcfl Duchamp
Apolinère Enameled

We should also acknowledge the nicknames used in his *Correspondance*, among them:

Dee
Dee *(Vorced)*
Duch'
Marcel Dee
Marcel Rrose
Marcel Totor
Marcelavy
Morice
Rose-Mar-Cel

I recall Duchamp's intuition. In 1962 he said to Katharine Kuh: "So man can never expect to start from scratch; he must start from ready-made things like even his own mother and father." The context of this comment points toward a certain rapport between a tube of paint, a readymade, and the father/mother. "Say that you use a tube of colour," said Marcel Duchamp in this interview. "You didn't make it. You bought it and used it like a ready-made. Even if you mix together two vermilions, it's still a mixture of two ready-mades. So man can never expect to start from scratch; he must start from ready-made things like even his own mother and father."

Throughout this slightly specious argument, a structural relationship makes two tubes of vermilion into parental figures. The tubes of vermilion—white caps on both—are proper mother and father figures. The name—since it is always already present—is the first readymade.

I see Duchamp as a married bachelor with/to his name. It's a quote. A graft. In Jacques Derrida's *Signéponge*, "Francis Ponge will then indeed have gotten married. To himself, in the first place. Francis is Ponge. Francis and Ponge form a harmonious heterosexual couple."[17] Doesn't this also fit Marcel?

Of Duchamp's seven children, Marcel is the only one who kept his name. Three daughters married: Suzanne became Crotti (a brother-in-law with a name that reminds me of a satyr); Jacques Villon didn't waste any time, changing his name not only from Duchamp to Villon but also Gaston to Jacques; Raymond became Duchamp-Villon. And then one son died; his name remained the same. "There are times when a name loses its flavour," said Marcel on this point.

The works of Marcel Duchamp called *Le grand verre* or *La mariée mise à nue par ses célibataires, même* (*The Large Glass* or *The Bride Stripped Bare by Her Bachelors, Even*) are nothing more than an implementation of the first name MARCEL. In each lineage, there are one or two major destinies to fulfill, to which specific first names are attached. Marcel is one of them. With *Le grand verre*, this destiny was fulfilled. I will note in passing that this first name is broken, like glass. The first name bears a contradiction: *MARié/CELibataire* (married/single). The undecidability, if not the indistinctness, are what's proper to the name Duchamp.

On this subject, we must cite Matisse's name. With Teeny Matisse—his second wife, or replica of a wife, with whom he would visit his birthplace in June or July 1958—Duchamp added his name to the history of painting, a gesture Cézanne's name was denying him. There is no need to elaborate.

Let's get to the *Fontaine (Urinoir)* (Fountain [Urinal]). What interests me more than anything, in this story, that seems moreover a bit forced, indeed unconvincing, is the modification of the name. We know that while Marcel Duchamp was one of the twenty-one directors of the Society of Independent Artists of New York in 1917, he, Stella, and Arensberg bought a porcelain urinal from the J. L. Mott Iron Works establishment. We also know that a certain Richard Mutt from Philadelphia would send it, signed R. Mutt, to that very salon under the name *Fontaine*.

This famous gesture echoes the rejection of *Nu descendant un escalier* (*Nude descending a staircase*) by the Independents of Paris in 1912 (refusal communicated by his brothers). In this case, Marcel Duchamp faulted the institution for not honoring its statutes: no jury, nor recognition. The committee debated: "You are saying that if an artist slaps some trash on a canvas and sends it to the exhibition, we should accept it? I'm afraid so." The refusal took on grand proportions. Duchamp resigned. He blamed the institutionalization of an initiative that claimed to be open and free of constraints by putting to the test his museum power, which consists of naming art, of determining what is art or not by incorporating it into culture. He was led to ask a question with such scope, and under such spectacular terms, that is, the death of art or of anti-art, that was to become one of the fetish questions of artistic reflection in the twentieth century.

Like in Paris, in New York the committee is shocked by the work and by its nomination or more so by its signature: Mutt signifies an imbecile, and alludes to the comic strip *Mutt and Jeff*. In common language, it signifies a bastard.

So, Mutt remains a mystery. Duchamp wrote to Suzanne on April 11, 1917: "One of my female friends had sent, under the masculine pseudonym Richard Mutt, a porcelain urinal intended as a sculpture." Indeed, we were blown away by this obstinate and tortured refusal to acknowledge the authorship of *Fontaine* at least at the time. While Marcel Duchamp had in fact eventually accepted to proceed with replicas of the object in signing them R. Mutt, without fear of demands by a third party, the fact that the work was not declared his own adds another level of meaning. How so? That remains to be explored.

The very innovative gesture that also has its own story is then the use of the pseudonym.

Rrose Sélavy is born in 1920 in New York City. On June 17, 1960, Marcel Duchamp recounts: "I decided that it didn't suffice for me to be a single individual with a male name, I wanted to change my name to change, for the readymades especially, to make another personality for myself, you understand, to simply change names." He elaborated further in an interview with Guy Viau: "I wanted to change my identity and the first idea that came to mind was to adopt a Jewish name. I was Catholic and it was already a change to go from one religion to another! I didn't find a Jewish name that tempted or pleased me. And then all of a sudden I thought, why not change my sex! Then the name Rrose Sélavy came to me. Now it may seem just fine, but in 1920 Rose was a silly name."

A Jewish name and a sex change, Rrose Sélavy condenses into a single form the Jewish name and the female name (according to Ronsard). There's keen intuition to the idea of taking a Jewish name at that time. Was it the same intuition that led James Joyce, at the same time, to give his character the name Bloom? I am not sure. Ulysses was published in 1922; Sélavy was born in 1920. And even if this name is not a Jewish name, the trace of one is present.

This name has its roots in a painting. "The double RR," said Duchamp during his interview with Pierre Cabanne in 1967, "comes from a painting by Francis Picabia *L'œil cacodylate* [Cacodylic Eye], which Francis had asked his friends to sign. I believe I put Pis Qu'abilla Rrose, *arrose* has two Rs, I was drawn to the second R to which I added Sélavy." On the painting Marcel Duchamp had written "En 6 qu'habilla Rrose Sélavy." Francis Picabia's painting is itself a painting of signatures. They foreshadow the replicas signed by Duchamp. However, for Picabia, it was a way of thumbing his nose at those who thought the signature determined the value of the work. Duchamp's *Tongue in Cheek*—tied to the cessation of the signature—is much more ambiguous.

It was a matter of understanding the signature in two different ways that don't have the same significance. Nevertheless, the circus of names had begun.

Rrose has the allure of a music-hall name, or a New York cover girl for a Dada magazine. She subverts society's message of ever-growing consumption by her transgender nature, her lewd wordplays, and her vulgar behavior. Man Ray and Duchamp invented a perfume, bags, and accessories line for Rrose. She's a transvestite, and the more elaborate readymades that she signs are always accompanied by moustaches and blows destined to counterbalance the increasing commercialization of art and its contrived ideals. She is a learned woman who offers the consumer an image of her desires before brutally delivering the ambiguous message of a prostitute; her promise is that "pleasure has a price."[18]

At the time of the auctioning of the Yves Saint Laurent and Pierre Bergé collection, organized by Christie's at the Grand Palace in Paris on February 23–25, 2009, *Belle haleine, eau de voilette* (*Beautiful breath: Veil water*), created by Marcel Duchamp in 1921 (with Man Ray), reached the price of €7.9 million, excluding fees. It fared better than one of the eight 1964 fourth edition replicas of *Fontaine* from 1917. It sold on November 17, 1999, at Sotheby's in New York for $1.76 million. Never mind the flask, provided you get the intoxication.

Let's recap. In a first sense, Duchamp's name bears the mark of multiplicity. The artist wears more than one name. What's in a name? Either the name belongs to an individual and it is called a proper name or it refers to many and is called a common name. For me, what has been overlooked in Duchamp's name is the quality of this proper name that is also a common name. The distinction between a proper name and a common name seems well established, and has been for some time as it goes back to the origins of Western grammar. And yet this certitude is swept away by the proper name that is also common. The resemblances between a proper name and a common name— from which it is often derived—are detrimental to the acceptance of a common name as a proper name, often first in the eyes of the person who wears the name. It is a question of borders between a common name and a proper name that are porous and inverted. It could even be that through smuggling (over borders) what is in play here is the relationship of the proper name to the common name: Duchamp, Mallarmé, Ponge, or others.

What are the benefits of a name change/sex change? Forgetting one's own name for starters. Marcel Duchamp leaves behind his own readymade: the proper name and the shifting border between the proper name and the common name, the debt that he carries with him. A double or triple benefit of the pseudonym: sexual, political (Jewish and female), aesthetic. And economic. "To quite simply change names" would be, for me, the key to Duchamp. However, Mutt, Marcel, Rrose Sélavy, and so on are once and for all a signature. The name change is not a refusal to sign but the will to sign another name. However, to sign another name has, of course, effects on the sense of the signature. The readymade inscribes under all its guises Marcel Duchamp's signature.

5

Let's now get back to the hand. The refusal of the hand was a refusal to touch: the refusal to touch and to be touched ("the beauty of indifference"). This question is posed by others; on June 5, 1958, Yves Klein experimented with his "living paintbrushes": naked women. "This way, I stay clean; I don't dirty even the tips of my fingers," explained the artist. Cézanne shared a similar angst. The father of the modern painter could not bear to be touched. "No one will get me in their clutches" was his refrain. His housekeeper confirmed: "Even I was ordered to walk by him without touching him, not even with my skirt." One day, he preferred they go fetch him an axe to knock down the door instead of staying put with his gardener's two magnificent daughters. He wanted to avoid the sexual shamelessness of men his age. Of his *Baigneuses* (*Bathers*), he explained that because he was the object of occult surveillance by the Jesuits, he had long since abandoned having models undress in his studio.

It is certainly not irrelevant that the same person who had Duchamp sign the cessation of the signature—Arturo Schwarz—was the one who uncovered the incest (with his sister Suzanne) that was at the heart of *La mariée* (*The Bride*). Arturo Schwarz was a Jewish anarchist. In 2007 he even published a work titled *Réflexion d'un athée anarchiste* (Reflections of an atheist anarchist). According to him, the principle of authority is the basis of Jewish thought. This means that Jews are violently attached to the coming out of slavery (an experience they repeat yearly) into freedom; it is because they are infatuated with this liberty that they can be anarchists while respecting the law. In the space between freedom and the law, there is room for commentary, criticism, and narrative. Finally, the old master obeys. Marcel Duchamp finally accepts the law: that of art, the market, sex, and society; to the licit exchange. To be decidedly free or freed.

On September 12, 1915, Marcel Duchamp gave his first interview in English in the United States, a mere three months after his arrival: "The war will produce a severe direct art. One readily understands this when one realizes the growing hardness of feeling in Europe, one might almost say the utter callousness with which people are learning to receive the news of the death of those nearest and dearest to them. Before the war, the death of a son in a family was received with utter, abject woe, but today it is merely part of a huge universe of grief, which hardly seems to concern any one individual." In this first interview, given in New York City, what comes through first is the indifference, the distance, the lack of sensitivity. Let us remember then the way he expressed these new thoughts and the man cut in half that they evoke: a choice dictated by "complete anaesthesia," a mental choice ("grey matter") and not an aesthetic one ("retinal"); the object should not be pleasing, it should not be pretty, it should not affect the artist; it is about coming to a "state of indifference" toward the object; the beautiful form has been totally pushed aside; there is no appropriation but a pure and simple displacement that calls for "neither talent, nor work, nor know-how"— all these words are Marcel Duchamp's. In the end, the readymade must be invisible. "It's a thing that we don't even look at, that we look at while turning away," declared the artist to Alain Jouffroy on December 8, 1961, in New York City.

I would voluntarily reproach the artist for his indifference regarding the war and military service. In the 1914 box, which bears his name, there is this reflection: "Disaffection for obligatory military service, a disaffection for each limb, for his heart and his other anatomic parts, each soldier could no longer put on the uniform, his heart would feed a distant arm by telephone, etc. Then, the nourishment would cease, each disaffected person, isolating himself. Then, a fixation on regrets." Here and there is the same will to push away pain. In 1915, intuitively, with quite surprising intelligence, Duchamp—when the conflict had but begun—distances himself, as if the young man he was had already become elderly or ancient; Duchamp takes into account what will be one of the defining traits of the twentieth century, that is to say, the loss of experience, and what comes with it, namely, the impossibility of mourning. The experience of mourning becomes impossible when death is generalized, when the deaths are countless. This diagnosis that concerns the spirit of the time is also reflected in the work of the artist, particularly with respect to the readymade. Duchamp re-creates the experience of impossible mourning with his objects. He possesses the same indifference toward his readymades as a family possesses toward a dead son.

6

Where are they? What are they? And even: Who are they? Let us recall Mar-cel Duchamp, André Breton, and Marc Dachy's definition: "The readymade is a choice made by Marcel Duchamp to raise an ordinary object to the level of a work of art." What interests me in this definition is that it includes the artist's name. Duchamp's readymades include the following:

> *Roue de bicyclette*, 1913, Paris (lost)
> *Trois stoppages étalon*, 1913–14
> *Porte-bouteille*, May–June 1914, Paris (lost)
> *Shovel*, Nov. 1915, New York (lost)
> *Peigne*, Feb. 17, 1916, New York
> *Pliant de voyage*, 1916, New York (lost)
> *Apolinère enameled*, 1917, New York
> *Fountain*, Apr. 1917, New York (lost)
> *Trébuchet*, 1917, New York (lost)
> *Porte-chapeau*, 1917, New York (lost)
> *Air de Paris*, 1919, Paris
> *Fresh Widow*, 1920, New York
> *Why Not Sneeze, Rrose Sélavy?*, 1921
> *L.H.O.O.Q. Mona Lisa*, 1919 (38 replicas)

I am not entirely sure of this list. I believe that there is no reference list, that there couldn't be one or even that there shouldn't be one. This series has no end; it is not fixed in stone, and we can add or subtract here or there. In some ways then it is an open list, even if a well thought-out catalog exists; if the list of Marcel Duchamp's works is complete, it will always be possible to uncover a readymade, to include a forgotten object—of course, there will always be something or other left out, indeed an unknown readymade.

Readymade objects are waste, residue, scraps. Precisely, in terms of details, "rags of history" (Walter Benjamin), these unworthy objects, doomed to the scrapheap, bear more ardor than the rest, for those who can perceive it, a sort of signature that links them to the present. Like those wounded, dead, or disappeared persons from World War I, one must understand the meaning of these original readymades as fictional characters: wounded sons for whom we cannot mourn. The invisible nature of the readymade is precisely what gives it its *signature* quality of the time, what gives these chosen objects a nonchosen quality: the things best suited to speak of the present, that of their election in 1913–21 or 1914–18. The sequence of their discovery, selection, or election coincides, in fact, to a certain degree of precision, with the event of the beginning of the twentieth century—World War I. The minute difference between the two sequences cannot obscure the superposition of the historic readymade period and the duration of the war. These objects have in common their contemporariness in relation to the butchering that occurred during the conflict. In my opinion, forgetting the hand responds to the situation of the amputees.

Also, the repossession of these same objects in 1964, indeed in the same time frame in which Ben Gurion declares, "The Jewish State is the only heir to the six million assassinated Jews" (1960), the repossession and these replicas, albeit one and the same, also then share another signature, one from another present, that does not erase the past.

These 1964 replicas are to the historic readymades of 1913–21 what those interned in death camps are to the amputees and the other soldiers of 1914–18. If the historic readymades are fictional characters, the dead sons for whom we cannot mourn, the replicas take into consideration the industrialization of murder such as it was during World War II. The industry, technique, and repetition of death are the signature that these readymade replicas bear, a signature that is now mechanized, reproduced, and duplicated. Arturo Schwarz donated the thirteen readymade replicas to the Museum of Israel in Jerusalem in 1972, before handing over his library (which contains a beautiful autograph collection) in 1991 and finally, in 1998, his surrealist collection.

So what of the two holes of *Etant donnés*? They are the two wars; they should no longer disturb us; they should remind us to face history.

I put forward an analogy here with Louise Bourgeois's situation during World War II. She describes the work done in 1947 and exhibited at the Galerie Péridot in 1949. What are these seventeen figures placed in a room about?

My first mature work (1945–51) was a direct wood-carving, executed at life-size scale. The forms were severe and simple, slender and upright and were painted (mostly black and white), not to get colorist effects, but just the opposite—to increase the visual unity of each and to avoid any romanticism of the material. These extremely reduced forms, although apparently abstract because they were uncomplicated, were conceived of and functioned as figures, each given a personality by its shape and articulation, and responding to one another. . . . These pieces were presences—missed, badly missed presences. . . . I was missing certain people that I had left behind. It was a tangible way of re-creating a missed past. The figures were presences which needed the room, the six sides of the cube. . . . It was the reconstruction of the past. . . . I did not need the presence of people who were the height of my brother, my parents.[19]

She elaborated: "I was French. I belonged to a certain milieu. Pierre Matisse and Duchamp came by and said, 'This is extraordinary!' I told them it was simply a manifestation of 'homesickness.' They looked at each other and understood, that's all there was to it."[20]

7

It is easy to think of the replicas as a gesture inspired by cynicism, peculiar to recycling past subversion through the production of multiples, a gesture controlled by the market, part of the spectacle of society and of triumphant consumption.

Most of Marcel Duchamp's works were either given away or owned by friends. A large majority of them belonged to two collectors: Walter Arensberg and Katherine Dreyer. Duchamp in part had dealings related to artwork that never left his studio. He was helping his friends (Breton, Brancusi). For a long time he chose to escape the economic regime for his own works by giving them away. In short, he was generous. Moreover, Duchamp left several accounts of what Ian Wallace calls "art about money." In particular, the *Tzanck chèque* (1919), revived under the form of the *Chèque bruno* (1965), merits attention. It is also a readymade, but a forgotten one, separated from the rest of his work. The dregs of the scrapheap, so to speak.

The *Tzanck chèque* is a facsimile of a check paid to the dentist Daniel Tzanck in the amount of $115. In other words, according to Michel Leiris, in *Brisées* (1946): "A blank cheque, is a stylistic ploy since it is a fake cheque but real due to the fact that its worth lies in the hand that signed it." It's not exactly that. Duchamp came up with the check to pay his dentist. The end product is first economic and then artistic. It was only later on that the document found the art world. The check constitutes an ambiguous mixture of the economic transaction, a barter and a donation based on reciprocity. Duchamp had been introduced to this dentist by Jean Crotti, his brother-in-law. The dentist gladly accepted to be paid in art. So, this object had neither aesthetic value nor economic value; it was only once the dentist accepted it as it was that it acquired a lavish value.

The *Tzanck chèque* is bound onto *Tongue in Cheek* by its teeth, so to speak—an object that constitutes alongside nails and hair one of the natural signs of identity, related to the nonnatural signs such as initials, autographs, or the signature. If the artist needed Daniel Tzanck's services, it is obviously because his cheek was already puffed out—*Tongue in Cheek*—by something painful (an abscess or a toothache).

The biography of the check—which in English is called *history*—is interesting; that is to say the check was the object of a history of transactions. Tzanck kept it in his collection for twenty years. Duchamp bought it back for 1,000 francs. It seems he then gave it to Matta, which his wife Patricia denies. She was the one who bought it with *L.H.O.O.Q.* In 1965 it was displayed at the Cordier and Ekstrom gallery, then integrated into the Mary Sisler collection. The latter dispersed her collection, which upset Duchamp. In the end, Mary Sisler sold it to Schwarz, who then donated it to the Museum of Israel.

This object must be linked to Duchamp's famous statement in August 1944: They don't make paintings, they make checks. It was his response to the question: "Why aren't you painting anymore?" He said: "I don't want to copy myself like others do. . . . Do you think they enjoy painting the same thing a hundred times? Not at all, they aren't making paintings, they . . ." Marcel Duchamp didn't write they sign checks, he does it. He made the check and signed it.

In order not to bounce a check I will say one more thing about the Tzanck check: it saves the cost of a canvas. It makes due without and does away with its mechanisms. The ternary effects of the check are dismissing retinal painting and putting the readymade in its place; linking art to the market and inversely the market to art and commerce; and authorizing the signature of the signature; in other words, initiating the signature machine.

8

The replicas of the readymade take with them a repetition of the signature and attest to a change in the economic world. At the time when Duchamp created *Tongue in Cheek,* when he was going to put a stop to his signature, a change was made in the rules of commerce that also represented a change in the way commerce relates to the body. A disturbance. The economics of the signature that Marcel Duchamp and Arturo Schwarz introduced primarily but not limited to the art market attests to this change. This gesture was economic, in the sense that the artist no longer signs (a subtractive value "disaffected, isolating," he pulls away) and that the replicated signature becomes a product in a neither pure nor impure economy that now idles.

The replica of the signature attests to a broken subject. If the years 1944–56 are a time of reconstructing an identity after World War II, the time period that Marcel Duchamp opens up by way of his gesture is the moment of this contrived identity's deconstruction. This work then takes place in philosophy, with the preface and the translation of *L'origine de la Géométrie de Husserl* (Jacques Derrida, 1961); and in literature, when the term *nouveau roman* is pronounced for the first time by Emile Henriot in 1957,[21] as well as in *Le vent: Tentative de restitution d'un retable baroque* (Claude Simon), *La jalousie* (Alain Robbe-Grillet), *La modification* (Michel Butor), and the new edition of *Tropismes* by Nathalie Sarraute. In criticism, there was *L'ere du soupçon* (Nathalie Sarraute, 1956) and the creation of the group Tel Quel (1960) with Philippe Sollers and about Georges Bataille, James Joyce, Jacques Derrida, Michel Foucault, and Roland Barthes.

It is also the period when Marcel Duchamp replicates or restores T. S. Eliot: "the more perfect the artist, the more completely separate in him will be the man who suffers and the mind which creates." T. S. Eliot's intuition in 1922 is taken up by Duchamp during a speech titled "The Creative Act," given during a gathering of the American Federation of Arts, in Houston, Texas, in April 1957, in other words, two years before the creation of *Tongue in Cheek* and six years before the cessation of the signature. T. S. Eliot's imperative was a sort of signature of the era; its reiteration by Duchamp was also significant. A postwar pairing can no longer be made between 1922 and 1957. After the reconstruction that followed the war, much like on the economic scale, a disruption occurred (Thomas Bernhard, 1967). Nor was it really about, as has already been discussed, the disappearance of the subject or the death of man.

It was more about a reflection on the purpose of man (Jacques Derrida, *De la Grammatologie*).

When Claude Simon wrote, with a certain simplicity, the following note on painting that situates him a bit aslant of what we are speaking of, it is again a postwar thought:

> A common point connects painters like Miro, Dubuffet, my friend Novelli or even Rauschenberg. What strikes me in their works, is the common desire to return to the source, the fundamental, the concrete. . . . Everyone in the Western world is confronted with the same situation, the same collapse of two thousand years of "humanist" thought coming to a close in the Nazi camps on the one hand and in the Gulag on the other. At the end of the war, we had to face this, this sort of *tabula rasa*, this questioning of values.[22]

This work done without the hand of the dehumanized man was a response to the dehumanization of man broken by the war. The cessation of the signature was also a broken response. But this cessation represents a mechanized reproduction of the same signature that no longer simply indicates the position of the modern subject denied the experience of mourning or even denied experience *in general*: it now indicates the break between man and his name. There is no longer identity between he who does and he who signs, nor between the name and the man who signs it. There can no longer be identity. The subject is ruptured. The signature no longer refers to a stable individual but to a name without depth, to an infinite debt, and, finally, to a debt without a name. If the signature is man, then for Marcel Duchamp's replicas it is about signing without validating man's name: his own name but also the name of humanism's man. Another tightening of the screw for the signature signed *Marcel Duchamp* or the initials that refuse to assign the signature to humanism's man. From that comes my hypothesis that will also serve as my conclusion—the signature machine is a machine without a (man's) name.

Today, who can fully bear his name? Marcel Duchamp's gesture—a gesture that resonated and was made heard over the course of a life—begs the question of transmission and therefore of the name in the twenty-first century. In the twentieth century, an ultrathin difference between man and his name came about that persists still today: a break in the proper name of man. It is what I call *man*, orphan of his humanity. For Duchamp, the cessation of the signature that is at the same time a repetition of the signature and a replica of the signature, that is also an erasure of the signature, attests to this breakage, this difference, the cracks in a broken man, with solemn irony.

Post-scriptum

The cessation of the signature, this decision, was not religious nor metaphysical nor negative. It was subjective and, therefore, in this case, ironic. The gesture of the last Duchamp belongs to modern irony, an irony that turns on itself. His gesture forewarns and reveals the ambiguity of the modern world: a paradoxical gesture like *Don Quichotte* that is both an epic novel and a criticism of the epic. Like every decisive gesture, it is right on the edge between the two. It is a "game of massacre" (Jean Genet). The turning point wasn't about reconstructing an identity or even quite deconstructing it: since that moment—1964—it has been about creating play. Duchamp's anarchical gesture, which put an end to the political anarchy of the signature, was radical and playful.

Who am I? In other words, how do we know one another? Or even "what to know, how to know" (Claude Simon, *La route de Flandres*, 1960)?

It is time to give a little explication in due form of *Tongue in Cheek*, 1959. It is about, one could have guessed, an *auto-portrait of a signature* and, at the same time, a *death mask*.

The name reveals the bloodline, much like smoke does the fire. The distinction between natural signs and artificial signs is not absolutely pertinent when it comes to identity: seals, notarizations, signatures, digital imprints (nails, hair, teeth), portraits, proper names. Because the signature needs to be an autograph it stands out from all other signs. An unstable universe that is not only the consequence of the heterogeneity of the signs themselves—some of which are several centuries old, some several decades—but also the indication of a major difficulty: the identification of the individual. A portrait alone, for example, cannot serve as the sole identifier of an individual. Inversely, a proper name, without the image of he who bears it, does not allow us to recognize him. Each of the signs, within the system, proves to be insufficient and seeks within the other a complement to its effectiveness. The reasons for this "perpetual identity *bricolage*," in Béatrice Fraenkel's terms, escapes the systems and stems from the notion of identity proper. It is in this void that artists or writers inscribe the diverse manipulations they subject to the signs of identity. A hidden auto-portrait, an encrypted signature, a name disseminated in a work: these practices of "exasperation of the signs of identity"[23] are as much the practices of the signature that assume the support of a work. In the end, (legal) identity rests on these elements: the proper name and the portrait. The proper name and the face are the ultimate signs desired by an identity search. To these signs, it would be suitable to add one more: the imprint. These three signs—the proper name, the portrait, and the imprint—could be considered the basic signs of identity. Symbol, icon, and indication, the signature subsumes all the possible relations between a sign and an object and these three basic signs of identity.

Is it this vertigo that grabs hold of Marcel Duchamp? In an astounding way, *Tongue in Cheek* brings together, seemingly intuitively, these three basic identity supports that are the proper name, the portrait, and the imprint. The portrait is drawn with a pencil, the cheek is a molded imprint of the artist's, and the work is signed *Tongue in Cheek*, Marcel Duchamp, 1959.

Through the question of the name, the signature is bound to the question of identity. Confronted with the mass production of objects, like packs of cigarettes or bottle holders, it is more difficult to maintain the humanist notions of identity or singularity. Marcel Duchamp puts the question like this: "At the same time, an object is not the same at a second's interval—what rapport is there with the principle of identity?" (posthumous note, MAT 7).

Tongue in Cheek materialized in an untimely way as Marcel Duchamp's death mask, which features, in a certain way, an amputated face; only the cheek is molded, as if the rest of the face has been taken away, has disappeared, erased. The signature dates it. The work evokes from these facts first birth, then death.

The letter from July 28, 1964, signed on the anniversary date of his birth, foreshadowed the death of the artist, in Paris on October 2, 1968. The spirit of *Tongue in Cheek* is precisely to represent this passage from life to death, from death to life, to represent life then art as they are brought together in the signature of the living.

Notes

I would like to thank Serge Guilbaut, without whose trust, friendship, and support, this chapter would not have seen the light of day; and Molleen Shilliday for her lovely work as reader and translator.

Epigraph: Guy Viau, "Changer de nom, simplement" [interview of Marcel Duchamp], *Fin*, no. 5, Galerie Pierre Brullé (2000): 14.

1. Letter to Suzanne and Jean Crotti, January 31, 1954, in *Affectt Marcel: The Selected Correspondence of Marcel Duchamp*, eds. Francis M. Nauman and Hector Obalk (London: Thames and Hudson, 2005), 337. All translations are mine unless otherwise noted.

2. Bernard Marcadé, *Marcel Duchamp: La vie à crédit* (Paris: Flammarion, 2007), 440.

3. Michel Deguy, "Le sens de la visite," *Critique*, no. 743 (April 2009): 262.

4. André Breton, *Littérature* (October 1922).

5. Hadrien Laroche, *Le Dernier Genet: Histoire des hommes infâmes* (Paris: Flammarion, 2010); Hadrien Laroche, *The Last Genet: A Writer in Revolt*, trans. David Homel (Vancouver: Arsenal Pulp Press, 2010).

6. Jean Clair, *Colloque de Cerisy, Marcel Duchamp* (Paris: 10/18, 1977), 258.

7. Béatrice Fraenkel, *La signature: Genèse d'un signe* (Paris: Gallimard, 1992), 170–71.

8. Jacques Derrida, *Signéponge/Signsponge*, trans. Richard Rand (New York: Columbia University Press, 1984), 24–27.

9. Thierry de Duve, *Pictorial Nominalism: On Marcel Duchamp's Passage from Painting to the Readymade*, trans. Dana Polan and Thierry de Duve (Minneapolis: University of Minnesota Press, 1991), 181.

10. De Duve, *Pictorial Nominalism*, 17.

11. De Duve, *Pictorial Nominalism*, 18.

12. De Duve goes as far as taking Marcel Duchamp's vague explanation as factual currency. One explanation he translates as follows: "In choosing an already made object, I didn't really break with painting because all painters do likewise as soon as they select a tube of colour." Thus, according to de Duve, if all paintings are readymades, the reciprocal conclusion is that "all my readymades are paintings." More Q.E.D. than *L.H.O.O.Q.*

13. Thierry de Duve, *Le nominalisme pictural* (Paris: Minuit, 1984), 244.

14. Derrida, *Signéponge/Signsponge*, 24–27, emphasis mine.

15. Clair, *Marcel Duchamp*, 152–53, emphasis mine.

16. Derrida, *Signéponge/Signsponge*, 42.

17. Derrida, *Signéponge/Signsponge*, 24–27.

18. Michael R. Taylor, et al., *Dada: Zurich, Berlin, Hannover, Cologne, New York* (Washington, DC: National Gallery of Art, 2008), 296.

19. Louise Bourgeois, *Destruction of the Father/Reconstruction of the Father: Writings and Interviews, 1923–1997* (Cambridge, MA: MIT Press, 1998), 77, 105–7.

20. Bourgeois, *Destruction of the Father*, 176.

21. *Le Monde*, May 22, 1957.

22. Entretien avec Claude Duverlie, *Diacritics* 7, no. 4 (winter 1977): 47–58.

23. Fraenkel, *La signature*, 194, 200.

THE YOUNG AND THE OLD

October 2, 1959, marked the opening of the first Biennale de Paris. This exhibition gave André Malraux, who had become the Minister of Cultural Affairs eight months prior, the opportunity to partner institutions with *art vivant*. In this regard, the situation was mediocre; for a century, the state had committed itself to the most reactionary conservatism and academic complacency. The director of National Museums, Georges Salle, inaugurated the reopening of the Musée National d'Art Moderne in 1947, speaking of this day as the end of the divorce between state and genius. This remark was as optimistic as it was premature. The museum reopening its doors did not have much in its collections to allow for such lyricism: a few works by Pablo Picasso, Fernand Léger, and Pierre Bonnard, which were mainly acquired thanks to the museum director's social skills. In short, it was about the late reconciliation of state and geniuses, most of whom were in their sixties and apt, in this time of moral reconstruction, to represent France, an eternal beacon of civilization.

This biennial and international exhibition of young artists had two major challenges: the international question, on the one hand, and the youth question, on the other hand; these two issues were very rightly seen as indissoluble. First, with the overwhelming domination of Art Informel and its uncertain outlines and definition, which made the Biennale, in the eyes of many, an exhibition of bad paintings, this event signaled the end of the fifties. It also marked the beginning of the sixties, with Affichistes François Dufrêne, Raymond Hains, and Jacques Villeglé entering the scene, or Jean Tinguely's "abstract art making machine" and, finally, among the American selection, Robert Rauschenberg's *Talisman*, which was for some a true revelation. Alain Jouffroy, who spoke of "the revolution of the *regard*"—which he made the topic of a book—understood at the moment of the Biennale the extent to which painting was "anachronistic, paltry and pathetically out of touch." He said, "It was in front of a painting by Rauschenberg, *The Talisman*, exhibited at the first Biennale de Paris, in October 1959, that I suddenly became aware of this reversal."[1] Some months later, Pierre Restany founded New Realism based on the same diagnosis of a "sclerosis of all established vocabularies."[2]

Even though the Biennale seemed to fulfil Malraux's wish, its history went back much further. It was a distant descendant of the *Salon des moins de trente ans* (Under thirty exhibition) created in 1941 and of the *Salon de la jeune peinture* (Young painting exhibition) that had replaced it after the war. Two years prior, a first version of the biennale format, *Biennale 57 de la jeune peinture et de la jeune sculpture* (Biennale 57 of young painting and young sculpture), was organized by Jean-Albert Cartier at the Musée des arts décoratifs. Many had remarked on the worldwide success of this format for the international meetings in Venice, São Paulo, and Kassel, which was inversely proportional to the decline in France's success rate in this kind of exhibition.

The first Biennale de Paris was organized by Raymond Cogniat, Chief Inspector of Fine Arts and commissioner of the French pavilion for the Venice Biennale for ten years. Cogniat belonged to the Association française d'action artistique (French Association of Artistic Action) that depended on the Ministry of Foreign Affairs. His action stemmed from the similar cultural policies or propaganda as the British Council or the United States Information Agency. Since 1948, the French strategy in Venice consisted of explicitly acknowledging the idea that the award was religious in nature. This allowed them, in times of "reconstruction," particularly moral, to evoke through big names—Georges Braque, Henri Matisse, Raoul Dufy, Jacques Villon—an indisputable and moreover, uncontested, history. It is therefore by way of the Venice Biennale that France wrote a history of modernity incarnated by names that marked the "phases in French painting," to quote the title of the comprehensive work published by Bernard Dorival between 1943 and 1946.[3] Jean Cassou, director of the Modern Art Museum, said "these phases were outlined in advance of the Modern Art Museum's program."[4]

France had to foresee the future given the Venice award was attributed to a living artist and the reservoir of old living masters was not by definition limitless. If the country wanted to continue to produce names that would assure the continuity of the nation's genius, they had to build a story from the thirties and forties. That is to say, they had to envision rewarding the less glorious

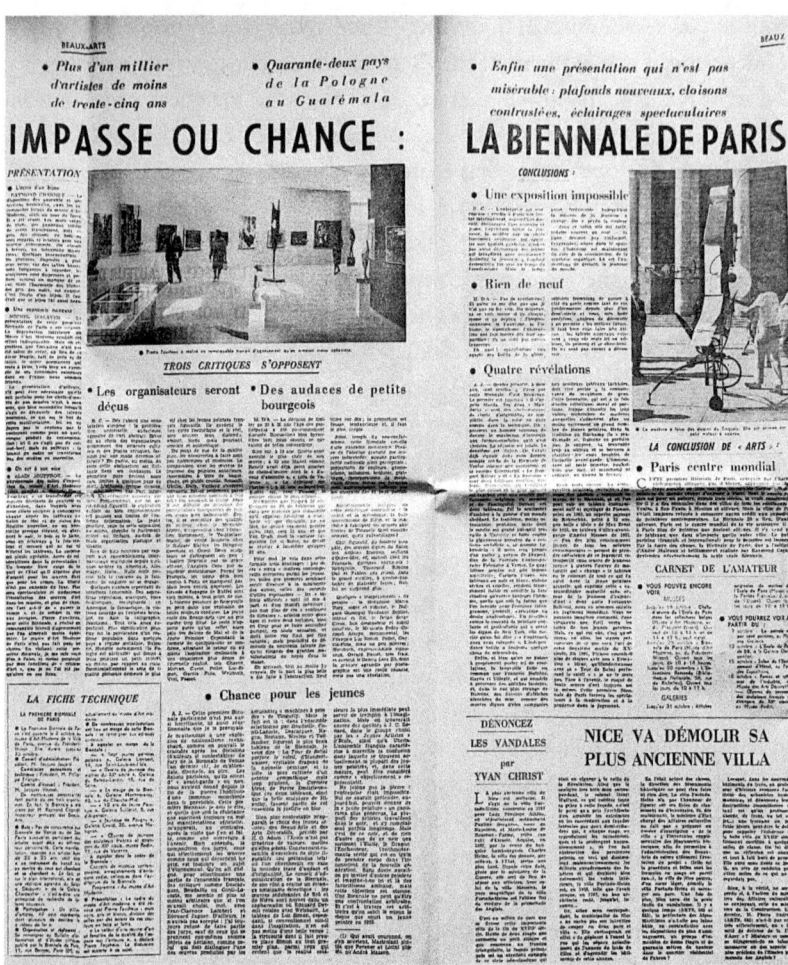

FIGURE 3.1 "La Biennale de Paris," *Newspaper Arts*, October 1959.

generation—somewhat of a euphemism—born around 1900. Cogniat therefore strung together, alongside some already historical celebrities, a group of
figural traditional artists from the interwar years: the putative heirs of cubism
and fauvism (Pignon, Tal-Coat, Marchand, Estève, Fougeron, Manessier, Ba-
zaine, Lapicque, Gischia); a realism characterized by the "fantastic" (Alfred
Barr went that route in 1936) bringing together Balthus, Tanguy, and Masson
with Goerg, Labisse, and Humblot, who were not particularly surrealist; an
expressionism *à la française* that was theorized in haste to criticize the "German propaganda," as Pierre Francastel said (Walch, Lorjou, Gromaire, Alix,

Gruber, Desnoyer); the painters of the "réalité poétique" (Brianchon, Oudot, Legueult) lumped together with Planson, Limouse, Cavaillès, Caillard, Poncelet, Aujame, Savin. In other words, in Venice Cogniat had to objectivize a history of the twentieth century that Dorival had taken on the task of writing in his *Étapes de la peinture française contemporaine*. This history assured the continuity of national genius, in a summary of fauvism and cubism, passion and reason, emotion and order, color and drawing: an art that would be *French*.

Youth

As of 1948, French critics—André Bloc or Léon Degand, for example—did not deprive themselves of deeming the French selections in Venise conservative and reactionary. The question of young artists was constantly being asked. Cogniat seemed to be attentive to the criticism that had been addressed to him. As of 1952, he had already opted for a generational presentation of his Venice selections with a room dedicated to artists under thirty. In June 1958 he indicated in a note that the objective of the Biennale de Paris was to compete directly with the initiative taken by the Venice Biennale the year before by dedicating a section to "young international creation."[5] This news, coupled with the untimely death of Georges Rouault, who had been nominated for the 1958 award—a withdrawal that allowed, or at least facilitated, giving the award to Mark Tobey, an American artist—prompted Cogniat to suggest, during the 1958 meeting, that the award be attributed to younger artists. By that he meant artists in their fifties, and he was thinking of Yves Brayer or Maurice Brianchon or perhaps even of painters whom his successor, Jacques Lassaigne, was to put forth for the award: Manessier (b. 1911), who was attributed the award in 1962 at the age of fifty-one; or the ill-fated Roger Bissière, who was put forth in 1964 at age seventy-eight but lost out to the young American Robert Rauschenberg. Yet, while young people could admit that the French institutions represented the grand and glorious history of French modern art, it also seemed to be absurd, irrelevant, and scandalous in 1958 to exhibit Anton Pevsner and Masson next to artists as dated, as behind the times, as Legueult or Auricoste, or to show Aujame next to Hans Hartung in 1960.

At the end of the 1950s, young artists had therefore become a challenge on the international scene. Moreover, Cogniat knew perfectly well that it wasn't up to him to take on artist selection. He had to put this task in the hands of young artists and critics themselves, Georges Noël (Hains, Villeglé, Dufrêne) or Pierre Restany (Jean Tinguely, Yves Klein). Two years later, for the 1961 Biennale, he had to explain himself without ambiguity in a televised interview when asked: "You are in charge, aren't you the organizer?" He replied, somewhat mischievously: "Organizer yes, responsible no."[6] He explained by saying that those in charge were the young artists, who "play their game, try their luck, pick their works."

An addendum to the catalog mentioning the awards attributed consisted of two texts; the first was an excerpt from the speech given by Malraux on the inauguration day; the second was a text by Jean Cocteau: "We are quite mistaken in our labels of youth, such as *nouvelle vague* (new wave) or *blousons noirs* (outlaw bikers and rockers). Youth is youth, with its power of disobedience that is able to disobey even if a harmful freedom prevents it. The power of youth is a revolt against conformism and if conformism is anti-conformism, then youth is advancing while seemingly backing away in horror from the old avant-garde. Vive the Biennale de Paris where young people throw caution to the wind." I should comment, at length perhaps, on this seventy-year-old academic's tone that is as paternalistic as it is reactionary (anticonformist conformism, etc.). Being the author of *The Terrible Children* made him the most appropriate godfather of this manifestation in the eyes of Malraux. However, I will limit myself to commenting on the reference to the more burning issue: the labels *nouvelle vague* and *blousons noirs*. Before becoming a term used to designate a group of filmmakers, the expression *nouvelle vague* derived from an inquiry on youth by Françoise Giroud in *L'Express* in 1957 and published by Gallimard in 1958.[7] As for the term *blousons noirs*, it was the big issue of the summer of 1959 when some widely broadcasted brawls took place in Saint Lambert square in Paris and Bandol in July. Three years later, in the preface to Émile Copfermann's book on the "génération des blousons noirs," Claude Bourdet, the founder of *L'Observateur* and of the New left, said, "We know that the French suddenly realized over the course of 1959 that youth existed in France and that it was time to take notice."[8]

Since I have mentioned Françoise Giroud and Émile Copfermann, I should note that this time was marked by the baby boom, and a number of studies of a sociological nature on youth appeared. In 1954 François Mauriac published *La France va-t-elle perdre sa jeunesse?* (Is France going to lose its youth?).[9] At the beginning of 1957, two studies appeared, one by René Matignon and Jean-René Hughenin in *Arts* and the other by Henri Perruchot in *Nouvelles littéraires*—the latter published a book about it in 1958 titled *La France et sa jeunesse*.[10] On October 10, 1957, Marcel Bluwal presented, as part of the television show *Si c'était vous*, the film *Délinquance juvenile*, which featured a generational conflict within a wealthy family. In 1959 Alfred Sauvy published *La montée des jeunes*.[11] That same year, Jean Jousselin spoke of youth as a "social fact."[12] Youth, which had become a political, social, and religious issue at the beginning of the twentieth century, particularly since the time that World War I decimated a part of Europe, became a *problem* in the fifties.[13]

Youth was a problem that cinema had been featuring for some time, from Ingmar Bergman's *Monika* to Nicolas Ray's *Fureur de vivre*; in France, Roger Vadim's *Et Dieu créa la femme* was the major success of 1958–59 and Marcel Carné's *Les tricheurs*, depicting idle middle-class youth brought to life by Laurent Terzieff and Jacques Charrier, was like an echo to the idleness that Françoise Sagan had been incarnating in film since the middle of the century.[14] It was a film by the old about the young, as Laurent Terzieff said himself, but a film that sold nine hundred thousand tickets, which in itself demonstrated if not a fact of society, at least a symptom.

It was in this context that a "rise of youth," according to Alfred Sauvy's title, inaugurated the "biennale and international manifestation of young artists." It must be noted that "youth," like "young people," are vague words that broadly designate everyone from adolescents to twenty-year-olds. The biennale "youth," often largely people in their thirties, are in fact those who turned "twenty in 1951," to quote the title of Robert Kanters and Gilbert Sigaux's study *Vingt ans en 1951*.[15] They were the ones who grew up during the war. Tinguely and Hains, born in 1925, Villeglé in 1926, Klein in 1928, Dufrêne in 1930, were all children and adolescents during the war. The youth that studies from the end of the decade allude to refer more to "new youth" who didn't know war and whom, according to the inquires cited, are more sensible or more conservative than the J3 and Saint-Germain-des-Près generation; they were more sensible and for that matter generally hostile toward abstract art.[16]

Even though the artists concerned were thirty-somethings, the "youth" Biennale situated itself at the crossroads of a specific history of French artistic institutions as it relates to their relationship with "current art" and a more general problem that extended to French society in the context of generations born between 1925 and 1940. In short, the latter was the "less than thirty-five" group that formed the contingents of artists represented at the Biennale. As shown through the mixture of condescension and paternalism in the comments made by André Chastel, Guy Dornand, or Robert Rey, this choice was not made without ruffling a few feathers.[17] Several months earlier, in August, Cogniat had given a few explanations in the first issue of the magazine *Perspectives*, where he spoke on the question of youth as "one of the most discussed of the next Biennale." He explained: "And we object not without reason that not only has an artist not yet had the time to express himself to the fullest extent by 35, but also that so very often artists who are much older have proven their freshness of mind, their vitality of discovery and their constant renewal that could be the envy of many young people. We do not deny and never wanted to insinuate that an artist had reached his destiny at 35 years of age."[18] Once this concession was made, he immediately added the opposite: "We are saying that at 35 years of age the games are already over and the following years witness their development." Cogniat, like the other supporters of the Biennale, considered that "all the important movements in contemporary art were shaped by men under the age of 35 and this was not a coincidence."[19] Namely he was referring to the impressionists of the 1874 exposition; the postimpressionists of the first exhibition of the Independents; André Derain, Raoul Dufy, Rouault, Maurice de Vlaminck, and Kees Van Dongen in 1905; Braque and Picasso in 1908; Robert Delaunay's windows; and Paul Klee's "new way" after his trip to Tunisia. The legitimacy of this argument was upheld at the *Jeunesse des maîtres* (Youth of the masters) exhibition that, in parallel with the Biennale, presented three generations of artists born between 1860 and 1900. This was done under the pretext, which was as fallacious as it was ironic, that these artists had all been under thirty-five at one point in their lives. This pretext allowed for the justification of Cogniat's idea that "the most important movements that have influenced modern art were created by artists between the ages of 20 and 35."[20] Furthermore, through the back door it let in the Matisse, Rouault, Vuillard, Marquet, Villon, Gromaire, and, in the end, all French painting since fauvism that had been chased out the front door.

In the Biennale magazine, the contradiction was remarked upon by the venerable Joseph Pichard, creator of the journal *L'Art sacré* in 1935 (then of the *Salon d'art sacré* in 1951 and of the journal *Art chrétien* in 1955), for whom "youth had no age"; "at 20 years of age one may not be young, one could be at 80"[21]—the most obvious example being Paul Cézanne, who was among the many listed by Pichard. In the same sense the critic Frank Elgar, who was in his sixties himself, affirmed in *Carrefour* that "the artist is old at 30, it is only during his later years that he acquires youth as Monet, Matisse, Bonnard have shown us."[22]

Thursday, October 29, at 9:00 p.m.—some days later—the young Michel Ragon dedicated his book *La peinture actuelle* to the Arnaud gallery.[23] In this book, destined for a wide readership, Ragon also evokes the question of youth. At first, he seems to reiterate arguments of the likes of Pichard or Elgar: "We believe that youth and newness are synonymous, meanwhile Kandinsky, Mondrian, Fautrier, Dubuffet were all forty when they became avant-garde painters."[24] And inversely, in this same vein: "Bernard Buffet has been a very old painter from the beginning." In fact, Ragon aims primarily to ruin Buffet, describing him as a "mundane *misérabiliste*" whose youth contributed to his notoriety—especially among older people—and in this kind of a battle all arguments are valid. For, at the same time, Ragon had spent the last ten years lashing out at Braque and Picasso, "inflexible old men," for their turpitude as "old painters vehemently opposed to youth who did not declare themselves their students."[25]

Therefore, it is not so insignificant that the first chapter of this same book is titled "Les vieilles gloires de l'École de Paris" (The old glories of the school of Paris). Ragon may be making a less reverential use of the word *old* when he used these terrible words in reference to Chagall: "It is a common trait among most painters that they become more and more [joli] by growing old."[26] This sentence is repeated almost word for word in his conclusion: "It is a sure fact, I repeat, that painters become more and more [joli] by growing old. Take Chagall, for example. What shall we believe? That old age dulls us or that success leads to compromise?" An advance copy of the book, dedicated to the critic Marcel Zahar, includes the latter's annotations in the margins. Like a teacher, Zahar marks with a "B" for "Bien" [good], or most often with an "idiotic," in Ragon's text. Next to the passage on Chagall's beauty and old age, this sentence is written in pencil: "what's the use of this kind of insult from a young person." That says it all: as Ragon, now a dashing young eighty-five-year-old, recently told me: "You understand, Zahar, Cogniat, Courthion, they were the old guys!" This is the same Ragon who just published a short book in which he evokes some failings of old age and which he aptly titled—as he confesses in the first line—the "sunset for the old."[27] As Terzieff rightly said of Carné's film, the "problem" with youth was above all a problem with the old. It was a conflict of generations that, at the end of the fifties, had become crucial. It was a problem with the old, but never named a problem with old age: an old age that General de Gaulle spoke of, in *L'appel*, the first volume of his *Mémoires de guerre*, published in 1954, as a "shipwreck."[28] This well-known quote often cited out of context—de Gaulle was speaking specifically of Marshal Pétain in 1940—has at least a symptomatic value if we relate it to others. André Gide, canonized as a Nobel Prize winner in 1947, evoked these "abounding examples of dishonourable old age."[29] Furthermore, Robert Badinter saw in Sagan "a young author who was as old as the others."[30]

The "old," "decrepit," "feudal," and "PPH" (*passera pas l'hiver* or will not live through winter) were some of the descriptors used by insolent and creative youth.[31] They were the important old men regularly crowned in Venice. They were the ones who claimed to represent a noble tradition of French modernity. They were the ones to whom Jacques Lassaigne, while mentioning Cogniat, was referring, for their "own tastes leaned towards the era of their youth, that is to say 1925."[32] They were the ones whom Pierre Restany, when evoking Gaston Diehl, described as "this intermediary generation to whom history gave a strong sense of responsibility . . . who had to take on the heavy task of bridging the times between before and after the war."[33]

International Relations

While the Biennale was aimed at young artists, it was also an international event. The international situation and the French situation are quite clear in this respect. Therefore, Cogniat could state in the preface to the catalog of the Biennale de Paris: "The large international match-ups are multiplying. Venice and São Paulo serve as examples and proliferate. France, who gives priority to the realm of arts, could not stay outside a movement of this nature that allows for ample information and extends intellectual exchanges."[34] In his address at the award ceremony, André Malraux emphasized this international dimension, drawing on the forty-two represented nations: "This exhibition . . . marks well, to a degree never before reached, the state of painting in the world. Each of us is forced to take stock."[35] But as the rest of the speech shows, this concession was just rhetorical:

> In no other city—be it the most powerful in the world—next to a river that runs alongside second-hand bookshops and the boutiques of bird dealers, are entire streets lined with paintings of the great masters informally opposed to the paintings of beginners, the genius of yesterday to the hope of today. It is only there that painting seems to grow through the cobblestones. . . .
>
> And in these paintings, chosen from all those the world has sent to Paris and of which Raymond Cogniat is now going to give you the list, I cannot prevent myself from seeing a tribute by all these painters to a city that once gone we will say: "There, painting lived in freedom."[36]

This pompous and grandiloquent lyricism that characterizes all of Malraux's speeches was quite common in this era where it was about expressing a chauvinistic vision of art history. The same commonplaces, the same conventional rhetoric, the same supposed "poetic" style is found, for example, in a documentary proposed by French news in 1950:[37] *L'art vivant*, to the famous tune of Vincent Scotto sung by Georgel in 1913, "Sous les ponts de Paris," aligns visual clichés (the Eiffel Tower, the bridges of Paris) and conventional rhetoric in an anthem that is, today, caricatural of the city:

> Under the bridges of Paris, the Seine runs like a miracle mood. Along its banks, each era leaves a story and, across from the Eiffel Tower, a giant gnomon marks the hour in Paris, the Palais de Tokyo hosts under its columns the most extraordinary of conferences, where each genius, where each current talent gave meaning to the visible universe. It's Matisse and rediscovered certainty. It's Picasso and the eternal search. It's Braque and internal rhythm. It's Derain and naked power. It's Rouault and the tragedy of the world.

The beginning of this documentary resembles so closely that of Vincente Minelli's film *An American in Paris* (1951) that it could be mistaken for it, and we must ask who in Hollywood or France, has, in this particular case, the advertising talent to produce postcards and universal clichés for the use of tourists. Whatever the case may be, ten years later, we notice that Malraux uses the same outdated images of the "bridges of Paris," just like Bernard Dorival, who, upon being asked why so many artists wanted to come live and work in Paris, responded: "The only explanation is that the Spirit still breathes in this old city and that the 'mood' is better suited here than elsewhere for the blooming of talents, in independence and freedom."[38] These commonplaces in Paris, its cobblestones, bridges, Eiffel Tower, and paintings, which are enduring and are still used today in particular to inform the American public of Paris in American television series like *Alias* (2001–6) and in French productions such as *Amélie Poulain* (2001), among others, weren't only the effects of a jingoistic nationalism since they were very popular *à l'étranger*, as we used to say. Edy de Wilde, director of the Stedelijk van Abbemuseum of Eindhoven, expressed his enthusiasm in comparable terms: "This is in Paris, more than elsewhere, that the entire range of painting becomes visible."

This rhetoric was accepted wholeheartedly by the very Gaullist Pierre Restany in an "inquiry" for the television program *En français dans le texte* made by Louis Pauwels, Jacques Mousseau, and Jean Feller and broadcast on RTF, the Radiodiffusion-télévision française, for the 1960 season, which debuted on September 23.[39] The show opened with the following question: "Fifty years ago, artists from all countries would arrange to meet in Paris. Is this still true today? Is Paris still the capital of the arts?" To ask the question was, in a sense, to anticipate the possibility of a negative response. But the journalist Jacques Mousseau responded without hesitation: "Yes, and it may be truer than ever." Interviews with artists who had chosen to live and work in Paris followed: Yozo Hamaguchi, Hisao Domoto, Paul Jenkins, James Metcalf, Agostim Cárdenas, Alice Penalba. Restany praised the virtues of solidarity, community, and especially freedom that Paris represents for the artists of the world that meet there: "Being in Paris is to learn a certain freedom." Restany became lyrical or even Malraucian when concluding: "Paris is the city of hope. Paris is the city that is indispensable to the acquisition of a universal language in the arts. It is up to Paris to create the universal language." And the report finished with a view of the Seine, Notre Dame, the bridges of Paris, the Eiffel Tower, the giant gnomon, and so forth.

Even though Paris' prestige and its syncretic vocation were still largely appropriate, as the testimonials of the artists interviewed show, these commonplaces of national genius and of Paris or the beacon of civilization and of the "universal language" already had, at the end of the fifties, a quality. Indeed, it seemed obvious to many that Paris no longer had, in terms of the arts as elsewhere, international preeminence. From 1958, in an open letter to Michel Ragon, the Belgian poet Christian Dotremont, cofounder of COBRA, was ironic about this nationalism and these postcard images that made Paris "a larger grotto of Lourdes."[40] As the critic Waldermar George clearly said, in *Combat*, while it was dedicated to young people, "the Biennale had other objectives," notably that of restoring "its place as the capital of the arts" in the context of a "plot hatched against French art," given credence by the awards attributed to Giorgio Morandi in São Paulo in 1957 and Mark Tobey in Venice in 1958.[41]

The target was clear. In the program *En français dans le texte*, Jacques Mousseau could not have been more direct when he asked the Argentinean artist Alice Penalba, in a more assertive than interrogative tone: "You chose Paris but couldn't you have chosen another city, New York for example?"

Precisely. Malraux spoke only of this at the Biennale. And we see clearly in the opening phrase of his harangue ("in no other city—*be it the most powerful in the world*") to whom this speech was addressed. However successful other biennales in the world may have been, neither Venice nor São Paulo nor Kassel were the "*most powerful* [city] *in the world*." He could not have been more direct had he pointed his finger at New York.

The message was received: some days later in the *New York Herald Tribune* Annette Michelson commented on Malraux's statements rebroadcasted the night before in *Le Monde* and identified within the Biennale a political signal: "The Biennale most certainly is a gesture, and a gesture most comprehensible and interesting. It has been precipitated by the tactical position of the School of Paris, and everything about it, including the unprecedented speed and efficiency with which it has been organized, indicates that it is essentially a defensive riposte in a duel to the death."[42] The Paris Biennale constitutes, according to Michelson, a response to Venice, São Paulo, and "indirectly but more importantly" to the United States. In a remarkable analysis of geopolitical finesse, she defines the Biennale as "a highly self-conscious enterprise, expressing a need for reassurance, for self-assertion and prestige inherent in France's general position today. The Biennale has a specifically Fifth-Republic character; it is one aspect of the general policy of the *rayonnement de la culture française*."[43] It just goes to show that already at this time we clearly saw the expectations of cultural politics. It also goes to show how much hostility was already therein engaged.

Times Are Tough

From the point of view of French cultural supremacy, times were tough. By a significant coincidence, the Paris Biennale opened its doors at the same time as those of the second Documenta at Kassel, which had taken place in the summer of 1959 (July 11–October 11, 1959) and had been consecrated exclusively to American abstract painting, were closing. Organized by artist and designer Arnold Bode and art historian Werner Haftmann, this exhibition— the theme of which was "art after 1945"—was quite unanimously considered the most caricatural illustration of an apologetic and teleological history of abstraction, a genre to which books by Franz Roh and Will Grohmann can be linked, and to which Haftmann had been the herald since the publication of *Painting in the Twentieth Century* in two volumes, which formed the theoretical basis of the first Documenta and afterward were regularly republished.[44] Jackson Pollock and Wols (Alfred Otto Wolfgang Schulze) were the heroes of this abstraction that we remember above all as a triumph of American abstraction.

The French, after several other European countries, were able to catch a glimpse of this triumph at the beginning of the year 1959, with the *Jackson Pollock et la nouvelle peinture américaine* (January 16–February 15, 1959) exhibition. While during the 1950s, American art was regularly presented by galleries, artists (Georges Mathieu), and critics (Michel Tapié), as well as by the National Modern Art Museum,[45] more regularly than other exhibitions of the same genre organized by the International Council of the MoMA, this particular exhibition could be considered a true war machine of this cultural war. The French edition of it combined two touring exhibitions: the retrospective *Jackson Pollock* and the exhibition *The New American Painting*.

The Pollock exhibition, organized by Sam Hunter at the time of the American artist's death in 1956, explicitly wanted a "historic moment" to the point that the critic Hilton Kramer considered it exemplary of the "prevailing tone of art criticism with its tendencies to dissolve all discrete objects and events in a headlong historical continuum, which, by purely rhetorical transformations, is itself made the new fulcrum of artistic meaning. This tendency has nowhere been so quintessentially embodied in overwrought rhetorical sophistries as in Mr. Hunter's brief monograph on Pollock for the exhibition which he has organized. It is a monograph which claims for Pollock the heroism of history to a degree which is absolute and unequivocal."[46] At the same time, Alfred Frankfurter, the director of *ArtNews* and former commissioner of the American pavilion at the Venice Biennale, published in his magazine, in a text with the perfectly clear title "The Voyages of Dr. Caligari through Time and Space," a version of this heroic story of expressionism born in Germany finishing its journey in America with Pollock.[47]

It was this exhibit that was shown in France, as elsewhere in Europe, but mixed with *The New American Painting* exhibit organized by Dorothy Miller as part of the MoMA's international program and that also toured in seven other European countries in 1958. It was an iteration of the American shows that were imagined by Miller in 1942 in the framework of war propaganda and continued until 1963.[48] The 1958 exhibit added to the historic group of the 1940s (William Baziotes, Adolph Gottlieb, Arshile Gorky, Pollock, Clyfford Still) younger artists, or less known in Europe, who constituted a part of the group in the exhibit *Twelve Americans* in 1956 (James Brooks, Sam Francis, Philip Guston, Grace Hartigan). This allowed for Abstract Expressionism to have a lineage that we could hold onto, thanks to a small chronological imprecision, the name of "second generation," supported by Clement Greenberg—the inventor of the notion of "American-Type Painting" in 1955—and Meyer

Schapiro. It wasn't quite a question yet of New York "stealing the idea of modern art," but with this exhibition, the Americans showed Europe that not only did they have "new painting" but also that this painting had a second generation, that is to say a history, an *indigenous* history.

In the wake of the exhibition *Cinquante ans d'art moderne* shown during the Brussels World's Fair in 1958, which was considered in France to be a veritable provocation toward Paris,[49] along with the award given to Tobey in Venice, these American exhibits seemed like they were showing off their power. It was becoming clear for many in Europe that "the unwavering fortress of the French school was shaken," as Will Grohmann put it in September 1958 in *Der Tagesspiegel*.[50]

Especially since, as the title of the report by Pierre Restany in *Cimaise* shows, "U.S. Go Home and Come Back Later" (in English in the original text), the *Jackson Pollock et la nouvelle peinture américaine* exhibition was not welcome.[51] Anti-Americanism dated back at least as far as the postwar years and was fed by American military presence on French soil and by the ideological war fought between communists and anticommunists. Although the external politics of the French Fourth Republic had temporarily calmed, it experienced a sudden jolt with de Gaulle's return to power, his memorandum to President Dwight D. Eisenhower and to British Prime Minister Harold Macmillan in September 1958, and the events of the year 1959 that ended with the retreat of French naval forces from the Mediterranean and the refusal to stock American nuclear arms on French soil. The beginning of the Fifth Republic was marked by growing tension between France—that is to say de Gaulle—and the United States.

America and Youth

In the meantime, in New York City, another happy coincidence took place. In precisely the year 1959, one month after the Paris Biennale, the exhibition *Sixteen Americans*, the last of Dorothy Miller's American shows, illustrated in a striking and even scandalous manner the politics of the museum in terms of its support for young artists.[52]

Placed under the patronage of Louise Nevelson—who surprised everyone by presenting a white collection, *Dawn's Wedding Feast*—the exhibit assured the filiation of Abstract Expressionism (in particular Alfred Leslie and Jack Youngerman) but also showed the two stars of the Castelli gallery, Robert Rauschenberg and Jasper Johns, who had been the main topic of conversation the year before. Above all, a newcomer—Frank Stella—who, discovered and supported by William Seitz and Robert Rosenblum among other Princeton professors, had had an exhibition at Tibor de Nagy in April and had just been taken on by Castelli, was shown. Dorothy Miller's account of her discovery of Stella leaves no doubt of the strong impression the young painter immediately made on Castelli and herself when they visited the painter's studio in the summer of 1959.[53]

After the exhibition the museum bought Stella's *The Marriage of Reason and Squalor*, but not without rousing the acrimony of the regular enemies of the MoMA, like Emily Genauer of the *New York Herald Tribune* and John Canaday of the *New York Times*. This purchase, like others, could not have shown any better the politics of the museum that supported both the potential successors of Abstract Expressionism and, despite the scandals, the "enfants terribles" of the New York scene such as Johns, Rauschenberg, and Stella, since their first exhibition at Leo Castelli in 1958 and 1959. It is true that Barr, to whom we owe a history of cubism, abstract art, and surrealism that had a lasting impact on French historiography,[54] had a totally different vision of the relationships between past and present. This is evidenced by this word of advice addressed to gallery owner John Myers: "The art of the past is something that takes care of itself. What is much more important for people like yourself is to do new—really new—things."[55] In 1958 Alfred Barr—and by his voice, the MoMA—deplored the academicism of Abstract Expressionism and called for a "revolution" by young artists.[56] In doing so, Barr and his team of curators created a historic follow-up to the American movement that began with Abstract Expressionism, a follow-up first seen from the perspective of the heirs of "American-Type Painting" but in some way sidetracked by Leo Castelli's burst onto the scene and his decisive and above all voluntary action in the construction of an American historiography. The "second generation of the New York School," also referred to as "Post Painterly Abstraction" by Clement Greenberg, had to face the growing power of an alternative principally portrayed by Rauschenberg as of the middle of the decade. In merely a couple of years, the "second generation" scene faced a collapse that was primarily linked to a major event: in February 1957 Leo Castelli, who had been evolving for several years on the art scene, opened his gallery. Now, for Castelli the sixties had to be anti-Expressionist; during his numerous interviews, he often recounted his strategy: "I studied art history and figured out that one movement followed another and that there were changes that occurred periodically. . . . I never showed the Abstract Expressionist painters because I didn't have a gallery at this time. But I knew them all, knew what they were doing. They dominated the scene for a while so I felt that something else had to happen. I tried deliberately to detect that other thing."[57] Castelli had known Rauschenberg's work since 1951. Moreover, he had chosen him to participate in the Artists Annual that he had organized at Sidney Janis's Ninth Street Show that same year. Rauschenberg and his white paintings already went against Abstract Expressionism.[58] In March 1957, one month after the opening of his gallery, Castelli discovered Johns at an exhibition organized by Meyer Schapiro at the Jewish Museum presenting artists from the "second generation of the New York School": it was "total and absolute" love at first sight.[59] The two artists were to become the "pillars" of the gallery.

Johns's first solo exhibition, in January 1958, was a scandal for supporters of the mainstream but, nevertheless, a big success: the cover of *ArtsNews* featured *Target with Four Faces*—the choice being that of Thomas Hess, who was ordinarily an ardent defender of Abstract Expressionists. Barr and Miller chose three works for the museum—and one each for their personal collections—facts without precedent for such a young painter. Two months later, the first exhibition of Rauschenberg and his works *Combine Paintings Bed, Odalisk, Gloria, Satellite,* and *Rebus* at Castelli's was another scandal. The MoMA did not buy anything but chose at this moment to include Rauschenberg and Johns in the future American show, and selected Rauschenberg, when the question was raised, for the new Biennale de Paris.[60]

The role of the MoMA in the selection of young artists—and therefore in the fabric of history to follow—was the object of numerous debates at the time. In her interview with Paul Cummings, Dorothy Miller remembered that they were constantly accused by the hostile art critics of making these careers, against which she defends herself. Three years later, in the conference on Pop Art organized by Peter Selz on December 13, 1962, Hilton Kramer was dismissing Leo Steinberg, who was surprised to be reproached at the MoMA for his actions regarding contemporary art and his naïveté on the subject: "I think, Leo, that you are completely ignoring the role that the Museum plays in creating history as well as reflecting it."[61] And Henry Gelzahler added: "It is too late for the Museum of Modern Art to step out of history. It is very much involved in the action and reaction of contemporary history."[62]

Stella himself would pass on an extremely pertinent anecdote on the subject. At the time of the opening, Stella met Margaret Scolari Barr, the wife of MoMA's curator, who was also an art historian: "She said 'Well, how does it feel to be here in the Museum of Modern Art which is the most important historical museum in the world' or something to that effect, 'this is going to affect art history, just the fact that you've been chosen for this.'"[63] In a very astute analysis, Stella very aptly interpreted this remark as an enormous "burden" that this "historic consequence" could put on the shoulders of a young painter, like a confession in regard to the enormous burden that was already weighing on the shoulders of his interlocutor, on her critical judgment: "In other words, she was really worried about how history was going to judge her critical evaluation of me."[64] Through Margaret Barr, this anecdote revealed, like a lapsus, the repressed intentions of the MoMA.

The fifties witnessed the emancipation of American art from European tutelage, which had become stifling after World War II, by the writing of a national American art history, from Winslow Homer to John Sloan to Jackson Pollock.[65] By the end of the decade, the next chapter of this history was already in play, with the artists of the "second generation," according to Greenberg's expression—like Grace Hartigan, Helen Frankenthaler, Theodoros Stamos, that is to say Schapiro and Greenberg's artists—largely supported by Alfred Barr and Dorothy Miller at the MoMA, or Castelli's "enfants terribles": Rauschenberg, Johns, and Stella. In short, in December 1959, the year Paris discovered an American art history from Pollock and Willem de Kooning to Francis and Frankenthaler, New York was already busy writing the next chapter of its history. France would discover this history some time later, in 1964, when one of these young Americans defeated an old French artist, in Venice.

An Old Country and a Young Nation

Another meaning of this opposition, or better put, of this *relationship* between the young and the old that constantly comes back to the discourse on time, exceeds the social framework of the "problem of society" to become something like a symptom of a problem of civilization, a problem stemming from anthropology or a more general historical psychology. Every now and then this rapport between "the young and the old" comes to define the relationship between the old world and the new. It is such that, in the American version of *The New American Painting* exposition catalog, where an international press review is published, André Chastel's article in *Le Monde* clearly demonstrated the paternalistic contempt in which France—or at least a certain France—held the United States. This attitude was brought to light also, some time before that, by the benevolent albeit a bit suspicious condescension offered by Jean Cassou regarding the "young American nation."[66] This stereotype has more recently resurfaced with the "historic" speech made by the Minister of French Foreign Affairs Dominique de Villepin addressed to the United States at the UN in 2003 at the time of the Second Iraq War: "it is an old country that is telling you."

As Pierre Bourdieu very rightly said, "youth is but a word."[67] It is a social, symbolic, ideological, construction, a problem in the balance of power. "Youth and old age are not facts but socially constructed, in the struggle between the young and the old."[68] It is whatever creates the two signifiers.

In the second chapter of his book, "'Blousons noirs' et 'croulants,'" Émile Copfermann cites in an epigraph a number of short quotes and beautiful texts on this relationship between the young and the old, such as the magnificent dialogue drawn from Jean-Paul Sartre's *Les séquestrés d'Altona*, a play written at the moment General de Gaulle took power and in the context of the Algerian War and the torture that the play serves to denunciate. It was performed for the first time on September 23, 1959, with Serge Reggiani in the role of Frantz; September 23 was one week before the youth Biennale:

The father—Do you remember the future that I had given you?

Frantz—Yes.

The father—I talked to you about it ceaselessly and you saw it. Well, it was only my past.

Translated from the French by Molleen Shilliday

Notes

1. Alain Jouffroy, *Une révolution du regard: À propos de quelques peintres et sculpteurs contemporains* (Paris: Gallimard, 1964), 193. Translations from French into English are by Molleen Shilliday, unless otherwise indicated.

2. Manifeste du Nouveau Réalisme, Milan, April 16, 1960.

3. Bernard Dorival, *Les étapes de la peinture française contemporaine*, 3 vols., vol. 1, *De l'impressionnisme au fauvisme, 1883–1905* (Paris: Gallimard, 1943); vol. 2, *Le fauvisme et le cubisme, 1905–1911* (Paris: Gallimard, 1944); vol. 3, *Depuis le cubisme, 1911–1944* (Paris: Gallimard, 1946).

4. Jean Cassou, Bernard Dorival, and Geneviève Homolle, "Introduction," in *Musée National d'Art Moderne, catalogue-guide* (Paris: Éditions des musées nationaux, 1954), vii.

5. Quoted in Marylène Malbert, "Les relations artistiques internationales à la Biennale de Venise, 1948–1969" (PhD diss., Université Paris I Panthéon-Sorbonne, 2006), 311.

6. "La biennale des jeunes artistes au musée d'Art moderne à Paris," accessed June 13, 2014, http://www.ina.fr/art-et-culture/musees-et-expositions/video/I04189963/la-Biennalee-des-jeunes-artistes-au-musee-d-art-moderne-a-paris.fr.html.

7. Françoise Giroud, *La Nouvelle Vague: Portraits de la jeunesse* (Paris: Gallimard, 1958).

8. Claude Bourdet, preface to *La génération des blousons noirs: Problèmes de la jeunesse française*, by Émile Copfermann (Paris: Maspéro, 1962), 7. On this subject, it is relevant that the admirable publishing firm Maspéro was founded in 1959 by a twenty-seven-year-old who thereafter had the sad honor of being harassed, due to his involvement as a leftist, by the political censorship of de Gaulle and Pompidou.

9. François Mauriac, *La France va-t-elle perdre sa jeunesse?* (Paris: Arthème Fayard, 1954).

10. Henri Perruchot, *La France et sa jeunesse* (Paris: Hachette, 1958).

11. Alfred Sauvy, *La montée des jeunes* (Paris: Calmann-Lévy, 1959). This book inspired, among other things, the creation of the TV magazine *Le journal des jeunes* that then became *L'avenir est à vous* by Françoise Dumayet and J.-P. Chartier in 1960. See the works of Marie-Françoise Lévy for information on the history of television during this period.

12. Jean Jousselin, *Jeunesse, fait social méconnu: La place des jeunes dans la civilisation française d'aujourd'hui* (Toulouse: Privat, 1959). Jousselin, director of the Centre d'études du Conseil français des mouvements de jeunesse, also published *Présence de la jeunesse: Structure sociale—Mouvements; Rôle des pouvoirs publics* (Paris: Privat, 1955).

13. On this subject, see Ludivine Bantigny, *Le plus bel âge?* (Paris: Fayard, 2007).

14. On the subject of cinema and youth, see Antoine de Baecque, *La Nouvelle Vague: Portrait d'une jeunesse* (Paris: Flammarion, 1998).

15. Robert Kanters and Gilbert Sigaux, *Vingt ans en 1951* (Paris: R. Juillard, 1951).

16. On this subject, see Perruchot, *La France et sa jeunesse.*

17. André Chastel, "Les plaisirs de la jeunesse," *Le Monde*, October 5, 1959; Guy Dornand, "La première Biennale de peinture," *Le Hors-cote*, October 7, 1959; Robert Rey, "N'est pas jeune qui veut," *Nouvelles littéraires*, October 8, 1959.

18. Raymond Cogniat, "L'âge de la jeunesse," *Perspectives, Bulletin d'informations et d'études critiques publié par la Biennale de Paris*, no. 1 (August 1959): 4. (The two-page spread is topped with the title "Pourquoi trente-cinq ans?")

19. Cogniat, "L'âge de la jeunesse."

20. Cogniat, "L'âge de la jeunesse."

21. Joseph Pichard, "La Jeunesse n'a pas d'âge," *Perspectives, Bulletin d'informations et d'études critiques publié par la Biennale de Paris*, no. 1 (August 1959): 5.

22. Frank Elgar, *Carrefour*, March 4, 1959.

23. Michel Ragon, *La peinture actuelle* (Paris: Arthème Fayard, 1959).

24. Ragon, *La peinture actuelle*, 59.

25. Michel Ragon, *L'aventure de l'art abstrait* (Paris: Robert Laffont, 1956), 74.

26. Ragon, *La peinture actuelle*, 23.

27. Michel Ragon, *Ils se croyaient illustres et immortels* (Paris: Albin Michel, 2011).

28. Charles de Gaulle, *Mémoires de guerre*, vol. 1, *L'appel, 1940–42* (Paris: Plon, 1954).

29. André Gide, *Ainsi soit-il: Ou les Jeux sont faits* (Paris: Gallimard, 1952).

30. *L'Express*, February 20, 1958, quoted in Bantigny, *Le plus bel âge?*, 44.

31. Bantigny, *Le plus bel âge?*, 41.

32. "Une interview de Jacques Lassaigne," in *Biennale de Paris, une anthologie: 1959–1967* (Paris: Fondation nationale des arts plastiques, 1977).

33. Quoted in the exhibition catalog *Un homme, une empreinte, Gaston Diehl, 1912–1999* (Paris: Venezuela Art Promotion, 2000), 24–31.

34. Biennale de Paris, 1959, vii.

35. André Malraux, *Perspectives, Bulletin d'informations et d'études critiques publié par la Biennale de Paris*, no. 2 (October 1959): 1.

36. André Malraux, *Perspectives*: 1.

37. *L'art vivant*, January 1, 1950, accessed June 21, 2014, http://www.ina.fr/art-et -culture/musique/video/AFE00003967/1-art-vivant.fr.html.

38. Bernard Dorival, *L'École de Paris au Musée national d'art moderne* (Paris: Éditions Aimery Somogy, 1961), 18–19.

39. "Une enquête," *En français dans le texte*, September 23, 1960, accessed June 22, 2014, http://www.ina.fr/art-et-culture/beaux-arts/video/CPF08009178/une-enquete .fr.html.

40. "Lettre ouverte de Christian Dotremont à propos du nationalisme artistique français" (1958) in *Vingt-cinq ans d'art vivant: Chronique vécue de l'art contemporain de l'abstraction au pop art, 1944–1969*, by Michel Ragon (Tournai: Casterman, 1969), 80.

41. *Combat* (Art section), November 1959, 9.

42. Michel Conil Lacoste, "Avec M. André Malraux à la Biennale de Paris," *Le Monde*, October 6, 1959; Annette Michelson, "About the Biennale," *New York Herald Tribune*, October 7, 1959.

43. Michelson, "About the Biennale."

44. Will Grohmann, *Neue Kunst nach 1945* (Cologne: M. DuMont Schauberg, 1958); Will Grohmann, *Art since 1945* (New York: Harry N. Abrams, 1958); Franz Roh, *Geschichte der deutschen Kunst von 1900 bis zur Gegenwart* (Munich: Bruckmann, 1958); Werner Haftmann, *Painting in the Twentieth Century*, 2 vols. (New York: Praeger, 1960).

45. Such exhibits included *Advancing American Art en 1946* and, via the international program of the Museum of Modern Art, *L'œuvre du XXᵉ siècle* in 1952, *Douze peintres et sculpteurs américains* in 1953, and *50 ans d'art aux États-Unis* in 1955.

46. Hilton Kramer, "Month in Review," *Arts* 31, no. 5 (February 1957): 46–51.

47. Alfred Frankfurter, "The Voyages of Dr. Caligari through Time and Space," *Art News* 55, no. 9 (January 1957): 28–31, 64–65.

48. *Americans*, 1942; *American Realists and Magic Realists*, 1943; *Fourteen Americans*, 1946; *Fifteen Americans*, 1952; *Twelve Americans*, 1956; *The New American Painting*, 1958–59; *Sixteen Americans*, 1959; *Americans*, 1963.

49. *Cinquante ans d'art moderne*, Brussels, Heysel, International Palace of Fine Arts, April 17–October 19 1958.

50. Will Grohmann, *Der Tagesspiegel*, September 7, 1958. Text translated and published in the American version of the catalog.

51. Pierre Restany, "U.S. Go Home and Come Back Later," *Cimaise* 6, no. 3 (winter 1959): 36–37.

52. This exhibit ran from December 16, 1959, to February 14, 1960. See Dorothy C. Miller, ed., *Sixteen Americans* (Garden City, NY: Doubleday, 1959).

53. See Dorothy Miller, "Interview with Paul Cummings," 1970, Archives of American Art, microfilms 4210–11: 137–38.

54. The expositions *Cubism and Abstract Art* (March–April 1936) and *Fantastic Art, Dada, Surrealism* (December 1936–January 1937) are regularly cited by Jean Cassou, *Panorama des arts plastiques contemporains* (Paris: Gallimard, 1960); and Bernard Dorival, *Les peintres du vingtième siècle* (Paris: Pierre Tisné, collection "Pictura," 1957), 2 vols., vol. 1, *Nabis, Fauves, Cubistes*; vol. 2, *Du cubisme à l'abstraction, 1914–1957*, among others. The famous diagram on the cover of *Cubism and Abstract Art* was moreover reprinted in Michel Seuphor's *L'Art abstrait: Ses origines, ses premiers maîtres* (Paris: Maeght, 1949).

55. John Bernard Myers, *Tracking the Marvelous: A Life in the New York Art World* (New York: Random House, 1983), 171.

56. Alfred Barr, speaking at the club in 1958, deplored what he called the "young academy" of Abstract Expressionism and called for a "'revolution' by younger artists." Calvin Tomkins, *Off the Wall: Robert Rauschenberg and the Art World of Our Time* (Garden City, NY: Doubleday, 1980), 133.

57. Leo Castelli, "Interview with Milton Esterow," *ARTnews*, April 1991, 75.

58. "I had met Rauschenberg many years before.... Already in 1951, when I organized the Ninth Street show, I spotted him [Rauschenberg] as an artist who was doing something different from the prevailing Abstract Expressionist mood." Castelli, "Interview with Milton Esterow," 73–74.

59. *The New York School: Second Generation* (New York: Jewish Museum, 1957).

60. See Miller, "Interview with Paul Cummings," 255.

61. "A Symposium on Pop Art," *Arts Magazine* 37, no. 7 (April 1963): 42–43.

62. "A Symposium on Pop Art," 43.

63. Frank Stella, "Interview with Sidney Tillim," March 1969, Archives of American Art, microfilm, 3418, 4.

64. Stella, "Interview with Sidney Tillim," 5.

65. On American art moving away from European influence, see Serge Guilbaut, *How New York Stole the Idea of Modern Art: Abstract Expressionism, Freedom, and the Cold War* (Chicago: University of Chicago Press, 1983), particularly chapter 4. The idea of a national American art history started to appear in 1936 with Alfred Barr. See Kirk Varnedoe, "The Evolving Torpedo: Changing Ideas of the Collection of Painting and Sculpture at the Museum of Modern Art," in *The Museum of Modern Art at Mid-Century: Continuity and Change*, ed. John Elderfield, Studies in Modern Art 5 (New York: MoMA/Abrams, 1995), 15–73, followed by Clement Greenberg in two articles for the *Nation* in June and *Les temps modernes* in September–October 1946. Still uncertain

in John I. H. Baur, Lloyd Goodrich, Dorothy C. Miller, James T. Soby, and Frederick S. Wight, *New Art in America: Fifty Painters of the 20th Century* (New York: Whitney Museum of American Art/New York Graphic Society, 1957), this history aligns itself clearly with Sam Hunter, *Modern American Painting and Sculpture* (New York: Dell, 1959); and Lloyd Goodrich and John I. H. Baur, *American Art of Our Century* (New York: Whitney Museum of American Art/Praeger, 1961).

66. Jean Cassou, "A French Viewpoint: Paris Critic Finds a Nomadic Element in Recent American Painting," *New York Times*, November 28, 1954, reprinted in Serge Guilbaut, *Be-Bomb: The Transatlantic War of Images and All That Jazz, 1946–1956*, exposition catalog (Barcelona: Museo d'Art Contemporani de Barcelona; Madrid: Museo Nacional Centro de Arte Reina Sofía, 2007), 641–43.

67. Pierre Bourdieu, *Questions de sociologie* (Paris: Minuit, 1984), 144.

68. Bourdieu, *Questions de sociologie*, 144.

REDEFINING THE BOUNDARIES OF CULTURE
The French Experience of Jazz

"Le jazz, c'est comme les bananes, ça se consomme sur place."[1] Jean-Paul Sartre's famous sentence exemplifies the complexity of the history of jazz in France: a French intellectual visits New York just after World War II, discovering this music in a jazz club and writing a short text in which he insists that jazz is an American phenomenon to be consumed "sur place"; this text is immediately used by French jazz fans to legitimize jazz and to give it a French touch through forever associating (at least in France) African American music and the world of intellectuals. In other words, Sartre's text suggests, though it was not the author's intention, that jazz is both an American exportation and a French invention. The history of jazz in France is indeed a curious one: developed between the 1920s and the beginning of the 1960s, it is the story of an American genre that became naturalized as French while also legitimized as an original art. This does not mean that France created a *French* jazz; rather, it created a *French* experience of jazz that emerged during these years that was not only the reinterpretation of American jazz but also a local coproduction. This process had two major consequences with respect to the breathless days of 1959–60: first, the integration of jazz in France helped to redefine the French cultural landscape, for it provided an example of the redefinition of the boundaries of national cultures at an age of growing transnational cultural exchanges; second, by redefining the aesthetic boundaries between high and low culture, between academic and avant-garde art, it contributed to the evolution of the hierarchy between arts. This chapter deals with the process of integration of jazz in French culture and examines the way jazz contributed to the explosion of the frontiers between high and low culture by mixing various forms of art.

The French Experience of Jazz

Jazz music encountered a great and lasting success in France from the end of the 1910s (when the first marching bands landed in Brittany in the summer of 1917 a few weeks after the United States entered the war) until today (as witnessed by hundreds of annual jazz festivals throughout France). As early as the thirties, one of the main ingredients of the French recipe of this success appeared: the birth of a group of jazz enthusiasts that grew from year to year and started to gather in apartments of the bourgeois districts of Paris in order to listen to and discuss their favorite music. The Hot Club de France was created in 1932 in Paris and was followed by many others in the provinces; after 1945 until the end of the 1950s, hot clubs were fundamental to the understanding of the success of jazz in France. In addition to listening and commenting, a small group of jazz fans were also acting as agents of diffusion of jazz in France: from the beginning of the 1930s, they organized concerts (Louis Armstrong in Paris in 1934) and worked toward a better understanding of jazz by the public, by way of public conferences and the writing of books (Hugues Panassié published *Le jazz hot* in 1934) and also by creating, in 1935, the first journal in the world exclusively dedicated to "hot" jazz (*Jazz hot*, which still exists). Two years later, in 1937, Charles Delaunay and Hugues Panassié created Swing, the first jazz record label in France. They were promoting American and French jazz at the same time, as is proved by their support of a band created by two young musicians, guitarist Django Reinhardt and violinist Stephane Grappelli, whose Quintette du Hot Club de France was considered an example of what France could bring to jazz. The first concerts and records of this orchestra were in 1934 and by the end of the thirties, the orchestra was recognized both in France and elsewhere in Europe, where it toured in 1938 and 1939.

However, the success of jazz in France remained low-key until World War II. Curiously, the German occupation of France between 1940 and 1944 was a moment of growing audiences for jazz, though this phenomenon was masked by the context of war. Indeed, World War II was perhaps the first moment of a crystallization of a French experience of jazz, given that for four years, French musicians and public lived in cultural autarchia, without the presence and concurrence of American musicians. Incidentally, this was also the moment of the greatest success for the Quintette du Hot Club de France. Though its violinist left Paris for London in 1940, Django Reinhardt stayed in France and was unquestionably one of the stars of the occupation. However, the real golden age of jazz in France occurred after World War II, between the end of the 1940s and the beginning of the 1960s: over the course of less than two decades, more than 500 American jazz musicians came to play in France,[2] and a number of them settled in France for months or years, including Jimmy Gourley and Bud Powell, or even for life, as did Kenny Clarke and Sidney Bechet. More than 950 concerts were organized and 700 recording sessions by French recording companies. From the beginning of the 1960s onward, the success of jazz decreased but it never lost its public as the creation of many festivals during the sixties clearly demonstrates. Today, there are more than 300 jazz festivals in France all year round. Though the success of jazz has known high and low periods between the 1920s and today, the presence of this music in France is undoubtedly a lasting one. France remains one of the most important places in the world for jazz.

JAZZ AND FRENCH CULTURE: A COPRODUCTION IN SITU

This great success and its lasting character was the subject of my research, published more than ten years ago, in which I interpreted the integration of jazz into French culture as a process of acculturation, using the theoretical framework elaborated by acculturation studies that were promoted by cultural anthropologists from the 1930s onward and greatly developed between the 1950s and the 1980s.[3] This framework was especially used in the 1950s and 1960s, both by anthropologists and then by historians, to analyze the relationship established throughout the American continent between immigrants coming from Europe and local cultures (especially Indian culture); it was also used, in a general way, to interpret the confrontation between traditional cultures and modernity. From the middle of the 1980s onward, this theoretical framework was used by historians in order to analyze the process of Americanization of national cultures, both in Europe and other continents.[4] Both European and American historians have extensively studied the processes of reception of American culture in many national areas since World War II. Americanization studies are indeed full of national case studies describing this process: one can read dozens of books pertaining to the Americanization of France, Australia, Austria, Sweden, Germany, and Canada.[5] According to this framework, the process of Americanization is in most cases analyzed in a unidirectional way, as if American culture was an export impermeable to other cultures and as if, symmetrically, other national cultures were importer only. As a consequence, most studies on Americanization have focused on the "reception" of cultural forms coming from the United States to other countries.

If one wants to go further in the analysis of the Americanization process, it is necessary to revise this framework, and especially the concept of "reception." From the 1990s onward, the development of new trends in history and anthropology has brought many tools and concepts seeking to revise the study of international cultural exchanges, among which we can mention the transnational anthropology illustrated by Arjun Appadurai, and also the large field of transnational/global/connected history, all of which have put into the spotlight the articulation of global and local scales and the local construction of transnational phenomena as well.[6] In the new trend of intercultural studies, which emerged from all these works, transnational circulations and local dynamics have proved to be more pertinent than the concepts of "diffusion" and "reception" that now appear as somewhat mechanical and having the disadvantage of naturalizing cultures instead of considering them as historical constructions.

These new perspectives have to be taken into account by historians of Americanization in order to rethink the relationship between the United States and other national cultures, and especially to revise the trilogy diffusion/reception/reinterpretation that characterized the framework of acculturation studies. It is especially important to consider that the local dynamics intervene not as a force of reception and reinterpretation of an imported form but as a factor of coproduction in situ of this form during the process of importation, not after, as was usually suggested by most acculturation studies. The two processes are indeed synchronic, not diachronic. In other words, the exportation and the reinterpretation intervene in the same course, a process that historians of Americanization have hardly underlined, as they were concentrated on the diffusionist perspective.[7] From this perspective, the internationalization of jazz does not have to be considered uniquely as the diffusion of American music coming from the United States that is then transformed by national cultures but as a transnational coproduction in which multiple national cultures participate in the construction of the artistic form called *jazz*, this process occurring synchronically to its development within the United States. France is thus not only the destination of American jazz but an important place of its construction as an aesthetic object.

If we go back now to the recipe of the French experience of jazz, all characteristics of the process of integration of this music in French culture testify to the importance of the local dynamics of the phenomenon: the diffusion of

American jazz in France organized mainly by the French, who came to the United States to find records and musicians and bring them back to France; the international recognition of a number of French jazz musicians from the 1950s onward (pianist Martial Solal being a case in point); the success of jazz not only in Paris but also in the provinces, where hot clubs were active and where concerts and festivals grew in the 1950s and 1960s; the creation of jazz curriculum in French musical schools from the 1960s onward; and, finally, the involvement of the Ministry of Culture in the 1980s, symbolized by the creation of a National jazz orchestra that is the most visible, the most important symptom of the process of naturalizing jazz in France and of institutionalizing the French experience of African American music.

FROM "NIGGER MUSIC" TO ART: A PROCESS OF LEGITIMIZATION

One other interesting aspect of the history of jazz in France is the process of legitimization of what was considered "nigger music" in the beginning of the 1920s, and became recognized as an original art form at the end of the 1950s. There are two main reasons for this recognition.

The first one is the aesthetic evolution of jazz after 1945, when modern jazz appeared with its complex harmonic and rhythmic structures, and was regarded more and more as a respectable music by people who were rejecting it twenty years earlier as a primitive music. The complexity of bebop and the virtuosity of musicians (Charlie Parker, Dizzy Gillespie, and Max Roach, among others), along with the development of orchestral forms represented by musicians like Stan Kenton, Gunther Schüller, or Gil Evans, contributed to the separation of jazz from the sphere of popular music and entry into the club of sophisticated forms of music. This is not the place to develop this aspect, as a number of musicologists have gone through the analysis of musical structures of jazz.[8]

The second reason for the recognition of jazz was the specificity of French alchemy. There are three main elements to be taken into account to understand the role France played in the legitimization of jazz.

First, one should consider the special relationship between France and popular culture and the important power of intellectuals in French culture.[9] During the twentieth century, much popular music was legitimized thanks to intellectuals who wrote and spoke in favor of it: this was the case for tango, jazz, rock, and, more recently, rap. In the category of intellectuals, one has to include not only famous novelists and philosophers like Jean-Paul Sartre (who is the symbol of the figure of the intellectual in contemporary France) but also *middle* intellectuals, having acquired an important knowledge in a specific field: jazz critics, who wrote extensively both in journals and books and in a theoretical manner, belong to this category. From the middle of the 1930s onward, jazz criticism became a literary genre, illustrated by authors like Hugues Panassié in the 1930s, André Hodeir and Lucien Malson in the 1940s and 1950s, or Michel-Claude Jalard and Alain Gerber in the 1960s. They all played a major role in the process of legitimizing jazz.

Second, one must consider the strategy of cultural propaganda organized by jazz enthusiasts as early as the 1930s: concerts, conferences, books, articles, radio talks, and records. Between 1935 and 1960, they succeeded in creating a special place for jazz in the music landscape, somewhere between classical music and variety.

Finally, there is the special relationship of love and hate between France and the United States. Both countries have had the ambition, since the eighteenth century, to deliver a Universalist message to the world. But as early as 1918—from exhaustion by World War I—France was not a great power anymore, whereas the United States became one and was confirmed as such after World War II. Moreover, after 1945, France was one of the European countries where the American influence was most important: it was one of the principal destinations of the Marshall Plan's dollars; American foundations funded many French academics and researchers; jazz music and Hollywood movies encountered a great success, not to mention Coca-Cola, which was commercialized in 1953. But at the same time, and partly because of this influence, France was one of the European countries where anti-Americanism was the most violent. This anti-Americanism has to be taken into account in order to understand the French interest in jazz: welcoming this black music and claiming it as art was a way to demonstrate that, even after the collapse of its military power, France was still a great culture, and was still superior to the United States, for American society at this time was unable to recognize the legitimacy of jazz because of racial segregation.

Jazz Encounters Other Arts: Beyond High and Low Culture

In the course of its integration and legitimization in France, jazz not only contributed to the redefinition of the boundaries of French culture but also acquired a specific place at the crossroads of high and low culture, being thus a symptom of the redefinition of aesthetic categories. Indeed, it would be a mistake to interpret this process of legitimization as simply its integration into the pantheon of classical culture: it is rather the emergence of a new category of art that required during the 1950s and 1960s a reconsideration of the boundaries between high and low culture. The multiple encounters between jazz and other arts in the course of its journey into French culture are highly significant, for they demonstrate that the traditional separation between high and low culture is no longer appropriate in the twentieth century, particularly after 1945. This phenomenon suggests that the evolution of boundaries between high and low culture is deeply linked to the process of cultural globalization, of which the internationalization of jazz is but one example.

POPULAR SONG

As in the United States, jazz was soon incorporated into popular songs in France. As early as the 1930s, Charles Trenet was using jazz rhythms in his songs, and after 1945 a new generation of singers influenced by jazz emerged, represented by artists like Yves Montand, Gilbert Bécaud, Charles Aznavour, and many others.

Not only did they compose songs influenced by jazz, but they were also accompanied on stage by French jazz musicians who thus had both the opportunity to earn a living between two jazz sessions and to be heard by a larger public in jazz clubs afterward. The most important bridge between jazz and popular song was created by Sidney Bechet, who began a spectacular second career in France in 1949, which lasted until his death in 1959, and was subsequently almost totally forgotten in the United States. During the fifties, Bechet became the first—and the only—jazz "star" in France, having sold more than one million records by 1955, which was exceptional for a jazzman. The success of Sidney Bechet was mostly due to the way the American musician mixed New Orleans jazz with French popular tunes and melodies, as in songs like "Petite Fleur," "Dans les rues d'Antibes," or, his last discography success, "Les Oignons." Through such popular melodies, he greatly contributed to the public's jazz education and also transformed it, making it a part of the patrimony of the "chanson française."

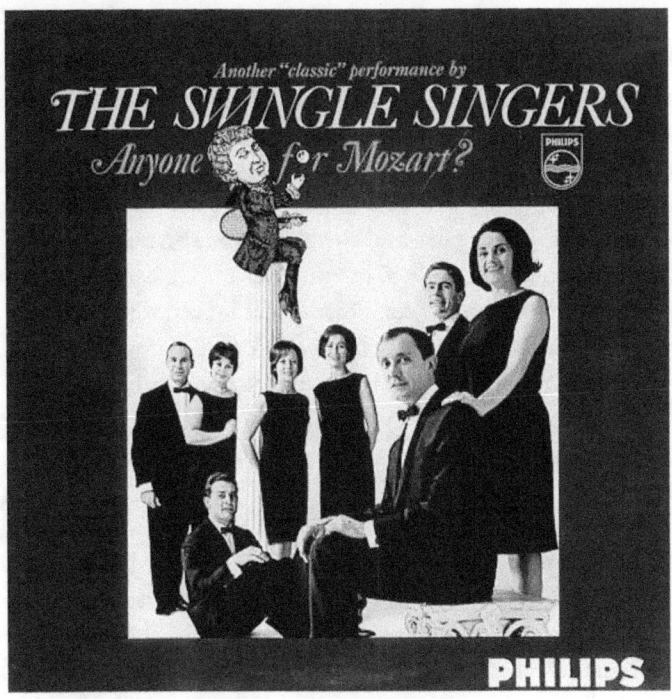

FIGURE 4.1 The Swingle Singers, *Anyone for Mozart?*, Philips, 1964.

CLASSICAL COMPOSERS IN THE INTERWAR PERIOD

The encounter between jazz and classical music occurred in France as soon as the end of the 1910s, when jazz was a source of inspiration for composers living in France. Darius Mihaud, Igor Stravinsky, and Maurice Ravel are the most famous. They all used jazz in works such as Stravinsky's *Histoire du soldat* (1918), *Ragtime pour onze instruments* (1918), and *Piano rag music* (1919); Milhaud's *La création du monde* (1923); and Ravel's *L'enfant et les sortilèges* (1925), *Sonate pour piano et violon* (1927), *Concerto pour la main gauche* (1929–30) and *Concerto en sol majeur* (1931). However, all of these composers considered jazz as a primitive, if interesting, music, and their interest did not last a long time. On the other side of the musical spectrum, jazz fans were seeking recognition from the classical world: in November 1937, Charles Delaunay, artistic director of Swing, asked Django Reinhardt, Stephane Grappelli, and the American violinist Eddie South (who was then in Paris) to record a jazz interpretation of Johann Sebastian Bach's *Concerto in D-minor*, released a few months later. Nonetheless, jazz did not gain a real recognition during the interwar period.

Things changed after 1945: a new generation of composers and interpreters, who had been in contact with modern jazz, claim their interest for it in the media and contribute to changing public opinion. Among them are the pianist Samson François, who was internationally considered as a great interpreter of Robert Schumann as early as the end of the 1940s; and Ravel and Claude Debussy, who came regularly to listen to jazz in clubs during the fifties. Also under consideration is the composer André Jolivet, who integrated some elements of jazz in his *Concerto for Trumpet* in 1948 and who declared in 1952 that "negro" spirituals were part of the universal musical language. In 1954 an academy of jazz was created in Paris (a sort of replica of the French Academy), and two classical composers, Georges Auric and Henri Sauguet, agreed to be part of its board.

At the same time, among professional musicians in orchestras, the prejudice against jazz disappeared little by little in the fifties, partly because classical musicians had heard the new forms of jazz and partly because they met jazzmen in recording sessions: in 1957 Eddie Barclay, manager of Blue Star, the most important French discography company, created an orchestra dedicated to the recording of the variety singers of the company. All the members of the orchestra were jazzmen (their drummer was Kenny Clarke) and were frequently rejoined by the string sections of the Paris Opera Orchestra in order to play special arrangements for singers. If the first generation of French jazzmen (before World War II) were frequently autodidacts, the second generation after 1945 had a more classical background and a good knowledge of their instruments. Little by little, they won the esteem of their classical colleagues.

JAZZ AND BAROQUE MUSIC

One of the most interesting phenomena in the 1950s regarding the relationship between jazz and the classical world is the encounter between jazz and baroque music. Before World War II, baroque music was almost forgotten in France as in many other countries. After 1948, the invention of the long-playing record, which was longer and cheaper than the 78 rpm, paved the way to an extraordinary development of the repertoire of classical music: in order to increase their sales, discography companies were in search of new composers to record. This is one of the reasons for the great revival of baroque music in the fifties. From 1954 onward, many composers, French or otherwise, were

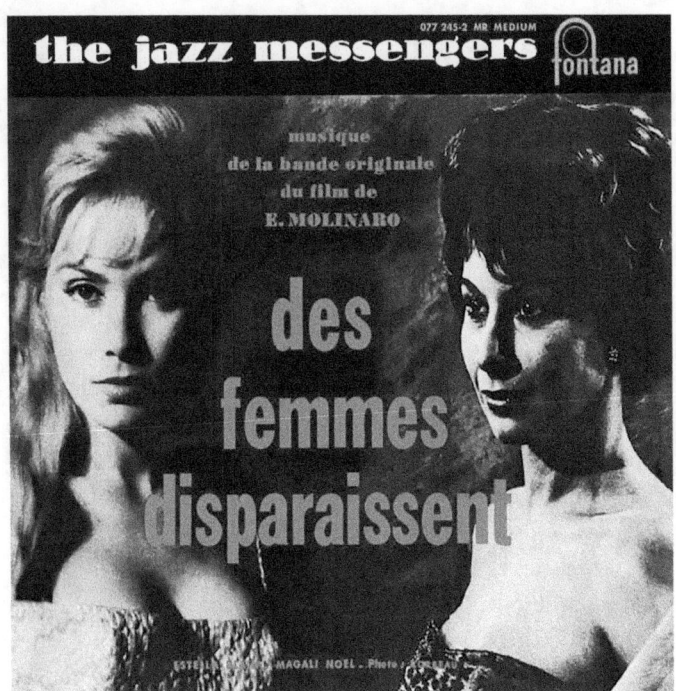

FIGURE 4.2 Art Blakey and the Jazz Messengers, *Des femmes disparaissent* (sound track from the film), Fontana, 1959.

recorded: Marc Antoine Charpentier, Michel Ricard Delalande, François Couperin, Antonio Vivaldi, and Johann Sebastian Bach. At the same time, a number of jazz musicians who were exploring new possibilities for jazz found some interest in baroque music because of its use of counterpoint and unbroken rhythm. For example, the Modern Jazz quartet, whose leader John Lewis had studied musical theory with the French composer Germaine Tailleferre at the American conservatory of Fontainebleau after World War II, played three times in Paris, in 1956, 1958, and 1959; and even if his exploration of the baroque universe did not appeal to French jazz critics, they used it to emphasize the fact that jazz was now classical music. On their side, classical critics discovered that jazzmen had a solid musical background and were able to play with virtuosity. Soon, French musicians started to record famous works from Bach. For example, the pianist Jacques Loussier recorded the *Well-Tempered Clavier* in 1959, and the Swingle Singers gained international success in 1963 with their album *Jazz Sébastien Bach.*

Mainly through critic and composer André Hodeir, jazz also entered the world of contemporary music. Born in 1926, Hodeir studied violin, harmony, and counterpoint at the National Conservatory of Paris and was one of Olivier Messiaen's students between 1945 and 1948, along with future figures of the contemporary scene like Pierre Boulez. In 1954, Hodeir was part of a group of young anticonformist composers who followed Boulez in the enterprise of renewing music and created the Domaine Musical,[10] an association dedicated to the organization of concerts of contemporary music; at the time, the doors of the temples of classical music were still closed to it. From the beginning of the fifties onward, Hodeir tried to include jazz in his quest for a new musical language and composed a number of pieces mixing African American music with concrete music (*Jazz et jazz*, 1952) or dodecaphonism (*Paradoxe I*, 1954). In 1954 he created the Jazz groupe de Paris, an orchestra of jazz musicians dedicated to playing his music, which was invited in 1957 to present Hodeir's work at the Donaueschingen Festival, then the most important meeting place of European avant-garde music.[11] Though Hodeir always remained marginal in the world of contemporary composers, he made his way as a composer and, after having experimented in many directions, became convinced at the end of the fifties that jazz and atonalism were incompatible, to say nothing about concrete music. He therefore abandoned his attempts in mixing jazz and dodecaphonism and serialism to come back to tonality. Then, he found his own aesthetic way and started to present himself as a "jazz composer." The first piece of this new stage in his production was *Flautando*, composed in 1960, which was followed during the sixties by a number of pieces that represent the maturity of Hodeir's work, among which is *Anna Livia Plurabelle* (1966), inspired by James Joyce's *Finnegans Wake*.

LITERATURE

The use of Joyce, beyond Hodeir's fascination for the Irish writer, is but one episode in a long relationship between jazz and literature that is fundamental in the French process of the legitimization of jazz, given the prestige of writers and philosophers in France. Three elements illustrate this key role.

The first is the construction of the jazz critic. As mentioned above, in 1934 Hugues Panassié wrote *Le jazz hot*, one of the first books written about

jazz in the world and the one that inaugurates the birth of jazz as a theoretical discourse. It was followed by a long series of books and articles in
French reviews that, despite their aesthetic divergences, have in common the
literary, rather than musicological, approach to jazz. The jazz critic, which
can be considered as a sort of literary genre, played a key role in the social
recognition of jazz because it explained to the public the rules on which jazz
was constructed.

The second point is the Saint-Germain-des-prés phenomenon. As a number of clubs were located in this district, jazz became one of the symbols of
Saint-Germain-des-prés and was associated immediately after 1945 with exis-
tentialism, a new philosophy that gained public recognition at this moment
mainly through Jean-Paul Sartre's plays, such as *Morts sans sépulture* (written
in 1941, but played for the first time in 1946), *La putain respectueuse* (1946),
or *Les mains sales* (1948). Saint-Germain-des-prés is important for the legitimization of jazz in France because it was the place where jazz and the Parisian
intelligentsia encountered one another. One of the symbols of this encounter
was the special issue "Jazz 47," released in June 1947, in which articles written by jazz critics were placed side by side with paintings by Jean Dubuffet
and Fernand Léger, along with the text by Jean-Paul Sartre mentioned above,
which immediately became famous.

The third point in this relationship between jazz and literature concerns the construction of the image of the jazzman in jazz fans' imaginations. An analysis of the articles and pictures in reviews shows that the
image of the jazzman is superposed on an existing symbolic figure of French
literature, which is the figure of the "poète maudit" or accursed poet. The
term *accursed poet* was assigned to a number of poets of the end of the nineteenth century, like Charles Baudelaire, Comte de Lautréamont, Arthur
Rimbaud, Jules Laforgue, or Paul Verlaine, who were the pioneers of modern poetry but also lived in poverty, were alcoholics or drug-addicts, and
died prematurely. According to French fans, jazzmen were the reincarna-
tion of accursed poets who were misunderstood during their lives. Charlie
Parker is the most significant example of this association: after his death
in 1955, articles in French reviews told his short, creative, and dramatic life
in detail and described him as a modern albatross, an explicit reference to
the poem "L'Albatros" in which Baudelaire compared the poet to this bird
whose wings were too big to enable him to walk on the earth; it was, then,
the French adaptation of the metaphor of the "bird," which was Parker's
nickname.

In the fifties, jazz was also associated with cinema thanks to the young generation of filmmakers who were also jazz fans and wanted to integrate jazz in their
movies. This association reached a climax in France between 1957 and 1961, for
over those four years, jazz soundtracks accompanied at least forty-one French
films. Most of them are just a sonorous illustration in which jazz is associated
with sex, prostitution, and detectives: this is the case of films like *Des femmes
disparaissent* (1959, soundtrack by the Jazz Messengers) and *Un témoin dans la
ville* (1959, Barney Wilen) by Edouard Molinaro, or *Les Liaisons dangereuses*
by Roger Vadim (1959, Jazz Messengers). However, a minority of filmmakers
tried to construct a real partnership between the music and the pictures. A
number of documentary films were realized in this perspective: Jean Pain-
levé's *Les assassins d'eau douce* (1947, music by Duke Ellington), and also some
fictional films such as *Ascenseur pour l'échafaud* by Louis Malle (1957, music
by Miles Davis), and *À bout de souffle* by Jean-Luc Godard (1960, music by
Martial Solal), the latter being obviously inspired by John Cassavetes's *Shadows* (1959, music by Charles Mingus). In all these movies, the music acts as a
partner of the picture, both filmmakers and musicians having tried to create
between them a real interaction, made possible, in the case of *Ascenseur*, by
the projection of the film in the studio when Miles Davis and his sidemen
(Kenny Clarke on drums, René Urtreger on piano, Pierre Michelot on double
bass, and Barney Wilen on saxophone) recorded the soundtrack.

AVANT-GARDE FESTIVALS

The last, but not the least, interesting aspect of the relationship between jazz
and the arts is its association with avant-garde movements of the fifties, as can
be seen in a number of festivals during this period. The formula of the festival
was invented after 1945. In jazz, the first festival was created in Nice in 1948,
six years before the Newport Festival in the United States. It is interesting to
see that both jazz and avant-garde movements used the festival as a way of
presenting their works.

The first festival in which the association between jazz and the avant-garde
is obvious is the Salon du jazz in 1950. This salon took place when the popularity of jazz in France was growing. It presented jazz concerts, a commercial exhibition of instruments, scores and phonographs, and an exhibition of
contemporary paintings at the same time. This point is not surprising when

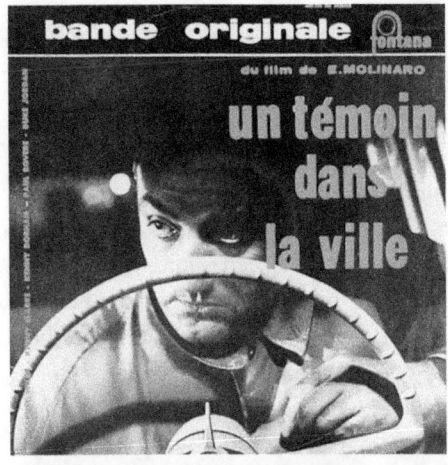

FIGURE 4.3 Barney Wilen, *Un témoin dans la ville* (sound track from the film), Polygram, 1959.

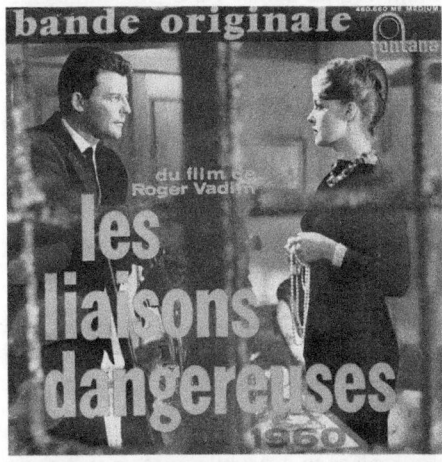

FIGURE 4.4 Art Blakey and the Jazz Messengers with Barney Wilen, *Les liaisons dangereuses* (sound track from the film), Fontana, 1959.

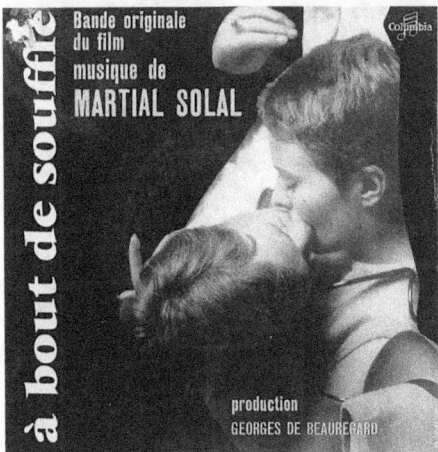

FIGURE 4.5 Martial Solal, *À bout de souffle* (sound track from the film), Columbia, 1960.

one knows that Charles Delaunay, the organizer of the salon, was the son of Robert and Sonia Delaunay. Charles Delaunay was aware that the presence of paintings was a way to increase the public of the salon and at the same time to give jazz legitimacy by showing that it could inspire other artists. He then asked his mother to gather a number of contemporary paintings from both established and young painters. In the first category, one finds Matisse, who was after 1945 at the top of his fame and had published a volume called *Jazz* in 1947, a part of which was presented at the salon; one also finds Fernand Léger, who had realized a canvas called *Jazz* in 1930; Jean Dubuffet, whose concept of *Art brut*, formulated in 1945, echoed the supposed spontaneity of jazz; and a number of abstract painters such as Robert and Sonia Delaunay and Piet Mondrian. Besides these recognized painters were young avant-garde artists such as Jean-Michel Atlan, Jacques Doucet, and Guillaume Corneille, who were members of the Cobra group created in 1948 in order to protest against what they called intellectualized painting.[12]

During the fifties, jazz was present in other festivals dedicated to the avant-garde. In April and May 1952 the Congress for Cultural Freedom, secretly in cooperation with the CIA, organized in Paris the festival *L'Œuvre du vingtième siècle* in order to respond to the cultural propaganda of the Soviet Union. A great number of writers, painters, sculptors, and musicians were on the program, such as Igor Stravinsky, Claude Debussy, Bela Bartok, André Malraux, Henri Matisse, and Vassily Kandinsky. One session of the festival was dedicated to avant-garde music, and the French jazz composer André Hodeir presented his work *Jazz and Jazz*. Hodeir was also part of the organizing board of the Festival de l'art d'avant-garde created in 1956 by Jacques Polieri.[13] The first festival took place in Marseille in 1956, in La cité radieuse, which was a large building constructed by architect Le Corbusier in 1952 and was then a symbol of avant-garde architecture. At this festival, works were presented by dancer Maurice Béjart, plays by Eugène Ionesco, an electronic sculpture by Nicolas Schöffer, and musical pieces by Karlheinz Stockausen, Pierre Henry, Pierre Schaeffer, and also the quintet of the French jazz pianist Martial Solal. In 1957 the second Festival de l'art d'avant-garde took place in Nantes, and Martial Solal was also present with his trio.

These examples suggest that the process of recognition of jazz in post-1945 France is not only a symptom of the evolution of the French cultural landscape but also a sign of the process of reconfiguration of boundaries between high and low culture, an alternative that became less and less pertinent from the 1950s onward. Obviously, jazz does not fit into this dualist framework, having clearly one foot in each side. This hybrid position was uncomfortable before World War II in a France marked by a return to the traditional artistic order after the aesthetic storm of the first decade of the century but became an advantage after 1945 when the quick evolution of the landscape, combined with the multiplicity of artistic encounters between jazz and other forms of cultural production (e.g., classical music, cinema, literature), facilitated its legitimization in a France that was more and more caught up in the accelerating process of the globalization of cultural production. This seems to confirm that globalization had, and still has, an important impact not only on the evolution of artistic production by stimulating exchanges of all kinds but also on the reconfiguration of the aesthetic categories and eventually on the conception of "culture."

Notes

1. Jean-Paul Sartre, "New York City," in "Jazz 47," special issue, *America* (May 1947). "Jazz is like bananas, it has to be consumed fresh and on site."

2. See the complete list in Ludovic Tournès, "Jazz en France, 1944–1963: Histoire d'une acculturation à l'époque contemporaine" (PhD diss., University of Versailles Saint Quentin, 1997).

3. See Ludovic Tournès, *New Orleans sur Seine: Histoire du jazz en France* (Paris: Fayard, 1999); Robert Redfield, Ralph Linton, and Melville Herskovits, "A Memorandum for the Study of Acculturation," *Man* 35 (1935): 145–46. This memorandum was republished in 1936 in the American review *American Anthropologist*.

4. See, for example, Rob Kroes, Robert W. Rydell, and Doeko F. J. Bosscher, *Cultural Transmissions and Receptions: American Mass Culture in Europe* (Amsterdam: VU University Press, 1993); Richard Kuisel, *Seducing the French: The Dilemma of Americanization* (Berkeley: University of California Press, 1993); Pascal Ory, "L'américanisation, modernisme et culture de masse," in *L'esprit de l'Europe*, vol. 3, ed. Antoine Compagnon and Jacques Seebacher (Paris: Flammarion, 1993), 252–61; Richard Pells, *Not Like Us: How Europeans Have Loved, Hated, and Transformed American Culture since World War II* (New York: Basic Books, 1997); Dominique Barjot and Christophe Reveillard, eds., *L'américanisation de l'Europe occidentale au XXe siècle: Mythes et réalités* (Paris: Presses de l'université de Paris-Sorbonne, 2002). For a more complete bibliography and a more developed discussion on Americanization, see Ludovic Tournès, "La philanthropie américaine et l'Europe: Contribution à une histoire transnationale de l'américanisation" (research paper, Université Paris-I Panthéon Sorbonne, 2008), chapter 2, "Américanisation: Un concept à repenser"; and Ludovic Tournès, "Américanisation," in *Dictionnaire d'histoire culturelle de la France contemporaine*, ed. Christian Delporte, Jean-Yves Mollier, and Jean-François Sirinelli (Paris: PUF, 2010), 18–22.

5. Kuisel, *Seducing the French*; Philip Bell and Roger Bell, *Americanization and Australia* (Sydney: University of New South Wales Press, 1998); Reinhold Wagnleitner, *Coca-Colonization and the Cold War: The Cultural Mission of the United States in Austria after the Second World War* (Chapel Hill: University of North Carolina Press, 1994); Günter Bischof and Anton Pelinka, *The Americanization/Westernization of Austria* (New Brunswick, NJ: Transaction, 2004); Rolf Lunden and Erik Asard, *Networks of Americanization: Aspects of the American Influence in Sweden* (Stockholm: Almqvist and Wiksell, 1992); Alexander Stephan, *Americanization and Anti-Americanism: The German Encounter with American Culture after 1945* (New York: Berghahn Books, 2005); Samuel E. Moffett, *The Americanization of Canada* (Toronto: University of Toronto Press, 1972).

6. See especially Arjun Appadurai, *Modernity at Large: Cultural Dimensions of Globalization* (Minneapolis: University of Minnesota Press, 1996). On the transnational history, see, for example, Frederick Cooper, "Conflict and Connection: Rethinking Colonial African History," *American Historical Review* 99, no. 5 (1994): 1516–45; Sanjay Subrahmanyam, "Connected Histories: Notes Toward a Reconfiguration of Early Modern Eurasia," *Modern Asian Studies* 31, no. 3 (July 1997): 735–62; Daniel T. Rodgers, *Atlantic Crossings: Social Politics in a Progressive Age* (Cambridge, MA: Harvard University Press, 1998).

7. For a more detailed discussion on the concept of Americanization, see Tournès, "La philanthropie américaine et l'Europe," chapter 2; see also Ludovic Tournès, *Sciences de l'homme et politique: Les fondations philanthropiques américaines en France au XXe siècle* (Paris: Éditions des Classiques Garnier, 2011), introduction; and Tournès, "Américanisation."

8. See, among others, André Hodeir, *Jazz: Its Evolution and Essence* (New York: Grove, 1961) (translated from the French); and Paul F. Berliner, *Thinking in Jazz: The Infinite Art of Improvisation* (Chicago: University of Chicago Press, 1994).

9. See a recent case about the failure of the French soccer team during the 2010 world cup in Alain Finkielkraut, "Des sales gosses boudeurs," *Le journal du dimanche*, June 20, 2010.

10. Jésus Aguila, *Le Domaine musical: Pierre Boulez et vingt ans de création contemporaine* (Paris: Fayard, 1992).

11. The Historic Donaueschingen Jazz Concert 1957, Album MPS Production 68.161, 1977.

12. Centre Georges Pompidou, *Paris-Paris 1937–1957* (Paris: Éditions du Centre Pompidou; Gallimard, 1992), 214.

13. Michel Corvin, *Art Avant-Garde: Marseille, Nantes, Paris (1956–1960)* (Paris: Somogy, 2004).

A CRUCIAL SEASON FOR ALEX KATZ

Fifty years on, it is none the easier to position Alex Katz within the annals of the history of art. Chronologically, Katz belongs to the second generation of American Abstract Expressionism: in the 1950s he hung out in New York's now legendary hot spots—the Club, the co-op galleries on Tenth Street, the Cedar Bar. While the speed with which he paints no longer displays the vigorous, expression-laden brushwork of the late 1950s, the aesthetics of directness that characterizes even Jackson Pollock's most paradoxical heirs finds its mark in Katz's early work. Iconographically, Katz exudes Pop sensibilities, for his main subject matter is the everyday event as presented in the media. Even if the emphasis is on the human figure—which would link him to an older, broader, established tradition—a Pop-ish insistence on the visible effects of fashion, run-of-the-mill consumption, and the commodification of beauty remains. However, under close scrutiny Katz fits within none of these canons and he is not in any way a *proto-something*—even if the most frequent, current pigeonhole for him is that of proto-Pop.

If there is a connection with *this* or *that* movement, indeed, it is because from the outset Katz's painting proceeds from a determination to produce pictures that reflect two potentially contradictory principles. For him, each work must slot into the long tradition of "man-made pictures"—I use this phrase to refer specifically to the moment when painting was freed from its liturgical, thaumaturgic straitjacket—while taking into account that access to the image (by which I mean Katz's access as creator as well as ours as viewer) is now rarely achieved other than through the new, "non-man-made" (*acheiropoietic* if we stick to Byzantium) images of the mechanical era: the photographic, cinematic, and digital.

Many aspects of Katz's pictures have plumbed this binary since the beginning of his career. I would like to linger here on one that might be described—at the risk of invoking the spirits of art historians with little pertinence in this particular instance—as the singular migration of images from one picture to another and, to go one step further, from one realm of reality to others. Many of his works of the late 1950s were painted with this migration in mind, as he himself has recalled: "Advertising images were fresh. The way they took a rectangle and broke it up was exciting. The composition ideas, some of them, were crazy! TV also used very aggressive imagery. They could take that 18-inch screen and really push it into your face. . . . Movies, television, and advertising were exciting sources from which to paint."[1]

Katz understood very early—without ever saying so except in deed, in his painting—that mechanical images affect our relationship with reality more by creating a new degree of reality, one characterized by the image's autonomy, reproducibility, and exponential dissemination, to use the vocabulary of Walter Benjamin, than a concern for faithful reproduction.

A Crucial Season

The basic tenet of Katz's earliest work would seem almost the opposite of the migration I previously outlined. The impulse to work directly from life—while emphasizing the defocalization of the subject—came to the young painter when he saw Pollock's great works: it was their spontaneous, abstract character that, in the early 1950s, sparked in Katz an urge to inhabit the same stance with respect to landscape and the human figure.[2] And yet, by the middle of the decade—after a relatively timid initial series of small collages on paper—a decisive first step was taken with the disappearance of the realistic, perspectival context in the pictures containing human figures, of which *George's Basketball* (1957) was one of the first examples. By treating the background as an abstraction—a more or less uniform color plane—the artist posits a fundamental detachment from directly observable reality in the interests of an authentic pictorialization, and so sets up a permanent tension. Subsequently, an endlessly renegotiated channel opens up between mimetic figuration and autonomous abstraction, a channel whose recourse to mechanical models of the image is one of its most effective tools—even if the critics generally settled for mentioning that aspect only in passing.[3]

The monochromatic ground, itself a dual movement of decontextualization (in relation to the setting the figures were in when they posed) and recontextualization (on the picture surface), would never culminate in total abstraction, even if initially, around 1958–60, it contaminated the figures to the point of actually dismantling them—at least partially—in the same way, for example, as the grounds of certain works by Henri Matisse in the 1910s.[4] In Katz's 1959 *Marcia*, you no longer know whether you are dealing with a naturalistic or an abstract background; the large area into which the model's feet and ankles disappear can also be read as a stretch of sand, while the spattering along the curve of its upper edge can be seen as an autonomous application of paint and/or—there being no absolute alternative—a natural phenomenon such as a gust of wind. In the painted version of *Joe and Jane* (1960), the background absorbs parts of the furniture—the arms and one of the legs of the armchair the female figure is sitting in—while there remains at the feet of the figures a horizontal bar just barely interpretable as a ground line otherwise obliterated by paint.

Katz came to grips with mechanical images and the aesthetic regime borne of the image's mechanization and infinite reproducibility in the 1959–60 season. To be clear about this: photography made its appearance more than a century earlier, and cinema half a century; I am making no claim that Katz was the first painter to examine the mechanical image. The history of this attention goes back a long way and represents an ongoing advance from Jean-Auguste-Dominique Ingres to Gerhard Richter. Neither am I saying that the images Katz used were literally mechanical, a point made by Willem de Kooning when Katz's 1959 solo exhibition was badly received by many visitors: "They look like photos, but they are paintings, and don't let them knock you away from it."[5]

In the early years of 1951–53, Katz worked from found snapshots, thereby influencing a two-dimensional look to his figurative painting. Thus *Old Photo* (1951) was a free interpretation of a small, square photo of three people against the backdrop of a forest: their features are blurred; the setting becomes an assemblage of colored patches echoing the flat fields of their clothing. Once out of this fledgling period, Katz rarely used a photograph, much less any kind of mechanical image, as his sole—and exclusive—starting point. At most, the photograph enabled him to settle on a feature he would reuse in a painting. In a manifestation of the already established duality, Katz chose to represent images seen firsthand—landscapes at certain specific moments, people who had posed for him—while at the same time treating them as distanced and autonomized, often allowing a lapse of time between the initial experience and its transformation into a finished work. Often, this lapse of time was that of the journey from his house in Maine to his studio in New York.

Katz's process helped to establish a detachment from the initial visual impressions that was freely controlled rather than submitted to mechanically (it could have been abridged by the use of an epidiascope or some similar device, as Roy Lichtenstein and James Rosenquist were then starting to do) via a process that could be called abstraction in the strictest sense. It enabled the artist to separate himself from his subject and to home in on certain characteristics at the expense of others. In other words, said process freed the image from its referent in the same way that photographic and filmed images acquire autonomy in relation to the reality they briefly signal and can then be used indiscriminately—as the tabloid press and political propagandists were quick to realize, retouching and fusing on a grand scale material long supposedly credited with the ontological status of truth. The images used by Katz were primarily free of the excessive constraints of external reality, except to the extent that it owed it to itself—to itself and nobody else—to maintain a certain link, of an edgy, unobvious kind, with that reality. Such images—whether of humans, animals, landscapes, or, much more rarely, inanimate objects—always had to be lifelike, so that their autonomy would not be broken down by an overabstraction that would absorb them unselectively into the technical means used to shape them; in the final analysis these images remain equidistant from abstraction and figuration and embody both simultaneously—with all the contradictions this stance implies.

The 1959–60 season also saw the appearance of three uses of the image, establishing Katz as an artist who achieved a concrete rethink of painting, nourishing it through a rapport of exceptional alertness to the image environment that is ours today and whose wellspring is the postwar United States. The chronological order of these uses, insofar as it can be established with any certainty—the pictures, when dated at all, are marked with the year and nothing more—matters little. Here I shall simply deal with them in order of complexity.

Framing

The first consequence of the paradoxically simultaneous autonomizing of figure and ground is the possibility of giving each a more or less important part in the composition. The ground can play the role, so to speak, of a

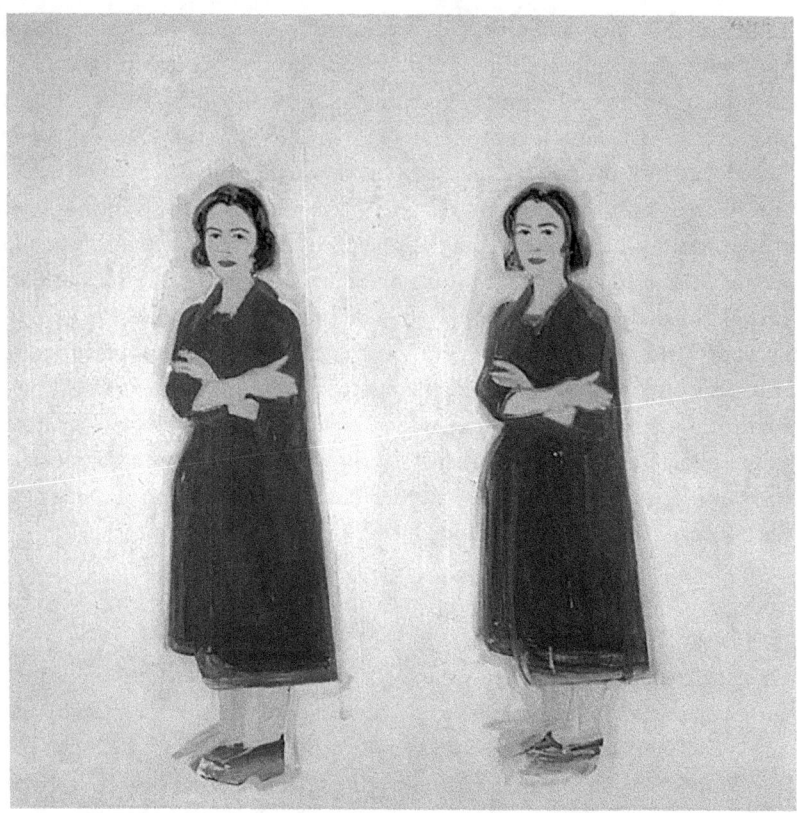

FIGURE 5.1 Alex Katz, *Ada Ada*, 1959. Oil on canvas. © Alex Katz/SODRAC, Montréal/VAGA, New York (2015).

frame, absorbing a part of the figure in such a way as to then make it appear reframed, as in the viewfinder of a camera. This way of proceeding—significantly observable in the work of Peter Blake in the same period, without the two artists knowing one other (whose subjects were film stars like Kim Novak)—finds its ideal material (if I may put it that way) in the image of Ada, the artist's wife. The portrait bust may stand out, frontally and in its entirety, against a green background, or be framed by a red diamond set into a dark green ground in such a way as to make it resemble a logo on a nonrealistic advertising poster.

In addition to the strict application of the logo procedure, the fragmentary face finds itself altered or moved about on the canvas to form all sorts of naturalistic compositions based either on page layout principles or on pictorial composition. The exemplars here are Alexei Brodovitch and Alexander

Liberman, designers and artistic directors of *Harper's Bazaar* and *Vogue,* respectively; the painters Giovanni Bellini and Edouard Manet; and the originators of the billboards gracing America's rural and urban landscapes. This is true not only of the works of literally monumental size, like *The Red Smile* (1963), in which the portrait bust, cropped by the right-hand edge of the picture, is set against a vast area of red. This is also the case in the paintings that, while of mainly modest size, apply a principle of relative scale to the detached face and the ground, just as in the big horizontal pictures of Matisse and Barnett Newman. In *Ada* (silver series) of 1965, for instance, the choice of a wood cutout for the face and the evident vigor of the brushstrokes outlining the bare neck and stylized hair make the figure stand out like a centrifugal sign on the long canvas whose spatial indeterminacy is augmented by its coating of silver paint. (In the same year, in *Ada, Right Eye, Blue Series*, a fragment of this same figure is placed in the lower left corner of a blue panel, leaving visible only part of an eye and a snippet of eyebrow, hair, and face.)

Montage

One outcome of Katz's various framing and reframing operations is his play with major spatial disjunctions: while ensuring the unity of the picture surface and the image presented on it as painting, he nonetheless leaves open the possibility of spatial fragmentation and of representation as story. Thus, given its autonomy, the image can be treated as a tool to be combined with others at will.

This principle of free use of objects may have been anticipated by Matisse, whose pictures were peppered with this sort of disjunction once he autonomized his images: thus, in a painting like *Music* (1939), the hands can be seen as out of proportion—by which I mean that the hands of the two models are literally as big as one of their arms—but this can pass unnoticed by the viewer insofar as the painted image becomes its own point of reference. Katz, however, is doing almost the opposite. He described Matisse as "my hero for realistic painting," given Matisse's awareness that realism lies not "in details" but in "an all-over light, and having every surface appear distinctive."[6] Katz does not permit this *incongruity* in objects—figures, furniture, trees, and flowers are rendered complete and closed in on themselves by habit and daily life—even while not denying the possibility of occasional *incoherencies*: limbs ending in claws in pictures from the beginning of the 1960s, and the disappearance of certain vital physiological details from people in works painted since then.

What he opted for, rather, was the principle of montage to which press advertising (as a static form) and the movies (as a dynamic form) have accustomed us. In this process, Katz anticipated various uses of digital imagery now being vaunted as evidence of a radical break with the past, when in fact what they involve is more of a change in degree than nature: at a stroke the possibilities for freely combining images and signs multiplied vertiginously. Each image that has been made autonomous, each *symbol*—for Katz the terminological opposite of the "signs" that, in his view, Pop artists were out to produce[7]— could be freely combined with the others.

The 1956–57 engagement with collage (the small formats notwithstanding) enabled Katz to establish his bearings. Even so, it was only with a certain timidity that he implemented the most radical consequences of this phase. The main example from 1959–60 remains the pair of collages titled *Red Sails*, in which we see that the same boat can change scale and visibility by being set against different grounds. Once again this was a subtle operation in that to register the change one has to see the two collages together, which was not the original intention. In the same way, the use of both sides of the picture is the earliest manifestation of the montage principle in painting. The opportunity clearly came with the creation of the first cutouts, stemming from Katz's dissatisfaction with the insertion of a figure into a ground: one day in 1959 Katz quite simply cut up his canvas and glued the figure onto a wooden support with the same outline—another way of announcing that the autonomy of the images was thoroughly achieved. Having a figure stand out on a shaped canvas could lead to the results simply being hung as if on a wall, as in *Blackie Walking* (1959). The artist chose instead to present the work as a kind of flat sculpture, signaling that the entire space in which it was situated—a space shared with the viewer—now constituted its ground and context and could be very densely peopled, given that Katz could juxtapose dozens of cutouts in a single room, as he did, for example, in the extraordinary *One Flight Up* of 1968. One of the outcomes of this decision was the creation of two-sided paintings, with the sides simultaneously visible only in a fragmentary way. The issue here was to approach each side according to the cinematic principle of parallel editing, either preserving anatomical consistency in both cases or making play with the possibilities for disjunction between the two.

Most of the cutouts, like some of the two-sided pictures from the beginning of the 1960s such as *Vincent and Ada at Ducktrap* (1961), opt for the first solution, their recto and verso united by a mimetic rationale. As early as 1959, however, some works were already displaying an awareness that they were still montages. The best-known example is *Maxine* (1959), whose obverse shows the figure in a swimsuit while the reverse shows the body naked. Conversely, one could consider that it is this nudity, little seen in the oeuvre with the exception of a few pictures from the 1980s, that is ultimately covered on the recto. Over the years some cutouts would make use of an effect of denaturalization of both sides, thus affirming the autonomy of the image in its transferals.

Katz's montage is seemingly less incongruous in the pictures that come across as an association on the same surface—sometimes comprising several juxtaposed panels, but making no fundamental difference to one's possible perception of the phenomenon—of several points of view of the same object or person. In 1959 *Blackie Walking* was one of the rare occurrences of a solution showing a subject in movement, heading off into the distance at a walk effectively rendered by changes in the position of the legs and arms of the figures whose size diminishes progressively from left to right, with a simple two by two duplication to which I shall return later.

Reproduction

One of the most striking occurrences of the montage principle in Katz's work appeared in *The Black Dress*, showing six female figures wearing a little black dress. In addition to the montage governing this picture—as it also governs the variations the artist would later draw from it—Katz infers a third consequence of the mechanization of images: one allowing for the duplication of an image so as to create a new image. Here the same model, Ada, is shown six times wearing the same clothes, although the repetition is attenuated in each case by variations in the pose and the point of view. This method was identified in 1965 by the dance critic and friend of the artist Edwin Denby as a separate genre in Katz's painting: the "reduplicative portrait."[8] The radicality of its first appearance in 1959 underscores just how accurately the artist grasped the fundamental issue. Several paintings and a cutout from that year contain exact duplicates of the same figure; the first of them, chronologically, was likely *Ada Ada* and is now sitting in New York University's Grey Art Gallery. Its importance is further emphasized by the fact that *Ada Ada* became the subject of a second version, this time in cutout form. Bearing the same title, this work is in the Whitney Museum of American Art. Despite its modest size, the work has a monumental character, doubtless because the repetition autonomizes its scale in relation to its external referents.

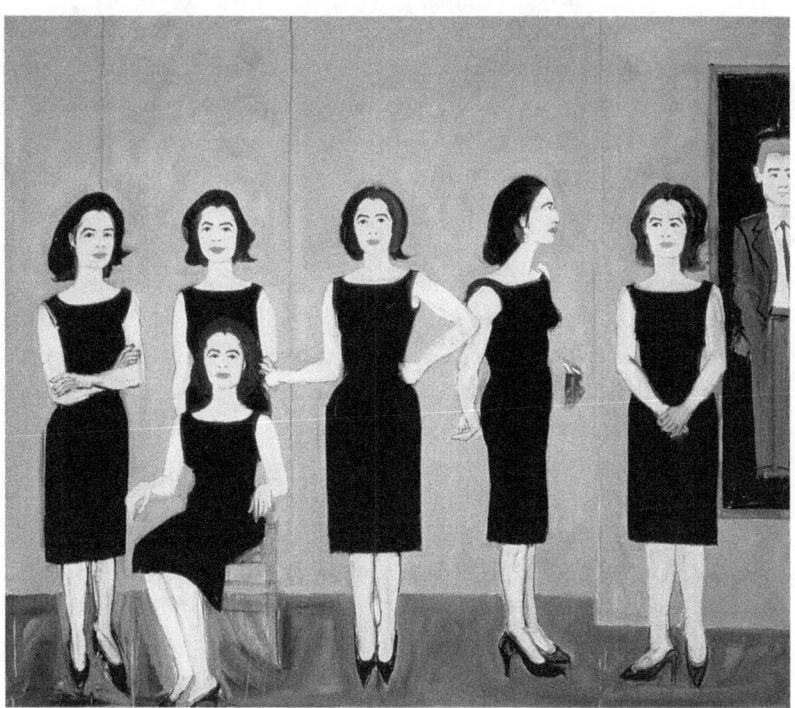

FIGURE 5.2 Alex Katz, *The Black Dress*, 1959. Oil on canvas. © Alex Katz/SODRAC, Montréal/ VAGA, New York (2015).

Both versions make use of the principle of photographic repetition— we have new prints made of photographs we like or need, notably for ID purposes—but make it painterly. The result is not an exact duplication, which cannot be the case without mechanizing the process of painting itself and thereby losing all the benefits of the game. At first glance, each figure is perceived as globally identical to the other and at the same time slightly different, but, surprisingly, without the viewer being led to pinpoint specific discrepancies. At the very most, and remaining at a fairly general level, in the picture the feet of the two figures are unequally defined, while in the cutout one figure is taller than the other. The work is still perceived as a unitary whole, made up of the repetition of the same colored shape. At the same time, the repetition ensures that there is hardly any point in looking elsewhere for the work's raison d'être, as each shape finds its justification and its referent in its replica, without it being possible to determine which came first and which second (theoretically if not in actual fact, since the artist may recall with which one he began). The rendering in paint of a photographic principle thus paradoxically ensures the autonomy of the picture or the sculpture, even though the invention of photography had its roots in the urge to achieve absolute mimetic capturing of reality.

When he painted the *Double Portrait of Robert Rauschenberg* (Paul Schupf Collection) the same year, Katz was applying this principle of duplication to the man who, at the time, seemed to be most convincingly establishing the consequences for gestural painting given the possibilities of mechanical reproduction. In *Factum I* and *Factum II* of 1957, Rauschenberg defused the prestige attached to inventiveness and demythologized the supposed subjectivity of the Abstract Expressionist method by producing two quasi-identical versions of the same composition, comprising not only collages but also, and above all, paint runs and spatterings. With *Double Portrait*, Katz imposed the same conclusion for figurative painting and especially for the portrait. He seriously undercut the gestural figuration of the de Kooning approach, including that practiced by Larry Rivers, who partially identified the problem by duplicating the figure of his model in *Double Portrait of Berdie* (1955) but failed to exploit the possibilities thus opened up out of a concern with maintaining an anecdotal narrative space. Katz also undermined any attempt at mimetic pictorial representation of reality that postulated absolute truthfulness. And in a further, ironic gesture, instead of simply duplicating the seated figure of the painter he also mirrored it, thus showing that image autonomy makes everything possible.

Reduplicative portraits would regularly raise anew this issue in the work of Katz, each time introducing inflections of which the how and when are worth establishing. (I make no claim to exhaustiveness here; I simply want to home in on some of the major inflections in his practice.) The 1959 *Blackie Walking* shows how the matter of duplication can be linked to that of montage and at the same time to the cinema model—or the pre-cinema model, for the closest rapport is maybe with the chronophotography of Étienne-Jules Marey and Eadweard Muybridge, long before Sol LeWitt adopted the same model in *Muybridge I* (1964). Significantly, in the LeWitt work the photographed figure moves toward the viewer, setting up a relationship evocative of the voyeurism suggested by the apparatus used—a black box. In the Katz work, the figure is seen in back view and moving away. The point is not only the four figures of diminishing size shown from behind, but also the repetition of a pair of images showing two different positions for the figure, who is returned to with a proportional reduction in size. The four images are different in their

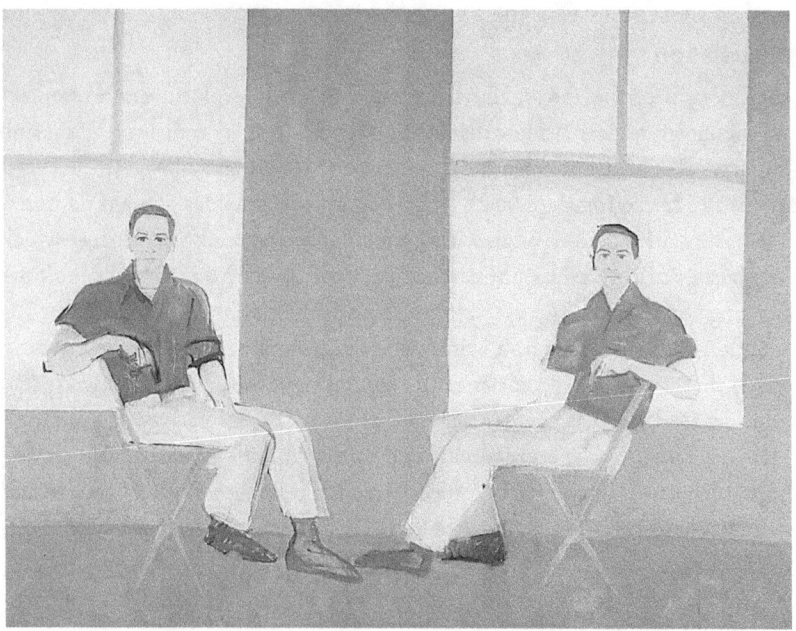

material form; they duplicate each other two by two in terms of their components, and they are all repetitions of the same figure.

The 1960 *Double Portrait with Frames (Double Ada)* explicitly combined, right down to its title, the issues of framing and duplication. Reframing the half-length, once-repeated Ada—a crude reframing effected by broad blue swipes of the brush that let the rest of the portrait bust show through lower down—Katz very slightly shifts the framing so that we no longer know whether this is exactly the same image (as the arrangement of the scarf and the placing of the large silver button lead us to believe) or its reversal in a mirror: the left edge cuts off the left shoulder in the image on the left, while the right edge cuts off the right shoulder in the image on the right. Moreover, the general effect is that of photo-booth anonymity, several years before Andy Warhol in turn—and on another scale—explored the parallel in a series of portraits that began in 1963 with *Edith Scull Thirty-Six Times*. This may be a way of returning to what so impressed the artist in the photographic work of Matthew Brady's team during the American Civil War: "They felt like images on top of images, to make a final image."[9]

Circulation

At the turn of the 1960s, Katz succeeded in freely exploiting the resources of the image regime Americans lived under, with all its transformations and inflections, and did so without recourse to any systematic program. He succeeded in rendering in paint the richly complex principles of framing, montage, and reproduction, often with a remarkable degree of prescience—which the beauty of the results has paradoxically obscured. More broadly, he took striking advantage of the possibilities these principles provide for the free circulation of images, not only within the same work but also externally to it, given that one of the premises of the aesthetics of mechanical images is that they demand a use that is not intensive but, rather, extensive. Depth is not their domain, but they are admirably suited to dissemination and "platitude"—a term I have used elsewhere in respect of a certain history of photography, and which would certainly be applicable to Katz's work in general, including its social dimension.[10]

From the start, what is involved here is a broad circulation of images, as illustrated in 1959–60 by the possibility of reusing the same image in two versions, one on canvas, the other on a wooden panel: thus there are two versions of *Ada Ada* in 1959 and two of *Joe and Jane* in 1960. This ongoing circulation has underpinned Katz's work since the beginning of the 1960s and continues to produce especially diverse and rewarding results today.

Translated from the French by John Tittensor

Notes

Originally published as "Reduplicative Painting," in *Alex Katz: An American Way of Seeing*, ed. Éric de Chassey and Roland Mönig (Tampere: Sara Hilden Art Museum; Grenoble: Musée des Beaux-Arts; Kleve: Museum Kurhaus, 2009), 10–57.

1. Alex Katz, "Katz Interviewed by David Salle," in *Katz: Unfamiliar Images*, ed. Vincent Katz (Milan: Alberico Cetti Serbelloni Editore, 2002), 9.

2. In 1967 he explained that Pollock "opened up areas of sensation painting and gestural painting, which wiped out all the rules I had been painting by." Alex Katz, "Jackson Pollock: An Artists' Symposium, Part 1," *Art News* 66, no. 2 (April 1967): 32.

3. In more precise terms than most other critics, however, even if keeping his focus fairly narrow, Frank O'Hara wrote early on, "For Katz the image, and his TV, billboard or movie close-up discovery, provided a way of both isolating and abstracting each separate feature, as if it were an arc, a rhomboid, an ellipse, within the psychological unity which the audience imparts to a recognizable form." Frank O'Hara,

"Katz," *Art and Literature*, no. 9 (summer 1966), reprinted in *Katz: Twenty-Five Years of Painting from the Saatchi Collection*, ed. David Sylvester (London: Saatchi Gallery, 1997), 159.

4. This decontextualization is made especially clear in the Rudolph Burckhardt photographs documenting the painting of *Incident* (1961) for James Schuyler's article "Katz Paints a Picture," *Art News* 60, no. 10 (February 1962): 38–41. In the photographs are various elements that later disappeared from the picture while, on the contrary, Burckhardt's camera appears in the picture but is missing—for obvious reasons—from the documentary shots.

5. Quoted in Alex Katz, "Starting Out," *New Criterion* 21, no. 4 (December 2002): 6.

6. Alex Katz, quoted in Richard Marshall, "Katz: Sources of Style," in *Katz* (New York: Whitney Museum of American Art, 1986), 15.

7. Katz, "Katz Interviewed by David Salle," 17.

8. Edwin Denby, "Katz: Collage, Cutout, Cut-up," *Art News* 63, no. 9 (January 1965): 44.

9. Alex Katz, *Erfundene Symbole/Invented Symbols*, ed. Vincent Katz (Ostfildern: Cantz, 1997), 60.

10. Regarding photographic platitudes, see Éric de Chassey, *Platitudes: Une histoire de la photographie plate* (Paris: Gallimard, 2006). Regarding the social reading of the Katz oeuvre, see Éric de Chassey, "Portrait of Katz as a Painter in the Jean-Jacques Rousseau Style," in *Katz* (Paris: Galerie Thaddaeus Ropac, 1998); and Éric de Chassey, "Painting, Reconciled," in *Katz: Small Paintings* (Kansas City: Kemper Museum of Contemporary Art; New York: Whitney Museum of American Art, 2001).

THE CACODYLIC MIND
Francis Picabia and the Neo-Avant-Garde, 1953–1963

for G. B.

"My heart beats only for Picabia" reads the inscription across Jean-Jacques Lebel's 1962 collage, a work that has been generally read as a straightforward homage to his much-admired predecessor. Appropriating an advertising poster in
which a woman affectionately cradles a small engine, Lebel overpainted the
bottom half gray and substituted "Picabia" for the original brand name, similarly appending the Dadaist's surname to the crankcase. Lebel's high regard
for Francis Picabia is well known, and the allusion of 1962 was nothing if not
timely: the Musée Cantini of Marseille mounted a retrospective in the spring
of that year, the first museum exhibition devoted to the artist. Both Lebel and
his father, the Duchamp scholar Robert Lebel, had loaned work to the show,
and Jean-Jacques would also author the preface to the catalog of another Picabia retrospective that year, held later in the summer at the Kunsthalle Bern. A
more direct motivation for the work may have been the fact that included in
the Marseille show was Picabia's *Cacodylic Eye* of 1921, on loan from the collection of Louis Henrion, who kept it on display in the bar of his uncle's chic
Paris restaurant, Le Boeuf sur le Toit. The small Musée Cantini catalog even
used the painting for its endpapers, making it something of an emblem for
the artist's work as a whole. On its graffiti-covered surface, toward the center
left-hand side, one can clearly read the greeting left by the artist Valentine
Hugo: "my heart beats." Forty-one years later, Lebel's *My Heart Beats Only for
Picabia* was a latter-day addition to this collaborative display of affection; for

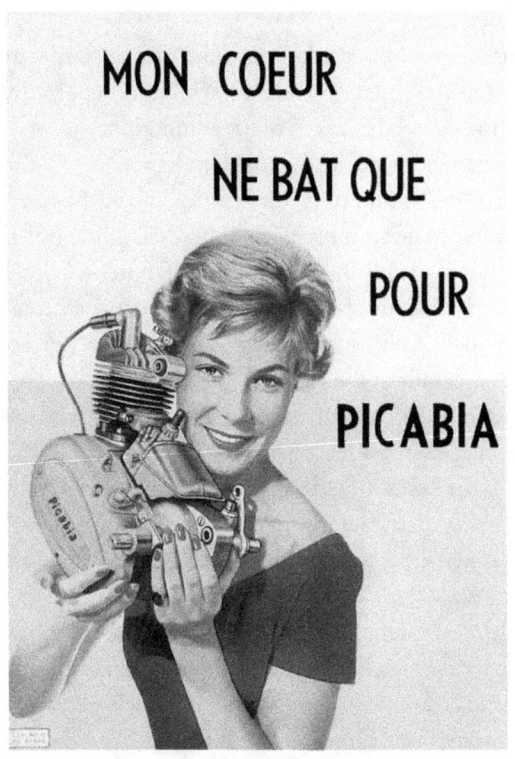

FIGURE 6.1 Jean-Jacques Lebel, *Mon coeur ne bat que pour Picabia* (*My Heart Beats Only for Picabia*), 1962. Collage and oil on canvas, Collection of Musée d'Art Moderne de la Ville de Paris. © Jean-Jacques Lebel/SODRAC (2015).

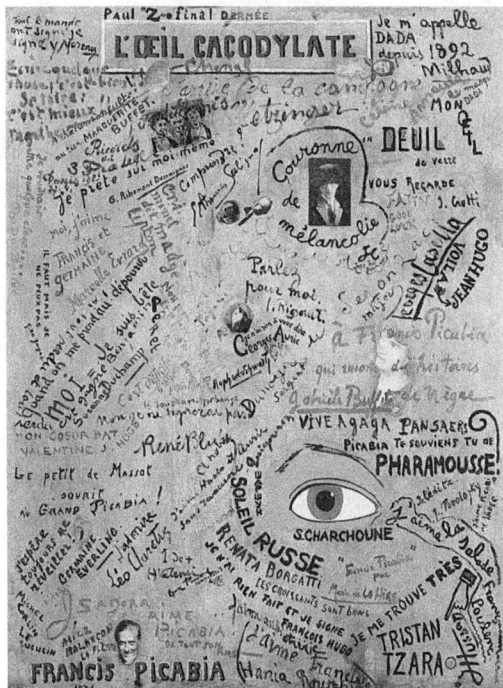

FIGURE 6.2 Francis Picabia, *L'oeil cacodylate* (*The Cacodylic Eye*), 1921. Oil with photomontage and collage. Collection of Centre Pompidou, Musée National d'Art Moderne. © Estate of Francis Picabia/ SODRAC (2015).

want of being able to append his own inscription onto the 1921 original—as one guest to the Salon d'Automne, where it was first exhibited, reportedly did, without invitation—he produced this token of his admiration.

But it is more than a modest homage. The immediate reference via the motor is, of course, to Picabia's "mecanomorphs" of the 1910s and to their mechanical imagery, as in the latter's famous portrait of Alfred Stieglitz. But if the photographer was presented as a study in impotence and failure—bellows falling away limply, the gear lever in neutral—Lebel appropriates the affirmative language of advertising to portray his subject as at least implicitly powerful, dynamic: Picabia appears precisely in the guise of a motor, which is moreover embraced by the ad's model as half baby, half lover. Troubling this image of a happy human-machine couple is the fact that the female model, in the logic of the work, is a stand-in for Lebel himself, suggesting confusion within the otherwise heteronormative dyad. In fact, the dyadic relationship of Lebel and Picabia is rather more a ménage à trois, with Marcel Duchamp as the third partner. For *My Heart Beats Only for Picabia*, by altering a brand name to convert an advertisement into a humorous reference to an artist, also assumes the logic of Duchamp's *Apolinère Enameled* of 1916–17. Something of Duchamp's challenge to artistic creation can also be seen in Lebel's play with his signature: *Apolinère Enameled* was signed "from MARCEL DUCHAMP," emphasizing its prefabricated nature; in the lower left-hand corner of Lebel's collage, a box reading "TIRAGE AU VERSO" stands in for his name in a frank acknowledgment of the mechanical origin of the work. A dutiful son displays the lessons of his fathers.

At approximately the same moment Lebel was declaring his admiration for, and insisting on his affiliation with, Picabia, the artist's widow, Gabrielle Buffet-Picabia, was accompanying *Le Monde*'s art critic through the galleries of the Musée Cantini retrospective. There, in the final room of the show, among his late abstract paintings, hung the *Cacodylic Eye*, "that photographic and lettrist collage," as the critic described it. Madame Picabia challenged him to recognize her among the friends whose signatures sprawled across the canvas, but he failed to rise to the challenge. Try as he might, he could not find it—surprising, perhaps, since hers is one of the largest, taking up much of the right-hand center and accompanied by a photograph, but the critic's blindness might well be emblematic: her inscription pointed precisely to the question of authorship and its abdication or displacement by Picabia, whom she called a teller of "ghostwritten stories." At the heart of the retrospective, she seemed to wish to emphasize, lay this painting that sought to undo the very logic of mastery, a painting that inscribed a radical emptiness in the place of the artistic subject. That was the lesson of Dada: look as hard as you might; it would not be found where you expected it. Before leaving the exhibition, Madame Picabia and the critic examined the extensive collection of Dada ephemera also displayed in the gallery; her last remarks might have echoed all the way back to Lebel's studio. Dada, she concluded, was "made not to last, and it is a mistake to try starting it again."[1]

There is indeed something counterintuitive in writing about Picabia's "legacy"; as Gabrielle Buffet-Picabia suggested, the notion of a Picabian lineage is a logical impossibility. We have recently been reminded of the inappropriateness, if not the evident absurdity, of the task by George Baker, who, in his book *The Artwork Caught by the Tail*, has analyzed Picabia's fundamental repudiation of patrimony in all its forms. In Baker's argument, Picabia's anti-program of purposeful failure (a key term for this history, by which the marginal, ephemeral, and incoherent is posed against the supposedly triumphal history of modernism) consisted of a kind of potlatch or sacrifice—the terms, of course, come from Georges Bataille—of aesthetic form itself as symbolic economy and, through structural analogy, of those diverse sociopolitical keystones upon which art rests: patriarchy, culture, capitalism. The theoretical model at work here derives largely from the French theorist Jean-Joseph Goux, whose work was introduced into art-historical discourse by Rosalind E. Krauss, in her *Picasso Papers*.[2] Goux extends the Marxist interpretation of the mode of capitalist exchange to incorporate other forms of substitution or equivalent processes in the social, legal, moral, religious, philosophical, and aesthetic realms; if Marx defined money as the "general equivalent" of commodities, Goux broadens the terms to encompass other kinds of exchange: phonetic language, the father, and the Lacanian phallus all become general equivalents in systems of meaning that are conjoined through structural homologies. Baker draws on this extension of the logic of Marxist exchange value into every aspect of the human life-world. Thus Dada is read as a series of attempts to rupture particular symbolic economies, or "to seize directly upon the 'general equivalents' . . . ruling these economies themselves (Father, Phallus, Language, Money)."[3] In Baker's reading, Picabia's project in these years around 1920 was nothing less than the subversion of each and every one of these pillars of bourgeois society. For example, when Picabia took a toy monkey, attached it to a blank canvas so that it holds its tail protruding from between its legs, and painted around it phrases like "Portrait of Cézanne, Portrait of Rembrandt, Portrait of Renoir," we are meant to understand one of these general equivalents being put to immediate use: "the phallus will be entered into the scene of representation, its exclusion denied, its substance used."[4] And this is what the general equivalents cannot abide—*use* rather than exchange, expenditure rather than reserve.

Even as Baker outlines a Picabia who had resolutely refused a filial heritage, this move nevertheless leaves him free to find the artist's "influence"— the mark of his strategies or operations—everywhere in postwar art, from Jackson Pollock's use of cut-out shapes to Lucio Fontana's pierced canvases. What this occludes, however, is the historically and geographically discontinuous reception of Picabia simultaneously within the neo-avant-garde and the museum during these years. While the influence of Duchamp and the readymade strategy on the production of the postwar neo-avant-garde has become a widely accepted and studied phenomenon, the significance of his erstwhile colleague and collaborator has hardly been acknowledged.

When Francis Picabia died on November 30, 1953, the Rose Fried Gallery on the Upper East Side of Manhattan was about to open *Duchamp Picabia*, a joint exhibition of these two artists' works. As described by one critic, in this "small but important documentary show . . . one sees how both of these artists invented imagery to express such concepts of the dada manifesto as 'Creation for its own sake destroying creation.'"[5] While the exhibition included a small-scale overview of his career—beginning with *Landscape, La Creuse* of around 1912, continuing with Dada works such as the 1915 mechanistic painting *Reverence* (consistently mistitled *Dedée d'Amérique* throughout this period) and a commemorative drawing of Guillaume Apollinaire made at the time of the poet's death in 1918, and concluding with a "transparency" and one recent painting—the works elicited a rather mystified response.[6] Confronted with *Reverence*'s geometric forms and metallic paint, the critic can summon only the notion that here "one finds a symbolical—perhaps a metaphysical— significance."[7] However, the ground of Picabia's reception in America was clearly shifting in these years, which saw the purchase of *I See Again in Memory My Dear Udnie* of 1914 by the Museum of Modern Art, after having been shown to critical praise at Sidney Janis.[8] The later 1950s and early 1960s indeed marked the gradual acceptance of his work within the museum, conditioned by two factors. The first, art-historical in nature, was the fiftieth anniversary of the Armory Show of 1913, which saw a spate of articles revisiting that famous exhibition where Picabia had exhibited four works, including *Dances at the Spring I* of 1912, originally sold to Arthur Jerome Eddy of Chicago, then acquired by Walter Arensberg, who donated it to the Philadelphia

Museum of Art in 1951.[9] The second, of course, stems from contemporary artistic developments—Pop Art, New Realism, and the like—that took Dada as a precursor. These two factors produced very different versions of Picabia, needless to say, with the first constructing a pre-Dada Picabia who might be properly inserted into a twentieth-century canon of post-Cubist painting, and the second generating a figure who might stand as an early instance of the kind of ontological questioning that Pop had once again brought to fore. When *Plumes* was exhibited in New York in 1963, a critic described it as "one of a number of brilliantly silly works" that nevertheless combines elements of assemblage, painting, found-object, and collage and raises questions about the nature of the painted illusion, the painting as a thing and not as a window, the problem of where a painting should stop, and what a painting is for.[10] Picabia was, then, the subject of an ambivalent acceptance into American art institutions—silly if brilliant, and in this sense not so different from his similarly inassimilable colleague Duchamp.

Certainly the most curious moment within Picabia's reception, however, was the essay published on his work in 1956 by Philip Pearlstein, who at the time was a young painter and recent recipient of a master's degree in art history from the Institute of Fine Arts (IFA). Pearlstein had moved to New York in 1949 after graduating Carnegie Tech and had quickly found himself in the commercial art world, working for the graphic designer Ladislav Sutnar; it was at the latter's urging that Pearlstein enrolled at the IFA in 1950. When it came time to start his thesis, his work on plumbing catalogs for Sutnar and his own subsequent paintings based on forms found therein led him to Picabia and Duchamp: "They also had made paintings based on machine shapes taken from catalogs, so I felt very much at home with their Dada work," he later remarked.[11] In "The Paintings of Francis Picabia, 1908–1930," completed in 1955, Pearlstein elaborated an iconographic study of the artist's work—a typical approach for the IFA at the time, even if the subject was unexpectedly modern for that conservative institution. As Pearlstein recalls, "While I was in the middle of putting this together, Picabia died, and I was suddenly the world's leading authority on Francis Picabia—at least in the English language. And I was asked to submit an article to a couple of art magazines."[12] This would become the 1956 article in *Arts Magazine*, "The Symbolic Language of Francis Picabia," the first scholarly essay published in English on the artist. In it, Pearlstein explored what he termed the "literary values" in Picabia's work, insisting on the latter's rejection of the formalism of Cubism—its dismissal of "subject matter" in favor of "the problems of painting per se"—so that instead "the plastic elements of the paintings exist for the purpose of conveying the subject."[13] Pearlstein traced how an initial abstract syntax of forms and colors conceived as language was transformed by the Dada years into a literal, if hermetic, use of words and phrases inscribed directly onto the picture plane; he proposed readings of a range of works produced between the teens and early twenties, and—in contrast to much of the critical reception at the time—was able to suggest the negativity operative in the art produced by Picabia and Duchamp. It seems telling that the two photographs of the artist reproduced with the article, which frame the text as the first and last images reproduced, revealed the move from painter captured amid the clutter of the studio in 1911 to anti-art provocateur, holding the *Danse de Saint-Guy* of 1921, an open frame strung with cord and cardboard—although it might also be noted that, in this era of "action painting," both photographs show him inactive, pensive in the first, sardonically breaking into a grin in the second. But whatever Pearlstein's insights into Picabia's work, he was careful to frame his article with a disavowal: in the contributor's list at the front of the magazine, he was careful to have himself described as "a young American painter *whose own work bears no relation whatever to Picabia's.*"[14] That disavowal would define the American reception of Picabia, whose historical actions could be assimilated to and neutralized within museum culture but could under no conditions be admitted into the realm of contemporary practice.

Something of the opposite condition would be the case in Paris, where younger artists might embrace the Picabian inheritance but where the conservative museum world had an exceedingly difficult time in admitting him within its precincts. When in 1959 the Musée National d'Art Moderne acquired *Rubber*, the purchase was legitimized only by characterizing the work as "his famous watercolor in which historians of abstract art generally agree to see the latter's first manifestation," that is, by claiming that the work, dated to 1909, represented the earliest example of nonfiguration. Although it could as easily be termed a still life, Bernard Dorival insisted on its primacy in the elaboration of abstraction, and in particular over Germany's claims in that arena through the work of Kandinsky and Der Blaue Reiter: "However crucial may have been the part of this painter and that of the Munich school in the development of abstract art, how can we not recognize that the School of Paris was even more important?"[15] Only through conscripting Picabia into the nationalist narrative of the School of Paris could the interest be justified. Otherwise, the mainstream of Parisian criticism was inclined to dismissal, as in the response of Pierre Schneider to a 1961 survey exhibition at the Galerie Mona Lisa; remarking indifferently on the successive metamorphoses through which Picabia had passed, he wrote: "The works now tend to look like period pieces—faithful reflections of passing modes, and yet Picabia initiated many of these."[16]

What critics noted with frustration—the artist's rejection of the sort of signature style so much in demand in the postwar moment—younger artists would precisely embrace. What Picabia offered Lebel or his Icelandic colleague Erró (Guðmundur Guðmundsson) was less a set of formal tropes susceptible to repetition than a counterparadigm of the negation and destruction of aesthetic form itself. Lebel and Erró had met in Florence in 1955, when both were studying at the Academy of Fine Arts. Although Lebel was four years his junior, he was undoubtedly the more cosmopolitan and knowledgeable figure, having spent his childhood in New York among the community of émigré Surrealists who were close friends of his father, Robert Lebel (who was soon to publish the first monograph on Marcel Duchamp).[17] At a moment when the experiments of Dada and Surrealism had largely been forgotten, and when a lyrical or gestural abstraction dominated the world of contemporary art exhibitions, Jean-Jacques Lebel offered a link back to the interwar avant-gardes that had pursued a program of conjoined political and artistic radicalism. Erró would attempt to make that program his own when he arrived in Paris in 1958.

The decision to settle in Paris should hardly be surprising; not only was the city still seen as the cultural capital of the West, but it was also home to the Surrealist and post-Surrealist avant-gardes among whom Erró clearly wished to stake his fortunes. The "Collages" series begun there in 1958 is, in many ways, the pivot upon which Erró's oeuvre turns, marking the transition from what were basically student works to his mature production. While modest in size, they announce his ambition to create an art out of the ephemera of everyday life, out of magazine advertisements, newspaper headlines, scientific photographs, and fashion plates; glue and scissors become the only tools in his scathing attacks on the *société du spectacle*. Guy Debord, who coined that phrase to describe the new dispensation of postwar capitalism, had just founded the Situationist International one year earlier, and Erró occupied a somewhat parallel politico-esthetic terrain. His collages could in fact be described as a form of Situationist *détournement*, the "diversion" or "subversion" of elements appropriated from mass culture and subjected to a process of Dadaist-type negation. So in an untitled work from the series we see two

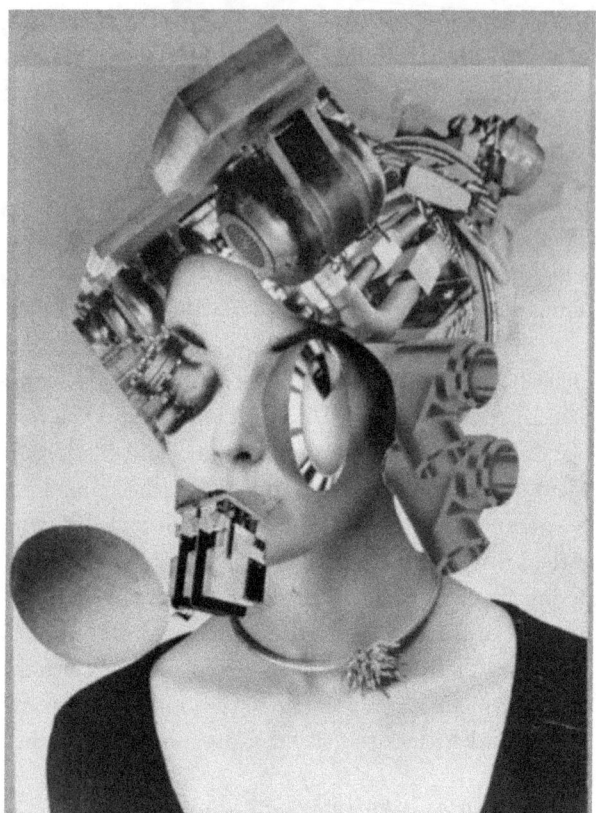

FIGURE 6.3 Erró (Guðmundur Guðmundsson), *Madame Picabia*,
1959. Photocollage on cardboard. Photo by Phillippe Migeat. Musée
National d'Art Moderne, Centre Georges Pompidou, Paris, France.
© CNC/MNAM/Dist. RMN-Grand Palais/Art Resource, NY/Erró/
SODRAC (2015).

heads of female models now sprouting mechanized appendages from their
eyes, mouths, and out of the top of their heads, the gray world of machinery
colonizing human flesh—a metaphor, perhaps, for the modernization that
was transforming not only the masculine workplace but the feminized domain of private life as well in these years. *Madame Picabia* similarly fuses the
female body and mechanical equipment in a work that is reminiscent of Raoul
Hausmann's Berlin Dada photomontages, but that more likely derives—as its
title suggests—from Picabia's ironic use of machine imagery.

Throughout this series the deformation of images of women is a repeated
theme (see, in addition to the works just discussed, *On My Lips, Do You Brush*

Everyday, and *Covema*), and if on the one hand imaginary violence against women's bodies is a venerable avant-garde gambit, on the other hand we should acknowledge that it has a more punctual meaning here. Kristin Ross has described the onset of postwar modernization in France as "headlong, dramatic, and breathless."[18] The arrival of consumer society in France by the late fifties entailed a new visibility for women in the public sphere—not so much as citizens or political subjects but as shoppers. It was precisely these years that saw the publication of new, glossy illustrated magazines like *Elle* and *Marie Claire* that touted the fashions and lifestyles of the upper classes, making them available to a mass audience; these were not coincidentally just the kinds of magazines from which Erró derived his source material. If the feminine (associated with the domestic, the private, the intimate) had once assured a patriarchal capitalist world that a realm existed sheltered from the instrumental demands of the workplace, the transformations of postwar society guaranteed the extinction of that preserve of humanity. Erró's "Collages" were the accurate seismograph of that extinction.

American Projects is perhaps one of the most opaque of this series. Under the fragmentary headline "American projects are born," we find four photographic elements: at the center, an advertisement for chocolate syrup, with the viscous liquid being poured from a can into a glass bowl; this is supported by the legs of a group of bathing beauties somewhat improbably wearing sashes bearing the names of folk-style wrestling positions (Escape, Reversal, Near-Fall, etc.); to the left, a well-appointed woman inserts a glass eye; and to the right we find Salvador Dalí in the guise of La Gioconda, a portrait made in 1954 in collaboration with the photographer Philippe Halsman. The meaning of the montage remains enigmatic, but it certainly pointed toward the unnerving artificiality of human life taking shape on the other side of the Atlantic, and the way that the human body and the "organic" more generally were being supplanted by strange new industrial products, whether prostheses, manufactured food, or the sorts of visual engineering involved in the Dalí self-portrait. Implicit too is a sense in which the defamiliarizing strategies of the historical avant-gardes have been overtaken by the inherent surrealist qualities of late-capitalist everyday life itself. And indeed in these years Dalí became a common target for the Picabian operations under discussion, as an artist who had by the later 1930s embraced a thoroughly reactionary politics and largely surrendered to the forces of commercialization—hence André Breton's derisive appellation of 1939, the anagram "Avida Dollars" (itself a reference to the forces of Americanization).

In his 1942 autobiography *The Secret Life of Salvador Dalí*, he had proclaimed his allegiance to "the flag of tradition, red and gold, of immemorial Spain," that is, the flag of Franco's fascist forces, and after World War II he spent much of his time back in Spain, even receiving an audience with Franco in 1956 at the presidential palace. That complicity, frequently attacked in postwar Surrealist tracts, was also condemned in Lebel's *Wife of the Caudillo Looking at Avida Dollars*, in which the simplified, winking face is composed out of plastic dog turds and nostrils made from coins contained within a gold frame and set on a floral wallpaper background. Money, shit, fascism, and sexuality merge in this savage caricature that literalized the scandalously scatological features once utilized by the artist and long since renounced in favor of the most conservative Spanish Catholicism. One could say that Lebel's work was little more than an ephemeral gesture, a crude joke—but it was Dalí himself who had placed his art in the service of Franco's reactionary regime, reducing it to a legitimizing gesture. Lebel did little more than to respond in kind. And here too, Picabia's precedent seems apposite, with his taste for scandal and mockery. (Curiously, however, Picabia's own flirtations with the reactionary ideologies of Vichy went unremarked in these years; he appears to have benefited from a complete rehabilitation that would only be called into question in the 1980s.)[19]

But this political condemnation of Dalí was also accompanied in these years by a critique of his commodification and commercialization of avant-garde practices—the "avidity" he had so ostentatiously avowed in Halsman's 1954 photograph. In the spring of 1953, the young "nuclear" artist Enrico Baj filed a complaint with the Milanese court against Dalí, claiming that the Spanish artist had improperly maintained that he was the originator of "nuclear art." Baj and his colleague Sergio Dangelo had founded a "nuclear art" movement in 1951, and insisted on their right use the term. As the critic Michel Seuphor reported:

> In Milan, at the end of last April, Baj, under international law procedure, introduced evidence of his alleged prior claim (over Dali's) to be known to posterity as the actual originator of "atomic art." He requested that Dali be restrained from furthering his aim of establishing himself as the pioneer in "nuclear art."
>
> In 1952, when Dali made his representations to the press concerning his own "nuclear art," he had not actually painted any works based on his new artistic conceptions. He did at that time, however, say that the first such picture that he would paint was to be an "atomic Madonna."

Baj's attorney in Paris has taken steps to summon Dali before the Court of la Senne [*sic*]. He will ask that an injunction be brought against Dali to prevent him from posturing as the creator of a new kind of art and that action be taken to punish the Spaniard for a violation of Article 6B of the Berne Convention.[20]

Now what may at first glance appear to have been a squabble for priority between an admittedly minor painter and a superannuated Surrealist was something rather different—that final invocation of the Berne Convention suggests the rather parodic aims of Baj in this matter, which took aim precisely at Dali's self-aggrandizing tendencies in order to paradoxically call into question the whole notion of authorship. The Berne Convention for the Protection of Literary and Artistic Works was an international agreement governing the legal rights of artists and publishers, first accepted in Berne, Switzerland, in 1886; the drafters of this agreement drew upon the French notion of a *droit d'auteur*, which empowered the author, rather than the Anglo-Saxon notion of "copyright" that focused exclusively on economic concerns. Article 6B concerned the right of an author "to object to any distortion, mutilation or other modification of . . . the said work, which would be prejudicial to his honor or reputation." Baj's recourse to international law was more than a prank, but it was not exactly in earnest either; his aim seems to have been to expose the purely legal fictions that underpinned avant-garde claims to originality, even as in his work he would undertake to dismantle those same fictions. The task of the neo-avant-garde, resuming where their Dada predecessors had left off, would be to systematically destroy the figure of the artist, and in his collaboration with the international movement *pour un Bauhaus Imaginiste*—a midfifties precursor to the Situationist International—Baj set out to do precisely that through operations of the "distortion, mutilation or other modification" of preexisting works, sometimes produced collectively. Taking up amateur paintings—realistic landscapes, nudes, and the like—Baj overlaid their subjects with monstrous figures that had evolved from his earlier "nuclear" canvases. He did so in conjunction with colleagues such as Asger Jorn and Daniel Spoerri, who were producing similar "modifications" in these years; it is a procedure with particularly Picabian echoes, in its questioning of authorship and signature, as in its flirtation with kitsch and bad taste. As with his Parisian counterparts Lebel and Erró, it was at least occasionally a technique whose overwriting of the female body assumed troubling and violent overtones. But it was intended above all else to question traditional, legal definitions of authorship and to propose a new, collective model of production that was directly opposed to Dalí's hyperbolic claims of genius.

This is only a sketch of a range of production that might be placed under the sign of Picabia. In Paris and Milan, those late 1950s centers of the neo-avant-garde, modernization and commodification were confronted by a set of practices that resisted the simple assimilation of his advanced strategies into the institution of art. At the horizon of the works of Lebel, Erró, and Baj stand two other crucial figures: Guy Debord and the Situationist International on the one hand, and Piero Manzoni on the other. As distinct as they are, their mutual development of strategies of negation are the untold element in this brief history.

Notes

1. Michel Conil Lacoste, "Au musée Cantini de Marseille: Visite à la rétrospective Picabia en compagnie d'un témoin de la grande époque," *Le Monde*, March 30, 1962.

2. Rosalind E. Krauss, *The Picasso Papers* (New York: Farrar, Straus and Giroux, 1998), 7, 242.

3. George Baker, *The Artwork Caught by the Tail* (Cambridge, MA: MIT Press, 2007), 13.

4. Baker, *The Artwork Caught by the Tail*, 117.

5. Margaret Breuning, "Pots, Pranks and Paintings," *Art Digest* 28, no. 6 (December 15, 1953): 14.

6. On the postwar mistitling of *Reverence*, see William A. Camfield, *Francis Picabia* (Princeton, NJ: Princeton University Press, 1979), 43, 88.

7. Breuning, "Pots, Pranks and Paintings," 14.

8. On the purchase of this painting, see "Painting and Sculpture Acquisitions," *Bulletin of the Museum of Modern Art* 23, no. 3 (1956): 15; for the critical reception of the work at the time of its exhibition at Janis, see especially Paul Brach, "Miniature Museum of Moderns," *Art Digest* 27, no. 9 (February 1, 1953): 14.

9. See Samuel Sachs II, "Reconstructing the 'Whirlwind of 26th Street,'" *Art News* 61, no. 10 (February 1963): 26–29, 57–58; and *1913 Armory Show, 50th Anniversary Exhibition, 1963* (Utica, NY: Munson-Williams-Proctor Institute, 1963).

10. Lawrence Campbell, "Reviews and Previews: Duchamp, Picabia, Schwitters," *Art News* 62, no. 1 (March 1963): 49.

11. "Philip Pearlstein: An Exchange with Robert Storr," in *Philip Pearlstein since 1983*, by Robert Storr (New York: Harry N. Abrams, 2002), 22.

12. "Philip Pearlstein," 22.

13. Philip Pearlstein, "The Symbolic Language of Francis Picabia," *Arts Magazine* 30, no. 4 (January 1956): 37.

14. *Arts Magazine* 30, no. 4 (January 1956): 3, emphasis mine.

15. Bernard Dorival, "La vie des musées: Nouvelles acquisitions, Musée national d'Art Moderne," *Revue des Arts* 9, nos. 4–5 (1959): 227.

16. Pierre Schneider, "Art News from Paris," *Art News* 60, no. 9 (January 1962): 51.

17. Robert Lebel, *Marcel Duchamp*, trans. George Heard Hamilton (New York: Grove, 1959).

18. Kristin Ross, *Fast Cars, Clean Bodies: Decolonization and the Reordering of French Culture* (Cambridge, MA: MIT Press, 1995), 4.

19. See, in particular, Benjamin H. D. Buchloh, "Figures of Authority, Ciphers of Regression," in *Art after Modernism: Rethinking Representation*, ed. Brian Wallis (New York: New Museum of Contemporary Art; Boston: David R. Godine, 1984), 107–35; and Yve-Alain Bois, "Francis Picabia: From Dada to Pétain," *October*, no. 30 (autumn 1984): 120–27.

20. Michel Seuphor, "Paris: Dali in Nuclear Theft Charge," *Art Digest* 27, no. 19 (August 1953): 10–11.

PART II

VIOLENCE, MACHINES, AND BODIES

THE PARADOX OF TIME
Nouveau Réalisme's Curious "Archaeology of the Present"

In 1960 French Nouveau Réaliste artist Arman (Armand Pierre Fernandez) created a series of haunting sculptures made from old alarm clocks. Each consists of a mass of clocks piled on top of each other in a shallow box-like case. Variously titled *The Paradox of Time, Untitled, Réveils,* or *La hora de todos,* they form part of a group of disquieting found-object accumulations produced by Arman during the early 1960s.

This chapter compares and contrasts one of these clock accumulations, *Réveils* or *La hora de todos* (1960) (referred to in this chapter as *Alarm Clocks*), with a Nouveau Réaliste sculpture titled *The Delbeck Family's Resting Place* (1960) by Arman's fellow Nouveau Réaliste artist Daniel Spoerri. Each artist responded to dramatic changes occurring in Paris in 1960 by seizing and freezing a quirky sample of the material culture of the period. Both attempted to simulate a type of "archaeology of the present" (to use a term employed by the French art critic Alain Jouffroy in 1961 to describe Daniel Spoerri's work), but they did so in ways that stage very different relations to memory and time.[1]

The "paradoxes of time" that structure Nouveau Réalisme's curious "archaeology of the present" are conveyed through its works' contradictory relations to memory, movement, and the changing tempos of contemporary life. Arman's and Spoerri's works illustrate different strata of memory-work buried in Nouveau Réalisme's multilayered repositories and recordings of the 1960s "present": the one associated with amnesia and traumatic realism, the other with remembrance and new envisionings of the future through the past.

"Le Nouveau Réalisme," or "New Realism," was launched in Paris in October 1960, following a series of controversial artworks and events in 1959

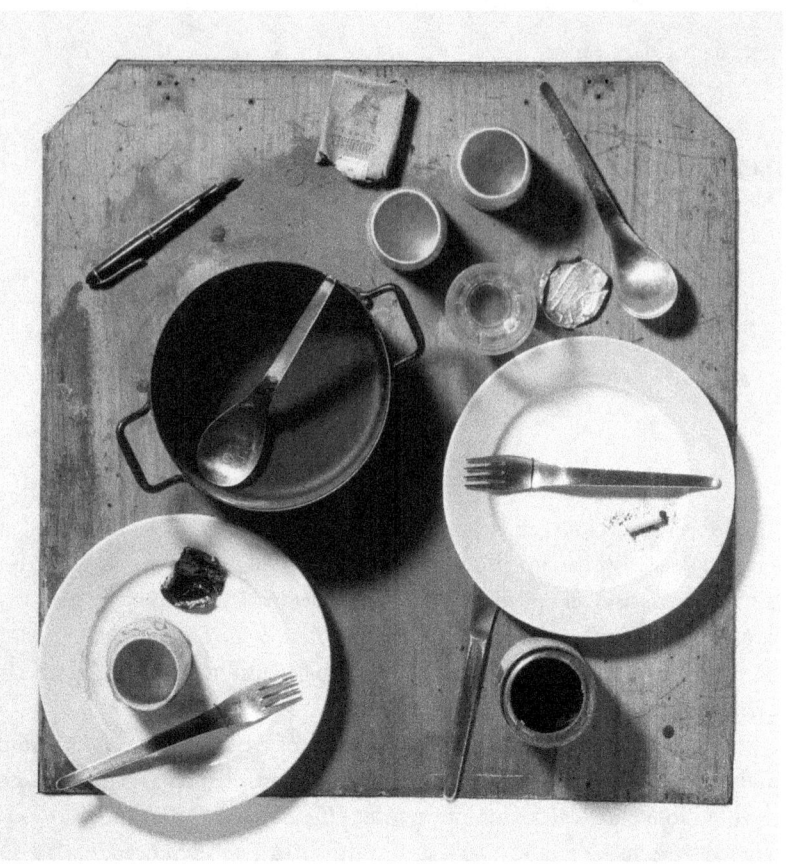

FIGURE 7.1 Daniel Spoerri, *Lieu de repos de la famille Delbeck*, 1960. Assemblage. Collection of Daniel Varenne, Geneva, Switzerland. © Daniel Spoerri/SODRAC (2015).

and 1960 in Europe and the United States. The new internationally focused artists' group was publicized by the French art critic Pierre Restany with a fanfare of manifestos, exhibitions, and promotional propaganda. Nouveau Réalisme, Restany argued, centered on the direct presentation of objects and materials drawn from everyday life. As he put it: "What, then, are we proposing? The thrilling adventure of the real perceived in itself and not through the prism of conceptual or imaginative transcription."[2] Restany contentiously presented Nouveau Réalisme as a "transparent," optimistic "art of the present." Nouveau Réaliste art, he claimed, attempted to both appropriate and celebrate the everyday.[3]

In his texts, Restany emphasized the power and aesthetic appeal of contemporary commercial products, a theme prominent in certain Nouveau Réaliste works such as Martial Raysse's *Display, Hygiene of Vision* of 1960. Raysse's assemblage of brightly colored supermarket products exemplifies the new consumerist cornucopia appearing in French supermarkets for the first time during the late 1950s and early 1960s. Broom, toilet brush, sponge, Génie washing powder, and Lux liquid soap—all examples of "Modern Nature," in Restany's opinion—swept away the old and heralded the dawn of a new, sanitized epoch.

The vibrancy of modern life was also captured, according to Restany, by the kinetic sculptures of Jean Tinguely. Tinguely's *Meta-matic* machines of 1959 such as *Meta-matic No. 12 (Charles the Great)* consisted of quirky "automatic" drawing machines of different shapes and sizes. When activated, they launched into a noisy frenzy of art production, producing scribbly parodies of abstract art. Tinguely staged a race between two of his *Meta-matics* in London in 1959 and, during the event, subjected his amused audience to a cacophonous, barely intelligible tape recording of his 1959 manifesto on movement. Intriguingly titled "Für Statik" or "For Statics," its declarations include the following:

> Throw away your watches! . . . Toss aside the minutes and the hours. . . .
>
> Live in time, with time. . . . Do not try to retain it. Do not build dams to restrain it. Water can be stored. It flows through your fingers. But time you cannot hold back. Time is movement and cannot be checked. . . .
>
> Let us be against stagnation and for static![4]

Despite Restany's paeans to the novelties of consumerism and Tinguely's more ambiguous celebrations of movement, acceleration, and change, however, much Nouveau Réaliste art gives the paradoxical impression of having suspended time's flight.

Daniel Spoerri's part-comic, part-lugubrious trap-pictures—also known as *tableaux-pièges* or snare-pictures—are a case in point. In 1960 Spoerri, an ex–ballet dancer, theater director, and poet, created his first trap-picture: *The Delbeck Family's Resting Place*. It consists of the glued-down remains of his meal, hung vertically from the wall in the manner of a three-dimensional still life or, to use the more resonant French term, a *nature-morte*. Its components include dirty plates, a stubbed-out cigarette butt, three yogurt containers, a jam tin, a pen, and a pack of Gauloises. Incongruous and droll, the trap-picture is allegedly a documentary record of his tabletop.

In a text of 1960 titled "Trap Pictures," Spoerri humorously described himself as the "arrogant and obedient . . . servant of chance."[5] Stating that he hoped his works would "make the observer uneasy," he elaborated:

> Why should my trap-pictures provoke malaise? Because I detest immobility, I detest all that is fixed.
>
> The contradiction of . . . extract[ing] objects from the flow of constant change pleases me. . . . Stagnation, fixation, death, should provoke change and life, or so I like to believe.[6]

Spoerri's words complement his friend Tinguely's reflections on movement and stasis. His use of quotidian objects, moreover, appears to exemplify Restany's notion of Nouveau Réalisme's appropriation or "artistic baptism" of the everyday (to use Restany's expression). Spoerri's theorization of his work in "Trap Pictures," however, differs from Restany's on two key counts: it rejects aesthetics and advocates provocation. As Spoerri succinctly puts it: "Do not take my trap-pictures for works of art. It's information, provocation, directing the eye to look at things it doesn't habitually notice. Nothing else."[7]

Spoerri's first trap-picture is in fact two-sided. The back of the wooden panel that once served as his table is covered with enameled signs, including an oval-shaped funerary announcement: *Ruhestätte der Familie Delbeck* or "The Delbeck Family's Resting Place." Spoerri describes how he acquired the panel while visiting the German city of Krefeld: "In town, in a sign maker's slightly old-fashioned display window, I discovered two panels covered with pretty enameled plaques hung as advertisements. I had to deploy a whole arsenal of persuasion to acquire these panels in their totality. It was only after the shopkeeper laboriously added up the price of all the little plaques, and calculated the total sum, that I was finally able to carry off these 'works of art.'"[8]

Spoerri's readymade time-trap contains a variety of signs announcing people's names and trades: shoemakers, such as Karl Höttger and Joseph Wiers; tailor and seamstress, such as L. Grünwald and Chr. Delchen. The signs on the right-hand side of the panel consist of German words such as *Expedition, Geschlossene Gesellschaft,* and *Durchgang verboten,* which I've loosely translated as expedition or dispatch, closed society, and at the bottom right, No Access. Wordplay and interpolation between languages are key in Spoerri's works. In this piece, when the words on the right of the image are read vertically, descending, Spoerri's graveside humor and sensibility as a multilingual ex–concrete poet comes to the fore:

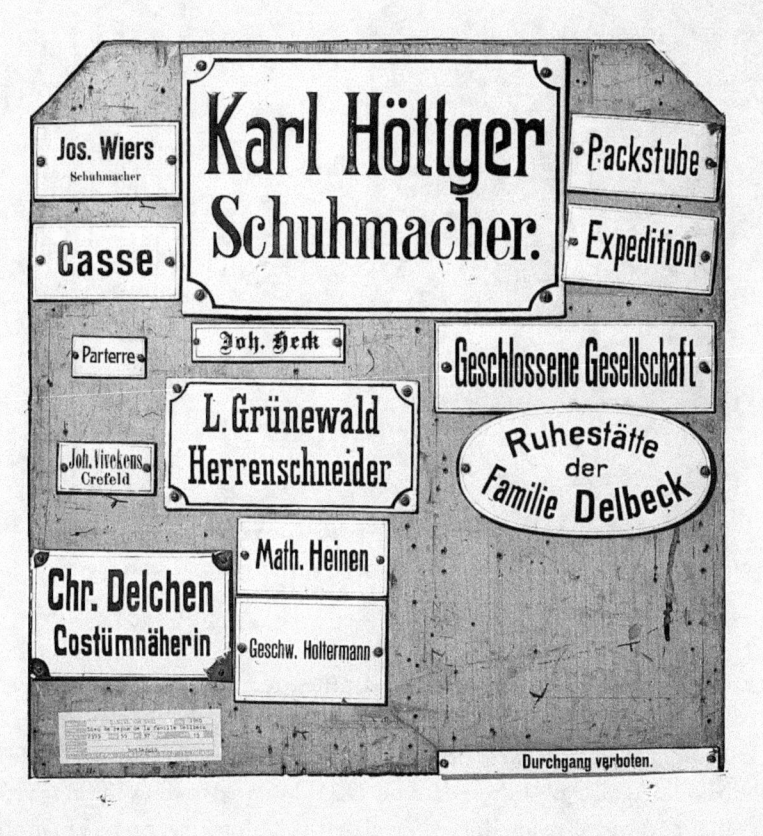

FIGURE 7.2 Daniel Spoerri, *Lieu de repos de la famille Delbeck* (back), 1960. Assemblage. Collection of Daniel Varenne, Geneva, Switzerland. © Daniel Spoerri/SODRAC (2015).

Baggage Room
Dispatch/Expedition
Private Party
The Delbeck Family's Resting Place
Access Forbidden.[9]

The tombstone-shaped back panel of Spoerri's trap-picture can be read as indirectly commemorating different types of extinction or disappearance. On the one hand, it irreverently alludes to the departed Delbecks. On the other, it references modes of production associated with certain skilled tradesmen such as a shoemaker or tailor, individual trades that by 1960 were giving way to mass-produced

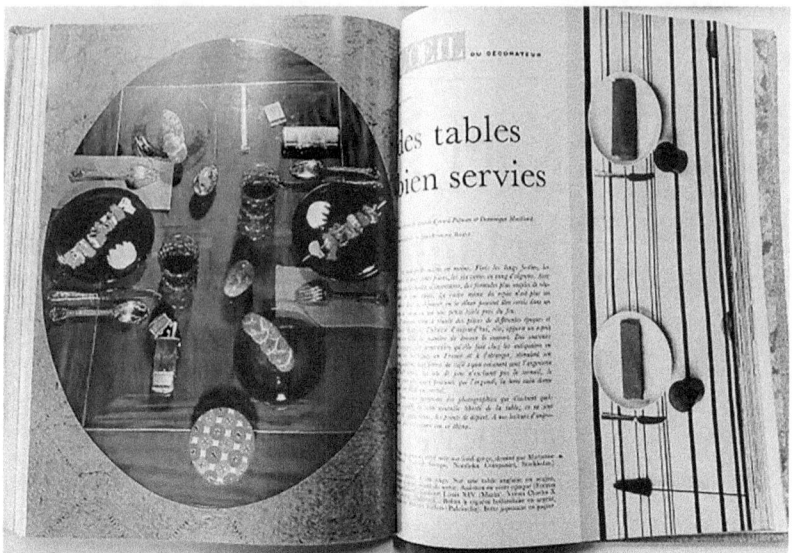

FIGURE 7.3 Daniel Spoerri, *Ci Git Jean Onnertz*, 1960. Assemblage. © Daniel Spoerri/ SODRAC (2015).

retail-marketed clothes and shoes. Against these reminders of the past, Spoerri juxtaposed a personal domestic scene from contemporary life. As he put it: "Editors, in those days, were bringing out books with titles like Daily Life in the Middle Ages, Daily Life under Louis XIV. I wanted to show life in 1960."[10]

The inexpensive yellow-and-white glazed plates ornamenting *The Delbeck Family's Resting Place* are typical of the modest everyday objects found in many of Spoerri's early trap-pictures. Many of these objects reference his poverty.[11] The items of sleek designer cutlery in Spoerri's first trap-picture, however, are an exception: they were a marriage present from his in-laws. The smoothly shaped forks, spoons, and knife were designed by Hugo Pott, a flatware brand synonymous, Spoerri has emphasized, with "the invention of modern cutlery."[12] When he married, he explained, "My parents-in-law thought that modern objects should fill me with happiness."[13]

The in-laws' enthusiasm for the modern was reiterated in art and interior decorating magazines of the period. The November 1960 edition of the French art and design magazine *L'Oeil*, for example, which appeared a few weeks after Spoerri created *The Delbeck Family's Resting Place*, featured an article on new fashions in table decoration (see fig. 7.3). Aligning the latest epicurean table styles with changes in French traditions of eating, it announced that the days of long, time-consuming banquets were over. People eat less and less, it observed, get-togethers are more informal, and "even the meal's frame is no longer fixed: lunch or dinner can be served in a corner of the living room or on a small table by the fire."[14] Its observations on changing alimentary modes proved apt: quick-to-prepare processed foods such as frozen supermarket products, for example, became increasingly popular in France during the early 1960s.[15] Modern eating habits, "L'Oeil du décorateur" proposed, were best suited by new "freer" table fashions such as the tabletop sporting a simple modern Swedish black-striped cloth pictured to the right of its page-spread, or the tabletop to the left sporting shish kebab, red wine, and a heteroclite collection of objects old and new.[16] Interestingly, both tabletops featured in L'Oeil employ a bird's-eye view reminiscent of Spoerri's trap-pictures. The "New Vision" that this angle connotes can be traced to photographic practices promoted by photographers such as László Moholy-Nagy in the 1920s. This visual language was more than familiar to Spoerri, who during the 1950s had personally typed a copy of Moholy-Nagy's 1925 illustrated book *Painting Photography Film* borrowed from a private collector in Switzerland.[17]

Visual parallels between Spoerri's first tableau piège (with its circular forms and lines) and the language of the Russian Constructivist and Suprematist avant-garde were thus not necessarily fortuitous. As Spoerri noted: "At the time, I was imbibed with the constructivist ideas of Malevich and Moholy-Nagy. I detested tachisme, Pollock, Mathieu.... I wanted to show that chance is as precise as construction. This idea is directly in line with concrete poetry."[18] Spoerri's attentiveness to the fortuitous yet potentially "precise" eruption of meaning that occurs in some concrete and found poetry is exemplified on both sides of *The Delbeck Family's Resting Place*. In addition to the German-language trade signs and funerary plaque, the "trapped" tabletop objects also include elements of written text. Printed on the outside of each yogurt container, for example, are the words "FOR THE PLEASURE OF CHILDREN WE OFFER IN EACH BAG AN ELEMENT OF A CONSTRUCTION GAME."[19] Here, Spoerri appears to have dispensed with the manufacturer's gift and transformed the commercial food containers into elements of his very own "construction game": a game ruled by chance, for sure, but informed nonetheless by avant-garde traditions such as Russian Constructivism, Suprematism, and the wordplays of Duchampian Dada.

In his trap-picture *Ci Git Jean Onnertz* of 1960 (see fig. 7.4), Spoerri offered viewers an equally rich game of word and image associations. Like *The Delbeck Family's Resting Place*, it consists of the remnants of a meal glued to

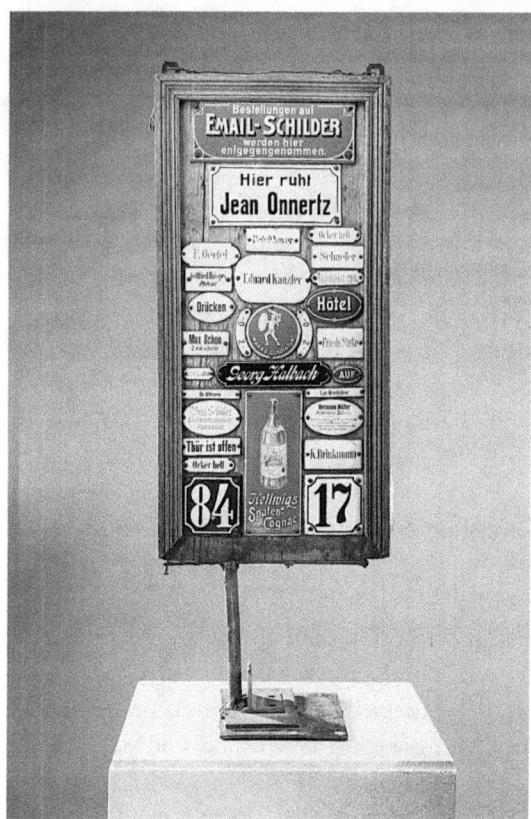

FIGURE 7.4 "L'Oeil du décorateur: Des tables bien servies," *L'Oeil*, November 1960.

a display board of signs—the second of the two panels bought by Spoerri in Krefeld. While the piece is named after the black-and-white funerary panel positioned in the upper center of the board—"Hier ruht Jean Onnertz" (or "Here lies Jean Onnertz")—other enameled signs leap out formally from the wooden ground through their eye-catching color and central positioning. A red circular plaque depicting a Roman gladiator occupies center stage, a black-and-white nameplate ("Georg Halbach") sits below it, and a prominent red sign at the bottom depicts a bottle of "Hellwig's Spaten-Cognac." Words such as *Hôtel* (in green and white), *Thür ist offen*, and *Ocker hell* are included on the sides of the panel amid names and numbers.

Spoerri's snare of signs lures the spectator to construct a multiplicity of narratives. Just how *did* the late Jean Onnertz meet his end? Was it in a fight? Was alcohol involved? Did it happen at the hotel . . . ? Questioned on the panel's word-image collisions, Spoerri responded: "That was the idea, like concrete poetry, where the reader has to finish it so everyone can imagine whatever he wants. . . . For me, it's always about the death of things. So instead of taking this drink, or the hotel, I took the negative, the death of Onnertz. But it's a readymade. Duchamp always made one-object readymades. In my tableaux-pièges it's the *contamination between* objects that makes a story, so it begins to be a drama."[20] *Ci Gît Jean Onnertz* was exhibited alongside *The Delbeck Family's Resting Place* in Milan in Daniel Spoerri's first solo exhibition in March 1961. Installation photos show *Ci Gît Jean Onnertz* positioned on its metal base on a table, while above, *The Delbeck Family's Resting Place* hangs suspended in the air, high above eye level and the surrounding tableaux-pièges on the wall.[21] Photos also indicate a slight shift in the position of meal elements in Spoerri's first tableau-piège: a knife resting across the rim of a glass toward the upper right of *The Delbeck Family's Resting Place* has since disappeared, while a glass and yogurt top have swapped positions.

Other snare-pictures such as *Kichka's Breakfast* (1960) and *The Draw* (1960) were included in the Milan exhibition.[22] *Kichka's Breakfast* features plastic red-and-green eggcups, a Nescafé tin, and Gloria condensed milk projecting into space. *The Draw*, in a jokey gesture of self-reflexivity, includes in its midst a tin of Henkel Pattex glue: a product invented in 1956 and marketed to handymen in 1960 just as the DIY movement began to take off in France. While both works focus attention on specimens of 1960s everyday material culture, they forgo the recto-verso interplay of words and images present in Spoerri's initial Krefeld works.

Some of the most perceptive critical commentary on the tableaux-pièges during the 1960s came from the art critic Alain Jouffroy, who coined the phrase *archaeology of the present* to describe the works; Spoerri, he wrote in 1961, displays "fragments of our daily reality as specimens, like an archeologist of the present. All art, we are told, is a document of its epoch. On that score, the snare pictures of Spoerri are documents of the first order, for they contradict completely our stream-lined and somewhat science-fiction picture of our own century."[23] A few years later, he elaborated:

> The enemy, here, is no longer industrial society, but time. . . . "Art" for Spoerri consists in giving objects a new existence in another space and time—those of an imaginary archaeology—without for all that changing the order in which life, chance, has them appear: this process brings to mind that of certain novelists, for whom "reality" must neither be changed nor deformed, but illuminated by the mental time envisaged for it by the

writer during the writing. . . . But, by a kind of unforeseeable turn-around, that which permits thought to attain this recognition is the light of an arrest, a petrification, death. Archaeology of the present, alas, makes of every object its own cemetery.[24]

Jouffroy's archaeological metaphor illuminates contradictory processes of arrest and excavation at work not only in the trap-pictures but also in other Nouveau Réaliste pieces such as Arman's accumulations.

The accumulations consist of imprisoned objects crammed behind thick display windows or massed together in wooden, glass, or plastic display cases. The similar or serial objects on show in each piece range from dog combs to crucifixes, perfume dispensers to padlocks, and broken dolls to human hair.[25] A majority of critics during the 1960s interpreted these works as illustrations of postwar commodity culture—a shop-window world overflowing with alluring material goods and object abundance.[26] Most of Arman's early accumulations between 1960 and 1962, however, consist of objects that were already outmoded by the early 1960s.[27] As such, they more closely resemble either stockpiles of hoarded, forgotten goods or abandoned modes of shop-window display. Arman's *Alarm Clocks* is no exception: it consists of a collection of dilapidated, broken, and rusty clocks pressed claustrophobically against a windowpane. Peering into this secular reliquary, one discerns a motley array of clocks, and details such as a torn clock face, hemorrhaging wheels and gears, and cracked shards of glass. Many of the clocks contain a bird motif in their center, indicating their fabrication by the twentieth-century French alarm clock company JAZ. Read as a commentary on modernity, the piece suggests conflicting notions of modern progress and its failures. Modernity's legacy of defunct serial products—here the very disciplinary tools used to help ensure production—are frozen in a melancholic display of extinguished use value.

If Arman's subject matter in *Alarm Clocks* consists of standardized products of mass production, his artistic output over time also occasionally evokes the repetition of serial production. Clock and watch accumulations from 1960 such as *Alarm Clocks, Les montres*, and *Un jour ouvrable* functioned as prototypes for further timepiece accumulations created throughout his life. Examples include *The Paradox of Time* (1961), *Accumulation of Clocks* (1972), and *O'clock* (1998).

What are we to make of Arman's recurrent focus on timepieces, and of the alternative title of *Alarm Clocks* (in Spanish *La hora de todas*, that is, "The

Hour of All" or "Moment of Truth")? Arman discussed his fascination with time in several texts and interviews. In the early 1990s, for example, he noted: "I'm attracted by celestial mechanics. Clocks, dials, watches, cogs come back in my work like the cult-objects of a universe subjected to time."[28] It is in a text titled "Time Is Not Innocent" written by Arman in 1971, however, that the implications of an "The Hour of All" are fleshed out and politicized:

> The true conscious anarchist, the coherent revolutionary should apply their determination and strength to the systematic destruction and sabotage of the clock . . . for without the effective measurement of time, a society cannot organize itself.
>
> This in remembrance of all, the first and last timed hours of the tick-tock of history, this in remembrance of the clocks of the Inquisition and the belfries of terror, in remembrance of the artillery's chronometers of the last five minutes, of dawn at 5:45 a.m., and of "I give you ten seconds," in remembrance of the timing of prisons and barracks, the clocks of the death camps and the watch above the Rosenbergs in the electric chair.[29]

The above list, with its references to death and terror, was preceded by earlier commentary by Arman emphasizing memory over time. In a 1968 interview, he declared: "I'm more upset by . . . memory than by time. . . . Time doesn't exist. I believe in memory. . . . Memory is the real inspiration. . . . Memory creates . . . time."[30] Such references to "upset" memory offer a useful key for reassessing important tensions in Arman's works between remembrance and forgetting.

Viewed retrospectively, Arman's allegorical tableau of arrested time simultaneously evokes the slow *durée* of entropy, and the more punctual freeze-frame of traumatic seizure or arrest. Writings on trauma and memory by Sigmund Freud, Cathy Caruth, and art historians such as Benjamin Buchloh and Hal Foster help bring into focus this latter aspect of the accumulations. In his texts on memory and traumatic neurosis, Freud emphasized the ways in which memory may freeze around the site of unassimilated knowledge. That which is repressed from memory, he suggests, may manifest itself after the fact via unconscious actions of repetition-compulsion and the return of the repressed.[31] Following Freud, Caruth proposed that trauma stems from "a break in the mind's experience of time," that is to say, a temporal split between sight and understanding involving an ungrasped "missed event" where one "saw nothing."[32] And Benjamin Buchloh, focusing on collective memory, has drawn attention to the impact of a "collective disavowal of the immediate historical past" upon European neo-avant-garde practices between 1958 and 1968.[33] The insights of these theorists illuminate instances of forgetting and unassimilated knowledge in Nouveau Réaliste art figured through structural features such as repetition and temporal fixation.

Buchloh's emphasis on postwar Europe's double project "of social modernization and amnesia" is particularly pertinent when seeking to contextualize Nouveau Réalisme's conditions of production and reception in France. [34] During the administration of Charles de Gaulle, France experienced a dramatic rise in consumerism and modernization. At the same time, de Gaulle pursued an agenda of reconciliation with Germany (arising from earlier government efforts to create economic cooperation during the Fourth Republic) that resulted in the 1963 "Treaty of Friendship" or "Élysée Treaty" signed by de Gaulle and Chancellor Konrad Adenauer.[35] Gaullist reconstruction, in its favoring of newness and erasure of older practices and sites of memory, promoted amnesia on a number of fronts. The new national administration attempted to excise memories of World War II from public consciousness alongside other so-called unwanted "remnants" of the past such as older proletarian neighborhoods and "unsanitary" cleaning habits. Key experiences to be effaced included France's defeat, and Vichy France's active collaboration with Nazi Germany.[36] If the French nation, in other words, had its own "unwelcome" memories, it employed the discourse of the modern to white out the past.

Processes of collective historical repression undoubtedly effected the early reception of Arman's art, and can be examined alongside the emergence of readings of a "Holocaust effect" in postwar art. During the 1990s, commentators such as Benjamin Buchloh and Ziva Amishai-Maisels began to note correspondences between Arman's accumulations and concentration camp imagery.[37] Examples of the type of works they refer to include *La vie à pleines dents* (an accumulation of false teeth), *The Hairdresser's Dustbin* (human hair), *Ainsi font font* (dismembered doll's hands), and *Argus extra-myope* (pairs of glasses), all created in 1960.[38] Such works, Buchloh noted, seemed "to echo" the accumulations of personal materials and possessions hoarded in concentration camps.[39]

Amishai-Maisels emphasized that the creation of these works by Arman paralleled ss officer Adolf Eichmann's capture, in May 1960, and trial and execution in 1961.[40] It is striking to observe, however, that during the 1960s few commentators in France referred to these associations. Instead, the accumulations were folded into discussions of industrial production, French consumerism, and the "new." Scouring Nouveau Réalisme's critical reception,

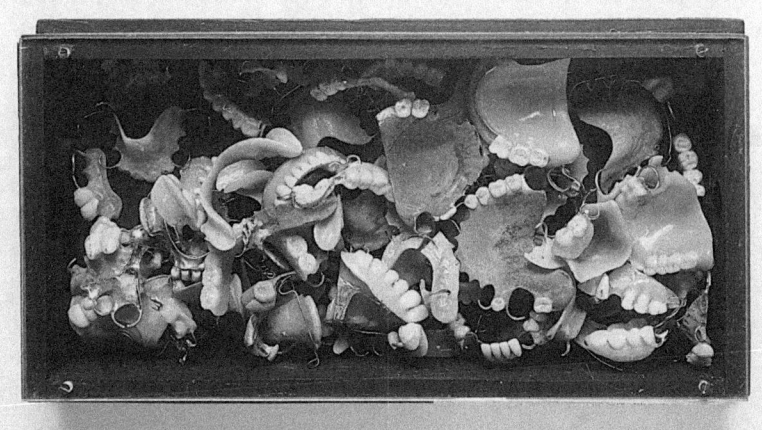

FIGURE 7.5 Arman, *La vie à pleines dents* (*Life with Plenty of Teeth*), 1960. Assemblage of dentures in a wooden box, resin, metal, wood. © Estate of Arman Fernandez/SODRAC (2015). Photo: Philippe Migeat. Musée National d'Art Moderne.

I found a rare exception. Robert Benayoun, interviewed in the Surrealist journal *La Brèche*, noted in 1962, "I can't help thinking despite myself of those mountains of combs and of hair that were refound at Büchenwald: is it possible to derive an aesthetic from this?"[41] For most French critics writing on these works during the 1960s, such associations were either unprintable or unthinkable.

Arman was generally dismissive of claims that his art evoked the Holocaust. Instead, he argued as late as 2004 that his early work, "rather than sadly celebrate the Shoah," was tied to "a certain denunciation of the mass production that was going to crush us."[42] When asked by his interviewer Tita Reut about the possible wartime associations of his 1985 twin bronze sculptures of accumulated clocks and suitcases at the Paris Gare St. Lazarre, Arman replied categorically: "As for the suitcases, there was absolutely no correlation with any kind of exodus, whether the Shoah or whatever."[43] Reut responded: "Would you accept, nonetheless, this second reading a posteriori, even if it escapes you?"[44] Arman replied: "I continue to not endorse it because, if I had wanted to evoke the exodus, I wouldn't have done it like that. I remember the exodus: I was on the road. The exodus passed by my grandfather's large field. I've seen what an exodus was . . . and I can speak about them. . . . It's always the same thing. I always have the same image in mind, and it isn't an accumulation of suitcases."[45] The interview continued, without mention of Arman's other (paternal) grandfather, a Sephardic Jew.

In an American oral history interview of 1968, Arman elaborated on his paternal grandfather's heritage: "My father had to escape because the Gestapo was looking. I was lucky with my very French and *paysanne* [peasant] mother to avoid many things. But my father and family had some trouble."[46] His more habitual silence on this aspect of his family history, however, can be contrasted with Daniel Spoerri's openness about his own family experience: Spoerri's father, Isaac Feinstein, a Christian Jew and missionary, was murdered in the Holocaust when Spoerri was five years old.[47]

Arman's responses to Reut's questions raise issues of unconscious repression and negation in Nouveau Réaliste art, a topic explored by Didier Semin in his 2007 essay "Pompéi mental."[48] Despite Arman's negation, it would appear that now, roughly fifty years after the creation of his first accumulations, knowledge pertaining to wartime and prewar experience is retrospectively "resurfacing" in Nouveau Réaliste works.

This coming to light of repressed imagery can be analyzed as an aftereffect of traumatic realism. I define "traumatic realism" as a form of amnesic repetition in Nouveau Réalisme that may retroactively provoke memory for future viewers.[49] The term has been used by theorists to designate possible relationships between representation and psychoanalytic theories of unassimilated knowledge. It is particularly useful, I contend, for understanding Nouveau Réalisme's refusals of knowledge and undidactic acting out of the past.

In his 1996 book *The Return of the Real*, Hal Foster referred to "a complex relay of anticipated futures and reconstructed pasts" in postwar neo-avant-gardes, noting: "On this analogy the avant-garde work is never historically effective or fully significant in its initial moments. It cannot be because it is traumatic—a hole in the symbolic order of its time that is not prepared for it, that cannot receive it, at least not immediately, at least not without structural change."[50] This *"failure to signify"*—a *trou de mémoire*, or memory lapse, or blank—helps elucidate Nouveau Réalisme's complicated relations to temporality. Foster argues that traumatic realism in art may both articulate a traumatic event through repetition compulsion and rehearse solutions by rendering "invisible" knowledge of the period retrospectively visible.[51] The latter operation functions retroactively, through the eyes of future viewers.

Traumatic realism frequently emerges in the intersection, as Michael Rothberg puts it, "of the everyday and the extreme."[52] The portrayal of "concentrationary" scenes of everyday objects has been examined in recent studies of

French postwar film, literature, and popular culture. As Max Silverman notes with reference to film, such scenes offer "a palimpsest-like effect in which one scene is visible behind, or within, another."[53] Throughout his career, Arman frequently referred to himself as a "witness of his times." The degree to which his archives of the everyday, however, either evoke memory or, on the contrary, stand in for memory as a form of "complacent closure" (to use a term of Andrew Hebard's) remains an open question.[54]

This same question can be asked of Daniel Spoerri's trap-pictures. *The Delbeck Family's Resting Place,* with its typographic games and the multiple readings these engender, would appear to militate against such closure. For Spoerri, the funerary inscriptions underlying *The Delbeck Family's Resting Place* transform its meal remains "into a vision of the Last Supper."[55] The Pompeii-like freezing of a moment conveys disaster and decomposition as well as preservation. Whether read as a figure of vanitas or even a Holocaust effect, however, the word fragments underlying Spoerri's trap-picture—with their references to names, dispatch, a grave, and forbidden access—appear to skirt both humor and horror, memorialization and loss.

Spoerri took steps to enrich his works the following year through the introduction of scripted narrative. In my introduction to this chapter, I suggested that two trajectories could be traced through Nouveau Réalisme's layered topographies of memory: the one associated with forgetting and the other with remembrance. Spoerri's *An Anecdoted Topography of Chance* most clearly exemplifies the latter.

The *Anecdoted Topography* first appeared as a fifty-three-page booklet to accompany a 1962 exhibition in Paris. The extendible map that folds out of the *Anecdoted Topography* reveals a series of numbered empty outlines of objects. These ghostly silhouettes come to life with the use of Spoerri's written key, which consists of eighty numbered anecdotes.

Spoerri explains the genesis of his project in the opening pages of the topography:

> In my room, number 13 on the fourth floor of the Hotel Carcassonne at 24 rue Mouffetard . . . is a table Vera painted blue one day to surprise me. I wanted to see what the objects on half of [it] . . . could suggest to me or spontaneously awaken in me while describing them; like Sherlock Holmes, who could solve a crime from a single object; or like historians who . . . reconstitute an entire epoch out of the most famous fixation in history, Pompeii. If, by chance, it is useful for understanding my experiment, I

should add that it was after constructing a pair of spectacles whose lens were equipped with needles to poke out the eyes [*crever les yeux*], that I felt the urge to re-create objects through memory rather than actually present them in reality.

Following the description of these objects you will find a foldout sheet whose irregular shape is the same as the shape of the table. . . . This foldout contains an exact tracing of a topography based on chance and disorder that I arrested on October 17, 1961 at 3:47 p.m.[56]

The "game," Spoerri explains, is thus to match each numbered object with its corresponding text, and in the process to retrace the history of an object in the manner of Sherlock Holmes investigating the scene of a crime, or an archaeologist reconstructing the petrified remains of Pompeii. Spoerri's aim, in short, is an excavation of hidden memories and histories embedded in each frozen object. The surprising result is a lively, rich, and humorous account of incongruous adventures and human interactions encircling each missing object.

Kishka's eggcup, a peanut, and an unused condom are but some of many itemized objects in *An Anecdoted Topography of Chance* that unlock a network of personal and societal relationships. While the work's procedure of recording and numbering appears to parody techniques of bureaucratic precision or scientific language, its deadpan documentation is ruptured by whimsical humor at every turn. A babble of voices erupts, and a cast of ordinary and eccentric individuals—neighborhood personalities, intimate friends, or strangers—flits across Spoerri's stage, at times intersecting, frequently not. *An Anecdoted Topography of Chance*, in short, functions not only as a fractured record of the everyday but as a ludic, darkly comic, and occasionally poignant account of human relations.

Item no. 55—an irregular curved oblong in the top right section of the topographic map—can serve by way of example. The object denoted is a peanut, and the annotation reads:

Peanut presented to me by "Mr. Peanut," the peanut vendor of the neighborhood, my brother (*"Toi tu es mon frère, oui Monsieur"*), an old one-armed Algerian with a completely wrinkled face who likes to recount the story of his missing left arm: "When I was little, I fell out of a tree, yessir, really. Then my arm turned completely black, yessir, really, completely black. Afterwards I was able to remove the hand and I threw it away, yessir, and later the whole arm turned black, and one day it fell off, yessir, really, because back home there aren't any doctors, nobody goes to a doctor, yessir, really."[57]

Cracks and tensions in French society of the early 1960s are represented along-side cultural crossings and celebration. Hence the voice of "Mr. Peanut," with his insistent declaration of equality—"You're my brother, yessir!"—movingly invokes colonial power relations between France and Algeria. The old Algerian's proclamation of brotherhood occurs at the culmination of over a century of French government repression of its Muslim subjects, who enjoyed equal rights with their French *confrères* neither in their Algerian homeland nor as exploited immigrants in the Hexagon.[58] The peanut vendor's familiarizing address, moreover, is spoken in the midst of the bloody Algerian war of independence—France's officially unrepresentable "dirty war" rife with terrorism and government-sanctioned torture. The one-armed street vendor's dialogue with Spoerri concerning the traumatic loss of his limb potentially conjures multiple subtexts of loss and displacement. In the *Topography*, the amputee's missing limb in fact becomes a mnemonic site in its own right—an occasion for "re-membering" aspects of his past in Algeria.

What role might Spoerri's spectacles equipped with needles "to poke out one's eyes" play in Spoerri's archaeological reconstruction? In contrast to Arman, Spoerri has stated: "What provokes me is not the realism of the object, but its placement in doubt."[59] Paradoxically, Spoerri presents his dark glasses as tools to restore sight and overcome blindness. His glasses, I suggest, are implicitly proffered as tools for puncturing modernity's illusions and combating its in-built forgetfulness. Spoerri's offer of lenses equipped with needles to "poke out" the eyes, moreover, suggests to me a call to address aspects of traumatic experience inscribed in Nouveau Réaliste texts. Spoerri's fiction of a traumatic rupturing of the real into the present challenges traumatic realism's *trou de mémoire* through its call (quoting Spoerri) "to re-create objects through memory."[60]

Spoerri's *Topography* can thus be reconceived as an interpellative grid or memory map. Readers are hailed to actively insert themselves into or in relation to its web of references to period, product, and place. As one of the *Topography*'s contributors noted, "The *Anecdoted Topography of Chance* is an *aide-mémoire* more reliable than memory itself."[61] For many readers in France in the early 1960s, the book offered them "a fragment of their own history" and, in so doing, countered processes of historical repression and amnesia such as those outlined earlier in this chapter.

In light of the *Topography of Chance*, how might we retrospectively reread *Alarm Clocks* and *The Delbeck Family's Resting Place*? Both pieces present us with material time capsules of French daily life in 1960 at a moment of unprecedented social and technological transformation. The memory work they engender, however, is built on multiple paradoxes, and as such, defies simple dichotomies such as amnesia versus memory. If Spoerri's piece in part appears diaristic and personal, and Arman's general and anonymous, chance and impersonality blend in both works alongside black humor and memento mori allegory. While the paradoxes outlined above in Spoerri's and Arman's works testify to a trapping of time, they also promise new possibilities for present and future readings of Nouveau Réalisme's curious "archaeologies of the present."

Notes

Elements of this chapter previously appeared in *Nouveau Réalisme, 1960s France, and the Neo-Avant-Garde: Topographies of Chance and Return* (Burlington, VT: Ashgate, 2010). My thanks to Christine Conley for her insights as I investigated Spoerri's first tableaux-pièges, and to the University of British Columbia and Queen's College at the University of Melbourne for offering me forums in which to present this scholarship. All translations from the French and German are my own unless otherwise indicated.

1. Alain Jouffroy, "The Snare-Pictures of Daniel Spoerri," in *Daniel Spoerri: 16–30 marzo 1961, mostra personale,* by Galleria Schwarz (Milan: Galleria Schwarz, 1961), n.p.

2. Pierre Restany, "The Nouveaux Réalistes Declaration of Intention," trans. Martha Nichols, in *Theories and Documents of Contemporary Art: A Sourcebook of Artists' Writings,* ed. Kristine Stiles and Peter Selz (Berkeley: University of California Press, 1996), 306; Pierre Restany, "Les Nouveaux Réalistes," in *1960: Les Nouveaux Réalistes* (Paris: MAM/Musée d'Art Moderne de la Ville de Paris, 1986), 265.

3. Pierre Restany, "A 40° au-dessus de Dada," in *1960: Les Nouveaux Réalistes* (Paris: MAM/Musée d'Art Moderne de la Ville de Paris, 1986), 267.

4. Jean Tinguely, "Für Statik" (1959), in *"Meta,"* by Jean Tinguely and K. G. Pontus Hultén (Boston: New York Graphic Society, 1975), 118–19.

5. Daniel Spoerri, quoted in Brandon Taylor, *Collage: The Making of Modern Art* (London: Thames and Hudson, 2006).

6. Daniel Spoerri, "Tableau-piège," in *Daniel Spoerri,* by André Kamber, Hans Saner, and Jean-Paul Ameline (Paris: Centre Georges Pompidou, 1990), 107. My translation draws on but alters the translation provided in Kristine Stiles and Peter Selz, *Theories and Documents of Contemporary Art: A Sourcebook of Artists' Writings* (Berkeley: University of California Press, 1996), 310.

7. Spoerri, "Tableau-piège," 107: "Ne prenez pas mes tableaux-pièges pour des œuvres d'art. C'est une information, une provocation, une indication pour l'œil de regarder des choses qu'il n'a pas l'habitude de remarquer. Rien d'autre."

8. Daniel Spoerri, "Lieu de repos de la famille Delbeck et Ci-gît Jean Onnertz," in *Restaurant Spoerri,* ed. Françoise Bonnefoy (Paris: Éditions du Jeu de Paume, 2002), 31:

"En ville, dans la devanture d'un fabricant d'enseignes un peu démodé, j'ai découvert deux panneaux recouverts de jolies plaques émaillées accrochées à titre publicitaire. Il m'a fallu déployer tout un trésor de persuasion pour acquérir ces panneaux dans leur totalité. C'est seulement lorsque le marchand eut additionné laborieusement les prix de toutes les petites plaques, et calculé la somme globale, que j'ai pu enfin emporter ces 'œuvres d'art.'"

9. "Packstube, Expedition, Geschlossene Gesellschaft, Ruhestätte der Familie Delbeck, Durchgang verboten."

10. Daniel Spoerri, quoted in Otto Hahn, *Daniel Spoerri* (Paris: Flammarion, 1990), 30: "Les éditeurs, en ce temps-là, sortaient des livres portant des titres comme *La vie quotidienne au Moyen Âge, La vie quotidienne sous Louis XIV*. Je voulais montrer la vie en 1960."

11. Daniel Spoerri, interview by Jill Carrick, Vienna, December 9, 2011.

12. Spoerri, interview by Carrick, December 9, 2011.

13. Spoerri, quoted in Hahn, *Daniel Spoerri*, 29. "Mes beaux-parents ont pensé que des objets modernes devaient me remplir de bonheur."

14. Andrée Eynard-Putman and Dominique Mailliard, "L'Oeil du décorateur: Des tables biens servies," *L'Oeil*, no. 71 (November 1960): 76–77: "Le cadre même du repas n'est plus un endroit fixe: le déjeuner ou le dîner peuvent être servis dans un coin du salon ou sur une petite table près du feu."

15. Frozen food brands such as Picard, Findus, and France-Glace (a division of Nestlé) were launched or expanded in France at this time.

16. Eynard-Putman and Mailliard, "L'Oeil du décorateur," 76–77. Photographer: Jean-François Bauret.

17. Archiv Daniel Spoerri, Schweizerische Nationalbibliothek NB.

18. Spoerri, quoted in Hahn, *Daniel Spoerri*, 30: "À l'époque, j'étais imbibé des idées constructivistes de Malevitch et de Moholy-Nagy. Je détestais le tachisme, Pollock, Mathieu. . . . Je voulais montrer que le hasard est aussi précis que la construction."

19. "POUR LA JOIE DES ENFANTS NOUS OFFRONS DANS CHAQUE SAC UN ÉLÉMENT DE JEU DE CONSTRUCTION."

20. Daniel Spoerri, interview by Jill Carrick, Vienna, July 28, 2013.

21. The two-sided panel *Ci Git Jean Onnertz* sits on a metal stand made by Jean Tinguely. Spoerri, interview by Carrick, July 28, 2013.

22. Galleria Schwarz, *Daniel Spoerri*, n.p. *The Draw* is cited in the Schwarz catalog as *The Table* (1961).

23. Jouffroy, "The Snare-Pictures of Daniel Spoerri," n.p.

24. Alain Jouffroy, "Les Objecteurs" (1965), in *Les pré-voyants* (Brussels: La Connaissance, 1974), 33: "L'ennemi, ici, n'est plus la société industrielle, mais le temps. . . . 'L'art' consiste pour Spoerri à donner une existence nouvelle aux objets, dans un autre espace et dans un autre temps—ceux d'une archéologie imaginaire—, sans changer pour autant l'ordre dans lequel la vie, le hasard les font apparaître: cette démarche fait songer à celle de certains romanciers, pour qui la 'réalité' ne doit pas être changée ni déformée, mais éclairée par le temps mental où l'écrivain l'envisage pendant l'écriture. . . . Mais, par

une sorte de retournement imprévu, ce qui permet à la pensée de faire cette reconnais-sance, c'est la lumière d'un arrêt, une pétrification, la mort. L'archéologie du présent fait hélas de tout objet son propre cimetière."

25. *La Parisienne* (1960), *Fetiches de la Secte des Théophages* (1960), *La Parisienne* (1960), *Home Sweet Home* (1960).

26. For an account of these works' critical reception in France and their relation to Benjaminian theories of the outmoded and Freudian theories of the uncanny, see Carrick, *Nouveau Réalisme*.

27. Pierre Baracca elaborates: "En effet le seul examen des objets contenus dans les 231 premières *Accumulations* d'Arman (1960–62), à l'aide des Catalogues de Saint-Etienne-Manufrance (1910–1963) . . . , montre que 96% des objets de ces *Accumulations* existaient dans l'Entre-deux-guerres, voire au dix-neuvième et même au dix-huitième siècles, donc provenaient de l'ère pré-fordienne." Pierre Baracca, "Art contemporain: De la peinture aux objets," *LMU—Le Mensuel de l'Université—Magazine interuniversitaire*, no. 27 (June 2008), accessed October 18, 2008, http://lemensuel.net/IMG/jpg/3 .ARMAN-web.jpg.

28. Arman, *Mémoires accumulés: Entretiens avec Otto Hahn* (Paris: Belfond, 1992), 53: "Je suis attiré par la mécanique céleste. Les horloges, les cadrans, les montres, les rouages reviennent dans mon travail comme objets-culte d'un univers soumis au temps."

29. Arman, "L'heure n'est pas innocente" (1971), in *Arman*, by Jean-Michel Bouhours (Paris: Centre Pompidou, 2010), 255: "Le véritable anarchiste conscient, le révolution-naire cohérent devraient appliquer leur détermination et leur force à la destruction et au sabotage systématique de l'heure en groupe et en détail, car sans mesure du temps ef-ficace, une société ne peut s'organiser. Cela en souvenir de tout, les premières et dernières heures minutées au tic-tac de l'histoire, cela en souvenir des horloges de l'Inquisition et celle des beffrois d'effroi, en souvenir des chronomètres d'artillerie des cinq dernières minutes, de l'auge [*sic*] à 5 heure 45, et de 'je vous donne dix secondes,' en souvenir du minutage des prisons et des casernes, des pendules des camps de la mort et de la montre au-dessus de la chaise électrique des Rosenberg."

30. "Oral history interview with Arman, 1968 April 22," Archives of American Art, Smithsonian Institution, Washington, DC. Listened to at the Archives for American Art, Washington, DC, June 10, 2011. http://www.aaa.si.edu/collections/interviews/oral -history-interview-arman-13125.

31. Sigmund Freud, "Beyond the Pleasure Principle" (1920), reprinted in *The Penguin Freud Reader*, ed. Adam Phillips (London: Penguin, 2006), 145: "The patient is unable to remember all that is repressed within him. . . . Instead he is driven to *repeat* the repressed matter as an experience in the present, instead of *remembering* it as something belonging to the past."

32. Cathy Caruth, *Unclaimed Experience: Trauma, Narrative, and History* (Baltimore: Johns Hopkins University Press, 1996), 61.

33. Benjamin Buchloh, "Plenty or Nothing: From Yves Klein's *Le Vide* to Arman's *Le Plein*," in *Premises: Invested Spaces in Visual Arts, Architecture, and Design from France, 1958–1998* (New York: Guggenheim Museum, 1998).

34. Buchloh, "Plenty or Nothing," 88.

35. The European Coal and Steel Community (La Communauté européenne du charbon et de l'acier [CECA]) was established in 1951, through the efforts of French Foreign Minister Robert Schuman, to ensure economic cooperation with Germany.

36. The latter included the rounding up of French Jews by French police.

37. Buchloh, "Plenty or Nothing," 88.

38. An uneasy tension arises in these works between their disconcerting materials and playful titles. The false teeth accumulation *La vie à pleines dents* or "Life with full teeth," for example, is a French expression meaning "life lived to the full." *Ainsi font font font* is the title of a children's song, and *Argus extra-myope* is named after the Greek mythological monster with one hundred eyes. Asked about the comic aspect of many of his titles, Arman responded: "Humor is like an exercise in bad or good taste. . . . You know the definition of humor from Ambrose Bierce: 'Humor is the politeness of despair.'" Arman added, "I don't feel that kind of despair," and elaborated: "The presence of death can be found in my work. But not with an attitude of despair—rather with one of calm acceptance." Arman, quoted in Marissa del Re, "An Accumulation of Conversations with Arman," in *Arman's Orchestra: May 11–June 11, 1983* (New York: Marissa del Re Gallery, 1983), 8.

39. Following an interview with Arman in 1998, he confirmed that Arman saw Alain Resnais's 1955 film *Nuit et Brouillard* "upon its release and remembers it as having had a profound impact on him." Buchloh, "Plenty or Nothing," 97.

40. Ziva Amishai-Maisels, *Depiction and Interpretation: The Influence of the Holocaust on the Visual Arts* (Oxford: Pergamon, 1993), 150.

41. Robert Benayoun and José Pierre, "Alchimie de l'objet, cabotinage du déchet," *La Bréche* 2 (May 1962): 53: "Je pense malgré moi aux montagnes de peignes et de cheveux, qui furent retrouvés à Büchenwald: est-il possible d'en tirer une esthétique?"

42. Arman, quoted in Tita Reut, "Quel charivari, les morituri! Guerre et puissances de destruction; Entretien avec Arman," in *Arman Armé* (Milan: 5 Continents Éditions, 2004–5), 32–33: "Il y a eu, au départ, une certaine dénonciation de la production de masse qui allait nous écraser."

43. Reut, "Quel charivari, les morituri!," 28: "Pour les valises, ce n'était absolument pas en corrélation avec un exode quelconque, la Shoah ou quoi que ce soit."

44. Reut, "Quel charivari, les morituri!," 28: "Acceptes-tu, néanmoins, cette deuxième lecture a posteriori, même si elle t'échappe?"

45. Reut, "Quel charivari, les morituri!," 28: "Je continue à ne pas la revendiquer, parce que, si j'avais voulu évoquer l'exode, je ne l'aurais pas fait comme cela. Je me rappelle l'exode: j'étais sur la route. L'exode est passé à côté du grand pré de mon grand-père. J'ai vu ce qu'était un exode . . . J'ai vu des exodes et je peux en parler. . . . C'est toujours la même chose. J'ai toujours la même image et ce n'est pas un accumulation de valises."

46. "Oral history interview with Arman, 1968 April 22." I have slightly modified the archive's typed transcription to correspond with the recording.

47. Spoerri's father was taken from his home in Jassy, Romania, in June 1941, and murdered with other Jews en route to a camp.

48. Didier Semin cites a passage from Freud's 1925 text "Negation" to suggest that negation may color the Nouveaux Réalistes' own vision of their art. Freud's text reads: "There is no stronger evidence that the unconscious has successfully been uncovered than when the patient reacts with the words: *'That's not what I was thinking,'* ... *'I ... (have never thought) any such thing.'*" Sigmund Freud, "Negation" (1925), reprinted in *The Penguin Freud Reader*, ed. Adam Phillips (London: Penguin, 2006), 99. Quoted in Didier Semin, "Pompëï mental," in *Le Nouveau Réalisme*, by Cécile Debray et al. (Paris: Galeries Nationales du Grand Palais, Editions de la réunion des musées nationaux/Centre Pompidou, 2007), 158.

49. Such a definition can be distinguished from Michael Rothberg's use of the term in his 2000 book *Traumatic Realism: The Demands of Holocaust Representation*. Rothberg elucidates the testimonial writings of Holocaust survivors, arguing that traumatic realism seeks "to instruct" or "produce the traumatic event as an object of knowledge." Michael Rothberg, *Traumatic Realism: The Demands of Holocaust Representation* (Minneapolis: University of Minnesota Press, 2000), 103.

50. Hal Foster, *The Return of the Real* (Cambridge, MA: MIT Press, 1996), 29.

51. Foster, *The Return of the Real*, 130–36.

52. Rothberg, *Traumatic Realism*, 9.

53. Max Silverman, "Horror and the Everyday in Post-Holocaust France: *Nuit et brouillard* and Concentrationary Art," *French Cultural Studies* 17, no. 1 (2006): 9.

54. In his discussion of Alain Resnais's film *Night and Fog*, Andrew Hebard warns: "In figuring archival material as evidence there is the dangerous potential that the archive will stand in for memory as a form of complacent closure, the closure of merely stating 'this happened' without negotiating its implications." Andrew Hebard, "Disruptive Histories: Toward a Radical Politics of Remembrance in Alain Resnais's *Night and Fog*," Memories of Germany, *New German Critique* 71 (spring–summer 1997): 111.

55. Spoerri, "Lieu de repos de la famille Delbeck," 31.

56. Daniel Spoerri, *Topographie anécdotée du hasard* (Paris: Editions du Centre Pompidou, 1990), 5: "Dans ma chambre numéro 13 de l'hôtel Carcassonne, 24, rue Mouffetard, au 4e étage, à droite de la porte se trouve une table entre le réchaud et l'évier que Véra m'a peinte un jour en bleu pour me faire une surprise. J'ai voulu voir ce que les objets qui se trouvaient sur la moitié de cette table ... pouvaient me suggérer, et ce qu'ils éveilleraient immédiatement en moi en les décrivant; comme Sherlock Holmes qui, partant d'un objet, pouvait résoudre un crime, ou comme les historiens qui ... reconstituent une époque entière à partir de la plus célèbre fixation de l'histoire, Pompei. Si, par hasard, cela peut être utile à la compréhension de cet essai, je dois dire que c'est après avoir construit une paire de lunettes dont les verres sont munis d'aiguilles qui menacent de crever les yeux, que j'ai éprouvé le désir de recréer les objets à travers la mémoire au lieu de les montrer réellement.

A la suite de la description des objets se trouve un dépliant, dont la forme irrégulière est la même que celle de la table. ... Ce dépliant contient un relevé exact d'une topographie due au hasard et au désordre que j'ai arrêté le 17 octobre 1961 à 15h47."

57. Spoerri, *Topographie anécdotée du hasard*, 40: "55. Cacahuète offerte par 'Monsieur Cacahuète,' le marchand de cacahuètes du quartier, mon frère ('Toi tu es mon frère,

oui Monsieur'), vieil algérien manchot au visage tout ridé, qui aime raconter l'histoire de son bras gauche perdu: 'Quand j'étais petit, je suis tombé d'un arbre, oui monsieur, parfaitement. Alors mon bras est devenu tout noir, oui monsieur, parfaitement, tout noir. Après j'ai pu enlever la main et je l'ai jetée, oui monsieur, et après tout le bras est devenu noir, et un jour il est tombé, oui monsieur, parfaitement, parce que chez nous il n'y a pas de docteurs, et personne ne va chez le docteur, oui monsieur, parfaitement.'"

58. French Premier Pierre Mendès-France had unequivocally declared in 1954 that "the Algerian departments are part of the French Republic. They have been French for a long time, and they are irrevocably French." Algerians in Algeria, however, were forbidden to freely organize public meetings or move within their country without permission, and Algerian immigrants in France were not allowed to vote unless they gave up their religion. "Algeria," *Library of Congress Country Studies*, accessed July 19, 2015, http://lcweb2.loc.gov/cgi-bin/query/r?frd/cstdy:@field(DOCID+dz0036.

59. Daniel Spoerri, quoted in Michel Conil Lacoste, "Spoerri: Le réalisme du tel quel," *Le Monde* 23 (February 1972).

60. Spoerri, *Topographie anécdotée du hasard*, 5.

61. Roland Topor, "Introduction," in *An Anecdoted Topography of Chance*, by Daniel Spoerri (London: Atlas Press, 1995), 22.

TO BE AN "EXEMPLARY" MACHINE
Tinguely's *Homage to New York*

On March 17, 1960 in New York City, after the St. Patrick's Day parade coursed up Fifth Avenue and its green-clad revelers had ducked into pubs or gone home, another, very different, display of "New York" appeared just steps away from the prior merriment of pipe bands and floats. At the Museum of Modern Art (MoMA), the Swiss-born artist Jean Tinguely presented his *Homage to New York*. Whereas the annual civic spectacle celebrated the long-standing presence of Irish in the life of the city, Tinguely's artwork was a first impression on his inaugural visit. It was his one chance to visualize his encounter with the city on such a grand stage. Taken aback by the novelty of the skyscraper capital, he was inclined to see things that others might pass by. Indeed, the promised tribute of the work's title was not obvious in the work itself. *Homage to New York* was a machine made of junk performing its own destruction. What kind of bizarre homage was this? What experience of the city could be embodied in such a machine?

When asked why he titled the work *Homage to New York*, Tinguely replied: "Listen, I found that in the garden of the Modern Museum, surrounded by those skyscrapers, those monsters, those cathedrals, those—I don't know what—New York is all the same a beautiful attempt to create a definitive *fixation of civilization*, and I thought that it was very nice that down there in the garden was a little machine that was beginning to conduct itself otherwise, or perhaps to conduct itself in an *exemplary fashion*."[1] Tinguely admired the city's constructed beauty yet felt a degree of trepidation as to its scale and power. Endeavoring to comprehend the experience,

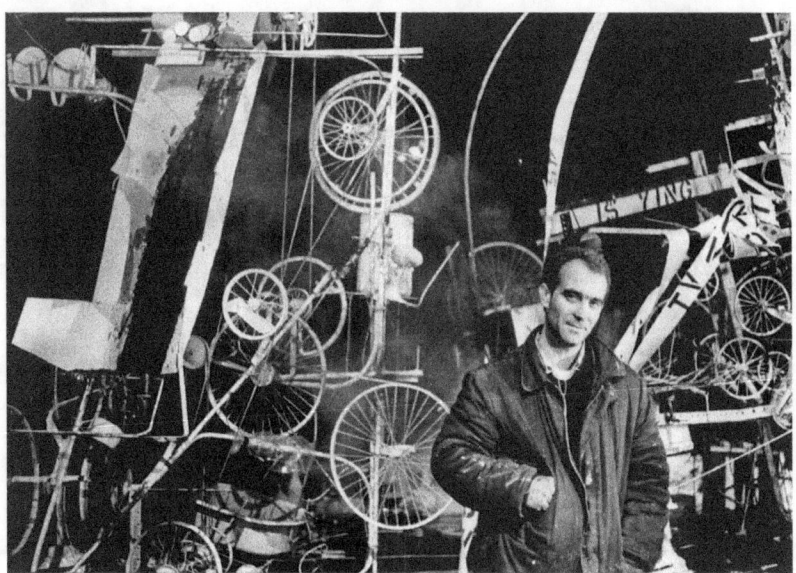

FIGURE 8.1 David Gahr, *Portrait of Tinguely in Front of "Homage to New York,"* 1960. Gelatin silver print. Courtesy of the estate of David Gahr.

he cast New York in familiar terms—materiality and movement—that he had been grappling with in his art for years. In this way, he could mediate a response. The city became an attempt at "fixation," while his machine conducted itself "otherwise." What this otherwise was, he did not specify, but clearly *Homage to New York* was not intended as a simple mirror reflection of the metropolis. Moreover, he was pleased to suggest that the conduct of his machine was "exemplary."

Motorizing sculpture was not new for Tinguely; he first did this in 1955. But New York opened up his interest in materiality and movement to new economies of materials and scale, and processes of mass production and consumption that were more intense and pervasive than anywhere in Europe at the time. The relationship between humans and machines and the possibilities of automation pressed with greater urgency. In New York, Tinguely began to show a heightened anthropomorphizing concern for the "conduct" of his own machine. What did it mean for a machine to be "exemplary"? This is the key question to ask about *Homage to New York*. Pursuing an answer will help one to understand the complexity of the image that Tinguely actually presented in 1960 and the ethical position it implied.

Getting "The Garden Party" Started

After three weeks of frantic production, *Homage to New York* was just barely ready for its audience. The two-hundred-some guests who arrived at the appointed hour of 6:00 p.m. had to wait for an hour and a half in the chill of MoMA's courtyard, while Tinguely and his crew raced to get the piece in order.[2] Finally, without any fanfare distinguishing the preparation from the performance, the machine began to work. Sort of. In order to get a sense of the proceedings, it is worth quoting at length from "The Garden Party," a first-person account written by the engineer and collaborator, Billy Klüver:

> The piano was to begin playing slowly as the flame on the keyboard was lighted. But the variac had broken in the transport, so the motor had to be started directly at full speed. The effect was that the driving sling jumped the wheel on the piano as the motor started. . . . No piano! Nervously I tried to put on the sling. . . . A fuse had blown. It was fixed. The piano was again working, but only three notes were playing. . . . After three minutes the first metamatic was on. But Jean had reversed the sling so the paper was rolling up instead of down. It was a bizarre effect. . . . The gasoline bucket was turned over the flame and the piano started burning. Rauschenberg's money-thrower went off in a big flash. The silver dollars were never seen again. . . . In the eighteenth minute the fire extinguisher in the piano was supposed to go off. It didn't. . . . In the twentieth minute the resistances in the first structure were connected. After a few minutes the metal had melted and the whole structure sagged, but it never collapsed and completely fell over.[3]

The performance ended when Tinguely, fearing that the extinguisher in the piano would blow up from the heat, called for the on-hand fireman to douse the flames, much to the chagrin of the excited crowd.[4]

Homage to New York was twenty-three feet long and twenty-seven feet high, had fifteen motors controlled by eight timers, and incorporated eighty assorted wheels and four hundred moving parts. The artwork's impressive scale was a fitting homage to a city whose prowess was so often measured by its sky-scraping towers. Yet, in an era characterized by the catchwords *automation*, *organization*, and *efficiency*, Tinguely's machine displayed breakdown, disarray, and excess as much as precision and control. How could this be exemplary?

The machine was made possible by the help and expertise of several individuals. Robert Rauschenberg's contribution—a "Money-Thrower" with a

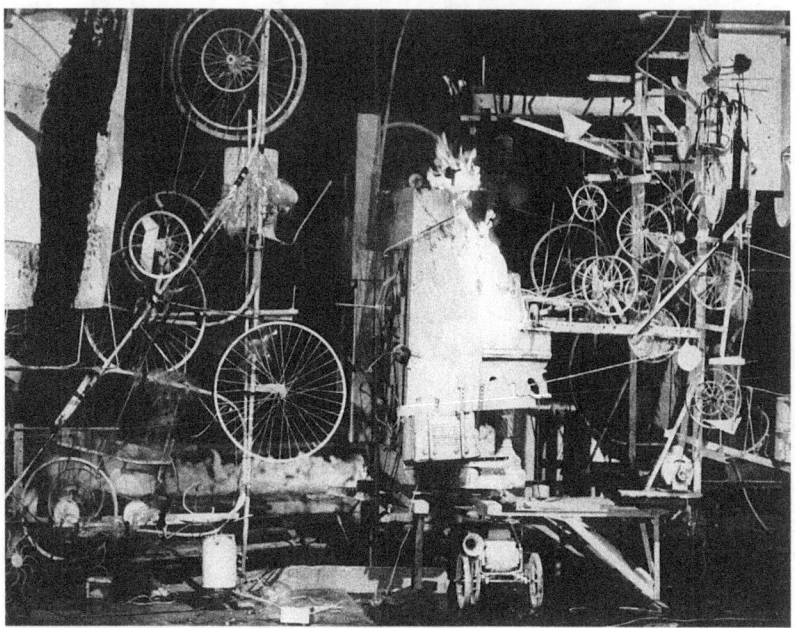

FIGURE 8.2 David Gahr, *Homage to New York*, 1960. Gelatin silver print. Courtesy of the estate of David Gahr.

small gunpowder blast that launched silver dollars from metal springs into the crowd—marked the beginning of the two artists' brief period of collaboration. It seems Rauschenberg gave the only positive response to Tinguely's call for New York artists to participate in his tribute to their city, and the humorous excess of his own machine—money-throwing as opposed to moneymaking—made it the ideal addition. The affinity of the two artists around issues of materiality and movement in this period was such that bringing Rauschenberg's practice into the fold of my analysis will help inform *Homage to New York*'s broader discursive connections.

The other instrumental figures in the production were Peter Selz, who had been appointed MoMA curator of paintings and sculpture less than two years before, and Klüver, who worked as a researcher at Bell Laboratories in New Jersey; MoMA also provided workers to assist Tinguely. Despite their lack of German or French and Tinguely's limited English, they understood what the artist wanted, if not why.

Featuring at one of New York's preeminent art museums was a fantastic coup for a European artist not yet known in the United States. It is doubtful this would have happened had Selz not been introduced to the work of

Tinguely in Paris the preceding year.[5] In October 1959 Selz served as the American commissioner for the first Biennale de Paris at the Musée d'Art Moderne de la Ville de Paris. Devoted to promising international artists under the age of thirty-five, the Biennale was an important organizational step for contemporary art in Paris, where only a few galleries were willing to take a risk on exhibiting new art. It provided a high-profile, state-sponsored opportunity for Paris-based artists to have their work set on par with artists from the forty-two participating nations.[6]

The United States showcased two artists who illustrated the artistic transitions then taking place in New York and to an extent the transatlantic art world at large. Helen Frankenthaler's postpainterly abstract canvases heralded the next wave of high modernism, while Robert Rauschenberg's "combines" addressed the gaps between painting and sculpture, art and life. The former seemed a perfect visualization of the American critic Clement Greenberg's aesthetic principles of medium purity and opticality, the latter an intentional challenge to them. For many young European artists the Biennale was among the first opportunities to see these recent American developments in person.

The Biennale certainly proved an important platform for Tinguely. As Selz oversaw the installation of the American entries inside the Musée Moderne, Tinguely was busy erecting a giant, gas-powered, drawing machine, called *Meta-matic No. 17*, on the grounds outside—the only place it was accepted for show. Like Rauschenberg, Tinguely disregarded traditional medium boundaries, but *Meta-matic No. 17*'s ability to actually move, the animation of the machine itself, took it to another level of attraction and meaning. The Parisian gallery owner Iris Clert marveled that *Meta-matic No. 17* "walked, danced, and made pictures."[7] The general public was no less enthralled. As the first work that Biennale visitors encountered, and with Tinguely on hand tending to it each day, the drawing machine enticed the largest crowds. Upon the insertion of a coin, a mechanical arm holding a piece of charcoal or a crayon moved around, up, and down to produce what looked like an Abstract Expressionist drawing. Thus, for one franc, viewers received automatic art. The impressive thirty-eight thousand mechanical productions generated over the course of the Biennale satirically resembled art that was much costlier by virtue of its handmade authenticity and originality, raising questions as to the nature and value of artistic labor in an age of automation.

What excited Selz the most about the "meta-matic," though, was its sense of humor. "Art hasn't been funny for a long time," he said.[8] The reference was to the postwar dominance of Abstract Expressionism and perhaps the ascendancy of Lyrical Abstraction in France. This art's angst-ridden rhetoric and heroic gestures with roots in Depression-era and wartime experiences were not things Tinguely and his peers related to easily. Their own coming of age as artists amid a rapidly developing, postwar, mass-consumer, mass-media society gave them a different outlook. Rauschenberg, for one, described his disaffection from the exaggerated pretensions on display at the New York School's famous watering hole, the Cedar Tavern: "They even assigned seriousness to certain colors. . . . It got to the poetry later, when the Beats started to hang around the New York artists. I used to think of that line in Allen Ginsberg's *Howl*, about 'the sad cup of coffee.' I've had cold coffee and hot coffee, good coffee and lousy coffee, but I've never had a sad cup of coffee."[9] It was a pithy yet profound insight into a major transatlantic shift in artistic sensibility. For the American and European artists, who were a half to full generation younger than the Abstract Expressionist painters, the literal and mundane became sites of immense fascination. Exploring the profusion of new materials and routines in everyday life felt fresh, exhilarating, and personal. The materiality of a real cup of coffee, or the act of drinking a real cup of coffee, inspired them; its "sadness" did not. They moved away from Abstract Expressionism, in its various national guises, toward new forms of realism in materiality and movement.

Marcel Duchamp was pivotal in this process of generational transformation. Like Selz, Duchamp felt a close rapport with Tinguely, stating: "He has that great thing, a sense of humor—something I have been preaching for artists all my life."[10] Tinguely met Duchamp in Paris in the summer of 1959, and the eminent avant-gardist's appearance with Tinguely at the Biennale a few months later might have lent the "meta-matic" credibility in the eyes of Selz. So too would the approval of Biennale founder André Malraux. Tinguely's machine was such a hit with the public that Malraux felt compelled to stop by and have his picture taken with the Swiss expatriate. The political cachet to be gained from supporting young artists was not lost on the French Minister of Culture.

These high-profile associations, bolstered by popular appeal, provided Selz with much-needed ammunition upon his return to New York City. The untenured curator pushed bravely, against disbelieving MoMA colleagues, to have one of Tinguely's machines "commit suicide" in their museum. After much convincing, the museum's hierarchy made a dramatic about-face. They granted Tinguely his show and relative freedom. He had full access to the courtyard, including the Buckminster Fuller Geodesic Dome for production and the garden for the exhibition. Given Director of Museum Collections

Alfred H. Barr's modernist vision for the museum based on a Greenbergian trajectory, and the temporary presence of Fuller's dome signifying an alternative narrative of a functional art-life continuum, MoMA's sculpture garden was at that moment an especially ideologically layered context in which Tinguely would intervene with his self-destructing machine. The directors revealed their lingering nervousness when they made Tinguely promise that as his machine combusted it would not also take down the museum!

Neo-Dada, Meta-Dada, Meta-Matic

The Museum of Modern Art attempted to set the tone of *Homage to New York*'s reception in a small broadsheet created for the event. Selz and Barr, plus a handful of select artists and critics privy to the behind-the-scenes making of the work, hailed Tinguely and his machines. Among them, founding Dada member Richard Huelsenbeck proclaimed: "I would call Tinguely a Meta-Dadaist because his machines not only turn traditional concepts upside down but also realize the old Dada love of movement. Tinguely is the inventor of the *perpetuum mobile*. . . . It is a giant step toward *la realité nouvelle*."[11] Tinguely, in Huelsenbeck's estimation, went "beyond Dada."

While the statements in the MoMA broadsheet were unequivocal in their praise, responses from outside the museum circle varied. Unlike Huelsenbeck, who generously asserted that Tinguely was doing something distinct from what he and his cohorts had instigated in the name of Dada at the Cabaret Voltaire in Zurich in 1916, several New York critics failed to see the evolution. They appreciated the playfulness of Tinguely's whizzing and whirling combustible contraption, but these critics considered the work to be at best "Neo-Dada"—where "neo" was shorthand for "retread." John Canaday of the *New York Times*, for example, published a favorable review of *Homage* the following day but ultimately concluded that Tinguely's work succeeded only "within the limits of Dada."[12] He wrote that "for the Dadaist, including the current crop of neo-Dadaists in the flourishing revival, despair may be assuaged by the act of negative creation, the creation of objects that offend others by denying hope, that shock them and thus affirm the personality of the despairer. It is an immature point of view, related to adolescent rebellion. . . . Mr. Tinguely received an ovation upon the death of his machine. Within the limits of Dada he deserved it."[13] Canaday's analysis demonstrates one of the potential shortcomings of the labels "Neo-Dada," and "Neo-Avant-Garde," namely, their propensity to obscure the truly productive contributions of postwar art, including *Homage to New York*. The historical links are undeniable, but accepting the ready-made notion that an artwork is merely a "neo" version of something that came before too easily defers the need and responsibility for close examination of how the art operated vis-à-vis its contemporary moment. At present, though, I am less interested in delving into the "Neo-Dada" debate than in taking up Huelsenbeck's notion of "Meta-Dada" as an alternative tool for understanding the historical specificity of Tinguely's machine.

Central to this analysis is the manner in which Tinguely's and his transatlantic peers' appropriation of castoff consumer items and incorporation of movement in their art contributed to the discourse on materiality at the turn of the 1960s. In other words, what made this generation of artists stand out was not so much that it created a novel visual language—Marcel Duchamp had gifted them the readymade, and Kurt Schwitters had granted them license to work with junk forty years earlier. Rather, what they produced was a distinct knowledge of the entire system of objects and exchanges within which they worked. It was knowledge encompassing new economies of material, scale, and value vis-à-vis the real economics of postwar international capitalism, knowledge not only of things but also of processes, relations, and the protocols that governed them. These artists' historical consciousness of their own implication within the advanced capitalist system—the commodity status of art, the role of the artist, political relationships to contexts of production and reception, and so forth—factored more than ever before in the creative process itself. The works of the "Neo-Dadaists"—or perhaps "Meta-Dadaists"—helped produce different understandings of materiality and individuals' relationships to it in postwar Europe and the United States. Whatever label is used, the art itself did "go beyond" the meanings produced by Dada.

"Meta-Dada" was an extension of Tinguely's own name for his mechanical wonders. He called them "meta-matics." The idea came to him via his good friend K. G. Pontus Hultén, a Swedish filmmaker, collector, and curator who became the director of the Moderna Museet in Stockholm in 1960. They had met in Paris in 1954 after Hultén was impressed by two exhibitions at the Galerie Arnaud of Tinguely's earliest motorized works—pictures with white geometric shapes that moved against a black background. Hultén described them as "meta-mechanical," appreciating the possible references to words such as *metaphysical, metaphor,* and *metamorphosis*; all of which resonate when trying to make sense of *Homage to New York*. Yet Hultén also made a point of consulting the *Grand Dictionnaire Larousse* to learn that the prefix *meta* means "with" and "after."[14] These seemed "just right," Hultén said. His certainty as to the appropriateness of these particular meanings elicits questions not only of how Tinguely's machines can be understood as operating "with" and "after," but also whether this relates to the apparent "exemplary" conduct of *Homage*. It is also worth recalling that Tinguely consciously refused to call his machines "automata": this was the name used by the editor in chief of *Cimaise*, a modern art monthly, in his introduction for the first Galerie Arnaud show. While some artists might simply have followed the lead of an influential editor, Tinguely charted his own "meta-matic" path.[15] Unlike "automata," "meta-matic" has a supernumerary register—a curious sense of operating above and beyond regular machines.

Materials and Materiality

Homage to New York was a surprising title for a work by an artist who had only just arrived in the city, and the piece itself seemed to complicate rather than clarify the nature of the relationship between the machine and the metropolis. Tinguely attempted to explain himself in an interview after the event: "Listen, I am not from New York, I see it for the first time, this was a way of responding, of making contact . . . it probably gave me a jolt. . . . I saw this magnificent accumulation of human power and I found I could calmly make a little unpleasantness there."[16] It is not unusual, of course, for first-time visitors to New York to gape at the sheer scale and concentration of its buildings and people. Francis Picabia, Marcel Duchamp, and other Dadaists and Surrealists are known to have marveled at the industry of the city in the 1910s and 1920s. But to conceptualize the city as an "accumulation of power" is striking. It suggests not only Tinguely's own sophisticated thinking informed by anarchist philosophies but also a wider discourse on the postwar geopolitical shifts that positioned New York as the world's new cultural and economic epicenter.[17]

Ironically, in order to collect the materials for his ambitious machine that would "speak" to the power of New York with its newly shimmering corporate monuments of glass and steel, Tinguely turned to the area's junkyards. Working with castoff materials was not unusual for the Swiss (he made his first sculptures incorporating old gramophone motors, scrap metal, wire, and everyday objects retrieved from the trash in 1954–55). He was not alone in doing so among his contemporaries. In Paris, Arman was filling vitrines with common household waste, and César was compressing old automobiles into blocks. In New York, Rauschenberg's combines, Richard Stankiewicz's discarded metal and machine-part sculptures, and John Chamberlain's auto-body assemblages all evidenced a broader junk aesthetic by the mid to late fifties.[18] Yet Tinguely spoke of the importance of seeing the Americans' work directly in New York: "I had been very struck by their work, and certainly very struck by Rauschenberg's withering personality, and by the phenomenons [sic] of John Chamberlain. Of course, I had used junk before, myself, but I could never have used it in the same spirit until New York opened the door for me."[19]

By 1960, the movement toward incorporating "lowly," castoff materials into art was significant enough for the British critic and curator Lawrence Alloway to identify what he deemed "junk culture." Alloway had a considerable transatlantic reputation due to his founding role in the Independent Group in London in 1955, numerous writings and exhibitions, and coining the term *Pop Art*, sometime between 1955 and 1957—all of which be recognized by his curatorial appointment at New York's Guggenheim Museum in 1961. His efforts contributed to a rethinking of how materiality in everyday life had changed in the postwar years.[20] In the essay "Junk Culture as Tradition," he wrote: "Objects have a history: first they are new brand goods; then they are possessions, accessible to few, subjected, often, to intimate and repeated use; then, as waste, they are scarred by use but available again. We eat 400 times our own weight in food, if we live long enough, and I don't know the figures for suits, shoes, beds, razor blades, records, friends. Assemblages of such material come at the spectator as bits of life, bits of the environment."[21] Alloway intimated that the increase in volume and kinds of goods was cultivating a growing self-awareness in relation to the process of consumption. Significantly, this awareness came about not only vis-à-vis the brand-name items fresh off store shelves but also the unprecedented excess and waste of their "afterlife." This could be measured intimately by the faster rate at which households filled their garbage cans.[22] Both types of material—new and disposed—might prompt a degree of reckoning with materiality's capacity to shape behaviors and a sense of identity. Among artists, perceptions grew as to how waste itself could become an artistic means for coming to terms with the rapid and complex changes in society. Objects thrown on a scrap heap or dumped in a lot were neither suddenly evacuated of meaning nor lost to reuse. As Rauschenberg stated: "I want it [a picture] to look like something it is. And I think a picture is more like the real world when it is made out of the real world."[23] The histories encrusted on their surfaces and dangling from their tatters made castoff objects seem less mediated from lived experience than oil paint from a tube.

"Junk culture" represented a particularly urban perspective, for it was in cities that individuals experienced the flood of new products, the mounting waste, and the rat race of routine most intensely. But even in cities, differential postwar economic development meant that junk, and experiences of junk, varied from country to country. For Tinguely, America afforded an unprecedented abundance and variety of consumer detritus. By 1960, the United States' unrivaled levels of postwar commercial production—its boom contrasting markedly with prolonged depression and rationing in Europe into the 1950s—also made it the leading generator of waste.[24] The Swiss artist had never witnessed anything like America's junkyards. According to Klüver, who also served as Tinguely's guide, New Jersey's fields of trash mesmerized the first-timer: "this would be a place where he [Tinguely] would like to live.... He would spend his days in the dump as a completely free man. Out of the debris he would build large, involved constructions."[25]

Rauschenberg delighted in picking up things as he came upon them on the streets, empty lots, and local beaches of Manhattan and its boroughs. His fascination with the city and the aspects of it he attempted to capture in his art were in sync with Tinguely. A 1960 photograph of Rauschenberg posing in a vacant lot on Water Street is instructive. Wearing a suit and overcoat, he sits in a chair against a backdrop of an old oil drum, a cracked washbasin, and other scattered debris. He looks more like a typical businessman than artist. It is as if he waits, calmly reading a newspaper, for his office tower to rise from the junk. Rauschenberg admitted his "excitement about the way in the city you have on one lot a forty-story building and right next to it you have a little wooden shack. One is a parking lot and one is this maze of offices and closets and windows where everything is so crowded.... It was this constant, irrational juxtaposition of things that I think one only finds in the city."[26] The statement had particular poignancy in New York around 1960, for Robert Moses had instigated his master urban renewal plan, including the wholesale destruction, carving up, and rebuilding of neighborhoods. While Moses's plan aimed for a totalizing uniformity, clarity, and control of the urban environment, artists working with junk could represent the urban experience as inconsistent, contradictory, and chaotic.[27]

For Tinguely, the dump—where "things" ostensibly go to die—was not the end of the line of a process of production and consumption begun in the big city. Instead, its decomposing mounds were an alternative iteration of that immense "accumulation of power." The skyscrapers, the hustle and bustle of people, and the trash were all of the same cycle. Yet materiality was experienced differently in the heart of Manhattan than at the dump. And it was, in part, the idyllic sense of freedom in materiality that Tinguely felt as a *bricoleur* at the junkyard that he hoped to infuse in the machine in MoMA's garden. As Klüver surmised, "It is against the background of the anarchy and chaos of the Newark City dump that I see the growth of his machine."[28] Coupling this statement with Tinguely's remarks about the city, we get a fuller picture of how the Swiss artist's first contact with New York influenced his work. It was the extreme contrast of the sites, mixed with the realization of their inseparability, that he found so compelling. If New York's awesome skyline seemed an attempt at fixity of civilization, the dump reminded one of its impossibility— of the perpetual change, chance, and entropy of life.

Movement

One of the most significant things we learn from Klüver's narrative and critical reviews at the time is the degree to which things "went wrong" and "did not work" in Tinguely's machine. By conventional operating standards this would be an embarrassing failure. Take, for example, the component of *Homage* called the "suicide carriage." The plan was for the carriage to move out from the main apparatus, zip over to the pond in the MoMA courtyard, and keel over into the water, thereby "drowning" itself in a variation of the suicidal performance at large. Klüver described what actually happened on that night: "The suicide carriage went off some ten feet. The motor was so weak that Jean had to help it along. It would never have made it to the pond anyway and Jean knew this all along. But he never exchanged the weak motor for a stronger one which would have been a simple operation. As a functional object the suicide carriage was supposed to move, as a work of art it wasn't."[29] This scenario was emblematic of the relationship Tinguely had with his machines. Instead of striving to ensure that everything ran like Swiss clockwork, mirroring the industrial aspirations of the day, he all but guaranteed there would be stoppages and repairs in a machine whose actual function was not even clear. In *Homage*, "malfunction" was wittingly built into the production process itself—such acknowledgment of its own mechanical fallibility lending further weight to the idea of it as a "meta" machine.

No matter how inutile the machine appeared it remained imperative that it was kept moving. Both Tinguely and Hultén made a point of distinguishing "movement" from "motion"—the former being of primary interest to them. Hultén addressed this in an essay published in his Stockholm-based anarchist journal *Kasark* in 1955: "When you want to talk about movement, Swedish is an unpractical language. English is much more convenient since it distinguishes between *motion* and *movement*. Motion appears to imply movement in general; for example a body's transfer from one place to the next, movement implies movement itself; for example the movement of the fingers in relation to each other when using a type writer. This belongs to this century's big events to allow an art work to move within itself like a motor."[30] Part of Hultén's objective was to counter the treatise on "motion" put forth by the Hungarian Bauhaus artist László Moholy-Nagy in his influential book *Vision in Motion* of 1947. As the art historian Patrik Andersson has explained: "Developing his own history of 'movement art' parallel to Moholy-Nagy's history [of] 'motion art,' Hulten increasingly understood Marcel Duchamp's visual and conceptual experiments to function as a genrebreaking toolbox which 'messed up' the rational and technocratic optimism of Bauhaus rhetoric."[31] For the purposes of this chapter it is not necessary to review the full significance of Hultén's claims about movement, but two points should be highlighted. First, one thread of his narrative of "movement art" is the progression from art that merely represents machines, especially in Futurism and Dada, to art that becomes a machine— moving "within itself like a motor." The same year of Hultén's *Kasark* article, Tinguely offered precisely this. He exhibited his first drawing machines at the Galerie Denise René in Paris as part of a group show called *Le Mouvement*. Of course, Tinguely was not the first to use motors in art. Moholy-Nagy's own *Light-Space-Modulator* (1930) stands out among the several precedents. But to dwell on this is to miss Hultén's real point. What made a drawing machine exceptional was not simply that it included a motor but rather that the motor was part and parcel of a work that itself had explicit creative powers. Moholy-Nagy's machine may have "modulated" space and light, but Tinguely's drawing machine was designed to supplant the artist as the creator of the end product that is traditionally recognized as art—the drawing. In conventional labor terms, Tinguely relegated himself to the roles of engineer and repairman. This likely appealed to his sense of himself as working class, and by the time of *Homage to New York* he adopted these roles with performative zeal. He made repairs as part of the main event in front of his MoMA audience and posed for photographs with his machine—all in his workman's coveralls.

The second point to emphasize is the "messing up" of Bauhausian "rational and technocratic optimism" that Hultén rightly ascribed to Duchamp.

This manifested, for example, in Duchamp's use of chance in composition, selection of mass-produced objects as "readymades," and motorized *Rotary Demisphere* (1925). Significantly, Tinguely's arrival in New York in 1960 afforded him the opportunity to renew his acquaintance with Duchamp, and the two traveled together to the Philadelphia Museum of Art to visit its famous Arensberg collection of Duchamp's work. Tinguely here had his first great exposure to the readymade. However, he also would have seen Duchamp's work titled *The Bride Stripped Bare by Her Bachelors, Even,* or, *The Large Glass* (1915–25)—the lower portion of which Duchamp referred to as a "bachelor machine." It is an impressive and, not surprisingly, humorous image of human-mechanical transmutation in which subjects emerge as desiring machines destined to autoeroticism and nonconsummation. The work both complemented and complicated Tinguely's own concerns, likely leaving a strong impression on him as he returned to New York. In *Homage,* frustrated desire in a mechanized world plays out through the constant breakdowns (Tinguely's repairs merely teasing the audience) and denial of any climactic explosion that would destroy the machine. The piece furthered Duchamp's questioning of Bauhausian "rational and technocratic optimism" by extending the unfortunate situation between "the bride" and "her bachelors" to the operations of the system as a whole.

Just prior to making *Homage,* Tinguely presented two texts in which he expressed his ideas on movement. The first, presented in 1959 and titled "Für Statik" (For static), was a manifesto as remarkable for its manner of "publication" as its contents. He wrote it for the Rhineland debut of his mechanical apparatuses at Dusseldorf's Galerie Schmela, one of the few important European galleries displaying new intermedia art.[32] At this point, Tinguely already felt frustrated by audiences' compliant acceptance of his work and cramped by the gallery system.[33] He planned to approach his German audience differently. Taking to the skies over Dusseldorf with a pilot in a low-flying airplane, he flung 150,000 copies of "Für Statik" onto the unsuspecting urban populace below. Or, so he thought. In actuality, none of the leaflets reached their intended recipients. Warm air rising from the city swept up the flyers and delivered them to the countryside several miles away, where very few, if any, people read them.

On the face of it, the stunt was a fiasco. Yet, as Calvin Tomkins concluded in an article on Tinguely for the *New Yorker* in 1962, the apparent misfire was in fact an excellent example of the "instability" and "continuous movement" propagated in the manifesto itself.[34] In Tinguely's words: "Everything

moves continuously. Immobility does not exist. Don't be subject to the influence of out-of-date concepts of time. . . . Resist the anxious fear to fix
the instantaneous. . . . Stop insisting on "values" which cannot but break
down. . . . Stop building cathedrals and pyramids which are doomed to fall
into ruin."[35] His call for received concepts and values to be challenged via
an embrace of life's perpetual change was redoubled in a longer text the following year. Publicized as "Art, machines and motion, a lecture by Tinguely,"
the text was read aloud by Tinguely in his limited English to a more captive
audience at the Institute of Contemporary Art (ICA), London. He stated:
"The constant of movement, of disintegration, of change and of construction is
static! . . . Get used to seeing things, ideas and works in their state of ceaseless
change. . . . Only in movement do we find the true essence of things. Today
we can no longer believe in permanent laws, defined religions, durable architecture or eternal kingdoms. Immutability does not exist."[36] Whereas "Für
Statik" proclaimed values and monuments to be impermanent, the ICA
lecture made this argument for civilization as a whole. From cultural symbols
and laws to the economic fortunes and military might upon which kingdoms
are built, the entire system, Tinguely implied, was no more solid than a perpetual movement of creative and destructive forces.

Creative Destruction

As one of the contributors to the MoMA broadsheet, Hultén offered a particular interpretation of the destruction in Tinguely's machines: "His machines
are not machines, they are anti-machines. . . . They make anarchy. The things
are freer than a human being can ever hope to be. They represent a freedom
that without them would not exist."[37] While Hultén's hyperbolic enthusiasm
for his friend is understandable, it undercuts an ability or willingness to see
the greater complexity of the machine. With its smoke and flames, *Homage
to New York* may have appeared on the surface to be an "anti-machine," but it
was not. To think of its breakdowns as symbolic acts of antagonism or protest
against machines is an oversimplification. The following remark by Tinguely
is much more indicative of his approach: "A machine like New York—and
it is a machine—needs to be ameliorated."[38] Here the analogy between metropolis and machine is complete. Moreover, he in effect construes the artist as an "ameliorator." This is quite astonishing vis-à-vis the history of the
avant-garde. Yet it resonates with his own wish for *Homage* to "calmly make a
little unpleasantness" at MoMA. Neither statement echoes the kind of nihil-

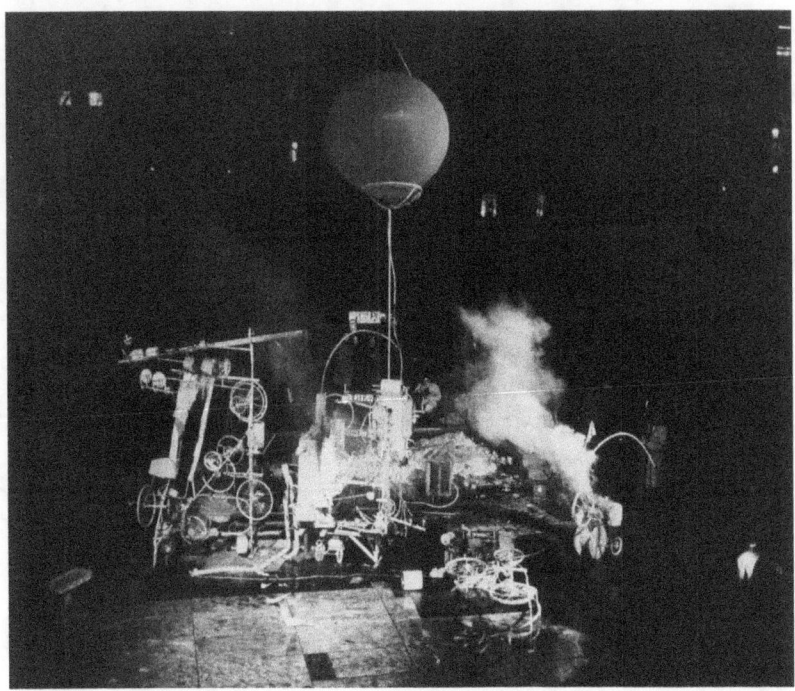

FIGURE 8.3 David Gahr, *Tinguely's "Homage to New York,"* MoMA, 1960. Gelatin silver print. Courtesy of the estate of David Gahr.

ist provocation heard in many early twentieth-century avant-garde quarters. Instead, they signaled the shifting attitude and political relations of Tinguely and his peers to their contexts of production and reception.

In the fall of 1960, Tinguely became a founding member of the Nouveaux Réalistes, the Paris-based art group dedicated to art's expansion to the limits of the real combined with its renewed powers of signification. They pitched themselves against an exhausted Abstract Expressionism, and staked their claim against the historical avant-garde. The group's leader, the critic Pierre Restany, stressed that he and his fellow artists acted "at forty degrees above the Dada zero, without any aggression complex, without typical polemical desire." Restany was making an important qualitative distinction. The Nouveaux Réalistes thought of themselves as "forty degrees above Dada" not only in terms of periodization—coming forty years after Dada—but also seeing Dada's nihilism as a necessary clearing ground from which positive meaning could once again be pursued in the new postwar, material reality. Fellow Nouveaux Réaliste Daniel Spoerri recalled how French critics pejoratively labeled them Neo-Dada: "We—the Nouveaux Réalistes—were not terribly pleased to be called Neo-Dada. . . . There was a very deep difference between our work and the Dadaists. For one thing, provocation was very important to Dada."[39] Restany and Spoerri gave voice to a greater transatlantic shift in historical consciousness taking place among young artists at the turn of the 1960s. Theirs was the first generation with the hindsight to see itself as part of a larger avant-garde history. With this came a realization of the new limits they faced. Tinguely expressed their sense of limitation in this way: "All the artists who have been compared to Dada—Rauschenberg, Johns, Spoerri, Saint-Phalle, Klein—no longer produce the same effects. . . . Thirty-five years ago Dada was a considerable shock, but today the bourgeois has got used to swallowing art monsters, like the canvasses of Jackson Pollock and Sam Francis; the bourgeois no longer dares to laugh."[40] Shocking the bourgeoisie was no longer possible. Instead, according to Tinguely, the artist had to try to "communicate" with the viewer.[41] Precisely what was to be communicated was often ambiguous, creating space for the viewer to become an active participant in the production of meaning. Yet the very idea that the artist was to be an "ameliorator" and "communicator" marked a significant change in thinking about the role of the artist.

Destruction was neither an end in itself nor even a primary concern for Tinguely.[42] His relationship to machines, and the city-as-machine, was too ambivalent for this. Evoking this ambivalence is precisely the strength of Hultén's more convincing term, "meta-mechanical." Here the pertinence of "meta" meaning "with" and "after" comes into sharper focus. Destruction as manifested in *Homage to New York* was a necessary means of both acceding to and critically negotiating with reality. In this respect, Tinguely's machine enters into an unexpected, yet productive, dialogue with the ideas of the Austrian economist Joseph Schumpeter. In 1942—with victory in World War II far from certain—Allied leaders were already anticipating the world's new postwar order in their own image of capitalist democracy, with the ideas of John Maynard Keynes in ascendancy to safeguard against another Great Depression. Schumpeter wrote a book asking whether capitalism could survive. His answer was no. But this conclusion is not of great pertinence where the work of Tinguely is concerned. Rather, it is Schumpeter's understanding of the development of the capitalist system that seemed also to turn the wheels of *Homage to New York* eighteen years later. Schumpeter theorized a process of "creative destruction" as the essential fact of capitalism: "Capitalism, then, is by nature a form or method of economic change and not only never is but never can be stationary. . . . The fundamental impulse that sets up and keeps the capitalist engine in motion comes from the new consumers' goods, the new methods of production or transportation, the new markets, the new forms of industrial organization that capitalist enterprise creates."[43] Innovation above all else, he claimed, enables capitalism to expand and thrive, but this cannot occur without innovation's dark underside—obsolescence and destruction. They coexist in a process that "incessantly revolutionized the economic structure from within, incessantly destroying the old one, incessantly creating a new one."[44] While Schumpeter formulated his ideas within the framework of economics and Tinguely in art, they both deduced the complementariness, indeed the necessity, of creation and destruction to a system in which "immutability does not exist." *Homage to New York* manifested a reverse logic to the condemnation of John Canaday—not "negative creation" but "creative destruction."

As a self-destructing machine, *Homage to New York* performed its own "planned obsolescence." This policy increasingly defined U.S. industrial production after the war, ensuring that the New Jersey dumps, and dumps across the country, would be regularly piled high with televisions, refrigerators, automobile parts, and a myriad other consumer items designed for shorter-term operability. The charming but antiquated feel of Tinguely's materials dramatized this life course of things within advanced capitalism. Rusty pram wheels in abundance spinning round appeared strikingly anachronistic in the post-Sputnik, Space Race era.

Black Market

Rauschenberg began to experiment more with movement in his combines after working with Tinguely and Klüver on *Homage*. The association bore further collaboration the following year in the form of the exhibition *Bewogen Beweging* (roughly translated as "Moving Movement"). In the summer of 1960, Hultén, director of the Moderne Museet, and Willem Sandberg, director of the Stedelijk Museum, Amsterdam, joined curatorial forces with their artist friends Tinguely and Spoerri to produce a showcase for the growing body of international kinetic art.[45] The exhibition ultimately included over 220 works by 72 artists, although Tinguely alone contributed 28 pieces.

Klüver was charged with collecting contributions from New York artists, and his request of Rauschenberg resulted in a new piece titled *Black Market*. As might have been expected from an artist not known for "kinetic art," *Black*

Market did not "move" in the usual sense. Alexander Calder's wind-powered mobiles, and Naum Gabo's or Tinguely's motorized sculptures, were more characteristic of the field as the exhibition's own prioritizing of these works in the galleries attested. Yet it is undeniable that *Black Market* functions as art essentially through its movable parts. It just so happens that any "kineticism" is dependent on an active viewer physically manipulating them. Today it is less interesting to valorize viewer participation for its own sake than to consider what knowledge is produced through the kineticism and/or performativity of the work.

Black Market consists of two main sections: a fairly typical Rauschenberg combine painting hanging on the wall, and a wooden valise resting on the floor (the reference is most certainly to Duchamp's *Boite-en-valise*, 1935–41). A rope connects them. Across the center of the canvas are lined four silver, metal, and flip-top clipboards. Inside the valise are four found objects, a flashlight, a photograph, a handkerchief, and a barnacle-encrusted light bulb.[46] In addition, the valise held an ink pad and four rubber stamps, each with the artist's name, the title of the work, and a number one through four. From two eyelet screws in the lid hung a card with the following instructions (in ten languages): "Objects 1, 2, 3 or 4 may be taken if a new object is put in its place. Please stamp the new object with the correct number, and trace or draw it into the book of the same number and sign your name."[47] Herein lies the "black market" of the title, as the work became at once a symbolic and real alternative site of exchange. Its most potent aspect was the eschewal of commodification and finance in favor of its very own barter system.

This all took place within the institutional confines of the art market. It was not illicit but sanctioned, and therefore not really a "black" market. The point here is not to naively claim art's ability to undermine the dominant system. Rauschenberg himself is said to have realized beforehand that the bartering process was doomed to break down (presumably due to the hold of commodity logic on viewers' consciousness, meaning that an ethos of individualism and private property would prevail).[48] When visitors did indeed begin taking objects without replacing them, he suspended the practice of exchange. On the one hand, *Black Market*, like *Homage*, was a failure. Both systems "went wrong" and "did not work." On the other hand, each artist created the work with this potential failure in mind. Tinguely used motors he knew were too weak; Rauschenberg employed a form of exchange by which he knew consumers would not abide. This systemic breakdown is the critical nexus between the two works, and where their most significant meanings are produced.

In April 1960 a *Time* magazine critic reviewing an exhibition of Rauschenberg's combines at Leo Castelli Gallery asked: "Do people buy Rauschenberg to share in his quiet protest against what they think is a cellophane-wrapped sort of world?"[49] Although suspicious of the merits of this junky art, the critic was willing to entertain the idea that buyers might actually have seen through the chic of newness to connect with a deeper cultural refusal in the work. In other words, the viewer's direct involvement was crucial, but it became part of a larger performative representation through which a particular knowledge of the system of advanced commodity exchange could be generated—bringing the work into the realm of "Meta-Dada." Rauschenberg structured the viewer's "creative contribution" toward the production of a historically specific discourse about the nature of the capitalist system itself. The performative nature of *Black Market* was an attempt to draw attention to the cellophane asphyxiation of lived relations in the commodity form by opening it up to the process of exchange. The work implicated individuals directly in symbolic and real acts of exchange of which the system is composed. It challenged them to recognize and consciously negotiate their role as viewer-consumers while also acknowledging its own implication as art.

"Exemplary" Conduct

Despite Tinguely's anarchist leanings, and his genuine wish to exist in a state of creative freedom, *Homage to New York* was not an image of romantic anti-capitalism. Like the absolutist notion of it being an "anti-machine," this reading loses sight of the machine's intricacies. *Homage* expended a tremendous amount of energy in a process of breakdown and revival, so much so that expenditure itself seemed exaggerated—the material always verging toward the immaterial, via movement, or fire, but never quite reaching this ultimate state. The self-destroying machine never actually self-destructed. Tinguely had to direct its final expiration, and even then the cycle continued. A few visitors collected souvenirs from the remains, but the rest of the machine was cleared away and returned to the dump.[50] Energy spent, without the pleasure and satisfaction of a great explosion that might also "take down the museum," the art/machine became junk once again.

The performative excess of Tinguely's "meta-mechanical" machine represented a desire to exceed the limits of the system, but at the same time demonstrated the capacity of the machine to arrest such desire through a controlled expenditure of the excess energy. Between 1946 and 1949, Georges Bataille theorized this within the economy at large as "the accursed share"—the surplus, nonrecoverable part of any economy that must be expended.[51] It was an idea central to his alternative economic model based on excess and expenditure as opposed to the classical principles of scarcity and utility. Economics that recognized only humans' capacity to produce, conserve, and consume rationally failed, he claimed, because it was unable to come to terms with the "loss" that occurs within the system. Bataille distinguished two types of consumption: that which is necessary for subsistence (rational consumption for continual productivity), and that which is useless (having no end beyond itself). Although seemingly contrary to the economics of balanced accounts, he argued that a principle of "nonproductive" or "excessive" expenditure is also demonstrated in, indeed is integral to, the life of the economy. Art belongs to this category, as do spectacles, such as parades in all their pomp and circumstance. This is because art and spectacles are creation by means of loss—apparently nothing comes of them. In actuality, of course, these ostensibly useless forms of expenditure do have social function and are productive, most crucially, of wealth, status, and power. They also produce knowledge about the character of the socioeconomic system of which they are a part. As Bataille stated: "The hatred of expenditure is the *raison d'être* of and the justification for the bourgeoisie; it is at the same time the principle of its horrifying hypocrisy."[52] Although Bataille's model taken in whole is problematic, his explanation of how expenditure functions toward the equilibrium (or disequilibrium) of the system illuminates both the historical specificity and "exemplary" conduct of Tinguely's machine.

The two very different expressions of New York that took place on March 17, 1960—the St. Patrick's Day parade and *Homage*—can both be construed as "excessive expenditure" in Bataille's terms. What distinguishes them most profoundly is the degree of design and discursive imbrication that enabled Tinguely's artwork to produce a more strategic knowledge to "communicate" to the viewers. While Tinguely himself was not fully conscious of all the procedures his work set in play, the work resonates within larger critical frames precisely because of his own aesthetic experiments and speculations about the role of the artist and art within the development of postwar advanced capitalism. Tinguely's (and Rauschenberg's) particular *activation of material*—through mechanical motors (or direct viewer participation)—staged an alternative understanding of the system beyond its protocols of efficiency, utility, and control. The system was exposed as a continuous process of recalibration, reproduction, and loss, in which minor breakdowns must be fixed repeatedly, desires get frustrated perpetually, and excesses are expended. This, ultimately, is what made *Homage to New York* an "exemplary" machine. It was an image of the system itself—totalizing, yet contingent.

Notes

1. Calvin Tomkins, "Interview with Jean Tinguely (no. 1)," transcript 5, IV.C.20, Museum of Modern Art Archives, New York.

2. According to Calvin Tomkins, 200 invitations went out, and uninvited people showed up as well. The critic John Canaday put attendance at 250. For these accounts, see Calvin Tomkins, "Profiles: Beyond the Machine," *New Yorker*, February 10, 1962; John Canaday, "Machine Tries to Die for Its Art," *New York Times*, March 18, 1960.

3. J. W. Klüver, "The Garden Party," Pl.II.B.193, 7–10, Calvin Tomkins Papers, Museum of Modern Art Archives, New York. Klüver's text was first published in Swedish in 1961 to accompany the *Movement in Art* exhibition cosponsored by the Moderne Museet, Stockholm, and Stedelijk Museum, Amsterdam.

4. Klüver, "The Garden Party," 10–11. Amid the great commotion at this stage of the performance many audience members were uncertain who authorized the extinguishing of the machine. They incorrectly blamed and booed the fireman. As Klüver emphasized, it was Tinguely who made the call.

5. The American critic Dore Ashton, then working for the *New York Times*, also knew of Tinguely before his arrival in the United States; she advocated for his work to be shown at the Museum of Modern Art.

6. For more on the Biennale, see the exhibition catalog, *1960: Les Nouveaux Réalistes* (Paris: MAM/Musée d'Art Moderne de la Ville de Paris, 1986), 63–65.

7. Calvin Tomkins, "Jean Tinguely—4/1/61 at 214 E. 51st Street," biographical notes, IV.C.20, Calvin Tomkins Papers, Museum of Modern Art Archives, New York.

8. Quoted in Tomkins, "Profiles: Beyond the Machine," 68.

9. Quoted in Calvin Tomkins, *Off the Wall: Robert Rauschenberg and the Art World of Our Time* (Garden City, NY: Doubleday, 1980), 89.

10. Quoted by James Johnson Sweeney in the exhibition catalog *Jean Tinguely: Meta-Maschinen* (Duisburg: Wilhelm-Lehmbruck-Museum der Stadt Duisburg, 1978).

11. *Homage to New York*, Museum of Modern Art broadsheet, CUR 661, Calvin Tomkins Papers, Museum of Modern Art Archives, New York.

12. For his initial review of *Homage,* see Canaday, "Machine Tries to Die for Its Art."

13. John Canaday, "Odd Kind of Art: Thoughts on Destruction and Creation after a Suicide in a Garden," *New York Times*, March 27, 1960. Other critics and curators at the time acknowledged the limitations of the term *Neo-Dada*. William C. Seitz, for example, included a section on "Dada and Neo-Dada" in the exhibition catalog for his groundbreaking 1961 exhibition *The Art of Assemblage*. In it he wrote: "The recent wave of assemblage, which has disturbed supporters of both figurative and abstract art, has repeatedly been designated, often in disdain, as 'neo-dada,' even though its manifestations

are far too varied to be so categorized." See William C. Seitz, *The Art of Assemblage* (New York: Museum of Modern Art, 1961), 32.

14. Jean Tinguely and K. G. Pontus Hultén, *"Meta"* (Boston: New York Graphic Society, 1975), 16.

15. Tinguely and Hultén, *"Meta,"* 10.

16. Tomkins, "Interview with Jean Tinguely (no. 1)."

17. Tinguely familiarized himself with the ideas of Pierre-Joseph Proudhon, Mikhail Bakunin, Max Stirner, Peter Kropotkin, as well as Karl Marx and Friedrich Engels and others. In his late teens and early twenties in Basel, he associated with a loose-knit group of anarchists, identifying from roughly 1944 on as anarchist in the individualist as opposed to communist tradition. See Tomkins, "Interview with Jean Tinguely (no. 1)," 14; and Tomkins, "Jean Tinguely—4/1/61 at 214 E. 51st Street," 2; see also Heidi E. Violand-Hobi, *Jean Tinguely: Life and Work* (Munich: Prestel, 1995), 14.

18. In 1960, two works in particular took junk culture to another level through the creation of total environments. Claes Oldenburg re-created the gritty Lower East Side indoors at the Judson Church for *The Street*. Arman used the occasion of his first major Paris exhibition to fill the Iris Clert Gallery with trash in *Le Plein*.

19. Tomkins, "Interview with Jean Tinguely (no. 1)," 11.

20. Alloway intended the term to refer not to an art that drew from mass culture but to the products of the mass culture itself. He and his colleagues from the Independent Group, including artists, architects, designers, and critics, wanted to help create a critical culture with the same vigor and appeal of popular culture, as opposed to the pure and disinterested culture of high modernism. See Saul Ostrow, "Lawrence Alloway: Challenging Modernism's Persistent Mythology," in *Imagining the Present: Context, Content, and the Role of the Critic*, ed. Richard Kalina (London: Routledge, 2006), xviii.

21. Lawrence Alloway, "Junk Culture," in *Imagining the Present: Context, Content, and the Role of the Critic*, ed. Richard Kalina (London: Routledge, 2006), 79. The text was originally published as "Junk Culture as a Tradition," in the exhibition catalog *New Forms, New Media I* (New York: Martha Jackson Gallery, 1960).

22. Arman marked the historical increase in waste, as well as the transatlantic differences in kinds and levels of waste, in his works called "accumulations." As he explained: "The first pieces I made with household garbage were in 1959. And I did some in 1960 and '61. . . . At the time I was making them in small glass containers, and I would say the quantity of garbage of a French household for two days was enough to make a piece that was two feet by one-and-a-half feet by four inches, with dust, little pieces of glass, little bits of thread, a box from Camembert cheese, things like that. . . . It took two days to fill up a case like that, from a normal three-person household. . . . By 1969, the garbage was totally different. It was about three or four times larger, and the colors, the contents, the containers, the plastic, and the packaging, and everything was so drastically different. What was more amazing, when I made similar pieces in Italy and France, they began to look exactly the same as the American garbage. . . . That means in those ten years the Americanization of consumption by supermarkets took place. It was quite incredible."

See Susan Hapgood, "Interview with Arman," in *Neo-Dada: Redefining Art, 1958–1962* (New York: American Federation of Arts, 1994), 110.

23. Quoted in Tomkins, *Off the Wall*, 87.

24. For a general history of this development, see Susan Strasser, *Waste and Want: a Social History of Trash* (New York: Metropolitan Books, 1991).

25. Klüver, "The Garden Party," 1.

26. "Painting: Most Happy Fella," *Time*, September 18, 1964, 84–87.

27. For an extended discussion of Rauschenberg's work in relation to urban renewal of the 1960s, see Joshua Shannon, *The Disappearance of Objects: New York and the Rise of the Postmodern City* (New Haven, CT: Yale University Press, 2009), 93–148.

28. Klüver, "The Garden Party," 3.

29. Klüver, "The Garden Party," 9.

30. K. G. Pontus Hultén, "Den forestållande Friheten eller om Rörelse i Konsten och Tinguelys Meta-mekanik," *Kasark*, no. 2 (October 1955): 2. Translated by Patrik Andersson. For an extended discussion of the significance of movement to Hultén and his efforts to distinguish his ideas from those of László Maholy-Nagy, see Patrik Andersson, "Euro-Pop: The Mechanical Bride Stripped Bare in Stockholm, Even" (PhD diss., University of British Columbia, Vancouver, 2001).

31. Andersson, "Euro-Pop," 46.

32. An ardent supporter of radical developments in postwar art, Alfred Schmela opened his gallery in Düsseldorf in 1957 with an exhibition of Yves Klein's mono-chromes. He was also an early supporter of Joseph Beuys.

33. See Hultén, "The Man and His Work," in the exhibition catalog *Museum Jean Tinguely Basel: The Collection* (Basel: Museum Tinguely; Berne: Benteli, 1996), 44.

34. Tomkins, "Profiles: Beyond the Machine," 63.

35. See the German version and the English translation in Tinguely and Hultén, "*Meta*," 77, 327.

36. Tinguely and Hultén, "*Meta*," 114–15.

37. *Homage to New York*, Museum of Modern Art broadsheet.

38. Tomkins, "Interview with Jean Tinguely (no. 1)," 5.

39. Susan Hapgood, "Interview with Daniel Spoerri," in *Neo-Dada: Redefining Art, 1958–1962* (New York: American Federation of Arts, 1994), 131.

40. Tomkins, "Interview with Jean Tinguely (no. 1)," 13.

41. Tomkins, "Interview with Jean Tinguely (no. 1)," 13.

42. This is evidenced as much in *Homage to New York* itself as it is in Tinguely's statements. See, for example, Tomkins, "Interview with Jean Tinguely (no. 1)."

43. Joseph A. Schumpeter, *Can Capitalism Survive? Creative Destruction and the Future of the Global Economy* (New York: Harper Perennial, 2009), 41.

44. Schumpeter, *Can Capitalism Survive?*, 42–43.

45. The exhibition began at the Stedelijk Museum, Amsterdam, as *Bewogen Beweging*, and subsequently showed at the Moderna Museet, Stockholm, as *Rorelse i Konsten* and the Louisiana Museum of Modern Art, Humlebæk, as *Bevaegelse i Kunsten*.

46. These were the found items Rauschenberg placed in the valise in 1969 when the work entered the collection of the Museum Ludwig, Cologne. They have not been exchanged since then.

47. Quoted in Branden W. Joseph, "Rauschenberg's Refusal," in the exhibition catalog *Robert Rauschenberg: Combines* (Los Angeles: Museum of Contemporary Art Los Angeles, 2005), 267.

48. Shannon, *The Disappearance of Objects*, 144.

49. "The Emperor's Combine," *Time*, April 18, 1960, 92.

50. Klüver, "The Garden Party," 13.

51. The book in which Bataille put forth his theory of "general economy" was first published as *La part maudite* by Les Éditions de Minuit in 1949, and was re-edited in 1967. It was translated into English and published as *The Accursed Share*, 2 vols. (New York: Zone Books, 1988–91).

52. See Georges Bataille, *Visions of Excess: Selected Writings, 1927–1939*, ed. and trans. Allan Stoekl (Minneapolis: University of Minnesota Press, 1985), 124–25.

NAKED LUNCH AND THE NEIGHBOR

This chapter considers not one but two texts from 1959–60: William S. Burroughs's *Naked Lunch* (first published in 1959 by Maurice Girodias's Olympia Press, in Paris) and Jacques Lacan's seventh seminar, *The Ethics of Psychoanalysis*, delivered at the Hôpital Sainte-Anne from November 18, 1959, to July 6, 1960 (*Seminar VII* was not published until 1986 by Editions de Seuil and 1992 in an English translation by Norton). So the texts, and their authors, are neighbors both historically and spatially—it is tempting to imagine Lacan and Burroughs passing each other on the street, perhaps when Burroughs was living at the Beat Hotel at 9 rue Git-le-Coeur in the late 1950s, just a few kilometers away from the Hôpital Sainte-Anne. Certainly there are more than a few similarities with the two figures—always courting scandal, textually adventurous, more politically incorrect than correct—and no doubt there are already theses at work on the obscene superego in Burroughs, or similarities between his favorite slogan from Hassan-i Sabbah, "Nothing is true, everything is permitted," and Lacan's declaration, following Friedrich Nietzsche and Fyodor Dostoevsky, that "God is dead, nothing is permitted anymore."[1] But the direction taken here in looking at these two texts is slightly different, and has to do with Lacan's concept of the neighbor, as developed in *Seminar VII*, and what that can tell us about reading Burroughs's *Naked Lunch*.

In a general sense, Lacanian ethics argues that the love of one's neighbor is intolerable for two reasons: on the one hand, one's love is limited, precious, and ought not to be doled out like the Welcome Wagon; on the other hand, the neighbor is a reservoir of some "fundamental evil" that in turn reflects the trauma of the Thing within our own subjectivity.[2] The demand to love thy

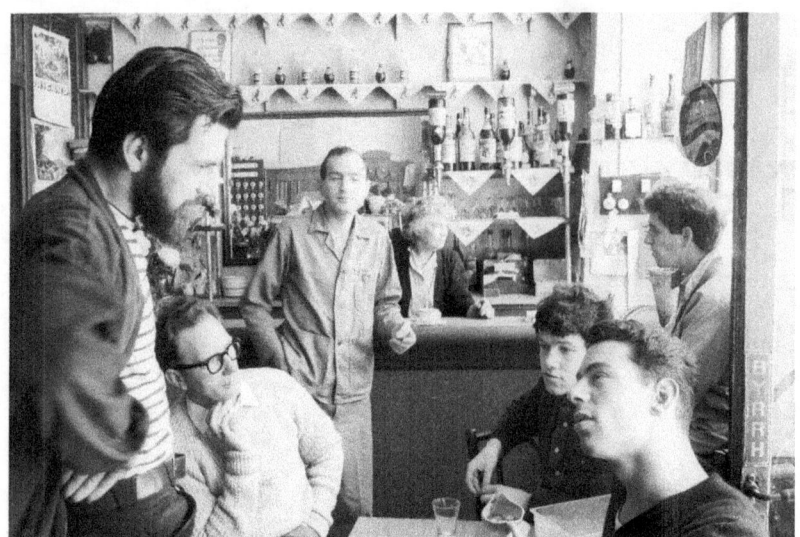

FIGURE 9.1 Harold Chapman, *The Beat Hotel Café*, 1957. Gelatin silver print. © Harold Chapman/Topham Picturepoint.

neighbor is, as Slavoj Žižek argues, nothing more than the gentrification of the Other *qua* Thing. With Burroughs's great novel one gets this sense of the horror of the neighbor in two ways: first, the obscenity of one character after another, of one scene after another—the junkie as neighbor as well as the talking asshole as neighbor, the queer as Thing and the fag as Other; then, second, there is the formal horror of the text, its collaged disarrangement in terms of plot, of coherence, its autodidactic hipster's insistence on defining every word of subcultural argot and slang starting on the second page of the novel, for example: "(Note: Grass is English thief slang for inform.)"[3]

But, to begin, let me unpack the Lacanian neighbor, by tracing its antecedents in Sigmund Freud, which occurs in two different texts: the 1895 *Project for a Scientific Psychology,* where Freud discusses the *Nebenmensch*, the neighbor as some primordial Other; and *Civilization and Its Discontents*, where he inveighs against the biblical admonition to love thy neighbor.

In *Project*, when Freud is discussing memory and judgment, that is to say, an ethical activity, he argues that when presented with a Nebenmensch (also translated by Strachey as a "fellow human being"[4]), the subject is reminded of "an object *of a similar kind* [that] was the subject's first satisfying object (and also his first hostile object)."[5] Freud remarks, "the complex of a fellow-creature falls into two portions. One of these gives the impression of being a constant structure and remains as a coherent 'thing'; while the other can be *understood* by the activity of memory—that is, can be traced back to information about the subject's body."[6] There is in perception a splitting of the ego, or a *Splatung* of the object into what is already known, and what cannot be known, what will perhaps stay the "Thing," ripping open a hole, as Joan Copjec puts it, in our signifying practice.[7] This Thing in the Other, in the Neighbor, comes to be quite important to Lacan in *Seminar VII*, where he keeps the word in its German as *das Ding* for a Heideggerian flavor. For Lacan, das Ding has two dimensions: it is the unknowable, the terrifying, dumb Real, but it is also an object of desire, connected to jouissance; some commentators, including Dylan Evans in his dictionary of Lacanian terms, argue that it is the precursor to the *objet petit a*, the object cause of our desire, a concept that will come to have tremendous importance for Lacan in the sixties (whereas the Thing is only discussed in *Seminar VII*). So the Thing is unknowable, it is a matter of, in Freud's words again, "residues which evade being judged."[8] It is the Kantian Thing-in-itself.

A similarly ambiguous—or is it ambivalent?—concept of the neighbor resurfaces in the late Freud, in *Civilization and Its Discontents* (1930), where he directly addresses the issue of the neighbor in the form of a commentary on the Judeo-Christian command to love they neighbor as thyself, a command that appears in the Decalogue of Leviticus (19:18) and then in the New Testament in both the Gospels and elsewhere (Matthew 19:19; Mark 12:1; Luke 10:27; Romans 13:9; Galatians 5:14). Freud takes an apparently naïve view of the injunction: "Why should we do it? What good will it do us? But above all, how shall we achieve it? How can it be possible? My love is something valuable to me which I ought not to throw away without reflection. . . . On closer inspection, I find still further difficulties. Not merely is this stranger in general unworthy of my love; I must honestly confess he has more claim to my hostility and even my hatred. He seems not to have the slightest trace of love for me."[9] Freud's point is not so much that one cannot or should not love a stranger, or one's neighbor (it is interesting how he slides from one to another; we might think of the contemporary term *frenemy*), but the essential strangeness, the immense difficulty, of this demand—a commandment, he goes on to say, "which is really justified by the fact that nothing else runs so strongly counter to the original nature of man."[10] So, this impossible demand is then what Lacan seizes on but in a way goes further than Freud was able to, arguing that what is most horrifying about loving one's neighbor is that in the neighbor's obscene jouissance, in his late-night partying or blocking one's driveway or suicide bombing or Iraq invading, we see our own desire, our own jouissance, we see the *Thing* as what Lacan calls the *extimité* or the ex-timate, both inside us and outside us at the same time. We can found our case on the following, Lacan writes in *Seminar VII*:

> Every time that Freud stops short in horror at the consequences of the commandment to love one's neighbor, we see evoked the presence of that fundamental evil which dwells within this neighbor. But if that is the case, then it also dwells within me. And what is more of a neighbor to me than this heart within which is that of my *jouissance* and which I don't dare go near. For as soon as I go near it, as *Civilization and Its Discontents* makes clear, there rises up the unfathomable aggressivity from which I flee, that I turn against me, and which in the very place of the Vanished Law adds its weight to that which prevents me from crossing a certain frontier at the limit of the Thing.[11]

What is horrible in the neighbor is what is also horrible, unapproachable, in ourselves. There are important implications here. Note the "unfathomable aggressivity" that Lacan describes here, an aggressivity that not only we flee from but that we cannot understand; this aggressivity is unknowable. This is the Thing, again—not merely that obdurate kernel of our own desire, our own jouissance, but our reaction to it, our hatred. The hatred or anger that the neighbor arouses in us—and I use *arouse* in all its sexual connotations—is actually an anger, a disgust, with our own jouissance. (The Lacanian psychoanalyst Jacques-Alain Miller has argued that our racism is founded on a discomfit with our own jouissance.)

So Lacan is not simply making a sophisticated form of the schoolyard taunt that when you point a finger at me, three fingers point back at yourself. Rather, Lacan is saying that the demand to love one's neighbor is the demand to confront our own jouissance, our own enjoyment; as Marc De Kesel puts it in his commentary on the Seminar, the commandment "is the moral law that enables us to see most clearly what constitutes the ultimate weight of ethics. Every ethical demand for the good is, in the final analysis, a desire for enjoyment."[12] This is the crux of the shift from Freud to Lacan, and where Lacan's treatise on the neighbor makes use of his play (which works in both English and French) on "goods" and the "good," a play that will lead, in particularly revolting ways, to Burroughs's *Naked Lunch*.

For Lacan is arguing that the ethical demand is not so much a demand not to indulge in one's desires but rather to acknowledge one's desires, one's enjoyment, indeed, never to cede one's desire. Thus our treatment of the neighbor indicates precisely how this would play out. Lacan gives examples of this injunction from the Christian tradition of brotherly or neighborly love: such as Saint Martin giving his cloak to a naked beggar; Lacan says that it is a mistake to think this is some magnanimous gesture: "As long as it is a question of the good, there's no problem; our own and our neighbor's are of the same material.... We are no doubt touching a primitive requirement in the need to be satisfied there for the beggar is naked. But perhaps over and above that need to be clothed, he was begging for something else, namely, that Saint Martin either kill him or fuck him."[13] That is to say, the beggar's demand is not merely for a material object, for a good, for a signifier in the economic realm, but also for love, to be desired, and perhaps for the ultimate jouissance of death. Which is not to argue, as De Kesel reminds us, that Saint Martin's neighborly act would have been to satisfy the beggar's erotic or suicidal desire (i.e., we should not follow the lead of John Woo's *Hard Target*, Brett Easton Ellis's *American Psycho*, or the British Columbia Liberals' *Safe Streets Act*) but, rather, to create a space for the neighbor's desire by confronting one's own. This is the crucial lesson of Lacan's intersubjectivity: one's desire is the desire of the Other, which means to desire the other, to be desired by the other, and to have the same desire as the other; the neighbor's jouissance is also a threat to our own (from which comes Žižek's analysis of racism: the racial—or sexual or class—other is always suspected of stealing our enjoyment).

I will make a final comment on the Lacanian ethic of the neighbor before I turn to how this plays out in *Naked Lunch*. In his essay "Neighbors and Other Monsters," Žižek warns against the domesticization or commodification of the Thing, of that essential strangeness, horror, unpalatability that lies at the core of the subject. The injunction to love your neighbor, he remarks, is not the politically correct form of multiculturalism or condescension toward the other, it is not the "New Age attitude which ultimately reduces my Other/Neighbor to my mirror-image or to the means in the path of my self-realization ... [rather, it] opens up a tradition in which an alien traumatic kernel forever persists in my Neighbor—the Neighbor remains an inert, impenetrable, enigmatic presence that hystericizes me."[14] The Neighbor is Other, Žižek goes on to say, for what bothers us so much in the neighbor is his or her desire—which, like our own desire, will remain unknowable. What bugs us about the Neighbor is what bugs him, but we don't know what it is. We don't know what bugs him, and that bugs us. The Thing that is in the neighbor triggers our aggressivity at our own Thing, our own jouissance. As my colleague at

Simon Fraser University, the geographer Paul Kingsbury, argues, "the Thing is first and foremost an intersubjective, that is, a social phenomenon." Which to say that it is also spatial, or a matter of extimité, and we will see how this functions in terms of the body and what comes into it and out of it with Burroughs.

I return to further implications of Žižek's theory in the conclusion of my chapter, but at this point I indicate some possibilities of rapprochement between psychoanalysis and historicism. There are three ways in which to orient such a discussion. First, think of how we historicize psychoanalysis itself. Thus Freud's neighbor is both the Nebenmensch of the 1895 *Project*, which itself splits off into das Ding—the too-close, unknowable object of maternal desire—and the biblical injunction he treats in *Civilization and Its Discontents*, an impossible demand due to our limited jouissance and the neighbor's essential evil. That is, we have here the stark difference between early and late Freud, a difference that is not so much elided by the trajectory of Freud's thought vis-à-vis the neighbor, as exemplified. A similar historicization has been offered of Lacan's thought by Jacques-Alain Miller, who periodizes Lacan into four periods (the structuralism of the fifties, the introduction of jouissance and *Seminar VII*, the four discourses of *Seminar XVII* as a reaction to May 1968, and the "society of consumption" of the seventies and *Seminar XX*).[15] Before Lacan furthered Freud's insights by arguing that really the impossible injunction is to love our own jouissance, our own Thing, he was also offering a historicist methodology for the clinical situation (remarkably similar, it should be noted, to Walter Benjamin's notion of history in his "Theses"), in his so-called "Rom Discourse" of 1953. There Lacan declared that the "unconscious is the chapter of my history that is marked by a blank or occupied by a lie: is it the censored chapter."[16] He elaborates, saying that this censored truth has also been written elsewhere, in "my body" as a monument, in the "archival documents" that are childhood memories, in traditions and legends, and in the distortion of same. But I do not mean by offering these brief histories of psychoanalysis to suggest that one should obliterate the real political and conceptual difficulties or antagonisms that separate historicism and psychoanalysis.[17] And while the subtitle of Copjec's *Read My Desire: Lacan against the Historicists* is suggestive, a more programmatic statement of the dialectic lies in Žižek's study of Gilles Deleuze, where he argues the following:

> One often hears that to understand a work of art one needs to know its historical context. Against this historicist commonplace, a Deleuzian

counterclaim would be not only that too much of a historical context can blur the proper contact with the work of art (i.e., that to enact this contact one should abstract from the work's context), but also that it is, rather, the work of art that provides a context enabling us to understand properly a given historical situation.[18]

This is to state baldly the antagonism, but also to argue that it is the very strength of an antihistoricist argument to reverse interpretive causality: rather than history explaining the work of art, the art explains history. Indeed, Žižek makes this case earlier on the same page of *Organs without Bodies*, when he writes that "a truly new work *stays new forever*—its newness is not exhausted when its 'shocking value' passes away." So Burroughs's "shocking" novel might be a test case here in two senses: First, is its newness exhausted when its shocking value has passed (although anyone who has read or taught the novel will surely find some satisfaction that readers inured to representations of violence by such "horror-porn" films as *Saw* or *Hostel* are still disgusted by the hanging/ejaculatory scene in *Naked Lunch*)? Then, if we follow Žižek's or Deleuze's reverse engineering of interpretation, what does *Naked Lunch* tell us about its historical context?

We can answer that second question first by turning back to Lacan for one final comment, and noting that his theorizing of das Ding and the neighbor in *Seminar VII* is only part of a trajectory of thought on ethics, culminating in his remarkable writings on *Antigone*; he notoriously smuggled this seminar in to Laurence Bataille, whose step-daughter had been jailed for her actions in support of the Front de Libération Nationale (FLN) in May 1960.[19] Perhaps the neighbor helps us understand French colonial politics in 1959–60 as much as the reverse. And then, in terms of *Naked Lunch*, surely it is no accident that Burroughs's formulation of its episodes had to take place both in an epistolary manner (via letters of "routines" to Allen Ginsberg) and a transnational one (between the United States, the Maghreb, and France). But is it possible to see the "newness" of the novel, of the neighbor in Burroughs, some fifty years later?

To answer that I suggest three ways to talk about *Naked Lunch* and the neighbor: the idea of the Thing in the human and the jouissance-filled reactions this engenders, the junkie or queer as neighbor, and formal alignments of the neighbor. In Burroughs's novel the Lacanian theory is not merely given its fictive, which is to say signifying, expression, but the novel's very attempts to go beyond language, beyond narrative—beyond the Symbolic—constitutes its embrace of the neighbor. First consider the following passage: "Blast of trumpets: The Man is carried in naked by two Negro Bearers who drop him on the platform with bestial, sneering brutality . . . The Man wriggles . . . His flesh turns to viscid, transparent jelly that drifts away in green mist, unveiling a monster black centipede. Waves of unknown stench fill the room, searing the lungs, grabbing the stomach. . . ."[20] As often happens in the novel, we have here first a spectacle; then, an account of some unfathomable substance in the human body, that Freudian *Thing* (here the black caterpillar); then, an inscription into the text of the working of affect, usually of disgust or eros, that indicates the libidinal quality at work (here the "unknown stench" that grabs the stomach), that enters the body of the subject.[21] Given the arguments of affect theory—surely a poor man's psychoanalysis—that disgust is to be distinguished from the libidinal, it is remarkable that in Sianne Ngai's *Ugly Feelings* (2005), she concludes with texts by Claire Lispector and Bruce Andrews, arguing that in one a character "eats the intolerable in an unsuccessful attempt to keep it down" and that the other "gorges on the alluring in order to throw it up."[22] In Burroughs's text we see a similar dialectic.

Naked Lunch is rife with scenes and substances that are both disgusting and sexual. Some are known from David Cronenberg's film version, and include the talking asshole; the Exterminator; Mugwumps, who "secrete an addicting fluid from their erect penises which prolongs life by slowing metabolism"; and the "Dream Police," who "disintegrate in globs of rotten ectoplasm swept away by an old junky."[23] Burroughs refuses the normalization of the neighbor; rather, he emphasizes the Thing in the neighbor, that "addicting fluid," the "globs of rotten ectoplasm," the talking asshole as "Undifferentiated Tissue."[24] But this Thing is simultaneously both revolting and alluring (as are, of course, the sexual organs viewed dispassionately), and it is this "question of beyond the pleasure principle, the place of the unnameable Thing" that Lacan insists on when he refers to thirteenth-century Saint Angela de Folignilio, who claimed to have drank the water in which she had bathed the feet of lepers.[25]

It is crucial that with Burroughs, the Thing here insists on being transitive: on being in the body being looked at but also the body that is looking, that is no sooner the superego (the Dream Police) than it disintegrates. It is worth noting that while various Burroughsian soundbites have made their way into popular culture—from the Steely Dan dildo to the term *heavy metal*, the 1979 Cheap Trick song "Dream Police" is remarkable both for preserving a sense of the neighbor ("the Dream Police they're inside my head") but also negating the dissolution of the same that is seen in *Naked Lunch*.

These are various versions of the Thing in the neighbor, and we also have the neighbor figured in terms of overwhelming proximity, as in the scene between a shoeshine boy and a sailor, who possesses "dead, cold, undersea eyes, eyes without a trace of warmth or lust or hate or any feeling the boy had ever experienced in himself or seen in another, at once cold and intense, impersonal and predatory."[26] The novel also gives us actual bona fide neighbors, as when "the whole clan of Europeans moved in next to me. . . . The old mother is having an operation, and her daughters move in to see the old gash receive proper service."[27] Indeed, the rich, Rabelaisian excess of Burroughs's writing—his lists, his obscenity, his chilly intelligence—folds back upon itself with this Calvino-like collapse of the space-time continuum: "Sooner or later the Vigilante, The Rube, Lee The Agent, A.J., Clem and Jody the Ergot Twins, Hassan O'Leary the After Birth Tycoon, The Sailor, The Exterminator, Andrew Keif, 'Fats' Terminal, Doc Benway, 'Fingers' Schafer are subject to say the same thing in the same words, to occupy, at that intersection point, the same position in space-time. Using a common vocal apparatus complete with all metabolic appliances—that is, to be the same person—a most inaccurate way of expressing *Recognition*: the junky naked in sunlight . . ."[28] And this same cohabitation, if you will, pervades the paranoid space of the Interzone: "The Zone is a single, vast building. The rooms are made of a plastic cement that bulges to accommodate people, but when too many crowd into one room there is a soft *plop* and someone squeezes through the wall right into the next house—the next bed that is, since the rooms are mostly bed where the business of the Zone is transacted."[29]

So the neighbors have dead eyes, are irritating spatially; they collapse into one another or the spaces they inhabit collapse into one another. In conceptualizing what Burroughs's text is doing here, the commentary of both Kingsbury and Copjec on Lacan is helpful, for both emphasize the spatial. Copjec, on the one hand, argues that the social is composed of a singularity that is not simply a matter of relations between individuals (Lacan's intersubjectivity) but a relation to unoccupiable places: "Someone dies and leaves behind his place, which outlives him and is unfillable by anyone else."[30] This is, of course, exactly contrary to Burroughs, where individuals are filled by each other, both sexually and in terms of their spaces. Kingsbury, on the other hand, argues that the enjoyment or anxiety we feel regarding the Thing has to take place in that shared space, in that intersubjective space: again, a space that *Naked Lunch* is concerned with negating.

What of the novel's twin fascination with addicts and homosexuals? This obsession originates, like some coeval bastardry, in Burroughs's two previous novels, *Junky* (1953) and *Queer* (unpublished until 1985). In *Naked Lunch*, Burroughs's take is that both practices—rampant drug use, sexuality *qua* perversion—involve the body as Thing, where the subject becomes the Thing, becomes the Neighbor. Thus we have a scene that reads as if straight from one of Burroughs's letters to Allen Ginsberg (in which the novel found its genesis): "Take a shot in front of D.L. Probing for a vein in my dirty bare foot . . . Junkies have no shame . . . They are impervious to the repugnance of others. It is doubtful if shame can exist in the absence of sexual libido. The junky's shame disappears with his nonsexual sociability which is also dependent upon libido."[31]

We can then think of the relationship between queers and junkies on the one hand, and the straights, the prototype for which is given on the first page of the novel, on the other: "Young, good looking, crew cut, Ivy League, advertising exec type fruit holds the door back for me. I am evidently his idea of a character. You know the type: comes on with bartenders and cab drivers, talking about right hooks and the Dodgers, calls the counterman in Nedick's by his first name."[32] For this square, the problem is that he doesn't see Lee, the novel's protagonist, as neighbor, and doesn't acknowledge his own desire. That is, just as the redneck philistine takes art more seriously than the complacent, bourgeois art lover, the homophobe who is threatened by the queer takes homosexuality more seriously than the untroubled straight with his married gay friends.

The junky and the queer are the neighbor but so, too, is the mark, the straight that the junky hustles (at a certain point the text introduces a distinction between the mark and the square[33]); in a remarkably Lacanian passage, Burroughs writes: "The Rube's attacks become an habitual condition. Cops, doormen, dogs, secretaries snarl at his approach. The blond God has fallen to untouchable vileness. Con men don't change, they break, shatter—explosions of matter in cold interstellar space, drift away in cosmic dust, leave the empty body behind. Hustlers of the world, there is one Mark you cannot beat: The Mark Inside . . ."[34]

There are also, it should be noted, ways to talk about the neighbor in formal terms, and not merely in the intersubjective relations I have been focusing on. In *Naked Lunch*, we can see that Burroughs's use of slang, his set-ups or routines (which he began in *Queer*), the broken or anachronic (to use Gérard Genette's vocabulary) narrative and repetition, all constitute such formal neighbors. One such strategy, of which there are many examples in the novel, is that, quite often, the text will interrupt itself, perhaps to define a term of slang like "people" (New Orleans slang for narcotic cops) or "hot shot" (junkies' term for strychnine as poison); or to provide quasi-medical or anthropological information on tribal practices or his imaginary political divisions; or, most metatextually, to refer to the appendix for his 1956 letter to the *British Journal of Addiction*.[35] This strategy does two or three different things: First, it foregrounds the various languages set into a dialogic relation with each other in the novel, discourses that range from medical to hipster, criminal to homosexual, literary to travel. In that self-conscious foregrounding, it makes the case for the impossibility of the dialogic relation; surely one of the hallmarks of various appropriations of Bakhtinian theory over the past few decades has been the withering away of its social antagonism—the notion of heteroglossia or polyphony as a form of discursive class struggle. In *Naked Lunch*, the discourses sit uneasily next to each other, signaled by the very awkwardness of these "notes." Then, such interjections into the text function in that neighborly or das Ding–like way of interrupting the flow of the text, interfering with the story, being too close—*Stop it, Bill*, you want to say, *I just want to read the thing*—but also in a dialectical way in that, unlike the stereotype of the hipster author (who seeks to preserve a hermetic subculture), here the narrator (or is it the implied author?) actually wants the reader to know the insider knowledge, the obscure slang. Finally, the origin of this strategy comes from a similar series of interruptions in the first, 1953 publication of *Junky*, in which more outré comments by the author were immediately followed by disclaimers in parentheses by the "Ed."[36] Those earlier intrusions in *Junky* were marks of the social, of the publisher's (Ginsberg and Burroughs's friend Carl Solomon and his uncle A. A. Wynne) anxiety about postwar repression. It is unfortunate that reprints of *Junky*, which restore deletions from the 1953 edition, delete those censors' comments.

So, to return to the historicist question earlier entertained, the foregoing is not the historicizing argument for Burroughs's conflation of the junky and the queer, such as is found by Jonathan Eburne, who contextualizes *Naked Lunch* in terms of "the pathologization of drug use and homosexuality [which] took place in the Cold War imagination as patently *psychological* ailments; ailments which, moreover, represented criminal breaches in the public health."[37] Eburne cites, in addition, Lee Edelman on the public concatenation of the two. Nor am I arguing, as Avital Ronell does in *Crack Wars*, that both Lacan and Burroughs falter before the addict as unanalyzable.[38] Rather, my argument has been more modest, concerned with tracing the appearance of the Lacanian Neighbor in *Naked Lunch*: first in terms of its hypostatization of the repulsive aspects of the body as the Thing (secreted fluid, ectoplasm); then, with its unsentimental and politically incorrect framing of proximity of the sailor, the collapse of the space-time continuum or the plastic rooms of the Interzone as the terrifying presence of the neighbor; and then the dyad of the queer and the junky as not merely dialectical neighbors but, in their turn toward the straight, or the Mark, as indication of the Mark within, one's own jouissance;[39] and, finally, in the formal device of taking the social insertion into the text of disclaimers (the social as the neighbor) in *Junky* and providing the same irritating device in *Naked Lunch*, a confrontation with his own desire, his own jouissance. Indeed, what is so remarkable about the novel is its power to engage and enrage both the body and the mind of the reader. The text as neighbor.

A recent work of poetry by the New York–based poet Rachel Zolf, *The Neighbour Procedure*, documents in particular the work by the Israeli Defense Force to use Palestinians as human shields and their reliance on the poststructuralist theory of Deleuze and Félix Guattari.[40]

> In the first house we took a Johnnie
> For a neighbour procedure blown through
> Autarkic swarm holes collecting inverse stuff
> Geometry ensuring nothing fractal booby—
> Trapped maneuvers inside rooms before you
> Do Germania so if a terrorist's inside Chicago
> He would be hurt and not you, war
> A matter of reading actually he is doing[41]

I close with a couple comments about extending this analysis to the present moment. Žižek comments on the "'gentrification' of the Other-Thing into a 'normal human fellow,'" and if there can be said to be a political project that connects Lacan and Burroughs, it can be located here.[42] Both writers were concerned with bringing to the fore that horror that underlies all love, all human interaction; a horror that, when we turn junkies into substance users, queers into married homosexuals, we disavow. And this pertains particularly to current debates (in Vancouver and internationally) around drug use, gentrification, and the transformation of urban areas into middle-class playgrounds. Gentrification involves not merely an urban policy of renewal and the removal of working-class and ethnic minorities but also the rendering of the lumpenproletariat, the crackheads and skid row drunks, into properly functioning citizens. In Vancouver specifically, for example, the Skid Row district was relabeled in 1973 (due to political activism by such resident groups as the Downtown Eastside Residents Association) as the Downtown Eastside, a form of semiotic gentrification, if you will (the term *Skid Row* or *Skid Road* had its origins in logging roads upon which one skidded logs down to the shoreline), but to no avail; if you look at real estate ads for condos in the neighborhood you will not see Downtown Eastside but instead the new gentrifying term *Crosstown*.

Notes

1. Ted Morgan, *Literary Outlaw: The Life and Times of William S. Burroughs* (New York: Holt, 1988), 305; Jacques Lacan, *The Seminar of Jacques Lacan*, book VII, *The Ethics of Psychoanalysis, 1959–1960*, trans. Dennis Porter (New York: W. W. Norton, 1997), 130, 106.

2. Lacan, *The Ethics of Psychoanalysis*, 186.

3. William S. Burroughs, *Naked Lunch: The Restored Text*, ed. James Grauerholz and Barry Miles (New York: Grove, 2001), 4.

4. Sigmund Freud, *Project for a Scientific Psychology*, in *The Origins of Psychoanalysis: Letters to Wilhelm Fliess, Drafts and Notes, 1887–1902* (New York: Basic, 1954), 392. Obviously Freud is talking about the mother or first caregiver.

5. Sigmund Freud, *Civilization and Its Discontents*, in *The Standard Edition of the Complete Psychological Works of Sigmund Freud*, vol. 21 (London: Hogarth, 1953–74), 331.

6. Freud, *The Origins of Psychoanalysis*, 391–92.

7. Joan Copjec, *Imagine There's No Woman: Ethics and Sublimation* (Cambridge, MA: MIT Press, 2002), 35.

8. Sigmund Freud, *Civilization and Its Discontents*, in *The Standard Edition of the Complete Psychological Works of Sigmund Freud*, vol. 21: 334.

9. Freud, *Civilization and Its Discontents*, 109–10.

10. Freud, *Civilization and Its Discontents*, 112. There's an entire tradition of commentary on the neighbor and also the enemy in Carl Schmitt, Jacques Derrida, Emmanuel Levinas, and so on; see also *The Neighbor: Three Inquiries in Political Theology*, by Slavoj Žižek, Eric Santner, and Kenneth Reinhard (Chicago: University of Chicago Press, 2005), for a useful survey.

11. Lacan, *The Ethics of Psychoanalysis*, 186.

12. Marc De Kesel, *Eros and Ethics: Reading Jacques Lacan's Seminar VII*, trans. Sigi Jöttkandt (Albany: State University of New York Press, 2009), 147.

13. Lacan, *The Ethics of Psychoanalysis*, 186.

14. Slavoj Žižek, "Neighbors and Other Monsters: A Plea for Ethical Violence," in *The Neighbor: Three Inquiries in Political Theology*, by Slavoj Žižek, Eric Santner, and Kenneth Reinhard (Chicago: University of Chicago Press, 2005), 140–41.

15. Slavoj Žižek, *On Belief* (New York: Routledge, 2006), 29–31.

16. Lacan, *The Ethics of Psychoanalysis*, 259, 215.

17. To these brief histories one could add such more specialized accounts as William McCarthy's fine-grained account, *Freud's Discovery of Psychoanalysis: The Politics of Hysteria* (Ithaca, NY: Cornell University Press, 1987), or Elisabeth Roudinesco's *Jacques Lacan & Co.: A History of Psychoanalysis in France, 1925–1985* (Chicago: Chicago University Press, 1990).

18. Slavoj Žižek, *Organs without Bodies: On Deleuze and Consequences* (New York: Routledge, 2004), 15.

19. Elisabeth Roudinesco, *Jacques Lacan*, trans. Barbara Bray (New York: Columbia University Press, 1997), 187.

20. Burroughs, *Naked Lunch*, 87.

21. The passage is introduced as "Schafer, the Lobotomy Kid['s] . . . Master Work: *The Complete All American Deanxietized Man.*"

22. Sianne Ngai, *Ugly Feelings* (Cambridge, MA: Harvard University Press, 2005), 353.

23. Burroughs, *Naked Lunch*, 110, 171, 46, 46.

24. Burroughs, *Naked Lunch*, 111.

25. Lacan, *The Ethics of Psychoanalysis*, 188.

26. Lacan, *The Ethics of Psychoanalysis*, 43. The boy is seeing his own jouissance.

27. Lacan, *The Ethics of Psychoanalysis*, 48.

28. Lacan, *The Ethics of Psychoanalysis*, 186.

29. Lacan, *The Ethics of Psychoanalysis*, 149.

30. Copjec, *Imagine There's No Woman*, 23.

31. Burroughs, *Naked Lunch*, 57.

32. Burroughs, *Naked Lunch*, 3.

33. Burroughs, *Naked Lunch*, 115.

34. Burroughs, *Naked Lunch*, 11.

35. Burroughs, *Naked Lunch*, 7, 4, 26, 30.

36. William S. Burroughs, *Junky* (New York: Penguin, 1977). See Ginsberg's introduction.

37. Jonathan Eburne, "Trafficking in the Void: Burroughs, Kerouac, and the Consumption of Otherness," *Modern Fiction Studies* 43, no. 1 (1997): 72.

38. Avital Ronell, *Crack Wars: Literature, Addiction, Mania* (Urbana: University of Illinois Press, 2004), 54.

39. Indeed, Burroughs's commandment that "hustlers of the world, there is one Mark you cannot beat: The Mark Inside" can be read as his version of the demand to love one's neighbor.

40. Eyal Weizman, *Hollow Land: Israel's Architecture of the Occupation* (London: Verso, 2007).

41. Rachel Zolf, *The Neighbour Procedure* (Toronto: Coach House, 2010), 61.

42. Žižek, "Neighbors and Other Monsters," in 144.

BODYBUILDING OR BODYCRUSHING?
FROM ART TO THEATER
From Bodies to Corpses, a Rhizomatic Meditation
on the Contemporary West

Muehl: Crushing the Body

Vienna, May 21, 1965: Otto Muehl performs his nineteenth and most significant material action (*Materialaktion*) in a Viennese basement. *Bodybuilding*.
The choice of title is a form of antiphrasis whose intention is sarcastic.
Bodycrushing? Muehl joyfully abuses the Western body: he turns it into a
monster, covered with *bandages*, between Golem and Frankenstein—a Viennese
mummy that does not fail to recall Sigmund Freud or the Anschluss. Muehl
is not the son of *anyone*: like all the Actionists, he claims a *father figure*—
Yves Klein. Not all the Actionists have read Wilhelm Reich. But all have
seen Klein, the great inventor of the modern, and not modernist, body that
is *ours*: a histrionic body that dreams of nothing but its own suppression in
weightlessness—Zarathustra revised by Buster Keaton.

Taking shape around 1960—Klein's big year—is something that is more
present than ever: the iconoclastic fabrication of an *anti*-body that never ends
up dying on stage. Klein's heritage passes through the *theater*. This will not
surprise anyone. In Europe, the theater is the liveliest of arts, above all in the
East, where it is *public*, while the plastic arts are becoming privatized under
the pressure of the market—of the supermarket—which cares for nothing
but the *top ten* of *art prices*. Sad tropics. We entered without warning into a
new era of cultural industry (the *Kulturindustrie*) where the museums rival
Hollywood and Disneyland by means of *blockbusters* and neocolonialist sub-
sidiaries, where the society of control, which is our own, blossoms.

Why so much hatred? Klein remains *unloved* by the critics, mainly North
American, who refuse to take him seriously since Klein did not do so

himself. This is a good sign. Serge Guilbaut showed us so well how the war machine of *Yankee* imperialism continues to remake history (and even art) to its own benefit. This chapter—this *rhizomatic* meditation—pays tribute to Guilbaut's theses: it is only interested in old Europe, whose postwar *twilight* was much more fruitful than people used to say, a lot more innovative than all the so-called modernisms. But forgive me if this meditation does it *blindly*, through lack of time; that is to say, of films, with only photographs that are, as Roland Barthes notes, images of *death*: art history, if it does exist, is at best nothing but a *mourning work*, which is, as we know from Freud, never-ending.

Klein: Suppressing the Art

IDEAL FLESH

Paris, March 9, 1960: A chic party takes place at d'Arquian's, International Gallery of Contemporary Art, rue Saint-Honoré. The master Klein is wearing a black *tuxedo* with a white shirtfront. He stands in the middle of the hall, the floor of which is covered with a white sheet resembling a *shroud*. On the back wall hangs a giant-sized blank canvas. To the right of the canvas is an orchestra of nine musicians, all with string instruments to produce a unique sound, the *monotone symphony*, by means of long bowings. Beyond that are the guests: a pretentious audience bearing the complacent expressions suited to fashionable *soirées*. The master introduces the actors, who are actresses: three naked women with perfect youthful figures. Everything is ready for the execution of the *rite*. Shaman, prophet, hierophant: the master is the great priest of this group liturgy that transforms art into *spectacle*, the public into *voyeurs*, and woman into *paintbrush*.

The artist has *clean* hands. One could even say that he has *no* hands at all. There is no question of touching the models' bodies or the flow of paint. Such a profane intrusion of the *tactile* element would jeopardize the master's status as an oracle. Painting here is just a concept: a principle of *power*. The man is dressed. The women are naked. But this unequal relationship entails *no* eroticism: the master is indifferent to these female bodies. What he looks for in them is substance, which is anonymous: *flesh*. But flesh itself is still too material for an idealist like him, an idealist who willingly expands his platonic theories. What matters above all is the *idea* of flesh: a carnal atmosphere that results not from desire but from necessity.

The painter's models are nothing but *tropisms* whose only talent is to combine the *three* kingdoms of nature: animal, vegetal, mineral. But they claim no real humanity. We are hardly surprised that he treats them like laboratory products: distant, directive, authoritarian. The *reification* of the female body culminates in the models' becoming-painting that is no more than a simple *prop* (a vector for paint) and a simple *matrix* (the mold of the imprint). Woman turns into *painting*: the ultimate fantasy of the male artist.

Klein explains: "I remained clean, I didn't dirty myself any more with the paint, not even my fingertips. Before me, under my control, in absolute collaboration with the model, the work was accomplished, and I was in a position to show myself worthy of it, wearing a tuxedo, to receive it as one must at its birth into the tangible world." This is Klein in his entirety, in the *crystal-clear* avowal of his *schizophrenic* ambition: the end of painting and the vertigo of the work; the hygiene of the concept and the prophetic nature of art; the primacy of the phallus and the work of sublimation; the language of sexism and the illusion of ascesis; the *démiurgie* of the creator and the dream of otherness; et cetera, et cetera.

JUMPING THE VOID

Fontenay-aux-Roses (near Paris), October 1960: A man leaps into the void. The leap is *posed*. And the void is cushioned. But what counts is what remains: an image. Or even a myth. Klein changes the world. We mean: the *art* world. But it is not so bad. We have difficulty nowadays; so much history is dependent on the *pictorial* model, to measure the depth of the event, that is to say its insignificance. For to jump off a wall, in a Parisian suburb with a tarpaulin underneath, is no more than a *dubious* exercise: a bad joke. But to make this episode a legendary act that our cautious minds struggle to recognize is an aesthetic *putsch*, where art at last becomes what it is (what it should never have ceased to be): a clever mix of rhetoric *and* ideology, without pathos or transcendence. The rest is all wind: all *void*. Where Klein jumps. With tied feet.

Note the posture. Some might say upright. Better to say: *erectile*. After all, this body points upward: bound like a bow (or almost). His arms are drawn back like coarse stumps. His head is no more than a bud on the stem of the body. One would not dare to say the glans on a penis. All in all, everything is reduced to the *main* member: firm, dense, compact. There is no point insisting. These aerial gymnastics are penis gymnastics. Klein plays the role of

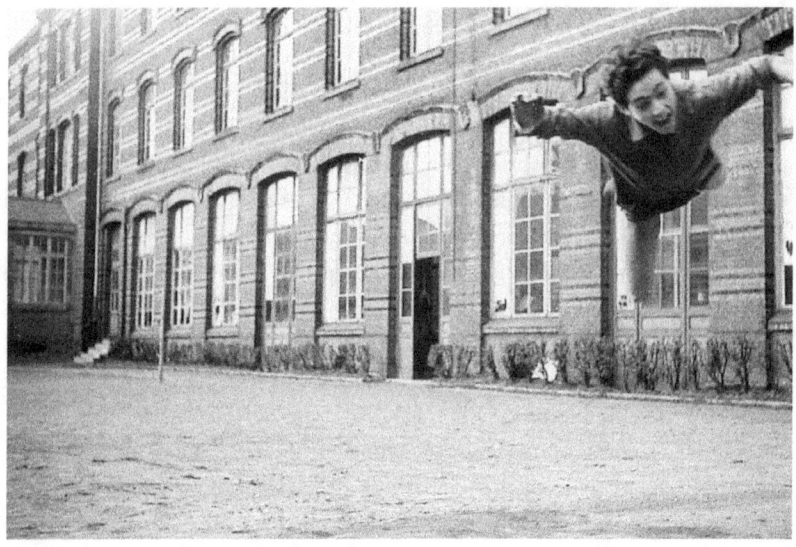

FIGURE 10.1 Unknown, *Leap into the Void*, 1959. Gelatin silver print. Archive of Serge Guilbaut.

the *phallus* in the suburban ether of a bourgeois city. This unusual exercise of Sunday acrobatics illustrates the *Traumdeutung*, the Bible of Freudian symbolism.

All is nothing but trickery, imposture, and lies. We do not know the date of the leap. We are not even sure that it was a *Sunday*. But we still have the *tarpaulin* that caught the jumper's body—I exhibited it myself at the Louvre as a sacrilegious relic: a parody of the Holy Shroud. And people were needed to hold the tarpaulin. One witness even mentioned *fifteen* carriers. These details are trivial. But they make sense: art is nothing but *theater*. With a backstage. The photographers were asked to remove the *show's* accessories that were unfitting—the canvas, the carriers, and the rest. The leap is nothing but a photomontage, where the jumper is king. Klein *finally* rids us of the ancestral bric-a-brac of Western art, paintbrush, painting, object, matter. Art is *life*: body, speech, play. And even a *trick*: illusion, mirage, pantomime.

GODARD: FETISHIZING THE SPECTERS

Paris, March 16, 1960: *Breathless* (*À bout de souffle*) is released. Michel Poiccard (played by Jean-Paul Belmondo), a small-time gangster and *French lover*, is heading for a fall with a bullet in his back: a New Wave–style *stations of the cross*, where the crosses are replaced by cars. Michel breathes out in his final fall: *a carp's leap* onto the pavement of Paris. This death will make its mark; after it, the French cinema resurrects. Belmondo doesn't die just *anywhere*, but on rue Campagne-Première, near Montparnasse: Klein's street.

Coincidence? It is puzzling. But it is not the only one. Jean-Luc Godard is obsessed by the leap into the void. The great novelty of *Breathless* is the *editing*, which turns the film into a race toward the abyss: everything goes badly but everything goes *quickly*—what matters is that we get there, even if it means losing breath. We pass from one scene to the next on a flying carpet. It is what the English call the *jump cut*. And what Barthes defined as anacoluthon: a rupture in syntax that causes the narrative to explode—a poetic elsewhere in which the great *curse* of the cinema, the effect of the real (the aesthetics of the spectacle), finally dissolves.

No way out. Another Godard film, *Pierrot le fou*, bursts into the air: it is the last scene of the film—a Godardian version of the leap into the void. This *mythical* epilogue is a tribute to Klein, who died two years earlier—the filming dates back to 1964. Belmondo paints his face blue. It is his final transformation: the human chameleon becomes a *human paintbrush*. He is now part of a revolutionary international with a chromatic vocation: that of International Klein Blue (IKB). And the world around him becomes *blue* like an orange, as Paul Éluard once said. This is not difficult: we are by the Mediterranean. But it is a blue that kills: *The Blue of Noon*, Georges Bataille's way.

For the hero destroys himself before our eyes, explosively. Pierrot, Klein, Godard leap into the void with the help of dynamite. Godard calls it *nitramite* (which does not exist). This death is a fable, a performance, a pantomime—the opposite of spectacle: an explosion of the void, in the style of Klein, the great pyromaniac, who *burns* his canvases, in place of bodies, in his *fire paintings*. "Since he who leaps into the void," Godard notes, "owes nothing to those who watch him." A self-portrait? Godard before Godard is already himself: a prophet of the *hiatus* who, Gilles Deleuze said, only dreams of breaking shots and emptying spaces. A great film, Godard insists, is a film in reverse: a film *in negative*.

Pierrot le fou meets high society: a society of spectacle where *publicity* replaces conversation. These people have nothing to say: *nothing* but advertising slogans. The men boast luxury cars (Alfa Romeo, Oldsmobile), and the women exalt beauty products (hairspray and body spray). "The spectacle," Guy Debord writes, "is the moment when the merchandise reaches *total occupation* of social life. Not only is the relationship with merchandise visible, *but* it is all that we see: the world that we see is its world."

We are there. Godard has not read aphorism 42 of *The Society of the Spectacle*. For good reason: *Pierrot le fou* was released in 1965, two years before the book. But he shows the fetishism of merchandise like no other: the *marketing* of the spectacular. Here the characters are automatons: *sandwich*-men or women who reify themselves before our eyes by reeling off their adverts in tones as cold as ice. They are the *robots* of capital. Godard fossilizes them in a dark-room *chiaroscuro*, partly red, partly blue: spectral light of the photographic negative. These false creatures are real *specters,* in the sense of Jacques Derrida—specters of Karl Marx: specters of specters. *Ad libitum.*

Debord: Blowing Up the Spectacle

Paris, October 1960: Debord ends the shooting of his third film, *The Critique of Separation.* The cinema, with Debord, becomes a system: a form of *anti*-cinema that encloses the image in the text to *blow up* the narrative. Debord is not Godard: he is a pure iconoclast. He distrusts images. But he does not know how to manipulate them. The text provides him with an antidote—an *antivirus*—to the infection of merchandise that corrupts images (ideology, marketing, propaganda) to the *separation* of the spectacle.

As the spectacular man is *separated from the world*, Debord writes in aphorism 33 of the *Society of the Spectacle*: "his life is now his product." And, consequently, it is no longer his life. It is no longer even life at all. Wherefrom comes the urgency for *destruction*. "We need to destroy the memory in art," Debord says in his film. You heard. Not just art, but its *memory* too. We pass from the anacoluthon to the anathema. And the screen goes *black*: it empties. This void is not the leap. But it is not so far.

October 1960: The very moment when Klein leaps into the void. His agenda is the same. He *wants to surpass the problem of art*, as his most famous text from 1959 states. Debord says the same thing in his aphorism 191, where he promotes the *surpassing of art*. Klein plays the situationist. He wants to create *states*, *zones*, *spaces* of pure sensibility where the medium (painting) and even the form (art) would be forgotten: this is what Debord calls the *construction of situations* where the viewer is removed from the spectacle (where the individual is no longer *separated*).

But Klein, like Debord, fears the lure of utopia. From there arises their common strategy, which is the only effective one: the *spectacular* criticism of spectacle, that art of *impossible change*, Debord notes, which is an *avant-garde* art, and which, consequently, *is not* art: it ceases to be. The *avant-garde*,

Debord writes, is the very principle of its own disappearance. A *paradox?* No doubt. But it is not the first; nor the last. Every blow is permitted in this game of *mirrors* (a game of dupes), where the body is but a shadow, and the image but a reflection.

Brus: Torturing the Organs

Munich, June 19, 1970: *Haus der Kunst. Zerreißprobe:* test of rupture. This title is a program. Günter Brus breaks with everything that makes Western art: old painting, ideal beauty, heroic bodies, and *tutti quanti*. It is Brus's most radical action and even of Viennese Actionism. A public descent into the hell of *sadomasochism*, where the artist is both victim and torturer? This is what the censors of Actionism say, as they see no art in it, only perversion. The *violence* of the action is so extreme that no one has yet seen anything of the kind.

In a raucous symphony of cries and groans, coughs and grunts, Brus stages the unbearable protocol of his own *mutilation* with lashing and slashing of scissors, razors, ropes, and whips. He urinates on his wounds. Then he drinks his urine. He tears off the top of his skull, hacks away at his thighs and finally sprawls in his filth in a paroxysm of convulsion. Self-torture is the ultimate *dramaturgy* of the pictorial body: the dismal body of the Christian West, which liquefies before our eyes in a maelstrom of *humors*, where the agony of the classical subject culminates: tears, sweat, urine, blood. A testament to Actionism? It is Brus's *final* and most memorable action: it is difficult to go further.

In opposition to analytic idealism, which was raging at the time (remember J. L. Austin and Ludwig Wittgenstein?), Brus exalts the *sub*language of the *subsignificant:* bodily language where the rough violence of the organic world and the impulsive expression of libidinal energy are unbridled. A return to *borborygm.* The Western man is a *semantic* man, saturated with meaning, and consequently inhibition. The only way to escape the rational control of articulated language, which is vocationally repressive, is to rediscover, as here, the false innocence of the primitive sound: the massive rebellion of *animal* phonetics, wherefore the body is not repressed by the puritan censorship of linguistic reason. Failing this, it is better to keep silent. It does not matter much. For, as Brus wrote in a diary from his youth, the world is already *mute*—from being dead.

Brus is the *counter*poet to the repressive State (the Austrian State), which has never stopped begrudging him with ferocious hatred. Hence the paranoiac *execration* of a Leviathan State that worms its way into the smallest part of the *intimate* sphere—the smallest crack in the body. *The State is everywhere*: in every one of my organs. There is only one way out: to remove them. Brus has not yet read Gilles Deleuze and Félix Guattari. For obvious reasons. *A Thousand Plateaus* was only published in 1980.

But Brus is ready to make himself an *organless body*: with *no sex* (that he symbolically castrates), *no head* (that he bleeds profusely), *no limbs* (that he slashes tirelessly). By the end of the action, his body is no more than a *chunk* of flesh at the slaughterhouse, rolling in its own blood. This is the Austrian variant to Chinese torture, dear to Bataille, who seeks the ecstasy of horror in photographs of *Lingchi*. But this dismembering is *voluntary*. It is the artist who quarters himself. No more organs, no more State? That is not entirely sure. But Brus pushes *resistance-art* to its extremity—to the ultimate extremity (of flesh).

Grotowski: Destroying the Stage

Wrocław, 1965: Ryszard Cieslak plays Pedro Calderón de la Barca's *The Constant Prince* in Jerzy Grotowski's staging. It is one of the most mythical postwar productions, which was the conceptual matrix of the so-called *poor theater*. No stage set nor costumes, no lighting nor props, no makeup nor machinery. Cieslak is naked, or almost: all he wears is a linen cloth around his waist, which is his ultimate patrimony. *Ecce homo*: a potential Christ, not far from Brus's *Zerreisprobe*. Such nudity is symbolic. Grotowski gets rid of all the rags of classic theater: a theater of *representation* that claims to reproduce the world by *aping* the real.

Grotowski is an Actionist in his own way. He repudiates the theater, and only keeps the action, or rather, the *actor*. It is the actor, and *only* the actor, that makes the spectacle, Grotowski writes. Now, this last term (*spectacle*) is proscribed. Debord published *The Society of the Spectacle* right in the middle of the Grotowskian years (1967). And it is since then that we speak of *performance* or *event*. Grotowski himself unearths to his own benefit one of the primary concepts of modern theater: *physical action*. A return to Constantin Stanislavski, the great theorist of actor's training?

Grotowski is no less famous for his *artistic exercises*, this breviary of the modern actor who turns into an athlete. Antonin Artaud would say: *an athlete of the breath*. For the actor *is* the action. Grotowski even said: *total action*, with no characters and (almost) no author, these scenic ghosts whose tutorship is parasitic. There is no more theater here. There is nothing left but the body.

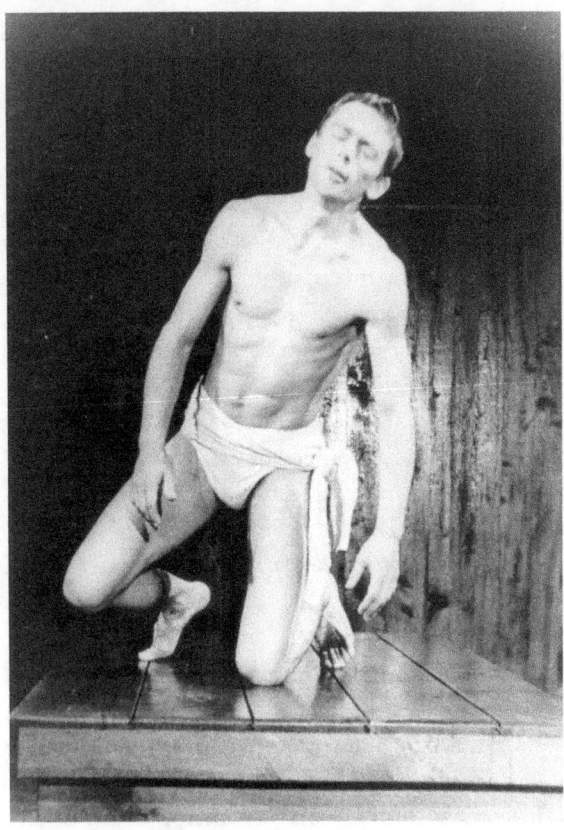

FIGURE 10.2 Rysard Cieslak, *The Constant Prince*, version I, Wrocław, 1965, photo of the Laboratory Theatre. Gelatin silver print. Courtesy of the Grotowski Institute, Wrocław.

But *what* body? Cieslak speaks no more. He murmurs some kind of *solitany*, a pale mixture of soliloquy and litany. It is what Grotowski calls the *somatization* of language. He is then as emaciated as Franz Kafka's *Hunger Artist*, in the slow convulsion of his imminent agony. By the end, Cieslak is no more than a living dead, who no longer has a voice or limbs—who no longer has a body. Grotowski does not only invent *poor* theater, but organless theater.

Kantor: Destroying the Actor

Kraków, 1975: *The Dead Class* is the most legendary spectacle of Tadeusz Kantor, who receives the public in his very own Caliban cave (his *ricoteka*, as he calls it). *Old* humans sitting on *old* benches tentatively raise their hands. And they leave. Then they return, one after the other, to the sound of a *popular* waltz, each carrying a wax figure on their back as an effigy of their own childhood. They are all clothed in black so that we cannot tell *who* is living and *who* is dead. The little oldies, Kantor says, resemble corpses even more than the puppets. For *they* are the *real* dummies that resemble men.

In the sixties, Kantor no longer knows *what* to make of the actor and the action, which are both overly *metaphysical*. How to rid himself of both one and the other? Kantor bundles his performers up in black bags that conceal their appearance, their identity: this is the *emballage* period. He submits them to random mechanical procedures that transform them into robots: the period of *informal theater*. But this becoming-thing is still not enough. He parts with the action, the event, the story: the period of *zero theater*. He finally seeks, in the practice of the *happening*, a way to find life *beyond* the stage.

This backstage work is a negative Graal: an endless quest for an *inferior* order of the world, which would at last be purged of the ideal. Poor theater? Grotowski is not far. Prosaic theater, in any case, or even *proletarian*, "without dignity, without prestige, defenceless and utterly despicable," he writes. What a scene! Suicidal theater: a *theater of death*, as Kantor himself called his last performances that made him famous.

Now the action changes nature. It becomes *total,* and even cannibalistic: it appropriates the space, then the public. It becomes collective, or rather *choral*, in the most Greek sense of the word: there are no more actors, but there is a choir, and of course a *choregos*: Kantor himself, in the position of master or demiurge, *deus* in *machina*, the ghost *within* the machine, the lord of puppets. Here lies the great invention of this iconoclastic enterprise. The theater of death is a theater of *puppets*.

But do not be mistaken: the real puppets are human. The actors become *robots*, be they tragic. The dummy here is the margin, or even the mud, that *reeks of sin*, Kantor says, in the spirit of Bataille. But above all it is *death*: the death of the actor, who is eventually reduced to the state of a mortal. And worse: the actor is now *less* than a man. And *less* than a doll: only just a novice dummy. That which no one has ever dared to do (neither Klein nor Brus), Kantor does before our eyes: *destroy* the actor with the action.

Jarzyna: Silencing the Dead

Warsaw, 2002: Sarah Kane's last play, *4.48 Psychosis*, debuts. The final suicidal scene: 4:48 a.m. It is the moment when the woman who says *I* hangs herself, as did Kane on a February day in 1999. Here there is no rope, but a wall that she breaks herself against: a *hospital* wall (a *psychiatric* hospital wall). And this block of concrete, which glows in the shadows, is a tombstone: a funerary stele. *Watch me*, says the woman who covers it with blood. The voice-over, a male, medical, patriarchal voice, ruled by all the usual *superegos* (the hospital, the State, society), provides her with a kind of funeral oration over the loudspeaker. And this preposthumous universe, which is cold as death, is no longer a theater. But a *morgue*.

And even a station. Grzegorz Jarzyna shows Sarah Kane in the Warsaw Main Rail Station (2002). The *unruly child* of the Polish stage is the most radical of iconoclasts. Jarzyna reads Kane backward. *I*, with Kane, is a voice. Nothing but a voice: words. The play is a monologue. And not even: scraps of phrases that get lost in the night. This shattered language is nothing but a mass of *phonemes* that the dizziness of aphasia threatens to silence at any time: the *silence* of psychosis. And yet, with Jarzyna, this text (this nontext) takes shape (the shape of a body). Magdalena Cielecka, his fetish-actress, is *not* silent. Far from it. She *screams*. And her scream is precisely what the psychosis inhibits: the grain of the voice, the exercise of utterance, the violence of the word.

But the action of suicide is *not* the suicide of the action. Jarzyna could well be the ultimate heir of Brus, who in turn is the heir of Klein. Like him, he displays an active nihilism that aims toward chaos. Jarzyna *destroys* the theater. Not just the actor. And he produces *monsters:* bodies in agony. On the brink of the grave. With Sarah Kane, there was still a last bit of humanity left: some remains of the subject—the stump of the *ego*. But here there is nothing but the void (barbarous): an inhuman theater of wild *urges* that contrasts with sickening supermarket music. Then come, then finally come, as the poet Stéphane Mallarmé said in "Funeral Libation (At Gautier's Tomb)," both *miserly silence and the massive night*.

PART III

TIME IS LONGER THAN
ANY DISTANCE

ACTION WRITING/ACTION READING

The twentieth-century novel openly and unabashedly establishes an instance of the subject who writes and narrates in the first person. Never before in literary history has the *I* been at once so "identified" and so prolix as subject and object of its own narration. Whether in the style of Marcel Proust in a continuous, undulating sentence made of crossroads, roundabouts, and divergences where the unfurling of meaning in its intermingling and interlocking durations constructs a labyrinth in which the subject wanders and gets lost. Or whether in the style of Louis-Ferdinand Céline, who shattered the sentence in the fifties, scattering its sparse fragments, debris of a dispersed subject who can no longer reconstitute himself into a center, a unity. Never has there been such access to the *I*, to the repeated inscription of the subject's sovereign instance in literary history, but correlatively, never has the instance been so suspect, deconstructed, or pulverized. Authors are ceaselessly exploring the limits of readability and meaning where the disintegration of the subject, as a unifying principle, is fulfilled by the creation of new forms of the novel. I am thinking of Franz Kafka's *Metamorphosis*, James Joyce's *Ulysses*, William Faulkner's *Pylon* and *The Sound and the Fury*, Malcolm Lowry's *Under the Volcano*, John Dos Passos's *Manhattan Transfer*, and Claude Simon's *The Flanders Road*. The twentieth-century novel is marked by multiplying of points of view, dispersion of voices, entropy of perception, madness, and alcohol, which function as uncertain, vague, unpredictable modes of thinking. Indeed, the twentieth-century novel opens an immense undertaking, a new reality for a being that configures himself in time's only immanence through the living. In the only immanence of duration rolled into a future, to construct the depth of the subject in a simple resultant. Faulkner wrote in *Absalom, Absalom!*: "Time is longer than any distance," which Henri Bergson underlines in almost identical terms when he writes: "Time is what prevents all from being given at one time. . . . Does the existence of time not prove that there is indecision in things? Is time not this very indecision?"[1] All transcendence disappeared from the rolling mill that was the twentieth century. Identity, subject, individual, and person are no longer vertical invariants that anchor us in the world with some universal necessity. "Man" is in pieces.

If being belongs to time, then there is no a priori sustainable and stable guarantee that can summon the subject at its leisure. It seems that in *La jalousie* (1957), Robbe-Grillet, theorist and author of the *nouveau roman*, proposes the form, the original invention of a form through the motif of jealousy as a concrete mode of masked visibility and as passionate affect. In this novel, the narrator obviously withdraws himself in order to ceaselessly lie in ambush behind his jealousy where he may watch the adulterous affair between his wife A . . . and Franck, a neighbor and friend, unfold:

> Two of the windows overlook the central section of the veranda. The first, to the right, shows through its lowest chink, between the last two slats of wood, the black head of hair—at least the top part of it.
> A . . . is sitting upright and motionless in her armchair. She is looking out over the valet in front of them. She is not speaking. Franck, invisible on her left, is also silent, or else speaking in a very low voice.[2]

The narrator and (supposed) husband's view of A . . . is necessarily partial, made up throughout the book of reconstructions that are at once incoherent, repetitive, and without real temporal logic, and yet perfectly interlaced; it constructs, if not the reality of the adulterous relationship, at least the coherent reality of jealousy and its fuel. The leitmotiv of scene reconstruction clearly depicts a narrative obsession inhabited by the affect of jealousy accomplished not simply by the architectural motif of partial visibility. However, the most distressing effect of this narrative device is the construction of quasi-ritualistic scenes of a drink for three on the terrace and dinner for three in the dining room: the narrator and husband's place, seat, chair, remain resolutely empty as if the narrator abandoned occupying this precise, prescribed, anticipated place that is his, as if the narrator saw himself as absent even while we know he is present by the minutiae of descriptive details: the position of A . . .'s hands on a glass, the condensation on the inside of the ice pail. "A . . . is about to pour the soda into the three glasses lined up on the low table. She distributes the first two, then, holding the third one in her hand, sits down in the empty chair beside Franck. He has already begun drinking."[3] Indeed, this chair and this glass remain, marking his existence and his inscription in this reality, that of the husband who maintains martial order and that of the narrator who maintains the narration's order, but there is precisely nothing in this place of the sovereign subject that is upheld any longer, that is any longer bearable. The narrator and husband is content with being nothing more than a voyeur, illegitimate in itself; the intermittent and partial vision is only constructed through rises of affect, precisely through the jealousy, always reconstituting late representations and meanings in afterthoughts that establish jealousy as a generic and metaphoric form of the subject's dismissal, a subject who is unaware of what he would desire to know, excluded as he is from the place where, for him, reality takes place. The place banned to the subject (so as not to say the banishment of the subject as unifying principle): the place where the scene begins, where the action takes place, where reality is threaded, and where time functions for the narrator and husband; powerless in being and acting, a part and partial role where his blindness and his clairvoyance, his ignorance and his lucidity, alternate. Instants remain when reality is captured—probably the actual reality of the adultery—and sovereign moments of subjectification where the reconstitutions quite rightly fit. And what asserts itself as essential, through the architectural motif of jealousy, is precisely the fact that there is no longer a continuous place or time of the referent subject, the central character of his own narration: there are only "moments of the subject" without place, instants of subjectification within which the principles of identity and the individual, the notions of the body and of bodily presence, become volatile and no longer guarantee anything.

What makes sense at present is this absence that Robbe-Grillet thematizes so well with the pragmatics of jealousy. If the chair is still there on the terrace no one yet dares to sit in it and pretend to play the referent subject and the center of perception. It is elsewhere, anywhere and anytime, that moments of subject readily happen such as flashes of conscience, fragments of memory, which may be a posteriori interlocked in an afterthought and which constitute a singular subject in the first-person singular. Bergson writes:

> Try, in fact, to represent today the action you will complete tomorrow, even if you know what you will do. Your imagination may evoke the movement to execute; but what you will think and feel while executing it you cannot know today, because your state of mind will understand tomorrow

the whole life you will have lived until then, with, moreover, what this particular moment will add.... Can you, without misrepresenting it, shorten the length of a melody? Inner life is indeed this melody.[4]

If the novel, in its just and cruel lucidity, knows how to activate this notion of subject better than any other narrative genre and, in our time period, damages it so much as to make it untenable and vacant, the passage to the subject *you* such as Michel Butor does in *La modification* (1957), is it not recourse to a "subject" that is outside the novel, recourse to the reader as the only reliable instance of subjectification? (Butor is also associated with the nouveau roman, though he has resisted the connection.) The narrator of *La modification* constructs his character on the constant *you* mode, on the mode of address, of interpellation. Further, if the reader identifies with the protagonist it is not due to a classic projection but because he accepts being the object of this address:

> Oh, already (you realize it now; at the same time there was only that uneasiness, that feeling of unaccountable anguish that crept over you as if something, some demon of weariness and cold, were concealing your real self from you; only now do you realize it, for you had put it out of your mind since then, you had been careful during these last weeks to avoid recalling such memories, for you hadn't had the time, you were fully occupied by too many cares at once; and it has taken this pause in your life made by a clandestine trip).[5]

This pause that constitutes this "clandestine trip" is also the personal, intimate, and "clandestine" time of reading. It is, in this sense, a situation of speech, a pragmatic that the reader accepts to espouse. It is then in the sovereign situation of a reader, accepting to occupy a particularly "exposed" place, that the modification of thought and affects takes place. This goes on during a train trip; the protagonist, Léon, alone, travels between Paris and Rome, which is also between Henriette and Cécile. All is reconfigured in Léon's imagination and psyche and upon his arrival in Rome he plans to finally abandon his future life with Cécile and foresees perhaps writing a book about this separation. This is also during the reading process; the reader alone with the text accepts, as reader, to be the subject of this modification. There is a confession or an affirmation of the impossibility of representing the subject, Léon, as a unified and complete evocation of an "equipped" story, at best, with a beginning and an end, as is authorized by the use of the imperfect, the pluperfect and the preterit. Butor himself substitutes, then, through his use of the present tense, the evocation of Léon in a present moment, without a beginning or an end, a moment for the subject corresponding to the train trip. But he turns to the reader as a possible guarantee that some sense is simultaneously being constructed during the reading and in the reality of the reading reader. Engaged in this action, the reader is himself confident to be in a moment of being. One and the other, the reader and the book, are established in their reciprocal reality. Indeed, to paraphrase Jean-Paul Sartre, *it is readers who make books*. But never has the place of the reader been inscribed in this way into the writing itself. *La modification* therefore inaugurated a formal dimension that solicits and objectifies the reader. The question of the arrival of the subject in a story finds itself transported to the reading situation, its duration, and the involvement of the reader subject. It is a considerable shift of the novel's center of gravity that reworks its meaning, no longer only regarding the material of the story but also in the pragmatics that link together the living, author and reader; instances of enunciation, narrator and reader; and an utterance, form and story.[6] The subject introduces himself like a twentieth-century sculpture that comes down from its pedestal to engage in a one-on-one link with its observers, in their space and on their ground where it now stands.

It is undoubtedly this *obligation* that constructs the contemporary novel inside its own writing; a place is hollowed and fitted for the subject reader so he may construct, in turn, a unity of experience and invent an outline of meaning that no other novelistic representation of a subject character can truly incarnate.[7]

Translated from the French by Molleen Shilliday

Notes

1. Henri Bergson, *La pensée et le mouvant* (Paris : F. Alcan, 1934), 1333.
2. Alain Robbe-Grillet, *Jealousy*, trans. Richard Howard (New York: Grove, 1959), 27.
3. Robbe-Grillet, *Jealousy*, 26.
4. Bergson, *La pensée et le mouvant*, 1261.
5. Michel Butor, *La modification* (Paris: Éditions de Minuit, 1957); Michel Butor, *A Change of Heart*, trans. Jean Stewart (New York: Simon and Schuster, 1959), 126.
6. We no longer find ourselves before an address to the reader, as Denis Diderot ceaselessly wrote in *Jacques le fataliste et son maître*, in which it was, above all, about limiting the novelistic convention of linking the author to the reader, and, for the author, of playing on the impatience and frustration of the reader who saw himself endlessly interrupted in his desire to pursue his reading of Jacques's story.

7. In Bergson's writing, there is reflection about teaching literature that particularly mirrors the work done by the contemporary novel: "It would be useful to speak of a great writer's work; this will make him better understood and enjoyed. Still, it is necessary that the student has begun to enjoy it. . . . That is to say, that the child should first reinvent it. . . . To read well and out loud is precisely that. Intelligence will come later to place nuances. . . . Before intellection as such, there is the perception of the structure and movement, there is, on the page that we read, punctuation and rhythm. Accentuating them properly, considering the temporal relationships between the diverse phrases of the paragraph and the diverse parts of a phrase, following without interruption the *crescendo* of the feeling and the thought until the point that is musically noted as being culminant, this is what the art of diction initially consists of. We are wrong to treat it as an ornamental art. Instead of beginning at the end of one's studies, like an ornament, it should be at the beginning and everywhere, as support. On it we shall place all the rest, if we do not give way to the illusion that the main thing is to discourse on matters, and that we know them well enough when we know how to speak of them. We know, we understand only what we can, in some way, reinvent." Bergson, *La pensée et le mouvant*, 1326–27.

FROM THE GENIUS IN THE MOUNTAIN TO THE PARTY IN THE DARK
Art, Cinema, and Cultural Politics at the
Beginning of the Cuban Revolution

The 1959 triumph of the Revolution threw a big party for the country.
Nonetheless, political tension in the air was already very high in 1961; some-
how, the lights had gone out on that party, but the people kept on dancing.
—Orlando Jiménez Leal

Around a Yacht and Two Palaces

The Palacio de Bellas Artes de La Habana is a concrete, stone, and glass prism
that was inaugurated in 1954 on the grounds of the old Plaza del Polvorín, site
of one of the city's principal markets since the late nineteenth century. After
a renovation that lasted almost five years, the building was reopened in 2001
to house the Cuban art collection of the Museo Nacional. While today this
hulking building retains much of its original elegance, the geometric shell—
which has always been adorned with sculptures and reliefs—bears witness to
various important transformations that have occurred during its sixty years
of existence.

From the main entrance of the Bellas Artes, visitors pausing to look across
the street have before them a plot of land the size of a city block, beyond
which resides the old Palacio Presidencial, today the Museo de la Revolución.
In the center of the square, between the palaces and surrounded by trees and
historical artifacts, rises an urn-like glass edifice that shelters a pleasure yacht,
the *Granma*. The English name reveals the American origins of a boat intimately connected to the history of the Cuban revolution. This *Granma* is
none other than the ship in which Fidel Castro and his initial army of about
eighty men sailed from Mexico to the coast of Cuba in December 1956,

effectively starting the armed insurrection that ended in January 1959, when the rebels entered Havana and seized control of Cuba.

As a result, edifices and artifacts associated with momentous events in the history of twentieth-century Cuba are lined up on a narrow stretch of land in La Habana Vieja, creating an urban landscape that can be surveyed in one sweep. These buildings and objects, whose roots we imagine intertwined under the hot city asphalt, are key to understanding, from a cultural and historic perspective, how the decade of the 1950s unfolded in Cuba.

In 1952, after a coup that ousted the legitimate president Carlos Prío Socarrás, the Palacio Presidencial—a jewel of Cuban architectural eclecticism— was occupied by Fulgencio Batista. Two years later and a hundred meters away, the Batista regime inaugurated the Palacio de Bellas Artes on the occasion of the II Bienal Hispanoamericana, an international exhibition organized in Spain by the Franco regime. Meanwhile, ex-president Prío Socarrás, exiled in the United States, was among Cuban emigrants who supported the young lawyer Fidel Castro. With the backing of various individuals, groups, and political factions, Castro was finally able to organize a rebel expedition in Mexico and buy a boat—the *Granma*—for sailing to Cuba. The December 1956 landing of the *Granma* forces was a military fiasco: the troops were decimated but managed to reorganize themselves and establish a guerilla cell in the Sierra Maestra mountains. The American journalist Herbert Matthews of the *New York Times* traveled there in February 1957 to interview Fidel Castro. The meeting between the veteran reporter and the little-known head of the rebellion occurred almost a month before a group allied to the nascent rebel army attacked the Palacio Presidencial. A striking relic remains of this bold urban guerilla action: next to the urn where *Granma* rests is the red-and-black truck that the assailants—very few of whom survived—drove on March 13 to the building where they did not find Batista after all. And as for Fulgencio Batista? He fled from Cuba with his entourage on the morning of January 1, 1959. One week later, Fidel Castro staged a tremendous triumphal entry into Havana that ended at the same Palacio where Batista had expelled Prío in 1952. There, before the joyous multitudes gathered to receive him, the commander of the insurrection greeted the provisional president, the lawyer Manuel Urrutia. Later that year in October, in the adjacent Palacio de Bellas Artes, the first great exhibition of Cuban art of the revolutionary period, the Salon Anual de Pintura, Escultura y Grabado was inaugurated.

This chapter focuses on the outstanding works and artists of that key moment of Cuban history—the year 1959—although it also deals with events that occur later during the sixties. Even then, almost everything discussed in these pages happens from the end of the fifties to the beginning of the sixties. I do not pretend to offer an overarching nor an exhaustive view of the art of the period; rather, this analysis concentrates on key works and artists in the visual arts and cinema at the time of the triumphal revolution and the years of postrevolutionary euphoria. I will attempt to underscore the originality of the artistic options that define the era, visions in which the aesthetic, the political, and the historical weave together in an illustrative and inextricable manner.

Regarding Cuban arts and especially Cuban painting, one should recognize that during the forties abstraction grew ever more influential. Along with this, some tendencies in figurative art favored a geometric and fragmented treatment of images; it became something of a rediscovery, albeit superficial, of cubism. More cosmopolitan interests emerged, a turn that served as counterweight to the traditions and styles that prevailed since the twenties and thirties. The generation that consolidated its importance during the fifties includes a very active nucleus—painters such as Antonio Vidal, Fayad Jamís, Guido Llinás, Raúl Martínez, Hugo Consuegra; the sculptors José A. Díaz Peláez, Augustín Cárdenas, Tomás Oliva, Francisco Antigua—organized as Los Once, a heterogeneous group that showed for the first time in Havana in 1953. Placed in the historical context of that decade—coup d'état, growing popular dissatisfaction, beginning of the armed rebellion against the government—the Abstract Expressionism preached by some of Los Once acquired a label of "insurgent," and in the hands of these young men it became an instrument of opposition and rejection. Opposition ranged from the preceding art (academic and avant-garde) to the politics of Fulgencio Batista's dictatorship (including some of his cultural initiatives). Perhaps the most outstanding example of this civic and finally political stance that "contaminated" these artists' works was the protest against the Bienal Hispanoamericana organized by the Franco government, a collective action that bore fruit in the 1954 exhibition *Plástica Cubana Contemporánea: Homenaje a José Martí*, also known as the Antibienal.

However, Los Once were not the only Cuban artists of the fifties. Other important artists, some who had experienced some success in the past, achieved a prominence during these years that established their careers; among them are Servando Cabrera, Manuel Couceiro, Raúl Millán, Zilia Sánchez, Jorge Camacho, Juan Tapia Ruano, Augustín Fernández, Antonia Eiriz, and José Luis Posada. Sandú Darié, a Romanian who immigrated to Cuba from Europe in the late forties, would be the staunch driving force behind concrete abstraction, supported by experienced painters like Luis Martínez Pedro and young artists such as José Mijares and Rafael Soriano. This direction was reinforced in 1956 with the exhibition *Pintura de hoy: Vanguardia de la Escuela de Paris*, which was presented in Havana's still young Palacio de Bellas Artes, gathered together current French and European art in which variations of geometric abstraction prevailed, and included works by two artists tied to the Paris art scene: Loló Soldevilla, who was in the 1955 Salon des Réalités Nouvelles, and Wilfredo Arcay, who showed at the Galerie Arnaud in 1952.

The first exhibition of the Diez Pintores Concretos group was in 1959 and included Soldevilla, Arcay, Darié, Martínez Pedro, Soriano, Mijares, Salvador Corratgé, and Pedro de Oraá, among others. In the following years, abstract art remained important, while other styles gained ground. One of these was the rise of a social and heroic realism, with tinges of Mexican muralism and Soviet-styled "socialist realism." Realism, in all its variations, was only one more option among the different possibilities explored in art to represent the profound changes shaking the country. Works by Adigio Benítez, Carmelo González, Servando Cabrera, Orlando Suárez, Enrique Moret, and others demonstrate this tendency. During almost the whole of the sixties the art scene remained varied, fertile, and polemic.

The year 1959—when the revolutionary forces seized power—does not mark a breaking point where strict "befores" and "afters" are defined in Cuban visual arts. Fragmented in tendencies and groups, the art was characterized by diversity. According to some critics of the time, the outcome of the moment was not very encouraging: "A cycle in our visual arts has ended. Everything that can be done with the forms and aims derived from the French School, Picasso, surrealism and what is called abstract art has already been done in Cuba. All that remains for our artists is to repeat unto tedium (the spectator's) variations on styles that are mummified in the museums of New York, Chicago or Paris. Apathy and uncertainty mark this incessant repetition of the same forms, colors and technical methods of the Europeans."[1] Beginning in that key year, radical transformations in art and culture were wrought, although the rate of change was never the same for the different areas of artistic creation: photography, cartooning, and book, advertising, and poster design, for example, evolved much faster than painting, printmaking, or sculpture. Meanwhile, the control of the revolutionary regime's cultural policies became the trophy in a struggle among the same groups and parties who, after Batista's flight, closed ranks as a body around Fidel Castro, the indisputable leader of the forces then in power.

The new regime at first assumed the complexity and fragmentation of the artistic panorama as a natural part of a historical-cultural process integrated into the future of the nation. But the relations between the incipient political power and the artistic and intellectual camp evolved as quickly as the changes in the society as a whole. Already in 1961, with the censure of the documentary *P.M.*, the closing of the weekly *Lunes de Revolución*, and the episode known as "Words to Intellectuals" (discussed later), that power drew inviolable limits on creative expression, and the divisions and disagreements between those in the world of literature and arts were very clear.

Some artists stood out in the first years of the revolutionary maelstrom for the accelerated pace of change in their works. The metamorphosis of their creations occurred at a rhythm that seemed synchronized with the effervescent dynamics of the surrounding society. In the case of these artists, an unrestrained maturation gave a characteristic direction to their respective works and placed them, almost overnight, at the very center of the artistic scene. Among them are Ángel Acosta León, Antonia Eiriz, Umberto Peña, and, perhaps as the emblematic figure of this phenomenon, Chago.

The Genius Who Came Down from the Mountain

Chago (1937–95) was the pseudonym of Santiago Armada, a young man who joined the rebels in March 1958 and was one of the troops closest to Fidel Castro in the Sierra Maestra. In addition to fighting as a guerrillero, Chago drew caricatures and cartoon strips for the newspaper *El Cubano Libre*, founded by Che Guevara. His evolution from political caricaturist to author of a book of satirical drawings (*El humor otro*, 1963), which are unique and unequaled in the history of Cuban publishing, and then to an artist of somewhat somber expressionist drawings and paintings, occurred at an explosive pace between his months in the Sierra Maestra and his first years in Havana in the early sixties. "Julito 26,"[2] the first important character he created, was born in the mimeographed pages of *El Cubano Libre* and its satirical supplement. Like his creator, "Julito 26" is not a very experienced guerrillero; the general tone of the cartoons is of a brazenness that oscillates between ingenuity and crudity. These early caricatures are carefully drawn and demonstrate a developing yet already effective graphic vocabulary.

When the rebels entered Havana in January 1959 they were received as heroes. Chago was just one in those triumphal ranks. He soon began to draw and design for the newspaper *Revolución*, which was directed by Carlos Franqui

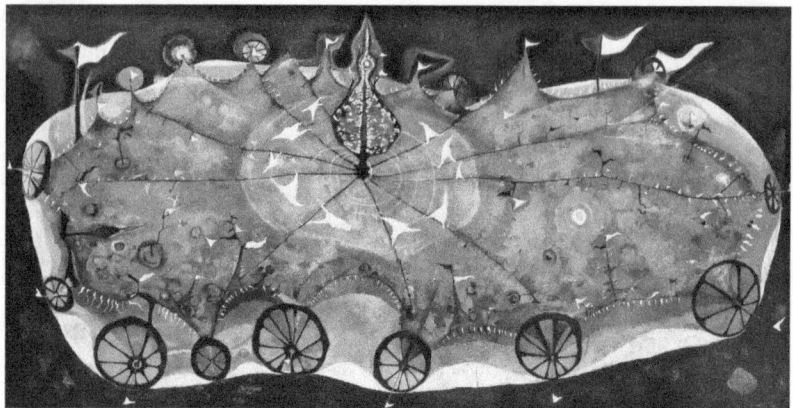

FIGURE 12.1 Ángel Acosta León, *Carrusel de la paz*, 1961. Oil on masonite. Cuban art collection, Museo Nacional de Bellas Artes, Havana, Cuba. Photo by David Rodríguez Camacho.

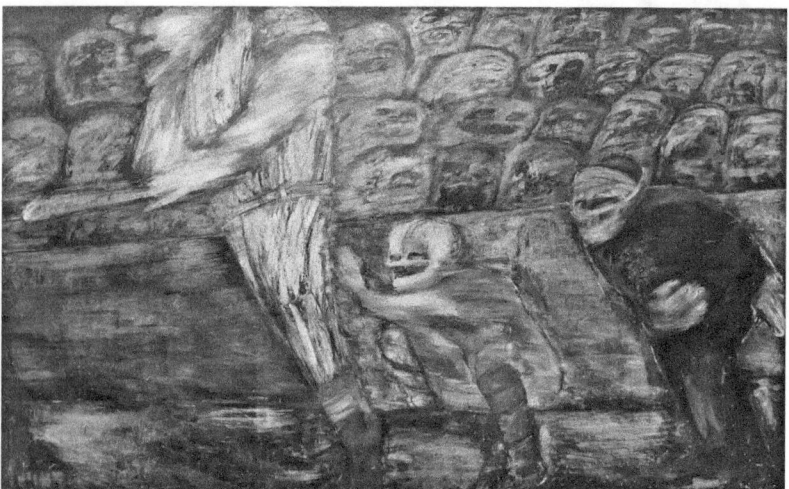

FIGURE 12.2 Antonia Eiriz, *La muerte en pelota*, 1966. Oil on canvas. Cuban art collection, Museo Nacional de Bellas Artes, Havana, Cuba. Photo by David Rodríguez Camacho.

(also an ex-guerrillero and a very influential journalist, editor, and promoter in the cultural life of the sixties). He also collaborated on the magazine *Lunes de Revolución*, an extraordinary tabloid dedicated to art and literature championed by the same Franqui, who gathered together some of the most brilliant writers and intellectuals of the time, including Guillermo Cabrera Infante, Ambrosio Fornet, Heberto Padilla, Jaime Sarusky, Humberto Arenal, Antón Arrufat, and Lisandro Otero.

"Julito 26" survived the arrival of his author to Havana, but no longer than absolutely necessary. Chago's horizons expanded rapidly and he decided to shelve "Julito . . ." at the same time he avoided pigeonholing himself as an editorial caricaturist. Attracted by complex new projects, in 1960 he joined the founding of another publication, *El Pitirre*, a magazine whose collaborators, almost all young—from Jean-Jacques Sempé and André François to Saul Steinberg and Jules Feiffer—drew on the best international caricature of the time in order to revitalize the satirical cartoon in Cuba. While he divided his attention among other fields beyond political caricature, the young rebel, with his hair recently cut and a beard he barely needed to shave, confidently entered a tunnel of fire: his own art. Soon he would be drawing and writing his most famous cartoon, "Salomón," a heuristic comic strip that synthesizes, better than any other work of the period, the speculations, guesswork, and uncertainty characteristic of the early sixties in Cuba.

In "Salomón," Chago created the perfect image of the confused intellectual, of the brilliant, distracted, and unpredictable dreamer; this thinker never stops philosophizing about the contradictions and harshness of the society in which he finds himself. Other artists recognized his importance and appropriated the character, by which they confirmed his stature as a cultural symbol and emblematic icon. "Salomón" appears in Antonia Eiriz's assemblages and in Raúl Martínez's paintings, and the screenwriter Edmundo Desnoes and the director Tomás Gutierrez Alea included him in one of the many memorable sequences of the film *Memories of Underdevelopment* (1968). Some years afterward Desnoes wrote about the character and his creator: "Chago, the only genius who came down from the mountain with Fidel, publishes 'Salomón,' a strip of 'humor otro' that reflects the courage and the doubts of a new reality."[3]

The expressiveness of "Salomón" is eminently visual: frequently he displays a pregnant silence, when he is not using a language that questions the validity of conventional dialogue. In this comic strip, the language veers between the poetic and the cryptic, as the texts elude facile and direct meaning. The language has the free feel of the soliloquy, and his enigmatic verbalizations can be seen as proof of his uniqueness. By expressing himself in words and sounds that only he must fully understand, "Salomón" reaffirms his idiosyncratic solitude. His cryptic balloons also express self-sufficiency: "Salomón" creates his own world, including planets and stars, so that his inventiveness with language is not surprising. His speech is full of onomatopoeia, babblings, and interjections, according to his surprise, fright, or feelings. Choking sounds emphasize a humor fed by absurdity, scatology, and anguished questions

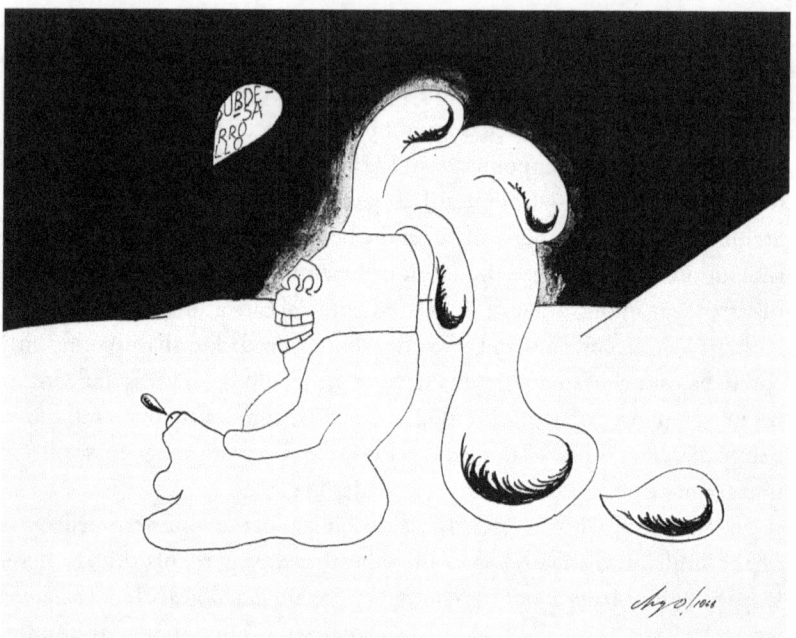

FIGURE 12.3 Chago (Santiago Armada), *Subdesarrollo: Eyaculaciones*, 1968. From the series Diarreas, esputos y eyaculaciones prematuras. Ink on cardboard. Cuban art collection, Museo Nacional de Bellas Artes, Havana, Cuba. Photo by David Rodríguez Camacho.

(question marks are a constant) before the unanswerable twists and turns of life: he questions death, sex, power, love, and friendship.

By presenting "Salomón" as a self-absorbed individual who is curious about his immediate environment, Chago underscored the centrality of the individual in a historic moment that was ever more dominated by the ideology of masses and collectivism. This facet of the caricatured figure undoubtedly made him more attractive to Desnoes and Gutiérrez Alea, who put a "Salomón" besieged by ever-greater questions on the screen to round out the portrait of Sergio Carmona, the skeptical and distant hero of the feature film *Memorias . . .* Although in differing degrees, Sergio, as much as "Salomón," who both lived in the same historical time, vindicates the importance of the autonomous person, differentiated from the crowd and in control of his own free will.

The years between 1959 and 1963 were sufficient time for Chago to tune into some of the most fertile artistic tendencies of the moment (neo-expressionism, neo-Dada, and the effects of "the Steinberg revolution" in caricature). The importance of these and other influences is evident in his book *El humor otro*, which brings together works from 1960 to 1963. The title announces his intention of breaking with his best-known work, which had been published in various newspapers and magazines. The "other" in this case is "humor that makes people think," as the novelist Lisandro Otero states in the prologue; he also notes that this thoughtful intention is the opposite of "laughter...as an escape." This is the concept that sustains the structure of this book: a thoughtful and knowing humor that leads to knowledge. Chago developed this idea years later in some articles and essays, in which he constructed a body of theory around his thesis of "gnosis humor."[4]

The book is also a beautiful object, carefully designed by the polyfaceted Raúl Martínez, one of the key artists of the time. To the disgust of Chago and his collaborators on this publishing adventure, it was censured. The edition, already printed, would lay dormant in government warehouses until the mideighties, when, without prior notice, it was put on sale in some Havana bookstores.

The drawings in *El humor otro* are deliberately deceptive in appearance: closely observed, they reveal an ever more complex and developed formal vocabulary. The drawing is very free, and arabesques, inkblots, and collage abound. The improvements in the richness and quality of drawing go hand in hand with a universal humor, at times somber, and far from the tone of a newspaper. The pages of the book reveal readings and affinities that clearly show intellectual growth: the young guerrillero has become an artist and has read Jean-Paul Sartre, Henri Bergson, and José Martí (he included several quotes throughout the book). The contents, grouped in sections, are treated with inventiveness and profundity touched with philosophy.

Chago's inclination toward a prickly, expressionistic visual language that emphasizes sexuality and the grotesque representation of the human body was being shaped in this book and others from this time. The imaginarium of the grotesque defines very important areas of art and literature produced in Cuba in the sixties, and Chago's contribution to this was personal and very early. Varying with the artists, that grotesque tone appears several times in crucial works of the period: Peña's truncated cattle and vociferous urinals, Acosta León's creaking bedsprings and steaming coffeepots, Eiriz's ubiquitous monsters, and Raúl Martínez's overworked painting surfaces. And also in literature: the acerbic poems of "Bamboleo Frenético" (Virgilio Piñera) and the ruthless verses of "La Pata del Palo" (Rafael Alcides).

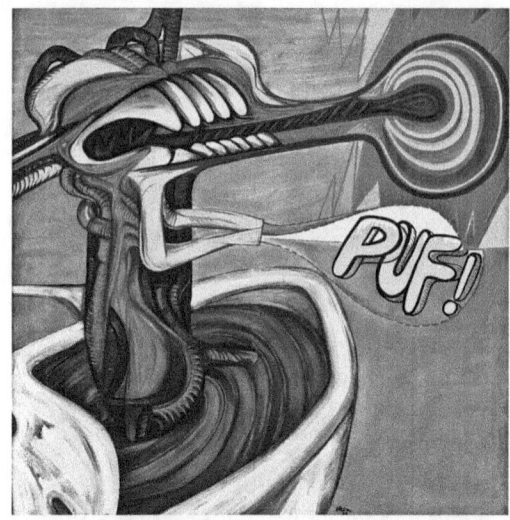

FIGURE 12.4 Umberto Peña, *El puf! De los caballeros*, 1966. Oil on canvas. Cuban art collection, Museo Nacional de Bellas Artes, Havana, Cuba. Photo by David Rodríguez Camacho.

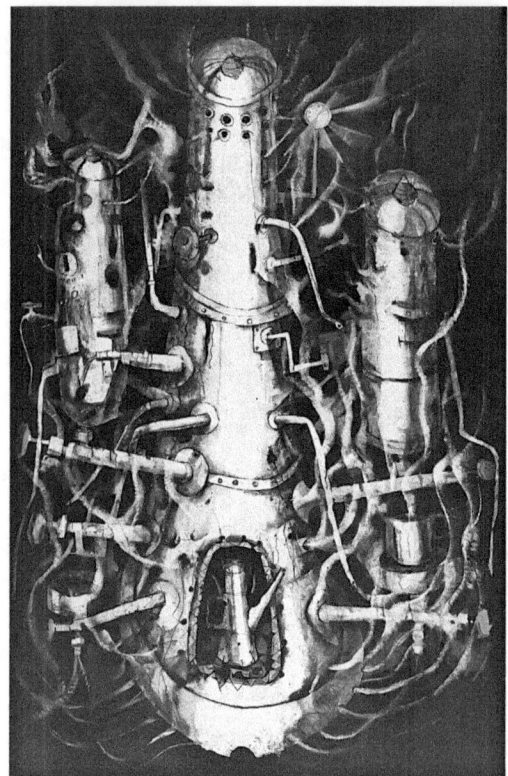

FIGURE 12.5 Ángel Acosta León, *Cafetera no.1*, 1960. Oil on board. Cuban art collection, Museo Nacional de Bellas Artes, Havana, Cuba. Photo by David Rodríguez Camacho.

In the following years the body, and particularly the male anatomy, were constant themes in Chago's work. The grotesque context incorporates the representation of events, substances, and objects (ejaculation, semen, condoms) that complement a dramatic vision that is somewhat self-critical of sexuality. The satiric tone and implications of violence that emanate from his work send us to the language of the street and Cuban popular culture, as well as to the mythological, philosophical, and religious foundation that feeds the cults and phallic representations of ancient art in Greece and Rome. The adoration of Priapus and Pan, the images of fauns and satyrs, the cults associated with fertility and powerful natural forces, as beneficial as destructive, are sources that connect to the irreverent character of his work and with his perception of the phallic as power, immeasurable energy, and mystery.

In July and August 1967 the Salón de Mayo, a famous event of the Paris art scene, was held in Cuba. Wifredo Lam, who served as intermediary between Paris and Havana, was key to this project that was presented in Havana and Santiago de Cuba. Added to this was the enthusiasm of important French and European artists and intellectuals toward Cuba and its Revolution, and the organizational talent and political influence of Carlos Franqui was paramount; he was a personal friend of Lam and, as we have seen, someone close to Chago first as a guerrillero and later during the days of the newspaper *Revolución* and the magazine *Lunes*.

In July 1967 Chago was invited to contribute to the *Cuba colectiva* mural, created in the Pabellón Cuba de La Habana by the foreign participants of the Salon and the contributions of some Cubans. There he painted *La llave del golfo* (The key to the gulf), and a version—a drawing in ink on paper—from the same year is in the permanent collection of the Museo Nacional. The title refers to an old expression by the historian José María Félix de Arrate, who during the colonial period baptized Cuba as "Llave del Mundo Nuevo" (Key to the New World), creating an emblematic image that was later canonized in the national coat of arms. Chago transformed Arrate's definition of the island as a geographical entity into a lesson on geopolitical anatomy. The popular cult of the phallus, an enduring feature of the machista culture of Cuba, is crystallized in this work: a defiant image that seeks to express, through specific anatomical features (the erect penis), the island's historic situation in the sixties. The figure's unbridled sexuality can be identified with a sometimes exhibitionist nationalism; the pose has as much implicit violence as it does potential life, and points to the turbulence and tensions so characteristic of that decade on a national and international level.

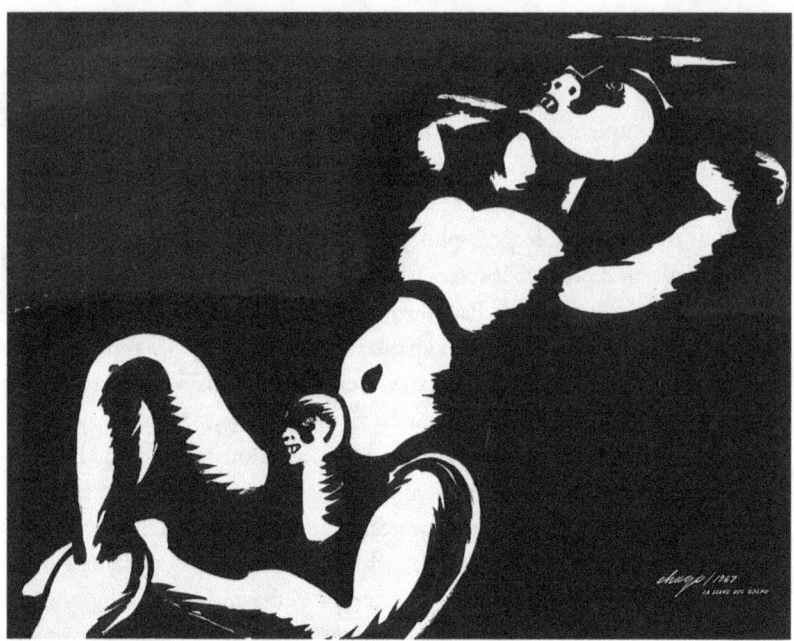

FIGURE 12.6 Chago (Santiago Armada), *La llave del golfo*, 1967. Ink on cardboard. Cuban art collection, Museo Nacional de Bellas Artes, Havana, Cuba. Photo by David Rodríguez Camacho.

In an expressionistic painting of vigorous brushstrokes and contrasting tones, the state of perpetual patriotic exaltation brought by the Revolution is translated as an erect, smiling, anthropomorphized penis. The feelings of bravery and virile energy, in Cuban nationalistic ideology traditionally associated with patriotism, take the shape of a huge obscene mass that is also a portrait of its complacent bearer. This penis-portrait rises like a point of reference, like a handle or a tower. Chago appears to parody a recurring phrase in the era's political discourse—"Cuba como faro de América" (Cuba, America's lighthouse)—and in a play on words transforms that expression into "Cuba como falo de America"—Cuba, America's phallus. The shining tower conflates with the fecund tower.

La llave del golfo is contained within Chago's broad area of production that focuses on the grotesque body and the emphasis on masculine attributes. This is one of the most significant themes in the art of the sixties in Cuba and affirms the central importance of the grotesque and carnivalesque as the platforms from which key works of art and literature are launched during that decade. From 1967—and even earlier—Chago's work copiously pictures the anatomical regions where the body flows, expands, and connects with its surroundings. Images of corporeal emanations abound (fecal matter, sweat, semen) in both masculine and feminine figures, while physiological and physical potentialities of the human anatomy (defecation, ejaculation, blowing) are privileged to define the bodies. Many works by Chago and also by his colleagues and contemporaries—among others the aforementioned Acosta León, Eiriz, and Peña—reiterate those components, which theorists such as Mikhail Bakhtin recognized in their conceptualization of the grotesque body.

With the same energy, these artists place their figures and stories in a living and changing environment. They capture spaces in their work where social interaction is usually accompanied by instability, and even the shock and inversion of established norms: Acosta León's circus big top, Eiriz's baseball stadium, and Peña's urinals. By using those spaces they channel what literary criticism recognizes as "carnival time": a time of liberation and change that implies the triumph of "'backwards' and 'contradictory' things," and "permutations between the high and the low, the noble and the grotesque." It is in these times when the sarcastic, destructive, and revitalizing laugh reigns, which ridicules "even the very mockers."[5]

The censure of *El humor otro* in 1963 was one of the first confrontations between Chago and the bureaucrats and functionaries in charge of the principal cultural institutions. His painting for the Salón de Mayo mural was not well received, and *La llave del golfo* became another excuse for the "guardians of the aesthetic canon" to keep his body of work out of the main circuits of exhibition and promotion. His isolation grew gradually, especially after 1967, and although he never stopped working, he had very few exhibitions after that. His artistic work was submerged for decades while he earned a living as a graphic designer. It is almost paradoxical, then, that his main work all those years was designing the daily *Granma*, the official publication of the Cuban Communist Party. That institution (particularly with the intervention of its director, Jorge Enrique Mendoza, also an ex-guerrillero) was a true refuge for the artist and there he found some support during a long period of ostracism. In the eighties, his comic strips, paintings, and drawings were rediscovered by a younger generation and his work was shown again sporadically. As for the appreciation and knowledge of that work among his countrymen, at least a modicum of historic justice was imposed: when the Palacio de Bellas Artes was reopened in 2001 and presented the Museo Nacional's permanent

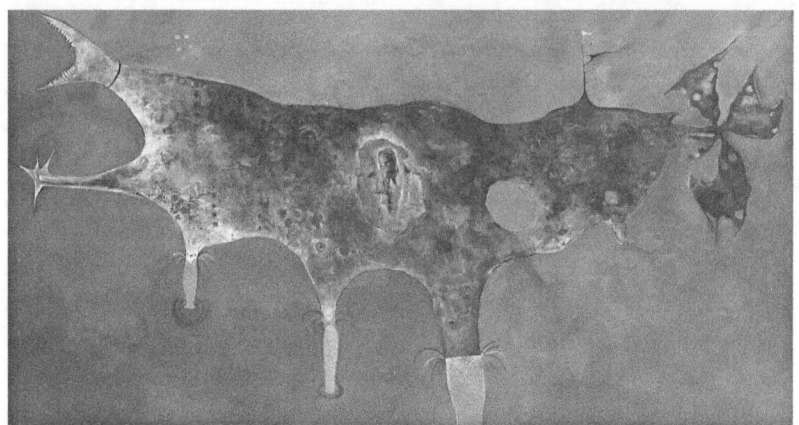

FIGURE 12.7 Angel Acosta León, *La nave*, 1961. Oil on cardboard. Cuban art collection, Museo Nacional de Bellas Artes, Havana, Cuba. Photo by David Rodríguez Camacho.

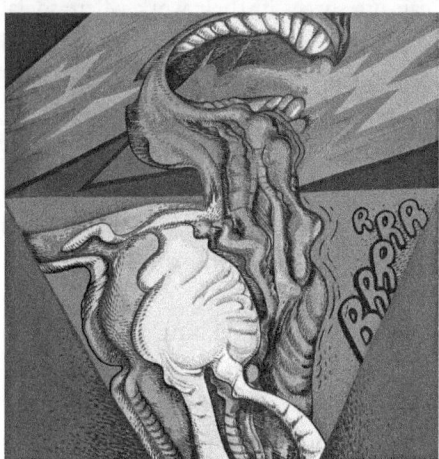

FIGURE 12.8 Umberto Peña, *Tu haces brrr con mi electricidad*, 1967. Oil on canvas. Cuban art collection, Museo Nacional de Bellas Artes, Havana, Cuba. Photo by David Rodríguez Camacho.

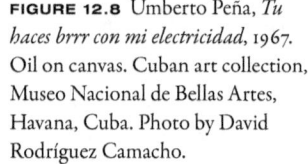

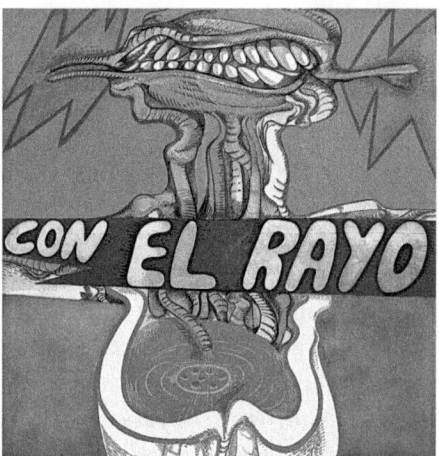

FIGURE 12.9 Umberto Peña, *Con el rayo hay que insistir*, 1967. Oil on canvas. Cuban art collection, Museo Nacional de Bellas Artes, Havana, Cuba. Photo by David Rodríguez Camacho.

collection, several of Chago's drawings were prominently displayed in the galleries dedicated to the art of the sixties.

Havana's Party in the Dark

Chago's close association with the highly regarded intellectual Carlos Franqui and the circle of like-minded individuals collaborating on his publications and projects—for example, the newspaper *Revolución*, the weekly *Lunes de Revolución*, and the publishing house Ediciones R—gave him a front-row seat to witness some of the dramatic events developing in the world of Cuban culture in 1961. In June of that year at the Biblioteca Nacional José Martí in Havana, three meetings were held between the principal political leaders of the Cuban revolution and the *crème de la crème* of the island's literary and artistic intelligentsia. Only a few weeks before, in April—and on the eve of the Playa Girón (Bay of Pigs) counterrevolutionary invasion, the military expedition organized by the United States government—Fidel Castro had proclaimed the socialist character of the revolution to a fervent multitude. On June 30, during the last of the library gatherings, the Cuban leader uttered his famous "Words to Intellectuals," a speech since then transformed into a doctrinal document (depending upon by whom, when, how, and where, it is seen as a straitjacket or protective cloak) for the revolutionary regime's politics of art and culture. Regarding this address by Fidel Castro, it has been pointed out that "its ambiguity, polyvocality and complexity have very often been reduced to its most famous (and sometimes misquoted) extract, thus precluding a comprehensive view of the speech's multiple functions: 'Dentro de la Revolución, todo; contra la Revolución, nada' ('Within the Revolution, everything; against the Revolution, nothing')."[6] As the meetings had been called in response to fears of censorship, the question of freedom of artistic expression was then analyzed, with Castro making a clear distinction between freedom of form and freedom of content, the latter being the essential area of concern to those assembled.

We should never overlook the fact that this meeting between intellectuals and politicians was held, above all, due to the tensions that arose around the production, distribution, and censorship of a film: the documentary *P.M. (Pasado Meridiano)*, directed by Sabá Cabrera Infante and Orlando Jiménez Leal and backed by the magazine *Lunes de Revolución*. That a fifteen-minute film, which one of its authors called "an unpretentious short,"[7] detonated the most significant polemic in the cultural history of the revolution tells us about the extraordinary importance of film in the political agenda pursued on the island since 1959. In terms of the events surrounding *P.M.*, Fidel Castro, in his 1961 speech, "recognised that the procedures used were arguably not the most effective, nor even was the final decision necessarily the right one: but again, with the interests of the people uppermost, cinema could be a powerful instrument of influence and must therefore be managed carefully."[8]

The film and the Biblioteca Nacional meetings that followed its television broadcast, which was sponsored by *Lunes*, and the refusal by the Instituto Cubano del Arte e Industria Cinematográficos (ICAIC) to screen it in a theater, were key elements of the aesthetic and ideological battles that colored Cuba's cultural scene in the early 1960s.[9] As remarked by the Haitian intellectual René Depestre, a first-hand witness to the upheavals in Cuba's literary and artistic life after 1959, "there are always contradictory interests stirring within every revolutionary process."[10] Here the lively and diverse artistic and literary camp engaged with the open or hidden conflict of groups contending for the control of cultural power. This was a dynamic that would be repeated, with new actors and in different circumstances, through the entire period dominated by the revolution up to the present.

After Fidel Castro's speech in the Biblioteca Nacional and above all after the closing of *Lunes de Revolución* in November 1961, the ICAIC (created by law in March 1959 and directed by Alfredo Guevara) absolutely controlled Cuban cinematography. Some of the important figures associated with the cultural weekly *Lunes,* and also with the making and promotion of *P.M.,* ended up, sooner or later, in exile, along with the intellectuals who were irreconcilably opposed to the revolutionary regime: among them the brothers Guillermo and Sabá Cabrera Infante, Orlando Jiménez Leal, Néstor Almendros, Carlos Franqui, and Heberto Padilla. Meanwhile, *P.M.* became part of a select list of mythical works. Shelved and afterward almost never available to the public, its reputation steadily climbed and during the following decades it became recognized as an essential milestone in the development of Cuban cinematography.

Beyond the scandal and the censure, there are powerful artistic arguments for considering *P.M.* as an influential work in its own historical moment and beyond, fundamental to twentieth-century Cuban art and cinematography. For now, I would like to focus on one of these arguments: the distinctive way in which this film assumes consciousness or sensibility toward the marginal environments and people of Havana. The documentary acutely captures, without any kind of condescension, the idiosyncrasies of the lower classes of Havana: "the characters on the docks, the lumpen with hats, suits and ties" who inhabit "an elegant . . . underworld . . . another Havana, secret and mildly illicit, parallel to the brightly lit, legendary Havana everyone knows."[11]

Camera in hand, the young filmmakers head for the underworld and margins of Havana. In its fluid movement through the nightlife of the streets around the Port of Havana and in the *playa* (beach) of Marianao, the film shows us picturesque characters, jammed together in a festive and relaxed environment of busy nightclubs and cafés, with people crowding up to the bars and the jukeboxes turned up to maximum volume. The filmmakers sidestep the lights and tinsel of the famous cabaret Tropicana; they also avoid the kitsch of the most expensive and pretentious nightspots in El Vedado. They guide us (reroute us) to those "marginal" places where the least privileged live their night to the fullest and with very little. That night, splashed with rum, wreathed in cigar smoke, and seasoned with the aroma of the fry stands, becomes a collective party, thanks to spontaneous dancing and music played by simple trios. The camera watches isolated individuals, but above all it captures atmospheres, movements, the relationships and interactions of the night crawlers as they cross paths, or meet at the same bar or in the claustrophobic room where a famous musician (El Chori, pseudonym of Silvano Shueg) performs his hallucinatory percussion show. Among the portrayed are blacks, mestizos, homosexuals, women, young, and old. There are heterosexual couples enjoying their celebration and their nightly drama.

The spontaneous merriment and vitality that bubbles out of the people—and by extension, the city that is the site of this party—would once again prove that Cuban culture, doubtless shaken by the cataclysm of 1959, flowed past that monumental date and still conserved, in its popular expressions and environments as well as in art and literature, many of its anterior characteristics. In any case, the banning of the film displayed a proactive attitude by the cultural and political authorities that decided against showing it in the theaters: those censors must have hoped to deal with a different film and a different reality. They probably would have approved a documentary that reflected a different people and a different Havana than those of *P.M.* An ICAIC document that laid the argument for the censure states that the movie is unacceptable because "it offers a partial view of Havana night life, that impoverishes, disfigures and detracts from the Cuban people's position against cunning attacks by the counterrevolution, ordered by Yankee imperialism."

The accusation of partisanship is nothing but a response to the filmmakers' decision to exercise a fundamental right of artists, that is, to choose their focus on this or that angle of reality. It is true that a movie like *P.M.*, bursting with music and alcohol, packed with humble people ready to party, dance, and drink, created an image of Cuba and its people that in the eyes of many ideologues in positions of power diminished the gravity of the circumstances besetting the country. The carefree attitude of the drinkers and dancers, according to the Manichean logic of the censors, was an unjustifiable concession, a corruption that was out of place considering the dangers and enemies—very real, by the way—that the new regime confronted. Fundamentally, the censure drew a false dichotomy by distinguishing between the drinking and partying Cuban and the revolutionary Cuban. That perspective, tinged with elitism and paternalism, did not take into account that, in the complex reality unleashed in 1959, the citizen capable of dancing and getting drunk was the same who sooner or later would take up arms to defend with his life the promises and hopes nourished by the Revolution. For those who decided not to show *P.M.*, the humble dancer in his jacket and tie could not represent, according to that artificial dichotomy, those tense and violent times. The cinema did need those people, just not at night, when the fiesta carried them away. It was much better if they appeared in the movies without their suits and ties, as militiamen carrying arms, workers sweating at the machines of the new factories, or peasants working the lands recently converted into cooperatives.

P.M., like so many of the works by painters and writers of the time, took an aesthetic position rooted in the carnivalesque and the grotesque. The censure was also a reaction against those premises: an opposition to those images of a world turned upside down, where authority is questioned and values inverted. The disproportionate reaction against the film proved its effectiveness as a work of art: Jiménez Leal and Cabrera Infante, two young filmmakers, share the credit for placing those aesthetic ideas at the very nucleus of Cuban filmmaking after 1961. They insisted on showing a chaotic world inverted, "turned upside down"—a world the camera brings in and out of focus, in constant movement—dominated by music, song, and dance, the profusion of raised arms and extended legs, gesticulations, wide and half-open mouths. Like every world marked by the carnivalesque, this universe has another side, that of threatening violence, of tragedy about to happen or already there.[12]

From today's advantageous perspective, these features of *P.M.* appear to presage what will be forthcoming in any number of Cuban films from the sixties and afterward: the many sweaty bodies stretching and reaching out; the sequences structured around crowds (with the characters situated at the edge of the drama, or in its epicenter) absorbed in the dance and the music. Party scenes and collective celebrations that will return in Eduardo Manet's *Un día en el solar* (*A Day in a Solar*) and Nicolás Guillén Landrián's documentary work *Los del baile* (*The Dancers*), both from 1965; in Sara Gómez's *De cierta manera* (*In One Way or Another*), 1974–77; Tomás Gutiérrez Alea's *Memorias del subdesarrollo*, 1968, and *Hasta cierto punto* (*Up to a Certain Point*), 1983; and Sergio Giral's *María Antonia*, 1990. I should reiterate that the emphasis on the grotesque and the carnivalesque remains one of the foundations of the art of the sixties, and influences a good part of the later artistic and literary production in Cuba.

The Party's Aftermath: In the Light of Day

Memorias del subdesarrollo was made in 1968, directed by Gutiérrez Alea, and adapted from the eponymous 1965 novel by Edmundo Desnoes. It is among the works made after *P.M.* in which we can detect the aura of that brief 1961 documentary. The action in *Memorias* essentially happens between the days after the failed invasion of Playa Girón in April 1961 and the October Crisis in 1962. Just the fact that the film is based in that historical period is reason enough to include it among the works discussed in this chapter.

Interestingly, Alea appears in his own film, as director: we watch him and listen to him characterize *Memorias* as a work into which he will attempt to put a bit of everything. He achieved this: the film, structured like a collage, contains fragments of what appears to be a soft-porn movie; citations (taken from the Cuban press) from the thoughts of Mao Tse Tung; the footage documenting a panel of Cuban and foreign intellectuals who argue "the fundamental contradiction of our time"; and the off-screen voice of John F. Kennedy announcing the start of the October Crisis to his country and to the world. And there is even room for an appearance of Fidel Castro on Cuban television in 1962, reporting the possibility of a U.S. nuclear attack on the island.

I am also lingering on *Memorias* for its paradigmatic quality in more than one sense: as a representation of the intellectual (upper-class bourgeois, in this case) who is determined to witness the triumph of a revolution; as an experiment in formalism that amasses a repertory of existing images and condenses them into a coherent whole; and as a "self-portrait" that its authors use to distance themselves critically from themselves and their works—Desnoes as well as Alea appear in the film, respectively, as Edmundo Desnoes and as an ICAIC film director. And another Sergio, an actor whose last name is Corrieri, plays the principal role, Sergio Carmona. *Memorias* is also admirable for its synthesis: Alea compresses an intense, partial version of Cuban history into a little more than an hour and a half. He achieves this by linking together a selection of extraordinarily eloquent images, many derived from documentaries.

Sergio is a curious and observant person, blessed with the conviction of doubt. He seems always conscious of his behavior and in a moment of self-reflection he says: "I am maintaining my lucidity. A disagreeable lucidity, an emptiness." Sergio's doubt is cynical and accompanied by an individuality that the film underscores by placing him among the hordes but almost never allowing him to become a part of them. Even when he appears disoriented as he navigates through the Havana carnival goers, Sergio manages to find his own space and remains against the current. More than once and not by accident, we see him through telephoto lens; he is portrayed at a distance, his silhouette slipping by erratically on the screen whose background is an often conspicuously gray city. That city is Havana, treated as a dramatic stage setting, and the cinematographer Ramón F. Suárez frames shots that will become archetypes—repeated ad nauseum—for portraying the Havana cityscape in film and photography: the malecón washed by huge waves, the rooftops and profiles of the buildings softened by the city's light smog, and the shady streets lined with doorways and columns. Keeping that same distance, Sergio's telescopic view (toward his urban surroundings, toward his fellow citizens, toward history) extends from a high balcony in one of those tall buildings that announced, in the Havana of the fifties, the never fulfilled promise of a city defined by a forest of elegant skyscrapers.

One of the central elements of *Memorias* is the portrayal of the popular celebration. Havana's carnival is like a collective personality, a fascinating and enthralling being that envelopes the actor and places him among a crowd of men and women who are very much like the ones we saw dancing, singing, and drinking in Jiménez Leal and Cabrera Infante's 1961 film.

The feature-length film by Alea opens with a powerful sound track, a refrain with a contagious cadence ("Where is Teresa? Dance Teresa!"), and music that blares out with drums, bells, and then trumpets. The avalanche of percussion immediately leads to the screen's most compelling image: the smiling, sweaty face of a musician, Pello el Afrokán, his hands frenetically beating the drum; behind him are other drummers and the dancers with their mediocre—and hypnotic—choreography. The camera opens, follows a cut, and registers faces, torsos, and arms of male and female dancers: bodies touching, their hands held high, white teeth in dark faces, their mouths confrontational. Close to the dancers, the camera follows the physical contact, the sweat, and ultimately the blood. In so many of the faces that parade on the screen, their mouths are emphasized: from the first face, recognizable as the famous Afrokán—his smile, his teeth—to the innumerable anonymous faces that sometimes blend together and almost always smile, revealing their teeth in half-open mouths. In this sequence of credits, the idea that "the confines between bodies and between the body and the world are overcome" is proven out.[13]

Make no mistake: we are at the very heart of the carnival. The disorder flows rhythmically and the sound track is integrated into an environment defined by the camera's instability: the handheld camera (the free cinema style that sets the documentary's tone is another point in common with *P.M.*) draws a zigzagging line full of anticipation. Guided through the multitude by this excited eye, we see an overflowing mass, the protagonist in a festive explosion where jubilation and violence seem predestined to come together. Then two, three shots are heard: a man falls, and while they lift him out of the puddle of blood where he has probably died, few people realize what has happened. The music and the dancing continue, the gestures and smiles become even more aggressive: in this carnival, like in all carnivals, the party is also a macabre celebration, merriment that is inseparable from the violent ritual of death. What then unfolds vertiginously before our eyes is the triumph of the carnival time: time of madness, leisure, and freedom. This is the collective party where the people act without limits, and where rejuvenation expressed through the theme of "birth-death-resurrection" is triumphant.[14]

The images in this sequence of credits "leave behind the feel of enigma, an unresolved tension which pervades everything that proceeds to unfold."[15] The carnival sequence returns, much later in the film, to be seen from another perspective. In this second version the band's Mozambique rhythm has been replaced on the sound track by an acoustic guitar solo. Coupled with the images of the multitudinous party and the undulating bodies, the new music creates incongruence; its inclusion emphasizes Sergio's confusion, as we discover that his lover has always accompanied him in the crowd. Disoriented, frightened by the violence that erupts near him, Sergio—who stands out for his European-like looks in a sea of blacks and mestizos—seems more like a discomfited witness than a willing participant in a peoples' festival.

I underscore an aspect of this initial sequence, which later in the movie is repeated from another angle. This is the placement of a white, bourgeois, indecisive intellectual in the midst of a carnival party, showing him at the height of his confusion before an act of extreme violence, a violence that in the midst of the carnival frenzy almost goes unnoticed, or regarded with in-difference by the other partygoers. Sergio, we are told in the movie, belongs but does not belong to that environment; he is there physically but he is a stranger, a distanced and fearful observer.

While the carnivalesque furor climaxes with the gunshots, the entire festi-val is a metaphor for the social upheaval that is taking place on the island: the violence that disorients Sergio is the violence of the revolution. Sergio's world has been overturned, unbalanced, by this violent convulsion that is soaked in sweat and blood; no one can now restore it to its prior state and at the same time no one can restore Sergio's social class to its dominant place in the social and cultural hierarchy.

Inarguably, *Memorias* is among the last of the extraordinary, transcendent projects of enduring influence dating from the late sixties in Cuban culture. Continuity can be established between this 1968 work and the artistic scene in real time (beginning of the sixties) in which the fictive narration takes place. The apogee of "Salomón," the censure of *P.M.*, the "Words to Intel-lectuals," and the closing of *Lunes de Revolución* are events that occur during the time span of *Memorias*. For Sergio Carmona, as for "Salomón," these inci-dents must have raised a great many questions.

I suspect that when Sergio refers to his "disagreeable lucidity," he expresses out loud what many Cuban intellectuals and artists, who like him witnessed the triumphant revolution, must have felt. After 1959, life placed them all in the vortex of a cataclysm that upended the geopolitical balance in Amer-ica and the world. Unlike Sergio, the distant and cynical figure created by Desnoes and Alea, and even unlike Chago's unpredictable and questioning "Salomón," the immense majority of artists, writers, and intellectuals who were present in Cuba in that faraway January gave of themselves generously, in body and soul, to that revolution: some for years, months, or weeks, others for their entire lives. Many of them—more or less successfully—attempted to transform their lucidity into creative brio, and from those attempts came works like the ones featured in this chapter.

Notes

Epigraph: Manuel Zayas, "Un baile de fantasmas: Entrevista a Orlando Jiménez Leal," *Encuentro de la Cultura Cubana* 50 (October 2008): 191.

1. José Rodríguez Feo, "El dilema de nuestra pintura," *Ciclón* 2, no. 2 (March 1956): 84. Unless otherwise noted, all translations are mine.

2. The name of this character is inspired by the "Movimiento 26 de Julio" (the July 26 Movement), the revolutionary organization led by Fidel Castro. He named it for the date in 1953 on which the members of this organization attempted unsuccessfully to seize two important army headquarters in Cuba's Oriente province, the Moncada and the Carlos Manuel de Céspedes.

3. Edmundo Desnoes, *Los dispositivos en la flor: Cuba; Literatura desde la Revolución* (Hanover, NH: Ediciones del Norte, 1981), 538.

4. Santiago Armada (Chago), *El humor otro* (Havana: Revolución, 1963), 6–7.

5. Augustin Redondo, "Tradición carnavalesca y creación literaria: Del personaje de Sancho Panza al episodio de la ínsula Barataria," *Bulletin Hispanique*, no. 80 (1978): 40–41.

6. Par Kumaraswami, "Cultural Policy and Cultural Politics in Revolutionary Cuba: Re-reading the *Palabras a los intelectuales* (Words to the Intellectuals)," *Bulletin of Latin American Research* 28, no. 4 (2009): 528–32.

7. Zayas, "Un baile de fantasmas," 191.

8. Kumaraswami, "Cultural Policy and Cultural Politics," 534.

9. William Luis, "Exhuming *Lunes de Revolución*," *CR: The New Centennial Review* 2, no. 2 (summer 2002): 274–77.

10. René Depestre, *Por la revolución por la poesía* (Havana: Instituto del Libro, 1969), 82.

11. Zayas, "Un baile de fantasmas," 191.

12. Mikhail Bakhtin, *Rabelais and His World* (Bloomington: Indiana University Press, 1984), 197–98.

13. Bakhtin, *Rabelais and His World*, 316–17.

14. Redondo, "Tradición carnavalesca y creación literaria," 41.

15. Michael Chanan, *The Cuban Image* (London: BFI Books, 1985), 237.

DISORDER AND PROGRESS IN
BRAZILIAN VISUAL CULTURE, 1959

In September 1959 Brazil hosted the annual meeting of the International Association of Art Critics (AICA). Titled "The New City—A Synthesis of the Arts" by the Brazilian art critic and intellectual Mário Pedrosa, the event was timely and utopian.[1] Sixty-five foreign delegates, including the organization's president James Johnson Sweeney, as well as many other members such as Meyer Schapiro, Giulio Carlo Argan, Bruno Zevi, and Tomás Maldonado, spent ten days touring the nation's three principal modern cities. First, in Brasília, President Juscelino Kubitschek presided over the initiatory session, even though the new capital, with modernist buildings designed by Oscar Niemeyer, was still under construction and would not be inaugurated for another seven months. The group then traveled to São Paulo for the opening of the V Bienal held in Niemeyer's Palace of Industry. The structure, a concrete box with glass walls and serpentine ramps throughout, was inaugurated just two years prior and was one of the newer buildings in the complex built in the recently rehabilitated Parque Ibirapuera. And finally, in Rio de Janeiro, the congress met at the Museu de Arte Moderna, despite the fact that only one of the museum's three projected buildings had been inaugurated. With sessions dedicated to such topics as fine art, architecture, urbanism, and art education, coupled with the dramatic backdrop of these modernist buildings, the delegates' attention was drawn to the cultural makeover Brazilians were carrying out.

Rio de Janeiro's Museu de Arte Moderna, AICA's third and final destination, was designed by the architect Affonso Eduardo Reidy. Boasting picturesque views of the city's famous landscape from its galleries, the complex sat at the water's edge of Guanabara Bay on freshly completed landfill, the

Aterro do Flamengo. There the congress initiated their activities with the vernissage of an Alexander Calder exhibition. The ambitious installation included thirty gouaches in the glassed-in gallery on the top level of the museum's School Block, and forty-four mobiles and stabiles placed outside on the surrounding terraces.[2] Not only was the installation remarkable for its use of interior and exterior spaces, calling attention to the potentiality of modernist architecture in a tropical climate, but the physical backdrop was also spectacular. Yet one cannot help but wonder why Calder, a famous sculptor from the United States, was selected to inaugurate the events in Rio. In every other respect, Pedrosa designed the congress's activities to showcase Brazilian achievements; Calder's prominence would seem to contradict the messages the organizers sought to convey. Although the reasons for this are manifold, the most important was that Calder was already well known internationally and his exhibition would have likely enhanced AICA's impression of the museum; the Museu de Arte Moderna was an institution that showed first-rate international art and was not reserved for Brazilian artists alone.[3] The itinerary and content of AICA's entire conference underscored one of the more prevalent desires on the part of Brazilians at that time: a celebration of nationalist achievements simultaneous with the embrace of postwar internationalism. These seemingly oppositional ideologies were perfectly united in many of the nation's most prominent cultural and political initiatives.

In 1959 Rio's modern art museum was still a relatively young institution.[4] Although founded in the 1940s, it was only in 1951 that Niomar Moniz Sodré assumed the directorship and scheduled exhibitions and programs on a continual basis.[5] Shortly thereafter she convinced city officials to donate a parcel on Rio's latest landfill as the site of the fledgling institution. She also persuaded Reidy, one of Brazil's most prominent modern architects, to design an elaborate complex of buildings. In 1958, with President Kubitschek at her side, Moniz Sodré unveiled the first building, the School Block.[6] However, the other two structures remained under construction for several more years as the Exhibition Block was not inaugurated until 1967 and the Theater Block was finally completed only in 2006.[7] It bears emphasizing that when Calder's exhibition opened for the AICA group in September 1959, the museum was still very much a construction zone.

The three cities on AICA's itinerary, Brasília, São Paulo, and Rio de Janeiro, were in various states of aggressive urbanization. The burgeoning domestic construction industry was a critical element in the dynamic and accelerated reconfiguration of Brazilian modernity on display for the art critics.[8]

These transformations, however, were fraught with complications and disruptions to everyday life. This chapter considers the discrepancies between the image of Brazil that was promoted as a modernizing nation with utopian aspirations and the actual confusion and disruption to daily life that was wrought by the very process of modernization. "Disorder and Progress" refers specifically to this state and draws from the positivist motto, Order and Progress, which appears on the national flag. My adjustment of the phrase is not intended as a critique but rather points out the polarity that describes Brazil's metropolitan centers in 1959, in their chaotic and disorderly march toward progress. Indeed, the image of Brazil has long been determined by dichotomies, going back to the first European imaginings in the sixteenth century when it was described as both a tropical paradise and dangerous land ruled by cannibals. The postwar period ushered in new contradictions, including the simultaneous embracing of nationalism and internationalism, as well as disorder and progress. This chapter points to a range of examples where these opposing concepts coalesced and converged in exhibitions, architecture, art criticism, and visual culture.

Calder's inclusion in the 1959 exhibition in Rio de Janeiro was also due to the way his unique formalism equally complemented the museum's architecture and the surrounding landscape, drawing the viewer's attention to the newness of the site both topographically and architecturally. In many of the photographs taken by Marcel Gautherot, one can see how the organic and geometric shapes of Calder's sculptures resonate with the curvilinear coastline of Guanabara Bay and the iconic silhouette of the Pão de Açucar, as well as with the rectilinear profile of the building and the shadows it cast in the intense tropical light.[9] The undulating arms on his sculptures synchronize with the subtle movements of the abundant flora in the coastal breeze on the Aterro do Flamengo, as designed by Roberto Burle Marx.[10] Certainly, Calder's work imagined the possibilities for successfully synthesizing art with architecture, thereby underscoring the theme of the AICA congress.

The resonance between Calder's sculptures and the natural landscape was interrupted, however, by Reidy's gargantuan Exhibition Block, which was under construction directly behind the sculptures and would have dominated almost every exterior view (see figure 13.1). As soon as someone circumambulated a sculpture, the Exhibition Block would have been impossible to ignore. Surprisingly, most of Gautherot's photographs documenting the exhibition manage to omit the Exhibition Block entirely.[11] And yet Calder's works harmonized with Reidy's unfinished modernist structure.[12] The angular bases of

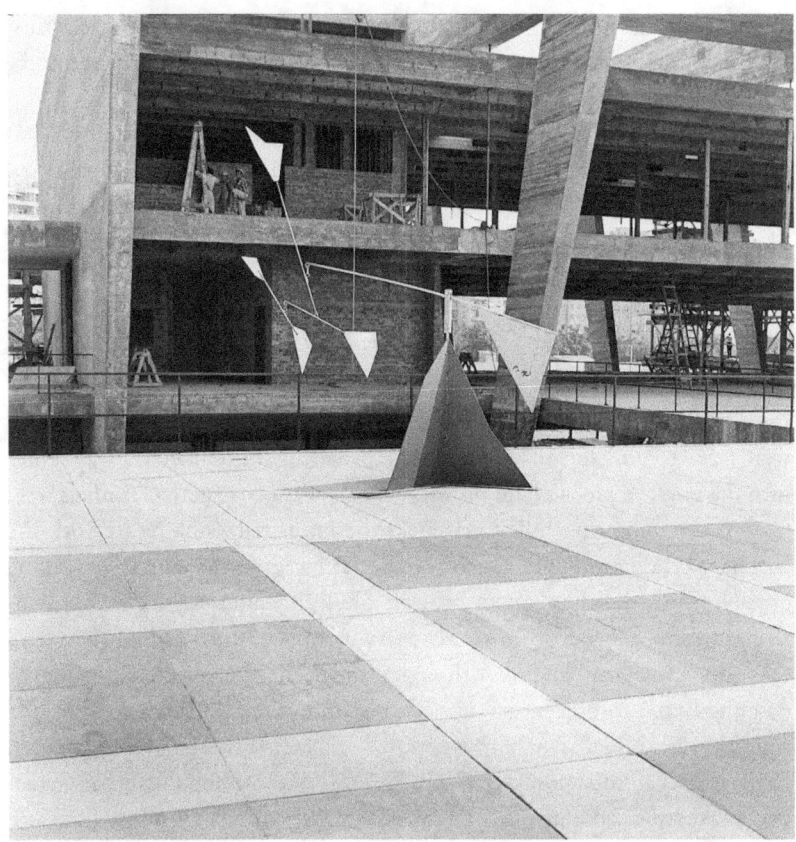

FIGURE 13.1 Marcel Gautherot, *The Museu de Arte Moderna's Garden during Alexander Calder Exhibition*, Rio de Janeiro, 1959. Collection of Instituto Moreira Salles, Rio de Janeiro.

the stabiles, with arms positioned at various diagonals, echoed the fourteen V-shaped ribs, the architectural hallmark of the campus, that extended the length of the building and served as an external framing device. Gautherot further emphasized this angularity by filling the lower half of the picture frame with the tiled terrace, so that the entire photograph has diagonals radiating in all directions. Moreover, the image is static and cannot capture the dynamic nature of the site. A constant stream of people, including foremen, engineers, and laborers, as well as city and museum officials, were coming and going from the construction zone. Machinery appeared and roared to life, as needed, only to be silenced and disappear later. In the photograph are silhouettes of workers, wooden scaffolding, ladders, sawhorses, pulleys, and cables, all of which would have been in constant motion during the work day, moving, lifting, foisting, and gradually placing the materials of modernist architecture—steel, concrete, and glass—into place. Despite what the photograph suggests, this site was not static but in perpetual motion.

By the end of the 1950s, building sites were increasingly ubiquitous and integral to the rapidly expanding urban landscapes of Brazil's principal cities, providing a potent visual symbol of the nation's rapid industrialization. In São Paulo, the city was under perpetual construction as it was transformed into Brazil's financial and industrial nerve center. Even soon-to-be bucolic spaces, such as the Parque Ibirapuera, home to the Bienal, had metamorphosed from a previously uninhabitable wasteland of run-off fluids from nearby slaughterhouses.[13] In Rio de Janeiro, new structures were erected and the city's topography was significantly altered.[14] Hills in the downtown area were razed to provide soil for the landfill project that extended the city center into the bay, the precise land on which MAM was constructed. Tunnels were blasted through other hills to connect the industrial Zona Norte with the beaches of the Zona Sul in an effort to better integrate the rapidly expanding city. Not only did these major projects physically alter cityscapes, but construction sites also occupied nearly every urban sightline, adding chaos and cacophony to quotidian life. Although utopian rhetoric is frequently used to describe Brazil at midcentury, it was a nation in the midst of a complicated transition and under actual construction.[15] Too often historians represent such projects only in their completed state. However, these ongoing urban makeovers taxed local populations in extreme ways. Associated noise, dirt, and odors permeated Brazilian urban life, overwhelming the senses of inhabitants and visitors alike, disrupting and complicating commonplace activities. Yet this reality was at odds with the perception circulated abroad. To the outside world, news of Brazil's building campaigns and cultural renovation was extraordinary, ultimately enticing AICA to travel there for its annual congress.

The most recognizable and audacious of all of these urbanisms was the planning and construction of the modernist city of Brasília, one of the most impressive symbols of Brazilian ingenuity and ambition.[16] Built from the ground up on an area of undeveloped land on the central plateau, Lúcio Costa's city plan and Niemeyer's modernist buildings were instant icons of Brazilian innovation (see figure 13.2). Costa and Niemeyer were already well regarded internationally for their roles in the creation of Brazilian modern architecture, which married Le Corbusier's principles of architecture and urbanism with the historical legacies and environmental conditions of the tropical nation.[17] Theirs was a wholly original, historically and regionally spe-

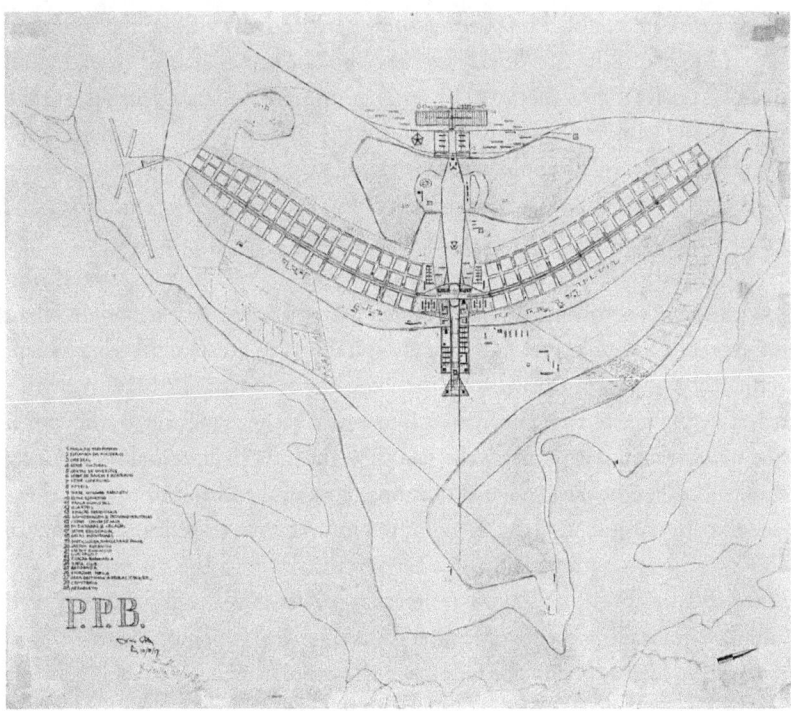

FIGURE 13.2 Lúcio Costa, *Plano piloto Brasília*, 1956. Collection of Lúcio Costa Archive, Rio de Janeiro.

cific, articulation of modernist architecture, and with Brasília they were given an extraordinary stage on which to present it to the world.

The building of Brasília was the fulfillment of a campaign promise made in 1955 by then-presidential candidate Juscelino Kubitschek and had both ideological and practical implications. Not only was it the embodiment of his slogan, "Fifty years of progress in five," but it was an opportunity for a tabula rasa and an antidote for the urban problems plaguing Rio de Janeiro, the historic capital since 1763.[18] Due to a national drive to shed Brazil's agrarian roots and industrialize the economy, many Brazilians left their rural homes and reestablished themselves in cities; between 1950 and 1960 the population of Rio de Janeiro grew from 2.3 million to 3.3 million inhabitants.[19] The coastal city had grown uncontrollably. This escalation in population caused many stresses on the city's services and accounted for the rapid growth of *favelas*.[20] Meanwhile in São Paulo, the situation was nearly identical. It was believed though, that these numerous and grave social ills would be avoidable in the new capital of Brasília because new perspectives could be incorporated into the fabric of the city. Social services could be provided more broadly and democratically if their modes of dissemination were integrated into the urban plan. City planners therefore focused on the idea of achieving an idealized circulation of goods, people, and services.

Brasília's meticulously thought-out transportation system, from the municipal bus network to a nationwide remapping of the roadways, is one example of this idealized circulation. With Rio de Janeiro's congested downtown and uncontrollable urban sprawl as an important reference point, albeit unfavorable, the objective in the new capital was to create perfectly efficient vehicular circulation throughout the city. The Residential Highway, which traverses the entire city, consists of fourteen adjacent lanes for traffic and is planned so that faster-moving vehicles utilize the interior lanes and slower, local traffic occupies the outer lanes. Additionally, all of the main thoroughfares are one-directional and, with the aid of ramps, underpasses, cloverleafs, and roundabouts, function without signals to keep traffic flowing. The automobile governed so much of the new city's design that pedestrians' needs were neglected and few sidewalks were incorporated into the plan, which ultimately would come to be seen as one of the failures of the utopian city.

For Kubitschek, one of the fundamental goals in founding Brasília was to establish a center of government that was equally accessible from all regions of the country, which would improve communication and travel between the individual cities and states and thereby create a more harmonious and unified nation. As economic, cultural, and political power had traditionally been concentrated in the South, particularly in the states and cities of São Paulo and Rio de Janeiro, the relocation of the capital to the interior was meant to destabilize the dominance of those locales. To further that end, there was a remapping of the country with the construction of a new network of thousands of miles of roads, built to link the various remote industrial, commercial, and agricultural regions with one another. For example, a newly constructed 2,500-mile arterial road connected the city of Belém in the far north with the southern state of Rio Grande do Sul, through Brasília. Brasília became the central node of an extensive hub-and-spoke national transportation system. However, rather than build multiple ports of arrival at the urban perimeter, where they are traditionally located, the bus station was located at the very center of the city where the two principal axes intersect.[21] The station was thus placed at the most central position possible, even more central than the seat of government, making this intersection a crossroad for anyone traveling by bus across the country or across town. Indeed, all local buses also made obligatory stops here. Kubitschek saw this feature as one of the most innovative and essential parts of the entire urban plan. It was such a priority that he insisted it be one of the few structures completed before the inauguration of the city.[22]

Costa's plan for Brasília was shaped like an airplane with two intersecting axes that represent the fuselage and the wings.[23] The Monumental Axis (the fuselage) houses the principal governmental and civic institutions, while the Residential Highway Axis (the wings) contains the dwellings and provides access to the interstate highway system.[24] The Praça dos Trés Poderes (Plaza of the Three Powers), located in the "cockpit," is home to the Supreme Court, the National Congress, and Palácio do Planalto, which houses the president's office. These entities reside in three of Niemeyer's most daring yet graceful architectural creations, in which he agilely integrated rectilinear and curvilinear form with smooth white surfaces. Niemeyer's curvaceous modern edifices were a defiant rejection of the Beaux Arts architectural style that had been used for government buildings in Rio de Janeiro. His designs were the formal antithesis of the traditional classical styles of the Biblioteca Nacional, the Teatro Municipal, or the Museu Nacional de Belas Artes, which framed Praça Floriano, one of downtown Rio's principal historic squares. All historical references seemed to have been erased from these buildings.[25] Instead, these new structures would host a perfectly efficient and democratic government. So confident were the planners of Brasília in the future success of these buildings and the city as a whole that no low-income housing was incorporated into the design, since they presumed that in the future, Brazilians would have no need for it.

The parabolas, domes, and arches Niemeyer designed were possible in Brazil for two main reasons, with one being construction codes that were far more liberal than in other places in the world. Significantly, the volume of concrete that was required over the steel reinforcing bars was approximately half the amount to that required in buildings constructed in the United States at the same time, which made slender walls and curvilinear forms possible.[26] The second reason why these unorthodox buildings were conceivable in Brazil was due to the incredibly low cost of labor and the near absence of workers' rights. In order to accommodate Kubitschek's accelerated timetable, construction took place twenty-four hours per day, seven days a week. The *candangos,* as the workers came to be called, worked long shifts often without days off.[27] It is ironic, then, that despite the planners' obsession with making

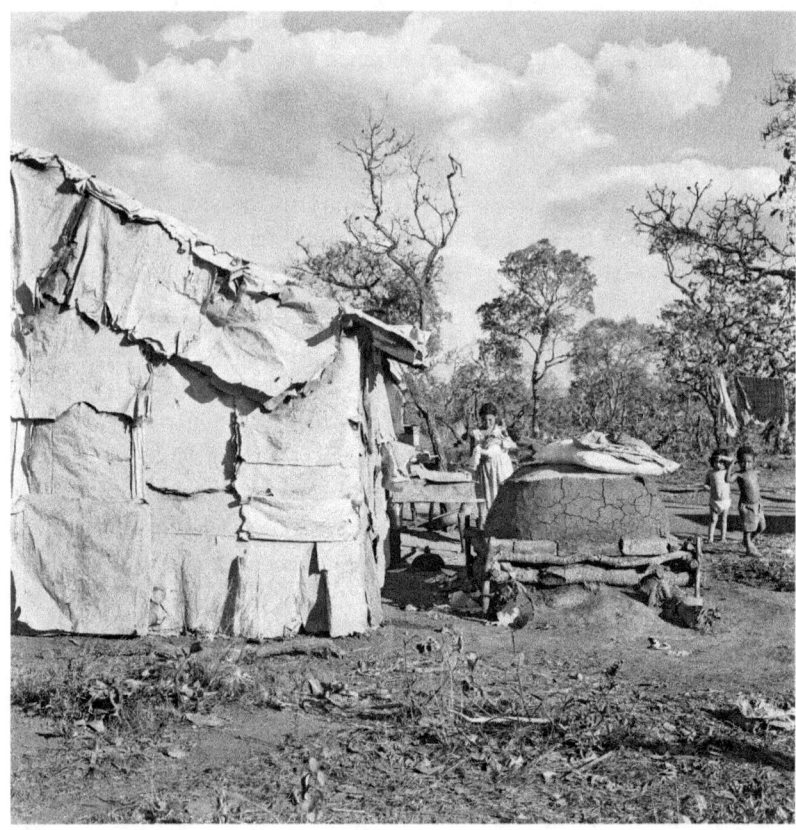

FIGURE 13.3 Marcel Gautherot, *House in the Suburbs, Sacolândia, Brasília*, 1959. Collection of Instituto Moreira Salles, Rio de Janeiro.

services easily accessible to the future population of Brasília, they neglected to take into consideration the needs of the candangos during the process of construction. These men had to build their own encampments where they lived during construction, assembling provisional dwellings out of cast-off materials from construction sites. Workers pilfered the empty sacks that the powdered concrete came in for the government buildings and draped them over the rudimentary frames of their small shacks, ultimately providing walls and roof. These places came to be known by such names as Sacolândia, or Bagland, and their inhabitants survived without even basic social services such as running water or electricity (see figure 13.3).

Despite the planners' obsession with systems of circulation and efficiency, these structures each required a high degree of specialized attention. Not

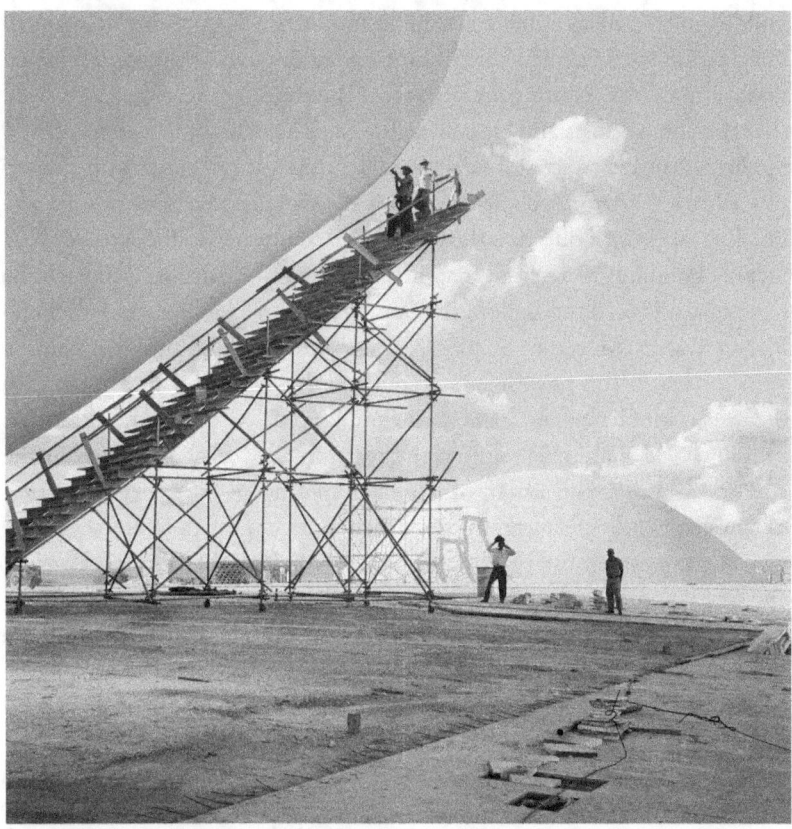

FIGURE 13.4 Marcel Gautherot, *National Congress, Brasília,* 1959. Collection of Instituto Moreira Salles, Rio de Janeiro.

only did each building, because of its unusual shape, necessitate customized scaffolding, but the smooth white concrete exteriors are an effect that must be achieved by hand. As Gautherot captures in his photographs of the construction of Brasília, scaffolding had to mimic the silhouette of the building so that workers, with finishing trowel in hand, could manually smooth the surfaces of the buildings (see figure 13.4). Indeed, despite the modernized appearances and the industrial ethos that was pervasive at the time in Brazil, these buildings were more like handmade sculptures than products of a truly developed nation, another example of the discontinuity between the perception and reality of Brasília.

Even though the site was physically removed from the urban centers of the south, and geographically difficult to reach while under construction, the building of the new capital took up an important position in the national imagination and occupied a significant role in the transformation of the national visual culture during the late 1950s. The entire Brasília enterprise, from the selection of Costa and his plan to the city's inauguration, was immensely publicized and it registered in the visual culture of the country in numerous ways. Even before people could visit the completed city of Brasília, the buildings were introduced to the public. For example, the silhouettes of Niemeyer's buildings and certain architectural elements, such as the parabolic form that was used throughout the Supreme Court building and Palácio do Planalto, were reduced to graphic symbols and started to proliferate in the visual culture.[28] This phenomenon is noteworthy in itself because it speaks to the way in which new modes of mass communication, such as the expansion of Radio Nacional, which during the 1950s finally reached all parts of the country, as well as the advent of television, promoted the wider circulation of news and images.[29] Furthermore, with the recent growth in literacy, many new magazines were established, including specialty publications such as art and architecture journals, and cultural supplements were added to newspapers. Simply put, there were many more outlets through which to spread the message of Brasília's potential and promise. Used widely in advertising in the late 1950s, these images signified not only the city of Brasília and Kubitschek's slogan but reinforced larger themes as progress, developmentalism, nationalism, and modernity.

The field of architecture and urban planning was only one field of many where profound changes were happening at the end of the 1950s. Describing the broader cultural landscape of this period, Paulo Venancio Filho writes: "Brazil wanted to be a new country for a new kind of man . . . the Brazilian fully emancipated from a patriarchal and enslaved past. It was for this new man that Brazilian artists created new architecture, painting and sculpture, literature, music and cinema. The keyword in the names of all the artistic movements of the day was 'new': Neo-Concretism in art, Bossa Nova in music, and Cinema Novo."[30] Visual artists, musicians, poets, and filmmakers were actively rejecting earlier national traditions throughout the decade, but it was in 1959 and 1960 that several of these movements crystalized.[31] By extension, the field of criticism grew simultaneously, filling the pages of the new magazines and newspapers. Equal in importance to the specific changes taking place in these arenas was the collaborative ethos of the period. Artists, critics, graphic designers, architects, poets, landscape designers, and filmmakers, among others, worked with each other and across traditional disciplinary boundaries, investigating a wide variety of materials and methods. As a result, many visual artists migrated between media, experimenting with painting, photography, graphic design, and three-dimensional forms, which included sculpture, installation works, and architecture to produce seemingly hybrid forms.[32] Moreover, in response to the ever-growing national industrial sector, many artists investigated the new technologies and industrial materials that were available and incorporated them into many of the visual works made in the late 1950s.

One of the best examples of this collaborative approach is the *Suplemento Dominical*, the primary site for the publication of reviews, criticism, manifestos, and debates among the members of the Brazilian avant-garde in the late 1950s.[33] Exemplifying how visual artists and poets collaborated and worked across media, in 1957 the poet Reynaldo Jardim, an editor at the *Jornal do Brasil*, invited fellow avant-garde artist Amilcar de Castro, a sculptor, to redesign the *Suplemento*.[34] De Castro conceived of a new layout for the paper, breaking with the traditional columnar format and approaching the page as a blank graphic space, juxtaposing empty areas with blocks of text and images, thereby creating a composition of geometric shapes in high chromatic contrast (see figure 13.5). Furthermore, he generated new graphic layouts each week depending on the content. In addition to art criticism and manifestos, the *Suplemento* frequently published works of Concrete poetry, photographs of exhibitions and artwork, as well as the work of regular contributors. As a result of its lively visual form as well as its radical content, the supplement is one of the most important works of Brazilian visual culture of the late 1950s. That de Castro, who was a sculptor and graphic designer, worked with Jardim, who was a poet and editor, to redesign one of the nation's premier newspapers is illustrative of the innovations that took place across the Brazilian cultural landscape in 1959.

The distinguished art critic and Concrete poet Ferreira Gullar was a regular contributor to the *Suplemento*, although at the time he was still a young instigator. Several of his most seminal texts appeared on its pages. Between March 1959 and October 1960, Gullar published more than four dozen essays in a series titled "Stages in Contemporary Art."[35] However, the title is somewhat misleading since these essays did not exclusively focus on contemporary art but instead dealt largely with the European avant-garde movements of the early twentieth century. Gullar's objective was to make European art history available to a wide audience of readers and covered a variety of areas including Cubism, Futurism, Russian Constructivism, Neoplasticism, Bauhaus,

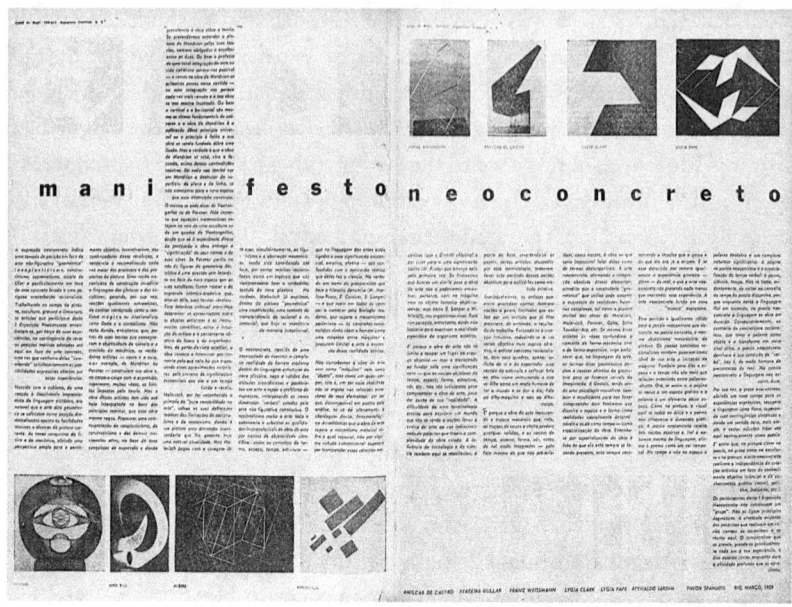

FIGURE 13.5 Amilcar de Castro (designer) and Ferreira Gullar (author), "Manifesto Neoconcreto," *Jornal do Brasil*, March 22, 1959. *Suplemento Dominical/Jornal do Brasil*, data, CPDoc JB.

Concrete art, and Brazilian Neoconcrete art. This was not a comprehensive history of art, nor even of the avant-garde, but was instead a carefully edited and teleological version or "new history" of the European vanguard, which all led, quite naturally, to Brazilian Neoconcretism, the only contemporary movement that Gullar addressed.[36]

The launch of Gullar's *Etapas* was timed to coincide with the opening of the *First Exhibition of Neoconcrete Art*, a landmark show staged at Rio's Museu de Arte Moderna, which appeared the same week that the "Manifesto Neoconcreto" was published in the *Suplemento*, penned by Gullar, designed by de Castro, and published by Jardim.[37] In addition to these three, Franz Weissmann, Lygia Clark, Lygia Pape, and Theon Spanudis also signed the manifesto. Within a few months the group had expanded.

In the *Etapas* as well as the "Manifesto," Gullar celebrated Neoconcretism as an aesthetic theory that not only originated in Brazil but also emancipated Brazilian artists from the European hegemony of the prewar avant-garde.[38] In Neoconcretism, he argued, artists created a new and authentically Brazilian approach to visual expression. In the manifesto he wrote, "We propose a reinterpretation of Neoplasticism, of Constructivism, and of various analogous movements, basing ourselves on their expressive gains and giving *precedent to the work rather than the theory.*"[39] Neoconcrete artists utilized the formal language of Art Concret, first theorized by the de Stijl artist Theo van Doesburg in 1930 and later proselytized by Swiss designer Max Bill, as a springboard for experimentation to create works that reintegrated expression into geometric abstraction. This principle is integrated into de Castro's layout in the *Suplemento*, which had ten columns of text, three large, open rectangular spaces, and eight small black-and-white reproductions of works: four by Europeans Nikolaus Pevsner, Max Bill, Josef Albers, and Kazimir Malevich, across the bottom lower left corner of the spread; and four by Brazilians Franz Weissman, Amilcar de Castro, Lygia Clark, and Lygia Pape across the top right of the page. Although it draws on geometry, it does not follow a rigid or prescribed order but rather reflects the designer's subjectivity. Gullar, like Kubitschek, Niemeyer, and Costa, believed he was witnessing the emergence of a new, modern, and culturally independent Brazil, a sentiment that registers in all of his texts from this period. In 1959 they were no longer laying the groundwork for a future nation but were watching it blossom.

Although he was not one of the original signatories, Hélio Oiticica was quickly incorporated into the Neoconcrete collective of artists and became one of the most critical members of the group. In 1959 he began a series of monochrome paintings in red and yellow in order to explore what he termed "metaphysical color." With these paintings he wanted to portray time, not space, and described his strategy for making a temporal work this way: "In order to do this I had to arrive at a one-color painting with various qualities, or change the direction of the brush strokes so that a single color could take on two aspects."[40] And indeed, on close inspection, one can still see traces of the brush: horizontal in the upper portion, and vertical in the lower, cleanly separated by a horizon line faintly running the width of the composition (see figure 13.6). Looking at the surface of this small monochrome painting, one has the sense of zooming in on the detail of a grid, with its perpendicular structure slowly coming into focus. Oiticica's "time" registers in this small object, which hangs on the wall like a painting but whose sides are also painted red, thereby emphasizing its three-dimensionality. The brushstrokes are indexical reminders of the process by which the work came into being, a rewarding visual experience for the slow and attentive viewer.

Oiticica, of course, was not working in isolation. He acknowledged the importance of foreign artists such as Piet Mondrian and Malevich, signaling his "reinterpretation of Neoplasticism, of Constructivism" mentioned in

the "Manifesto," at the same time that he was actively participating in a local avant-garde. His desire to create "metaphysical color" was aligned with other Neoconcrete artists who wanted to liberate geometric abstraction from the frame and pedestal and create expressive and intuitive forms that engaged with viewers phenomenologically. However, that the paintings in this series were deliberately and laboriously handmade out of traditional artist materials— an oil-casein emulsion on board—is at odds with the spirit of the day, which was committed to an aesthetics of industrialization. Most of the other Neo-concrete artists had been experimenting with industrial paints and supports for years. Yet Oiticica's *Red Monochrome* manages to slyly straddle this ideo-logical divide, reconciling the seemingly incompatible forces between the handmade object and the industrial product. In its chromatic uniformity, the painting looks, at first, like it could have been made with industrial tools and the paint applied in an even and regular fashion. Only on closer inspection are the traces of the artist's hand revealed. And it is on this level of very close inspection that Oiticica's small monochrome begins to feel like a handmade object, much like Niemeyer's buildings in Brasília. No matter how visionary Oiticica might have been, he was still a product of his place and time, Rio de Janeiro in 1959. His work's formal and material qualities cannot be separated from the sociopolitical conditions in which it was conceived, making it even more resolutely Brazilian. Indeed, no formal style, not even geometric abstraction, is ever truly neutral or universal—despite what artists such as Mondrian, Malevich, and Oiticica claimed—but is always motivated, expressive, and resolutely tied to the social and historical circumstances in which it emerged.

On April 21, 1960, Brasília was inaugurated as the new capital of Brazil. Although not all of the projected buildings had been completed, the fundamental principles of the urban plan as well as several of the most important edifices, such as the Supreme Court, the Metropolitan Cathedral, and the bus station, were already functional. In addition, the man-made Lago do Paranoá had been filled with water and the telephone lines were operating, only thirty-seven months after ground had been broken on the project. President Kubitschek defied expectations by adhering to the accelerated timetable he had set to build a new capital in the middle of the country's desolate Central Plateau in just three years. The populace had no knowledge of the reality of Brazil's grim future when a military coup took the reins of government in 1964 and oversaw the nation for the following two decades in an authoritarian style; in April 1960 Brazilians were still filled with optimism and energy. If, as the editors of this volume have suggested, there was a breathlessness and a pall of melancholy across the West in 1959, the Brazilian context represents an alternative scenario. Artists, designers, architects, poets, musicians, and critics responded enthusiastically to the contradictory nature of their rapidly changing and dynamic milieu. Despite the chaos and cacophony of daily life, as cities bulged with people and were built at breakneck speed, the mood was positively electric.

Notes

1. Details about this conference are available on the organization's website as well as in Mário Pedrosa's papers in the Biblioteca Nacional do Brasil, in Rio de Janeiro. Of particular help in writing this chapter was Henry Meyric Hughes, "Art Criticism Comes

of Age: Brasilia, AICA and the Extraordinary Congress of 1959," 8th DOCOMOMO Congress, Rio de Janeiro, Brazil, 2009, http://aicainternational.org/en/henry-meyric -hughes-art-criticism-comes-of-age-brasilia-aica-and-the-extraordinary-congress-of -1959/. The AICA is a nongovernmental organization that emerged after World War II and is affiliated with UNESCO (United Nations Education, Scientific, and Cultural Organization). The objective of this professional organization was to serve as a central body for those working in various capacities in the art world, including curators and critics as well as art historians and art educators. Members came together out of a sense of responsibility toward artists as well as the public, and because they wanted to communicate developments in the fields of art history and art criticism internationally. A significant amount of historical information can be found on their website, http:// aicainternational.org/en/.

2. This show, which ran from September 23 through October 25, is described and photo-documented in Roberta Saraiva, *Calder no Brasil: Crônica de uma amizade* (São Paulo, Cosac Naify, 2006), 199–201. This volume, published on the occasion of an exhibition of the same name at the Pinacoteca do Estado de São Paulo, exhaustively catalogs all of Calder's relationships and exhibitions in Brazil.

3. I have written about Calder's reception in Brazil and the logic behind his exhibition during the AICA Congress in "Traveling through Time and Space: Calder in Brazil," in *Calder and Abstraction: From Avant-Garde to Iconic* (Los Angeles: Los Angeles County Museum of Art; New York: Prestel, 2013).

4. My doctoral dissertation covers the founding and early years of this institution. Aleca Le Blanc, "Tropical Modernisms: Art and Architecture in Rio de Janeiro in the 1950s" (PhD diss., University of Southern California, 2011).

5. The founding of Rio's Museu de Arte Moderna is more or less contemporaneous with the founding of the previously mentioned Bienal de São Paulo in 1951, as well as the establishment of AICA in 1950.

6. Photographs of this event were published in many periodicals in Brazil, including *O Cruzeiro* and *Manchete*. Both were current-events magazines founded in the early 1950s that featured large-scale photographs paired with short articles about fashion, movies, and popular culture.

7. Descriptions and renderings of Reidy's plans, as well as his own writings about the complex of buildings for the museum, are available in Klaus Franck, *The Works of Affonso Eduardo Reidy* (New York: Praeger, 1960).

8. Numerous books have been written about Brazil's rapid economic development during the twentieth century. The following is only a small selection. Robert Jackson Alexander, *Juscelino Kubitschek and the Development of Brazil*, Monographs in International Studies, Latin America Series 16 (Athens: Ohio University Center for International Studies, 1991); Celso Furtado, *Development and Underdevelopment* (Berkeley: University of California Press, 1964); Luiz Carlos Bresser Pereira, *Development and Crisis in Brazil, 1930–1983*, Westview Special Studies on Latin America and the Caribbean (Boulder, CO: Westview, 1984); Thomas E. Skidmore, *Politics in Brazil, 1930–1964: An Experiment in Democracy* (New York: Oxford University Press, 1967).

9. In fact, the surrounding landscape was an important element in Reidy's design. His objective was to create a series of buildings that did not obstruct views of the bay, one of the reasons most of the second-story galleries have glass walls. Franck, *The Works of Affonso Eduardo Reidy*, 66–84.

10. Indeed, many of the titles of Calder's works refer directly to tropical vegetation, such as *Eucalyptus* (1940) and *Jacaranda* (1949).

11. Marcel Gautherot, a French photographer who relocated to Brazil in 1940, dedicated his career to photographing Brazilian architecture, both colonial and modern. He worked for the Serviço do Patrimônio Histórico e Artístico Nacional. His photographs of the building of Brasília are some of the most iconic images of the city. He also documented the construction of Rio's modern art museum and Calder's installation in 1959. Gautherot worked closely with many of the modern architects in Brazil, especially Niemeyer, documenting the process of construction. It is remarkable how the visual rhetoric of architecture photography is deployed in his images, similar to those by Julius Shulman in the case of Richard Neutra's buildings and Lucien Hervé's of Le Corbusier's structures. Marcel Gautherot, *O Brasil de Marcel Gautherot: Fotografias* (São Paulo: Instituto Moreira Salles, 2001); Marcel Gautherot et al., *As construções de Brasília* (Rio de Janeiro: Instituto Moreira Salles, 2010).

12. Although I have only seen a single image published that reveals the construction on the site, it is likely that there are more of these images at the Instituto Moreira Salles in Rio de Janeiro, where his archive is kept.

13. Personal conversation with Ana Gonçalves Magalhães, São Paulo, August 31, 2012.

14. Maurício de A. Abreu, *Evolução urbana do Rio de Janeiro*, 4th ed. (Rio de Janeiro: IPLANRIO, J. Zahar, 2008); Norma Evenson, *Two Brazilian Capitals; Architecture and Urbanism in Rio de Janeiro and Brasília* (New Haven, CT: Yale University Press, 1973).

15. The same can be said for the political situation. Kubitschek won the presidency with only 36 percent of the vote and over the course of the 1950s the "democratic" government was almost overthrown on multiple occasions.

16. Although there are many books about the architecture of Brasília, James Holston's text provides a very thorough anthropological reading of the creation of the city. James Holston, *The Modernist City: An Anthropological Critique of Brasília* (Chicago: University of Chicago Press, 1989).

17. Although Niemeyer had been preselected as the project's architect, Costa's city plan, referred to as the Plano Piloto, was only chosen in 1957 through a juried competition. Niemeyer and Costa had collaborated on several projects prior to the building of Brasília, dating back to the 1930s. Niemeyer and Kubitschek also had a preestablished relationship as they had worked together on an urban renewal project in the late 1940s. Kubitschek, then mayor of Belo Horizonte, hired Niemeyer to design and construct several municipal buildings in the suburb of Pampulha. Many consider this collaboration a dress rehearsal for Brasília. Celina Borges Lemos and Elizabeth A. Jackson, "The Modernization of Brazilian Urban Space as a Political Symbol of the Republic," *Journal of Decorative and Propaganda Arts* 21, Brazil Theme Issue (1995): 233.

18. Kubitschek was not the first to have the idea to build a new capital. In fact, there are at least two well-documented moments in Brazilian history when the idea of constructing a metropolis in the nation's interior came into the national consciousness. On the night of August 30, 1883, Dom João Bosco, an Italian priest, supposedly dreamed of a Promised Land located between the fifteenth and twentieth latitudes in Brazil and in 1891, the first Republican Constitution included a new capital in this location and set aside 14,400 square kilometers on the Planalto for this use. Holston, *The Modernist City*, 16–17.

19. Abreu, *Evolução urbana do Rio de Janeiro*, 115–35.

20. Costa and Niemeyer were both lifelong residents of Rio de Janeiro and had built their careers in the capital. They would have confronted the frustrations of the growing city on a daily basis at the precise time they were designing Brasília. Rio, therefore, is the most important urban reference point in the design of Brasília and it would seem that Costa and Niemeyer did everything they could to mitigate the coastal city's urban shortcomings. In 1956 the mayor of Rio de Janeiro was quoted in the *New York Times* as saying, "We are a besieged city. There is no water, no transportation, no food supply system, no usable thoroughfares, no hospitals, no schools. We have a deficient light, telephone and gas service, not enough homes for everybody, no room for recreation and no place to bury the dead." Tad Szulc, "Brazil's Capital a Bursting City: Rio de Janeiro Chops Hills and Fills in Bay to Find Space for Its Millions," *New York Times*, September 30, 1956. Found in University of New Mexico, Special Collections, Latin American News Clippings, Brazil folder.

21. Holston, *The Modernist City*.

22. Holston, *The Modernist City*.

23. It is worth noting that Brasília is one of the few planned cities in the world carried to fruition. The two other famous planned cities, both capitals, are Canberra, Australia, whose design was selected in 1913; and Chandigarh, the capital of the Indian state of Punjab. Le Corbusier was selected to design this city in 1951.

24. This description comes principally from Holston, *The Modernist City*. Despite the highly organized plan, the effect is rather disorienting on the ground (versus an aerial view). In addition to the cloverleafs and roundabouts, many of the streets curve and so it is difficult to retain North-South-East-West orientation. Additionally, it is impossible to quickly correct any directional errors one might commit. If one misses a turnoff, it will take considerable negotiating to find another turnoff and return to the original point. Moreover, because each neighborhood is uniform, differentiation becomes difficult. Holston points out that "it is almost impossible to give practical directions because there are very few memorable reference points . . . even long time residents regularly have difficulty finding the location of a place even though they . . . have been to it many times." Holston, *The Modernist City*, 138, 149.

25. Niemeyer has acknowledged that Brazilian Baroque architecture of the eighteenth century was an important reference point in his creations because he understood it as an entirely Brazilian creation free of European intervention, a status he strove for in his own designs.

26. Adrian Forty, *Concrete and Culture: A Material History* (London: Reaktion, 2012), 120–29.

27. Advertisements were placed on the radio and in the newspapers calling the nation's unskilled labor force to come and help construct Brazil's future. In 1957, when construction began, it is estimated that 2,500 workers were in residence, and by 1959, the year that AICA visited, between 50,000 and 80,000 candangos were contributing to the effort.

28. Fernando Luiz Lara, *The Rise of Popular Modernist Architecture in Brazil* (Gainesville: University Press of Florida, 2008), 9.

29. Francisco de Assis Chateaubriand started Brazil's first television station, TV Tupi, which took its name from one of Brazil's indigenous groups, in São Paulo in 1950, and began broadcasting from Rio de Janeiro in 1951. He owned the media conglomerate Diarios Associados, which also included newspapers and magazines. He also founded the Museu de Arte de São Paulo in 1947. As Paulo Herkenhoff writes, the expansion of Radio Nacional was the "most important bridge uniting the whole country." Paulo Herkenhoff, "Rio de Janeiro: A Necessary City," in *The Geometry of Hope: Latin American Abstract Art from the Patricia Phelps de Cisneros Collection*, ed. Gabriel Pérez-Barreiro (Austin: Blanton Museum of Art, University of Texas at Austin, 2007), 53.

30. Paulo Venancio Filho, "Rio de Janeiro 1950–64," in *Century City: Art and Culture in the Modern Metropolis*, ed. Iwona Blazwick and Tate Modern (London: Tate Publishing, 2001), 182.

31. Bossa Nova, a style of music frequently described as a blend of Brazilian Samba and American Jazz, also emerged in the late 1950s. Musicians composing in this style rejected the polished commercial products of an earlier era and instead favored dissonance and instrumental experimentation. Christopher Dunn, *Brutality Garden: Tropicália and the Emergence of a Brazilian Counterculture* (Chapel Hill: University of North Carolina Press, 2001).

Young filmmakers, based largely in Rio de Janeiro, looked to the examples of Italian neorealism and French New Wave cinema, combining European avant-garde models with some of the grittiest of Brazilian subjects, such as the *favela* and the *sertão*, to create a new national cinema. Robert Stam, *Tropical Multiculturalism: A Comparative History of Race in Brazilian Cinema and Culture* (Durham, NC: Duke University Press, 1997), 157.

Architecture is a somewhat unique situation and different from the other examples given. The modern style of architecture exemplified by the work of Oscar Niemeyer, Lúcio Costa, and Affonso Reidy, among others, employed in the fifties had already gained acceptance in the thirties and forties.

32. This collaborative ethos is not unique to the postwar period but a hallmark of much Brazilian production. In the 1920s, members of the *modernismo* generation, such as composer Heitor Villa-Lobos, poets Mário de Andrade and Oswald de Andrade, sculptor Victor Brecheret, and painter Tarsila do Amaral, collaborated with one another in publications and exhibitions.

33. The *Jornal do Brasil* ceased publication of the supplement in 1961. It is probable that it was the result of the death of the journal's owner, who championed the *Suplemento Dominical*, but whose nephew was not interested in it.

34. De Castro was a graphic designer by trade and worked for numerous other publications in Rio de Janeiro. He was employed at the *Jornal do Brasil* until 1961. Reynaldo Jardim collaborated with other artists as well. Most notably he worked with Lygia Pape on her *Neo-Concrete Ballets*, performances staged in 1958 and 1959. Yanet Aguilera, ed., *Preto no branco: A arte fráfica de Amilcar de Castro* (São Paulo: Belo Horizonte, Discurso Editorial, Editora UFMG, 2005), 86.

35. Ferreira Gullar, *Etapas da arte contemporânea: Do cubismo à arte neoconcreta* (Rio de Janeiro: Editora Revan, 1998).

36. Irene Small, "Exit and Impasse: Ferreira Gullar and the 'New History' of the Last Avant-Garde," *Third Text* (February 2012): 91–101.

37. Ferreira Gullar, *Experiência neo concreta: Limite da arte* (São Paulo: Cosac Naify, 2007).

38. Of course, Gullar was, perhaps unconsciously, deeply invested in European theories of the avant-garde that championed rupture with convention and prized originality.

39. Ferreira Gullar, "Neo-Concrete Manifesto," *Jornal Do Brasil* (March 22, 1959), reprinted in *Readings in Latin American Modern Art*, ed. Patrick Frank (New Haven, CT: Yale University Press, 2004), 173; emphasis mine.

40. Mari Carmen Ramírez and Luciano Figueiredo, *Hélio Oiticica: The Body of Color* (London: Tate Publishing, in association with the Museum of Fine Arts, 2007), 190, 361.

THAT TINGLING SENSATION
1959 and William Castle's *The Tingler*

The 1950s was a tumultuous decade for American cinema. With the downfall of the classical Hollywood studio system, new modes of film production and exhibition emerged. In the aftermath of this turmoil appeared William Castle's *The Tingler* in 1959. This film today might appear as an anachronism, attracting interest as a remarkable one-off film that belongs to a foregone era. More importantly, *The Tingler* calls for scrutiny not merely as a nostalgic reminder of outmoded forms of entertainment; the film presents an innovative juxtaposition of potentials inherent to cinematic practices that have since been left aside by later trends and tendencies within the motion picture industry.

The Tingler stars Vincent Price as Dr. Warren Chapin, a pathologist who makes the discovery that the site of fear is literally located in our spine. When we experience fear, a parasite inside the spine is nourished and grows, causing a tingling sensation. Naturally, the parasite is named "the tingler." The only way to still the growth of the tingler is to let out a scream when experiencing the sensation of fear. If you fail to let out a scream, certain death is imminent. This premise lays the foundation for the film's prologue, when William Castle, the producer and director of the film, appears on screen, directly addressing the audience. He delivers the following monologue:

> I am William Castle, the director of the motion picture you are about to see. I feel obligated to warn you that some of the sensations—some of the physical reactions which the actors on the screen will feel—will also be experienced, for the first time in motion picture history, by certain members

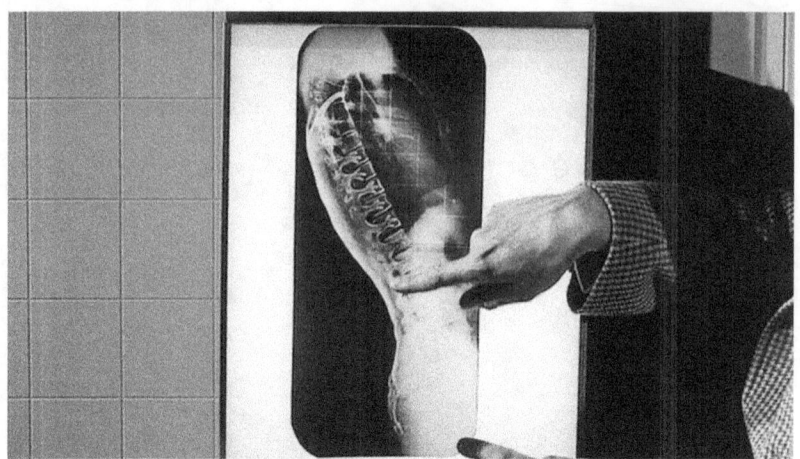

FIGURE 14.1 William Castle, *The Tingler*, 1959. Publicity still.

of this audience. I say "certain members" because some people are more sensitive to these mysterious electronic impulses than others. These unfortunate, sensitive people will at times feel a strange, tingling sensation; other people will feel it less strongly. But don't be alarmed—you can protect yourself. At any time you are conscious of a tingling sensation, you may obtain immediate relief by screaming. Don't be embarrassed about opening your mouth and letting rip with all you've got, because the person in the seat right next to you will probably be screaming too. And remember—a scream at the right time may save your life.

The audience is advised to scream—indeed, to scream for their lives. The tingling sensation described by Castle is not caused solely by audiovisual stimuli: in the first-run screenings of *The Tingler*, small motorized vibrators were implanted in a number of seats in the theaters. Triggered during key sequences of the film, these vibrators would help to further along the screams by giving unsuspecting audience members a jolt to the spine. This gimmick, labeled "Percepto," became an imperative part of the film's marketing campaign. Besides Percepto, and its vibrating seats, Castle would customarily hire a young woman to feign fainting during the climax of the film, causing a preplanned stop in the exhibition for her to be carried out of the theater and attended to by medical personnel.

In terms of exhibition and audience address, Castle followed a format close to the traveling side show or carnival, promoting gimmicks and showman-

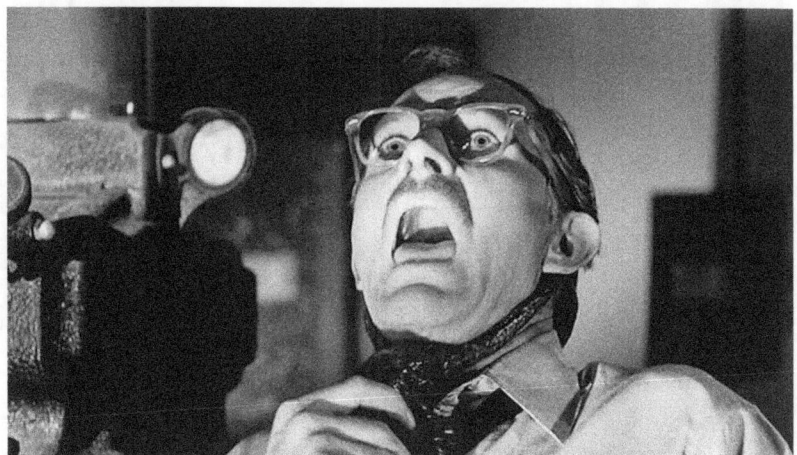

FIGURE 14.2 William Castle, *The Tingler*, 1959. Publicity still.

ship. As noted by *Variety* magazine: "The film abounds in hokum, camouflaged in science, and it has been successfully gimmicked to insure maximum exploitation."[1] This emphasis on exploitation and (extra)cinematic attractions locates *The Tingler* in the midst of a transitional era in the American movie industry where filmmakers sought new avenues leading audiences back into movie theaters.

New Attractions and the End of an Era

The 1950s marked the end of the classical Hollywood studio era.[2] The system of vertical integration came to an end following the Paramount decree of 1948, and the Hollywood production model was furthermore under challenge from the lower costs associated with movie production outside the studio lots.[3] At the same time, audience numbers were diminishing rapidly due to factors such as the advent of television, which went together with the baby boom and young families settling in the suburbs. Whereas in the classical era audience turnout was more or less guaranteed and the studios produced movies in an assembly-line manner, films increasingly came to be financed and produced as individual package units, often by independent producers.[4]

Under the earlier studio system, motion pictures were divided into A and B features. The A productions were the most expensive, attractive, and prestigious, with well-known film stars, lavish sets, and top-notch directors and personnel. These films received top billing in theaters and were the ones to harvest the major profits as well as audience acclaim and recognition. Billed alongside these A studio productions were the B movies, cheaply made genre pictures produced by the major studios or by small independent companies such as Republic or Monogram.[5]

Outside this circuit, at the bottom of the movie industry, operated a relatively small group of producers, distributors, and exhibitors of what came to be known as exploitation films. Produced on a shoestring budget, these films offered sensational and often atrocious topics and imagery. Films on sexual hygiene and reproduction, crime, illegal drugs, exotic cultures, and other sensational fare were presented as lessons to be learned about social ills and curiosities. To lure audiences to their productions, exploitation filmmakers had to offer something not to be found in mainstream movies such as nudity, violence, or drug use. The only ways such explicit visual imagery could be displayed were by providing socially redeeming and educational information about factual matters and potential dangers lurking in society. Films such as *Birth of a Baby* (1938) or *Mum and Dad* (1945) could, under the guise of teaching the biological facts of life, portray actual live human birth and thus also human genitals—imagery out of reach for mainstream Hollywood productions. Unlike more earnest educational films, exploitation films operated solely on a commercial basis and their educational messages were not backed by any authentic imperative to improve the living conditions of the masses. Audiences were, for the most part, in on the scheme, seeking out exploitation films for the sake of entertainment and titillation rather than any genuine search for socially redeemable information.[6]

This three-tier division between A studio films, studio and independent B films, and independent exploitation films was paramount throughout the studio era. The three categories were separated in terms of factors such as budgets, production schedules, use of sets, and access to skilled personnel behind and in front of the camera. Each category had a look and style distinct from the others. Besides differences in production value, the films also differed in content. While the A and B movies were fictional narratives, the exploitation films relied heavily upon factual content and the sensational exposure of shocking "truths." Also, the films differed in terms of marketing, distribution, and exhibition. A movies and B movies were exhibited together as double bills. The A movie, being superior in terms of production value and big-name stars, was the main attraction, while a B movie was designed to fill the bottom half of the bill.[7] Exploitation films, on the other hand, were channeled through separate chains of distribution and exhibition. Unlike the B movies, exploitation films had to be marketed in their own right; they had to create enough of a buzz to attract audiences into the theaters. As Eric Schaefer explains in his study of classical exploitation films, "lacking conventional narratives, stars, or genres with which to sell their films, exploitation producers relied on a marketing address that transposed to paper the key attributes of their films: spectacle in the form of education or titillation."[8] The exploitation film itself was often only one of many features of a carnivalesque exhibition event where the audience experience of witnessing an exploitation roadshow would differ dramatically from attending a regular mainstream double bill. According to Schaefer: "The act of seeing a film during the heyday of the exploitation roadshow was like attending the theater, the carnival, and the lecture hall. Exhibition of exploitation films was far from orderly. Films stopped and started for lectures and book pitches. Depending on the type of exploitation movie being shown, a range of 'unacceptable' responses could emanate from the audience, including hooting, groans, fainting, vomiting, and more."[9] Both as a spectacular exhibition event and as a cinematic style, the exploitation films differed from Hollywood products—a distinction that was obvious to these films' original audiences.

Schaefer explicitly links the centrality of spectacle in exploitation films to the "cinema of attractions," as defined by Tom Gunning.[10] This concept was developed in relation to particular emergent tendencies within early cinema. Prior to around 1906, Gunning argues, the cinema of attractions was the dominant format for motion pictures before it eventually became subordinated to a cinema dominated by narrative. Early filmmakers like the Lumière brothers and Georges Meliès saw cinema "less as a way of telling stories than as a way of presenting a series of views to an audience."[11] The relation to the viewer here is key, for the cinema of attractions is characterized by "its ability to *show* something."[12] These exhibitionist tendencies of the cinema of attractions are, according to Schaefer, "at the heart of exploitation."[13] He stresses that it is through their focus, as Gunning states, upon "exhibitionistic confrontation rather than diegetic absorption"[14] that classical exploitation producers managed to "differentiate their films from the mainstream."[15] The divisions between fiction and nonfiction were "consistently erased" in the exploitation film, as these films repeatedly assured "that their audience would 'See! See! See!' Fiction and nonfiction merged in the classical exploitation film, and spectacle served as their organizing and unifying principle."[16] This exhibitionistic address to the audience depends upon what Gunning in his comments on the cinema of attractions describes as "arousing and satisfying visual curiosity through a direct and acknowledged act of display."[17] In various ways, more or less integrated within some sort of narrative or message, the classical exploitation films attracted their audiences through spectacles markedly different from the classical Hollywood films.

As the era of classical Hollywood cinema was forever shattered in the 1950s, the era of the traditional B pictures and the classical exploitation films also came to an end and the divisions between exploitation and mainstream features became less clearly defined. In this terrain, hybrids of B movies and exploitation films emerged, where primitive modes of production were often reminiscent of exploitation films, while at the same time sticking to a format of fictional genre pictures in the tradition of the earlier B movies.[18] The new independent films were low budget and formulaic but differed from the B movies in terms of distribution and exhibition. These films were not being targeted toward the bottom half of a double bill and often utilized different chains of distribution than the studio productions.[19] No longer benefitting from the luxury of a guaranteed audience or the appeal of an attractive A feature on the top of a double bill, these films had to attract their audience through marketable gimmicks or exploitative elements.[20] Produced independently or by companies such as American International Pictures (AIP) or Allied Artists, new kinds of motion pictures flourished. Genres such as horror and monster movies, science fiction, teenage romances, and rock 'n' roll pictures gained popularity, explicitly targeting the emerging teenage demographic.[21]

The films' sensationalism and spectacular imagery could now take on an explicitly hedonistic tone, without any socially redeeming merits. Imagery of a sensational and titillating nature could be integrated within fairly traditional narrative formats, as can for instance be seen in monster movies such as *I was a Teenage Werewolf* (1957) or *Attack of the Crab Monsters* (1957). Further, the marketing of these films would be as important as their content, which could result in titles, posters, and trailers promising far more than the films could actually offer.[22] *The Tingler* emerged in this new terrain, drawing inspiration from B horror movies about monsters and mad scientists, while at the same time being organized around spectacles to be exploited in the film's promotion. Unable to compete with the high-end pictures in terms of sheer production value and star quality, *The Tingler,* in line with the classical exploitation films, went in another direction, offering something completely different in order to attract its audiences.

This drive toward gimmicks and technological novelties was not unique to low-budget independent productions of the 1950s. New methods and devices for film production and screening had already been around for some years but it was not until the 1950s that these were fully utilized, as Hollywood studios tested a number of technological advances and experiments in order to differentiate their product from what was on offer through the television screen.[23] Widescreen formats and color, displaying spectacular vistas and scenery, were a key attraction of major studio productions of the mid to late 1950s. Perceived and marketed as a more participatory mode of cinema, the widescreen format would enmesh the spectator in a sensory environment.[24] Films such as *Ben Hur* (1959) and *The Ten Commandments* (1956) were made for the big screen, emphasizing the experience of the cinema as distinct from television. This was even more obvious with the short-lived 3-D craze of the 1950s, starting with *Bwana Devil* in 1952 and culminating with titles such as *House of Wax* in 1953 and *Creature from the Black Lagoon* in 1954. Although an initial success, 3-D quickly faded away partly due to the increase in costs for exhibitors.[25] More low-budget gimmicks such as Psychorama (insertion of subliminal images) or AromaRama (smell) were applied by small-scale producers, with moderate success. William Castle attempted to fully explore the artistic as well as commercial potential of such stunts. Having already established a career as a B movie director, in the late 1950s, Castle made his name as a producer and director of horror movies[26] helped along by his skills in showmanship and marketing as much as by the qualities of his movies.[27] His two films preceding *The Tingler*, *Macabre* (1958) and *House on Haunted Hill* (1959), were both accompanied by marketing stunts that foreshadowed the spectacular gimmicks he put in motion for *The Tingler*.

In *Macabre*, Castle took out a life insurance policy from Lloyd's of London against anyone in the audience dying of fright during the film's screenings.[28] This policy was exploited in the film's marketing alongside gimmicks such as Castle arriving at the theaters inside a coffin in a hearse, having uniformed nurses in attendance inside the theaters, as well as having an ambulance outside, to take care of any panic-stricken audience members.[29] The campaign was a success, and, unsurprisingly, no one in the audience actually happened to die. For *House on Haunted Hill*, Castle came up with a gimmick he labeled "Emergo" where a glowing plastic skeleton would seemingly float about in the theater during the climactic scene of the film.[30] But none of these gimmicks could match "Percepto," Castle's spectacular idea for *The Tingler*. More importantly, while for both *Macabre* and *House on Haunted Hill* the gimmicks were made after the production of the film itself was finalized and thus went unnoticed by the events unfolding within the films' diegetic universes, such was not the case with *The Tingler*. Already in *The Tingler*'s production phase, Castle set up a dynamic interaction between events unfolding on the screen and in the theaters during the film's screening. What makes *The Tingler* unique is the close interplay between gimmick and diegesis, and its exploration of the interrelations between events on the screen and audiences in the theater. The gimmicks were not merely a marketing stunt but were closely integrated with the film's formal structure and mode of audience address.

The Tingler and Audience Address

The story of *The Tingler* revolves around the character of Dr. Chapin and his research into the physiology of fear. Fear is here represented by the organism of the tingler and given a visual presence in the shape of a lobster-like monster. The climax of the film happens when the tingler escapes the human body and roams about on the loose. This takes place in an apartment above a movie theater where the tingler flees under the floorboards, enters the theater below, and attacks unsuspecting patrons during the screening of an old silent movie. Panic unfolds. The tingler then disappears and the screen goes black. A voice emerges, declaring that the tingler is loose in the theater. Only this time the events do not take place in the theater on the screen but in the "real" theater where *The Tingler*—the movie—is being screened. During this intermission, mayhem unfolds in the theater: seats start vibrating and a woman faints and has to be carried out, before the tingler is captured and the movie can continue. Of course, everything is part of the show.

During this intermission the attention shifts from the screen to the theater, and an experiential event is generated through the relations unfolding between the people present. Staged scenes and unexpected reactions intersect and audience members become participants in the events that unfold. This participatory aspect sets *The Tingler* apart from other marketing gimmicks introduced in the 1950s. Although technological advances like widescreen formats and 3-D were promoted as participatory innovations, the mode of audience participation was that of an individual spectator enmeshed within the spectacle on display. Widescreen formats and, to an even greater extent, 3-D, enclose the individual audience member off from the surrounding space and enhance the connection between spectator and screen. With 3-D, the eye-screen relation becomes encapsulated, and other visual distractions guarded

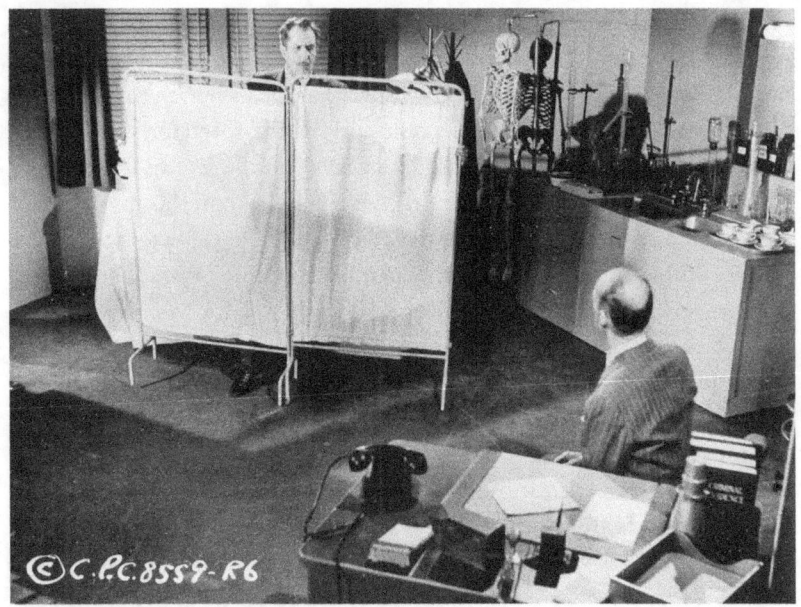

FIGURE 14.3 William Castle, *The Tingler*, 1959. Publicity still.

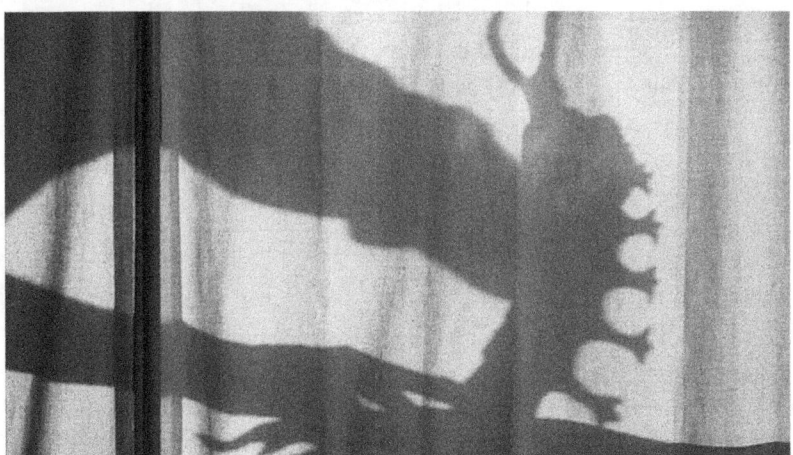

FIGURE 14.4 William Castle, *The Tingler*, 1959. Publicity still.

off. The film exhibition takes the form of a series of individual spectator experiences rather than a shared, collective event. Each viewer experiences the film on their own, in the role of a pacified spectator. In a similar vein, technologies such as Cinemascope and Technicolor put the spectator in a position of awe, while taking in the spectacular imagery on the screen. One relation is enhanced, while others are shielded away. Television in this historical period became a site of distracted viewing, accommodating interaction between viewers during shows, while cinema increasingly turned toward an isolated experience of individual spectatorship.[31]

In contrast to such high-tech endeavors, Castle's gimmicks, especially Percepto, are of a social nature and work all the better when experienced collectively. Percepto establishes a relationship between the events on the screen and the audience members in the theaters, while addressing the audience as a collective. To an even stronger degree than Castle's other gimmicks, Percepto is enacted through the relations between members of the audience. As screams and other visceral reactions are provoked by the vibrations in the seats by a few, this experience is communicated to others in the theater, and a chain reaction is triggered. Interactions among audience members are encouraged rather than prohibited. In this regard, *The Tingler* falls closer to the traditional exploitation film than to Hollywood's technological adventures of the 1950s. Similar to the earlier exploitation roadshow tradition, *The Tingler* functions more in the vein of the carnival than the passive spectator event—both in terms of its collective nature and in terms of its emphasis on active participation.

Psycho

This emphasis on audience participation can be contrasted with that of another and far more influential film from this period: Alfred Hitchcock's *Psycho* (1960). Following a string of major film productions during the 1950s such as *Rear Window* (1954), *Vertigo* (1958), and *North by Northwest* (1959), Hitchcock was at the peak of his career. Further helped along by the success of the ongoing television series *Alfred Hitchcock Presents*, Hitchcock was one of very few movie directors at the time to become a household name. The stamp of a "Hitchcock picture" was a marketable force in its own right.[32]

As Linda Williams argues, *Psycho* "fundamentally altered viewing habits" of American audiences upon its release in 1960.[33] As an advertising stunt, Hitchcock implemented a policy that would allow no one to enter the theater after the screening of *Psycho* had begun. Immensely successful, this stunt would have a lasting influence in terms of disciplining American cinema audiences into arriving at a specific time in order to catch a movie from beginning to end. Previously, audiences would enter and exit the theaters throughout the opening hours, often arriving midway through a film and then catching up with its beginning during the next screening.[34] With *Psycho*, audiences would arrive on time and patiently wait in line before the start of the movie. They would then enter and exit the theater collectively, and the same group of people would be present throughout the screening from beginning to end. In addition, *Psycho*'s trailers and marketing stressed the importance of letting the film remain a mystery; audiences were strongly discouraged from telling anyone the details of the film's plot.[35]

Further, *Psycho*'s visual style put the audience in a position of spectatorship. Hitchcock's choices in terms of lenses and camera positions were made to mimic a "natural" mode of seeing[36]—as if the spectators were to look in on real-life events unfolding in front of their eyes—thus establishing a voyeuristic spectator position. This positioning of the subject became a familiar and characteristic trope of Hitchcock to be found in several of his earlier as well as later films, such as *Rear Window* and *The Birds*. *Psycho*'s mode of exhibition encouraged individual viewing experiences. This is not to say that the film does not provide visceral pleasures. According to Williams, *Psycho* "does mark the important beginning of an era in which viewers began going to the movies to be thrilled and moved in quite visceral ways, and without much concern for coherent characters or motives."[37] Williams points to Gunning's concept of "cinema of attractions" to describe this renewed interest in the display of visceral sensations that would supplant narrative and characters as its main audience appeal; this constitutes a key characteristic of what Williams labels "postmodern cinema" that she traces back to *Psycho*. In her words, "*Psycho* thus needs to be viewed as a film for which disciplined audiences arrived on time in order to be attentively absorbed into the filmic world and narrative, and in which distracted 'attractions' of the amusement-park variety are equally important."[38]

The cinematic attractions evoked by *Psycho* are of a distinctly different nature than the attractions of earlier exploitation cinema. Gunning himself draws a distinction between the attractions of avant-garde and early cinema (or, for that sake, early exploitation cinema), opening for experiments with ways of shocking, moving, and disturbing the audience, and what he labels as the "tamed attractions" of contemporary special effects–driven action spectacles.[39] What Gunning finds lacking in contemporary blockbusters is a willingness to explore the radical potentials of the attractions put on display. Rather, in contemporary cinema, the attractions tend to be reintegrated within the film's narrative structure and discursive terrain. The attractions, which are of a conservative nature, startle and titillate but carry no impetus toward change. Rather than disrupt, the attractions thus function in support of the film's narrative structure. This synthesis of attractions and narrative integration within popular cinema serves to maintain a balance, to keep attractions subdued and carefully calculated. Although startlingly original compared to most of the later sensational blockbuster endeavors, *Psycho* opened a path toward a new mode of organizing attractions and integrating them within a narrative structure. The film puts its audience in a position of spectatorship, voyeuristically gazing at the events on the screen, while experiencing the sensations of watching macabre scenes of murder, titillating sexual imagery, and startling narrative twists. Indeed, in *Psycho*, the spectacular events are all integrated within the film's tightly constructed plot. Everything is neatly packaged together and Hitchcock's orchestration is superb in manipulating the audience's responses. As Hitchcock himself stated when interviewed by François Truffaut: "I was directing the viewers. You might say I was playing them, like an organ."[40]

Playing the Audience

According to Williams, *Psycho*'s paradigmatic position as a forerunner of the postmodern blockbuster is established through its successful integration of attraction and discipline; the film offers visual pleasures in a sensational and visceral manner where audiences are led from one intense moment to the next. The sensations triggered by *Psycho* are closely bound within the film's narrative structure, for the extradiscursive conditioning of the film's screening further emphasizes and strengthens the relations between the spectators and the diegetic events on the screen. *The Tingler*, on the other hand, follows a radically different formula. Although this film depends upon spectacular attractions, it is not accompanied by a disciplinary regime in the way of *Psycho* and later blockbusters, where the sensational elements neatly join together as an integrated whole and where audiences are put into individualized positions of spectatorship. This is not to say that *The Tingler* is free of any tendency toward disciplining its audience, but its mode of address and establishment of relations toward the audience operate in a different manner and enable greater potential for more varied and unforeseeable reactions and engagements.

The mode of address in *The Tingler* is not voyeuristic. It does not place the audience in a position of spectatorship, taking in through their eyes events unfolding on the screen that are beyond their control. Rather, the film establishes connections with its viewers, reaching out and involving the audience in its actualization. These connections are multisensory and not predetermined from the screen. *The Tingler* operates through embodied, haptic, and auditory responses generated through the physical space of the theater as much as through visual images projected on the screen. The impact and appeal of the film stem from how its images and participatory gimmicks operate together in triggering audience reactions. The question then becomes what the film sets in motion and how it brings about connective potentials. In other words, what is important is what *The Tingler* triggers and how it affects the experiences of viewers present during the screening. The main appeal of the film is visceral and interactive, and it evokes reactions that are not fully reintegrated within the film's narrative and discursive constitution. Its attractions are not tamed. *The Tingler* takes the audience along on a ride, the destination of which is not fully determined in advance.

This is not to say that the film's plot and storyline is irrelevant. Quite the opposite. The imperative question, however, concerns how the audiovisual images on the screen potentially connect with the events in the theater. What happens when the tingler roams about in the theater is a breach in the separation between audience and diegesis, between spectator and screen. Nonetheless, this situation is conditioned by the preceding events and composition of the film—starting from the film's marketing campaign and followed by William Castle's on-screen introduction, before the audience is invited into the film's plot and fictional universe. The film's sensational elements operate within—or rather, enter relations and connections with—discursive formations.

After being presented with the premise of a tingler that can potentially be lethal, the audience initially follows the discovery of the tingler within the universe of the film. When the tingler then escapes, the film comes to a halt and a "live" event unfolds in the movie theater. A warning is heard over the loudspeakers, seats vibrate, screaming ensues—which provokes more screaming—a woman faints, and so on. The resulting visceral reactions and effects are not dependent upon whether people in the audience actually believe in the real existence of the tingler or not. Most likely they do not believe.

The affective and interactive impact of the tingle is not merely a matter of interpretation. The effects of the tingler are not determined by its signifying content. An analysis of the signification or meaning of the object of the tingler in this film would not fully explain the film's impact and the radical singularity of its mode of audience address.[41] *The Tingler* operates materially and relationally. The tingler, as a physical object, *does* things within the film's diegetic universe, as well as in relation to the film's audience.

While the audiences are willing participants and the film conditions their interactions and responses, this is a very different form of conditioning than the disciplinary regime implemented by *Psycho*. Through startling images, vibrating seats, and interactive events, *The Tingler* actively encourages and accommodates screams and other physical reactions at given moments in the film. These reactions are not reintegrated into the film's narrative and signifying structures. The film climaxes at the moment of mayhem when the tingler escapes and flees into the movie theater, before the theater eventually calms down as the tingler is captured and the film comes to an end. The ending ties the narrative together after the preceding tumultuous outbreak. However, this does not tame the sensational attractions unfolding during the tingler's escapades in the theater. A status quo is not restored. The audience is left energized and bewildered. The film leaves a rush, leading many to return to the theater to experience the film yet again, and each experience might be different from the next.[42] In this sense, the film is made anew during each performance. No two screenings are alike.

While the tingler is on the loose, the audience's relation to the screen is disjointed and new sets of relations erupt. Through these relationships, a myriad of interactive practices unfold. The visceral sensations experienced by the audience are conditioned by the film's narrative and discursive constitution without being fully reintegrated within signifying formations where audiences can make sense of these experiences. The film may come across as a bewildering experience. The vibrations, screams, and tumbling bodies provoke further reactions among audience members and a process is set in motion where the film sets up events that can only be actualized in the movie theater. What the film sets in motion are affective potentials rather than fully realized responses. This contrast can be understood through Gilles Deleuze's distinction between *actualization* and *realization*. Realization, for Deleuze, is the making real of already existing possibilities that does not bring anything new into the world. Actualization, on the other hand, operates according to potentials, not possibilities. Unlike the possible, the potential is not already defined but can rather bring different realities, taking unforeseen and unknown directions. Hence it is "difference that is primary in the process of actualization."[43] This potential for difference is arguably the unique quality of *The Tingler*'s mode of audience address. While the sense-attractions evoked by *Psycho* are contained, captured by the signifying grid established by the film's discursive structure, the affective potentials evoked by *The Tingler* resist such categorizations. The screams and turmoil provoked by *The Tingler* evoke reactions in different directions. Furthermore, these reactions shift and change as the relations within the theater unfold. Even for an audience member who anticipates the staged gimmicks, the final outcome cannot be predicted. Screams, laughter, and other embodied reactions intermingle with the staged happenings, and the result is a potentially unpredictable and open-ended event.

The Tingling Subsides

The Tingler was in many ways a cinematic dinosaur, a dying breed of attractions ill-suited for later modes of cinema exhibition and distribution, as well as for the model of spectatorship that eventually became imperative from *Psycho* onward. By labeling *The Tingler* as a cinematic dinosaur, I explicitly position the film in the tradition of the traveling roadshow and classical exploitation cinema, and thus as distinct from later trends exemplified by Gene Youngblood's concept of *expanded cinema*.[44] Devoid of visionary philosophical ideas or new media technologies, Castle's gimmicks belong to what Youngblood would dismiss as "commercial entertainment" lacking in artistic value. Rather than seeking to transcend the human condition, Castle stands as an example of a filmmaker who, according to Youngblood, "copies, repeats, or imitates that which already exists within the grasp of the so-called average man."[45] Youngblood's hyperbole misses sight of the transformative powers of copying, repetition, and imitation, where a film like *The Tingler* could, by reassembling familiar elements, provide for potentials for the actualization of new and unexpected events. What makes *The Tingler* unique is its combination of elements of the 1950s sensational horror genre with the classical exploitation roadshow, with live gimmicks and the promotion of audience participation.

Today, contemporary movies, such as *Avatar* (2009) and other recent high-tech gimmicks, are closer to the tradition established by *Psycho* than the potentials exemplified by *The Tingler*. A captivating 3D-spectacle, *Avatar* takes each audience member along on a ride, from one thrilling and sensational moment to the next, but where you have no influence on the outcome, and, most importantly, where your experience is isolated from the experiences and reactions of others present. Like *Psycho*, *Avatar* and similar contemporary blockbusters provide joys and pleasures, although accompanied by a disciplinary regime. Of course, this does not say that these films necessarily operate in a disciplinary manner. Considerable interpretative leeway is possible, and the films can be incorporated and utilized in a number of different settings, with different potentials. Nonetheless, the audience members are positioned in a unidirectional relationship to the screen, where their main role is to process the information on offer. The extratextual conditioning of the cinematic experience further emphasizes the position of individual spectatorship, where the key information is provided from the screen, not from other members of the audience. Contemporary cinema multiplexes, as pointed out by Julian Hanich, offers audiences a movement toward individualization and absorption to an even greater extent than earlier venues for movie viewing. These tendencies are codependent and provide for an experiential realm where each isolated viewer is invited to be absorbed even more strongly into the atmosphere of the film, something that again further increases the individualization of the viewer.[46]

This situating and conditioning of the spectators differ markedly from the experience of a film like *The Tingler*. The joys and pleasures provided by *The Tingler* are not located solely *within* the film's diegetic universe but rather established through an interactive and dynamic relationship between the screen (audiovisual informational content), the theater (material infrastructure), and the people present (concrete social participants). The disciplinary regime offered by *The Tingler* is centered on making the audience members into willing, and enthusiastic, participants in this interactive relationship. Without the audience's participation, the collective experience would be stifled. The audience members are thus not conditioned into a position of passive recipients but are rather partakers of their own, collectively mediated, pleasures. Indeed, these pleasures are dependent upon disciplinary conditioning but, unlike films in the tradition following *Psycho*, this conditioning is fundamentally interactive. Audience members are invited, indeed encouraged, to actively partake in the creation of the cinematic experience. The film provides raw materials and instructions on how to enact and assemble these into an enjoyable experience, where the eventual actualization is left to the audience members.

Although later films have accommodated a certain degree of audience participation during screenings—most notably *The Rocky Horror Picture Show* (1975)—these films tend to take the form of a ritual more than a potentially open-ended event, often being as predictable as the screening of any mainstream movie. The potential exemplified by *The Tingler* points in a different direction, where surprise is one of its main elements of attraction. When going to see *The Tingler*, you would not know whether your seat would start vibrating, you would not know the reactions of the person sitting next to you, and you would not know how these events would intersect and create chain reactions between those present. The film would provide potentials whose actualization would be inflicted by a number of shifting factors and relations. Regardless of whether these potentials were actualized, or whether the screenings turned into stale rituals where audiences would scream on cue, *The Tingler* did point in a different direction for American cinema—a potential for a cinema radically different from the cinema of the disciplined individual spectator.

The Tingler designates a historical moment when it was still not quite determined what a cinematic experience would be like, and the film exemplifies other potential routes that the motion picture industry could have followed. The experiments with gimmicks and new modes of audience address in the American film industry during the mid to late 1950s were not one uniform movement but pointed in different directions, with different potentials for spectatorship and audience involvement. *The Tingler*, with its ties to the traveling roadshow, provided for a unique combination of the participatory and the open-ended. However, these same ties also indicate why the potentials pointed to by *The Tingler* were unable to traverse into the modes of cinematic production and exhibition that were to follow. Unlike the sleek attractions offered by *Psycho*, that could easily be assembled into a product readily available for mass distribution and standardized exhibition practices, *The Tingler* remained a one-off product, too cumbersome and unpredictable to be replicated in the era of the blockbuster.

Notes

1. "The Tingler," *Variety*, July 29, 1959.

2. Thomas Schatz, *The Genius of the System: Hollywood Filmmaking in the Studio Era* (New York: Pantheon, 1988.

3. Under the system of vertical integration, the Hollywood studios were in charge of production, distribution, and exhibition of their movies. This practice, where studios

would operate their own theaters, booking their own productions, were deemed to be a violation of antitrust legislation, and as a result the studios were required to divest their exhibition venues. Severing exhibition from production and distribution meant that the studios were no longer guaranteed a venue to book their films. This further raised the stakes in terms of financial risk for movie productions. See Thomas Doherty, *Teenagers and Teenpics: The Juvenilization of American Movies in the 1950s* (Philadelphia: Temple University Press, 2002), 16–17; Robert Sklar, *Movie-Made America: A Cultural History of American Movies* (New York: Vintage, 1994); Schatz, *The Genius of the System.*

4. Schatz, *The Genius of the System,* 435, 469–70; Janet Staiger, "The Package-Unit System: Unit Management after 1955," in *The Classical Hollywood Cinema: Film Style and Mode of Production to 1960,* ed. David Bordwell, Janet Staiger, and Kristin Thompson (London: Routledge, 1985), 330–37; Blair Davis, *Battle for the Bs: 1950s Hollywood and the Rebirth of Low-Budget Cinema* (New Brunswick, NJ: Rutgers University Press, 2012).

5. Charles Flynn and Todd McCarthy, "The Economic Imperative: Why Was the B Movie Necessary?," in *Kings of the Bs: Working within the Hollywood System; An Anthology of Film History and Criticism,* ed. Todd McCarthy and Charles Flynn (New York: Dutton, 1975), 13–43; Eric Schaefer, *"Bold! Daring! Shocking! True!": A History of Exploitation Films, 1919–1959* (Durham, NC: Duke University Press, 1999); Davis, *Battle for the Bs.*

6. Schaefer, *"Bold! Daring! Shocking! True!"*

7. Flynn and McCarthy, "The Economic Imperative," 14–15; Davis, *Battle for the Bs.*

8. Schaefer, *"Bold! Daring! Shocking! True!,"* 105.

9. Schaefer, *"Bold! Daring! Shocking! True!,"* 122.

10. Schaefer, *"Bold! Daring! Shocking! True!,"* 77.

11. Tom Gunning, "The Cinema of Attraction[s]: Early Film, Its Spectator and the Avant-Garde," in *The Cinema of Attractions Reloaded,* ed. Wanda Strauven (Amsterdam: Amsterdam University Press, 2006), 382.

12. Gunning, "The Cinema of Attraction[s]," 382.

13. Schaefer, *"Bold! Daring! Shocking! True!,"* 77.

14. Gunning, "The Cinema of Attraction[s]," 384.

15. Schaefer, *"Bold! Daring! Shocking! True!,"* 78.

16. Schaefer, *"Bold! Daring! Shocking! True!,"* 79.

17. Tom Gunning, " 'Now You See It, Now You Don't': The Temporality of the Cinema of Attractions," *Velvet Light Trap* 32 (September 1993): 3–12.

18. Kjetil Rødje, "Seeing Red: Blood Images in American Cinema, 1958–1969" (PhD diss., Simon Fraser University, 2011).

19. Flynn and McCarthy, "The Economic Imperative," 34–35.

20. Doherty, *Teenagers and Teenpics,* 30.

21. Doherty, *Teenagers and Teenpics,* 30.

22. This practice was often reflected in these films' mode of production. In the early days of AIP, a director like Roger Corman could at times be offered the task of directing a movie, as cheap and fast as possible, based on an already predesigned poster and

title. See Roger Corman and Jim Jerome, *How I Made a Hundred Movies in Hollywood and Never Lost a Dime* (New York: Delta, 1990), 26; Mark Thomas McGee, *Faster and Furiouser: The Revised and Fattened Fable of American International Pictures* (Jefferson, NC: McFarland, 1996), 54.

23. Doherty, *Teenagers and Teenpics*, 21–22; Sklar, *Movie-Made America*, 283–85; John Belton, *Widescreen Cinema* (Cambridge, MA: Harvard University Press, 1992); David Bordwell, "Widescreen Processes and Stereophonic Sound," in *The Classical Hollywood Cinema: Film Style and Mode of Production to 1960*, ed. David Bordwell, Janet Staiger, and Kristin Thompson (London: Routledge, 1985), 358–64; Davis, *Battle for the Bs*, 25–27.

24. Belton, *Widescreen Cinema*, 187–96.

25. Kevin Heffernan, *Ghouls, Gimmicks, and Gold: Horror Films and the American Movie Business, 1953–1968* (Durham, NC: Duke University Press, 2004).

26. Castle himself describes going to see Henri-Georges Clouzot's 1955 horror film *Diabolique* (*Les Diaboliques*) as a turning point. Enjoying the movie immensely, and observing the exhilarated reactions from screaming kids in the theater, Castle reached the conclusion that "young audiences are starving for this type of picture, and I want to be the one to satisfy their hunger." William Castle, *Step Right Up! I'm Gonna Scare the Pants Off America* (New York: Pharos, 1992), 134.

27. See Castle, *Step Right Up!*; David Sanjek, "The Doll and the Whip: Pathos and Ballyhoo in William Castle's *Homicidal*," *Quarterly Review of Film and Video* 20, no. 4 (2003): 247–63; Heffernan, *Ghouls, Gimmicks, and Gold*.

28. Castle, *Step Right Up!*, 137–39.

29. Doherty, *Teenagers and Teenpics*, 138; Sanjek, "The Doll and the Whip," 251; Castle, *Step Right Up!*, 144–45.

30. Castle, *Step Right Up!*, 147–48; Doherty, *Teenagers and Teenpics*, 138; Sanjek, "The Doll and the Whip," 254.

31. The 1950s was the heyday of the drive-in theater, a mode of exhibition that accommodated distracted and collective viewing practices more closely associated with television than with the new technological experiments associated with the production and exhibition of Hollywood productions of the time. While the drive-in was ill-suited for high-budget endeavors, it provided a key exhibition outlet for the new breed of sensational youth pictures that emerged in the 1950s. See Doherty, *Teenagers and Teenpics*; Heffernan, *Ghouls, Gimmicks, and Gold*.

32. Schatz, *The Genius of the System*, 482–83.

33. Linda Williams, "Discipline and Fun: Psycho and Postmodern Cinema," in *Reinventing Film Studies*, ed. Christine Gledhill and Linda Williams (London: Arnold, 2000), 351. Or in the words of Thomas Schatz, *Psycho* "was one of those rare movie experiences that forces viewers to rethink the very nature of narrative cinema and of screen entertainment." Schatz, *The Genius of the System*, 489.

34. This practice would live on in more marginal and alternative film exhibition practices, where the films would often merge together with other activities within the exhibition space—a practice perhaps most infamously exemplified by the porn

and exploitation theaters around Times Square in New York. See Samuel R. Delany, *Times Square Red, Times Square Blue* (New York: New York University Press, 1999); Bill Landis and Michelle Clifford, *Sleazoid Express: A Mind-Twisting Tour through the Grindhouse Cinema of Times Square* (New York: Simon and Schuster, 2002).

35. The gimmick of not letting anyone into the theaters after the start of the movie was thus also motivated by its plot, as the presumed main character, Marion Crane (Janet Leigh), is killed off early in the movie. This element of surprise would be lost to audiences wandering in halfway through the film. See François Truffaut, *Hitchcock* (New York: Simon and Schuster, 1966), 206.

36. Stephen Rebello, *Alfred Hitchcock and the Making of "Psycho"* (New York: Dembner Books, 1990), 93.

37. Williams, "Discipline and Fun," 356.

38. Williams, "Discipline and Fun," 366.

39. Gunning, "The Cinema of Attraction[s]," 387.

40. Truffaut, *Hitchcock*, 206–7.

41. For one analysis, see Mikita Brottman, "Ritual, Tension, and Relief: The Terror of *The Tingler*," in *Planks of Reason: Essays on the Horror Film*, ed. Barry Keith Grant and Christopher Sharrett (Lanham, MD: Scarecrow, 2004), 265–82.

42. For instance, the filmmaker John Waters recalls gleefully how repeat visits to watch *The Tingler* upon its initial release constituted the "fondest moviegoing memory" of his youth. John Waters, *Crackpot: The Obsessions of John Waters* (New York: Vintage, 1987), 17.

43. Gilles Deleuze, *Bergsonism* (New York: Zone Books, 1991), 97.

44. Gene Youngblood, *Expanded Cinema* (New York: Dutton, 1970).

45. Youngblood, *Expanded Cinema*, 67.

46. Julian Hanich, *Cinematic Emotion in Horror Films and Thrillers: The Aesthetic Paradox of Pleasurable Fear* (New York: Routledge, 2010), 57–58.

ATOPIC ATOMIC
Piero Manzoni's Space-Age Subtext and the "Ins and Outs"
of the Modern Intellectual

This is the art I prefer. The one I think we'll need tomorrow. Clean, neat,
without rhetoric, that doesn't lie, that doesn't flatter.
—*La dolce vita,* 1960

In early December 1959, Piero Manzoni's drawing *Linee* formed the inaugural
exhibition of his newly founded Galerie Azimut in Milan (see figure 15.1).
Undeniably radical, the *Linee* (or *Lines*) have come to exemplify Manzoni's
split from the nuclear painters in 1959 and his subsequent rejection of pictorialism and painting. Since his unexpected death in 1963, Manzoni's works
post-1959 have been lauded for their prescient anticipation of minimalist,
conceptual, and performative strategies. Described as "the last of the avant-
garde,"[1] the posthumous placement of Manzoni's works within a teleological
trajectory of twentieth-century avant-garde movements has tended to evacu-
ate their historical and cultural specificity in favor of analyses of the artist's
antagonistic stance toward consumer culture and the reification of the art
object.[2] But what if there was, in the middle of Manzoni's neo-avant-garde
tactics, an alien invasion of pictorial proportions? What could a series of extraterrestrial invaders have come to tell us about Manzoni's anti-aesthetic *Linee*
or egg-eating performances? Could they recast our understanding of his role
as progenitor of postmodern art? Would their sci-fi futurity require us to be
more attentive to Manzoni's historical present?

    In fact, such an invasion exists. In 1960, a year after the exhibition of the
Linee, Manzoni produced a series of thirteen drawings that are alien both
in relation to his recent antipictorial turn and in relation to their explicit

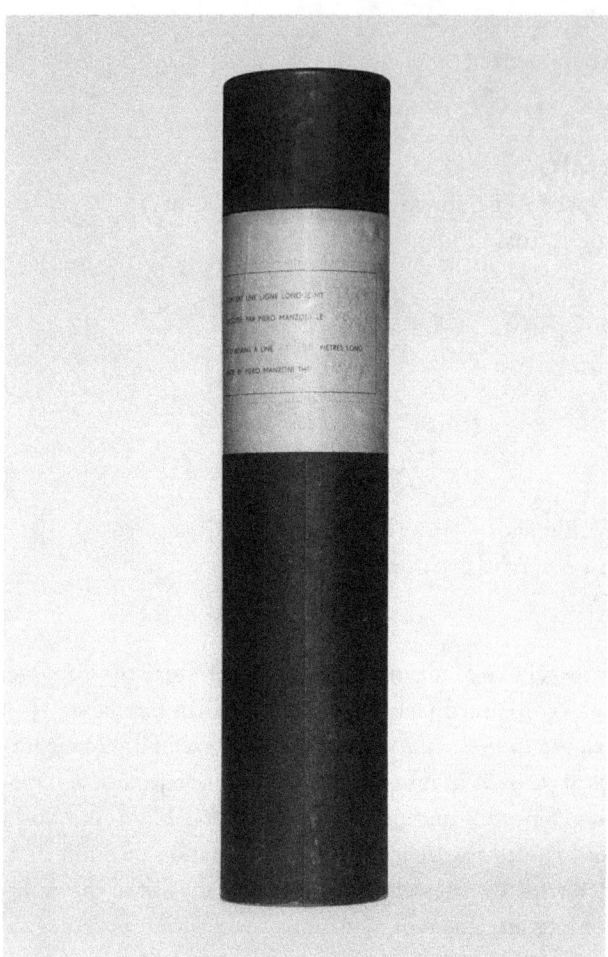

FIGURE 15.1 Piero Manzoni, *Linee m. 33,63* (*Lines 33.63 m.*), 1959. Ink on paper in cardboard cylinder. Collection of Archivio Opera Piero Manzoni. © DACS 2015.

references to outer space (see figures 15.2 and 15.3). Hovering humanoid figures are depicted frontally, emphatically, in undiluted black ink. Their heads are as round as astronaut helmets and antennae ascend and descend from the ears toward the earth and sky. Below the head, a long neck or torso is bisected by legs or limbs that curve downward as though frozen in place like the wings of a hovercraft, leaving an ambiguous protrusion that is alternately phallic or testicular. The titles of these drawings suggest that the figures are more human than alien. There are two self-portraits of Manzoni in *Io e il "mio gatto*

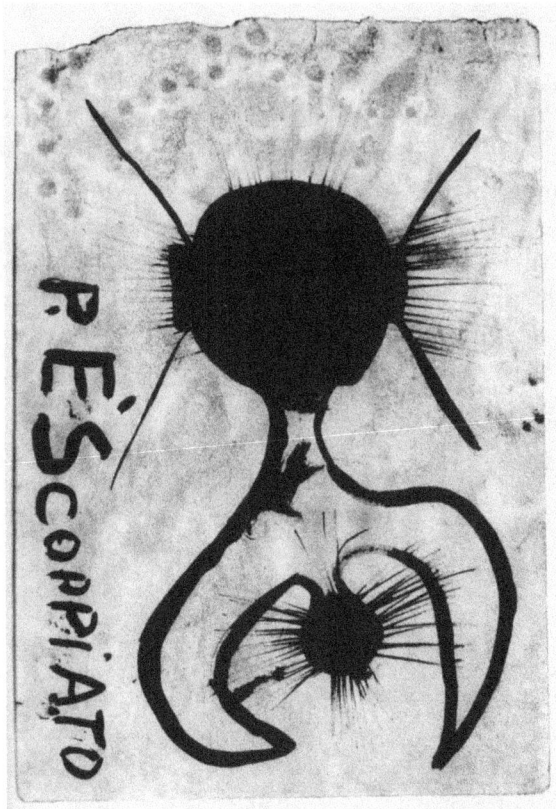

FIGURE 15.2 Piero
Manzoni, *P. è scoppiato*,
1960. Ink on paper.
Collection of Archivio
Opera Piero Manzoni.
© DACS 2015.

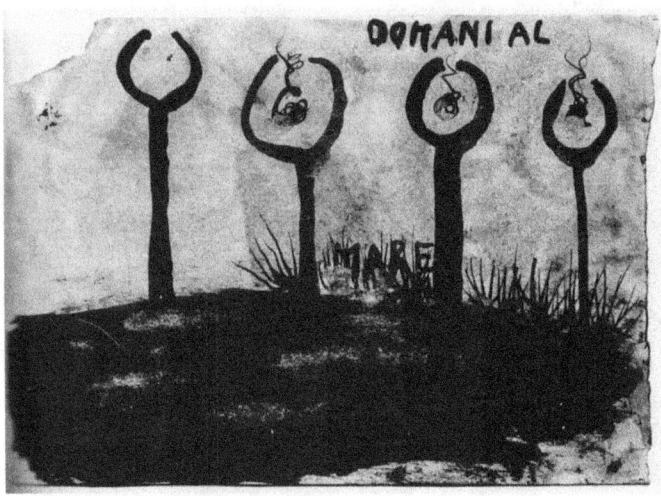

FIGURE 15.3 Piero Manzoni, *Domani al mare*, 1960. Ink on paper. Collection
of Archivio Opera Piero Manzoni. © DACS 2015.

(*Me and My Cat*) and *P. è scoppiato (P. Is Burst)*, a drawing of a traditional nuclear family in *Giovanni Smith e Signora (Giovanni Smith and Wife)*, and a number of unnamed "Ominidi" or "hominids": humanoid progenitors of a new human race. Manzoni had depicted similar hovering humanoids in many of his "Nuclearist" paintings of the late 1950s, and his fleeting return to this subject matter in 1960 could be considered a regression by critics who privilege his more conceptual works. Instead these drawings suggest Manzoni's continued investment in his atomic present after his break with the nuclear painters, complicating our understanding of Manzoni's meta-artistic commodity critique. Using the *Ominidi* drawings as a starting point, I argue that the thrust of Manzoni's neo-avant-garde invasion was not simply a unidirectional frontal attack on visual convention but an irreverent, multidirectional movement up and down and in and out. It is through the rhythms of Manzoni's practice that he resisted both utopic and dystopic positions by hovering between them delicately, deliberately, and, ultimately, with great difficulty.

In-and-Out (Ominidi)

The first drawing in Manzoni's series, *Paradoxus 60*, contains the most explicit references to outer space (see figure 15.4). The central alien figure is composed of a torso, coned head, and wrench-like legs. Holding what appears to be a ray gun, explosions burst on either side while an antennaed creature floats below. In the background of the drawing, vertically oriented lines evoke a lunar landscape inhabited by additional insect-like alien entities. The title *Paradoxus 60* provides a crucial frame for the narrative contained in the series of *Ominidi* drawings.[3] The Latin term *paradoxus* translates as "strange" or "contrary" to type and is used in the naming of a species whose features deviate from the dominant nature of their genus. *Paradoxus 60* thus introduces a deviant hominid whose mutation is historically located in the year of the drawings' production.

Invasions from outer space were pervasive throughout the 1950s and intensified in the later half of the decade. The fear of invasion that followed the Soviet launch of Sputnik and Sputnik II in 1957 was founded on earlier atomic rhetoric in which profound leaps in science and technology played a pivotal role. Such anxieties are manifested in the trailer to the American sci-fi film *War of the Worlds* (*La guerra dei mondi*): "The Second World War involved every continent on the globe and men turned to science for new devices of warfare which reached an unparalleled peak in their capacity for destruction.

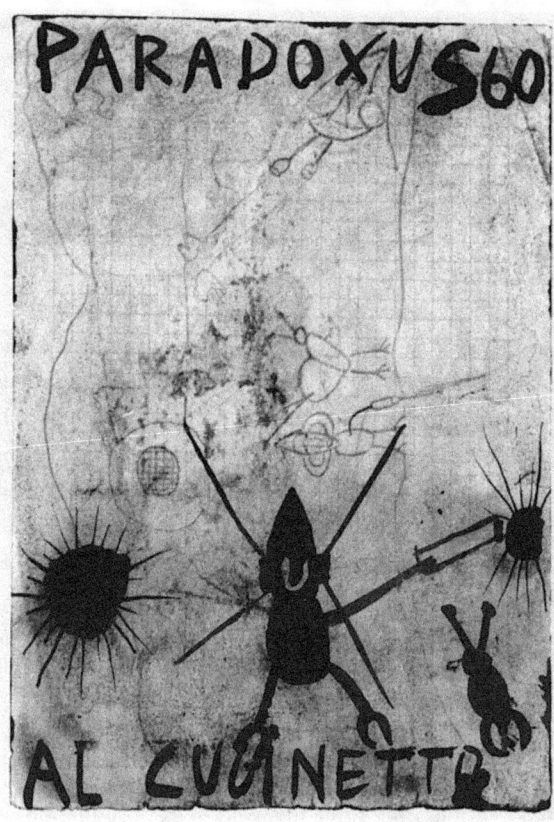

And now fought with the terrible weapons of super-science menacing all
mankind and every creature on earth, comes . . . the war of the worlds."[4] This
1953 film adaptation of H. G. Wells's novel chronicled the invasion of earth
by violent aliens that arrived on a meteorite, propagated through nests, and
attempted to annihilate the human race with ray guns and a scythe-like military strategy that swept around the globe. When *The War of the Worlds* was
released in America in 1953, the "terrible weapons of super-science" played on
popular fears surrounding atomic technologies and the threat of nuclear annihilation. Five years later, these earth-bound anxieties were turned on their
head to descend from the sky. Following the successful launch of the first
Earth-orbiting satellite by the Soviets, a "second postwar moral panic" ensued
whereby the threat of earthly destruction at the hands of nuclear arms and
missiles was compounded exponentially by the palpable presence of the Soviet satellites circling overhead.[5] By late 1959 the Soviet space program made

contact with the moon and produced images of its far side through the Lunik space program.[6] In Italy, the Lunik mission was foregrounded in the January 1, 1959, issue of the Milanese newspaper *La Corriere della Sera*. The role of space travel was central to the newspaper's predictions for the coming year, and between 1959 and 1961 Italy formalized its own national space program.[7] In Italy, as elsewhere, connections between the Cold War space race and popular science fiction were ubiquitous. The aliens and monsters of the Hollywood space operas were imported into Italy throughout the 1950s. Following the devastation of the Italian economy after the war, American films were imported for Italian consumption and included science fiction films such as *The War of the Worlds*.[8] By 1952, the term *science fiction* entered the Italian lexicon and by 1959 the expression was translated to refer to a native form of film production, the genre of "fantascienza."[9] The super-scientific lines of hovering Martian invaders are echoed in an Alpha Romeo concept car named the "disco volante" (or "flying disc") in 1952–53, an Italian term that dates from 1947; there were numerous sightings of extraterrestrial visitors on the Italian peninsula in the decades that followed.[10] Linguistic designations of this phenomenon developed as the Italians adopted the American terms *hovercraft* in 1960 and *UFO* before 1964. Indeed, the smooth lines and protrusions of the early Lunik satellites, the aliens in *The War of the Worlds*, and the disco volante sports car are echoed in the sleek silhouettes of Manzoni's *Ominidi*.

In the *Ominidi* drawings, the normative demands of communism and capitalism are implicated as a mutating force involved in the production of Manzoni's deviant genus. The drawing *Avanti* references the popular Socialist newspaper once coedited by the political theorist Antonio Gramsci in order to undermine leftist optimism.[11] Support for the Communist Party in Italy after the war weakened following the Soviet suppression of the Hungarian uprising in 1956 when there was a mass exodus from the Partito Comunista Italiano (PCI), particularly on the part of leftist intellectuals.[12] The drawing *Avanti* seems to have been shaped by the leftist intellectuals' disillusionment following 1956, offering a darker vision of Marxist ideals of vanguardism and progress. Likewise, the drawing *Duplex chinato* questions partisan politics. Its title translates to "party line" and "bow," thus calling up the deferent gestures demanded by absolute adherence to party policy. Conformity is raised in relation to domestic norms in the capitalist context in *Giovanni Smith e Signora* through a re-envisioning of the stereotypical domestic portrait. In this work's title the indigenous Italian name for John, "Giovanni," is appended to the surname Smith, forming a hybrid Italianate version of the quintessential

American title.[13] The presence of Soviet communism and American capitalism were acutely felt in postwar Italy. Geographically and ideologically positioned between the two superpowers, Italian politics were divided between the Catholic Democratic party that held power (the Democrazia Cristiana, or DC) and the national Communist Party. The PCI was the strongest Communist Party in Western Europe following the war and maintained ties to Soviet policies.[14] The popularity of the PCI in Italy after the war resulted in the Americans' economic and cultural occupation of the country for over a decade. With Italy under the sway of American interests, it is not surprising that the American defensive thermonuclear Jupiter missiles were placed on Italian soil in 1959.[15] Although these warheads were an invasion of sorts, their presence speaks more to the Italian government's complicity with—rather than the submission to—their American allies.[16] In the 1950s the Marshall Plan and the development of Fordist industry had resulted in what was known as the "economic miracle" in Italy. The incursion of films, televisions, personal automobiles, Vespas, fast food, and celebrity culture into Italy from the United States was combined with the rapid urbanization of a largely rural country. Ostensibly the most rapid modernization in the history of Europe, this new wealth was concentrated in the industrialized North, and Milan in particular.[17] Social and cultural upheavals were accompanied by the development of new technologies and medias that implicated the country within an emerging global order of social control through which a postindustrial, neocapitalist system entered the minds and bodies of Italians.[18] Linguistic recognition of this phase in the capitalist West occurred when the term "neocapitalismo" entered the Italian lexicon in 1958.[19] These changes were, in fact, connected with an insidious control of social life that Michel Foucault has termed *biopolitics*: political control that is enacted through the subject's own bodily self-regulation.[20]

In the *Ominidi* drawings, a narrative of mechanized reproduction explains the humanoid's hybrid morphology.[21] The procreation of the genus is the direct result of the utilitarian, wrench-like tools that surround, approach, and attach to the male Ominidi. In the drawing *Avanti* a single wrench directly approaches the phallus of the centrally placed figure (see figure 15.5). "Avanti," meaning "forward," could signify either a military command or a sexual come-on. By calling up the former, Manzoni seems to be making an implicit critique of modernist faith in progress that accompanied the optimism of the postwar economic boom in Italy while, at the same time, questioning the logic and purpose of the modernist artistic avant-gardes. The reference to sexual innuendo suggests that the wrench will perpetrate an act of mechanized ejaculation upon the faceless

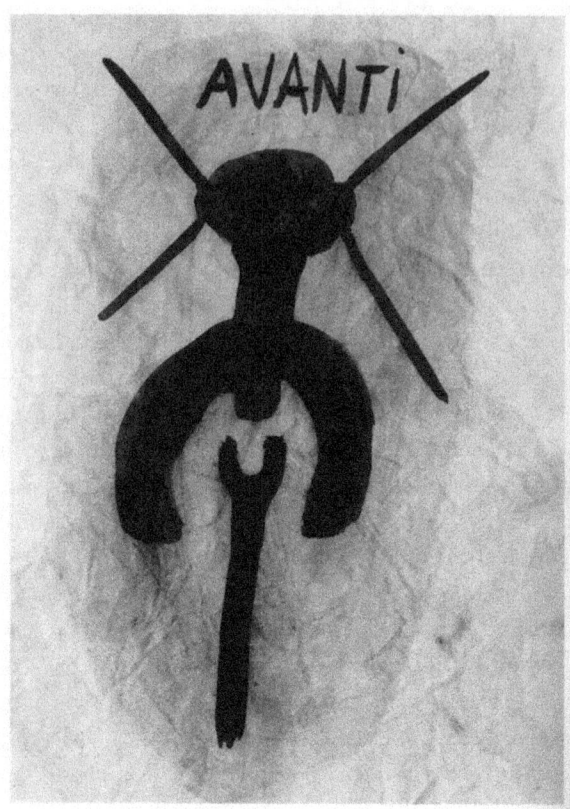

FIGURE 15.5 Piero Manzoni, *Avanti*. 1960. Ink on paper. Collection of Archivio Opera Piero Manzoni. © DACS 2015.

humanoid in *Avanti*. Manzoni had depicted similar tools swarming Omin-idi figures in earlier paintings such as the oil and tar painting *Genus* in 1957, although in these works the wrench-like shapes enact a more generalized threat than those depicted in the *Ominidi* drawings.[22] The narrative specificity of the *Ominidi* series is borne out in the drawing *Domani al mare* (*Tomorrow at the Beach*). In this drawing, a desolate shoreline is inhabited by wrenches that incubate inseminated eggs, a perfunctory role that obviates any pretense to intimate union or human connection in the process of social reproduction. The wrench-tools now act as a kind of nest or disembodied womb, a function that is underscored by the term *Ominidi* itself, which evokes the plural form of man, "uomini," and the plural form of nest, "nidi." Whereas the nests of aliens in *The War of the Worlds* threatened the human race with military annihilation, however, Manzoni's wrench-nests suggest a new kind of threat to mankind. Manzoni's 1960 genus is already invaded through the mind and body before it emerges from the super-scientific womb. The greatest threat to man is now man himself.

Manzoni's hybridized techno-humans stand in stark contrast to a contemporary series of painted collage works by the Milanese Nuclearist artist Enrico Baj. Baj's series of *Ultracorpi* depict gargantuan two-legged monsters invading idyllic mountain scenes using crudely applied brown-and-green paint that evokes the bodily and the abject (see figure 15.6). Through *detournement*, Baj superimposed these farcical monsters onto flea-market paintings of questionable artistic and moral value produced for bourgeois sensibility and taste. The juxtaposition between nostalgic pictorialism and scatological surfaces creates an absurd narrative in which an oblivious rural peasant could pass under the pseudo-triumphal archway created by an Ultracorpo's column-like legs and misshapen head-body. Cartoon eyes peer through the thick layers of paint, lending an irreverent comedic benevolence to their looming scale. These creatures and their invasion of bourgeois art thus demonstrate none of the anonymous technological infiltration of Manzoni's Ominidi. Instead, they seem to extricate the threat of invasion from the mind to the body of the subject, only to displace it even further through parody.

Enrico Baj was nearly a generation older than Manzoni, and his work participated in the utopic enthusiasm that the atomic age had inspired in artists working in Milan during the early 1950s. The postwar milieu was generally optimistic in tone, as Italians sought to recover from the dark years of isolation and repression under Fascist rule. In Italy following the war, mainstream artistic production was dominated by Social Realism on the one hand and the Art Informel on the other. Social Realist artists were supported by the PCI, which modeled the ideal of Zdoanovist cultural programming for the masses. The Art Informel (consecrated by the French critic Michel Tapié in 1952) was embraced by the centrist Italian government in the decades following the war. The Informel was dominated by an aesthetic of the humanist gesture embedded in processual materiality and abstraction. Even so, the movement was not immune to space-age rhetoric in which one artist allegorized the freedom of the paintbrush with that of a rocket.[23]

In this context, Lucio Fontana and Enrico Baj worked in Milan in the early 1950s, seeking to counter the empty abstraction and mindless stylistic replication that had led to the commercial success of the Art Informel. Milan had

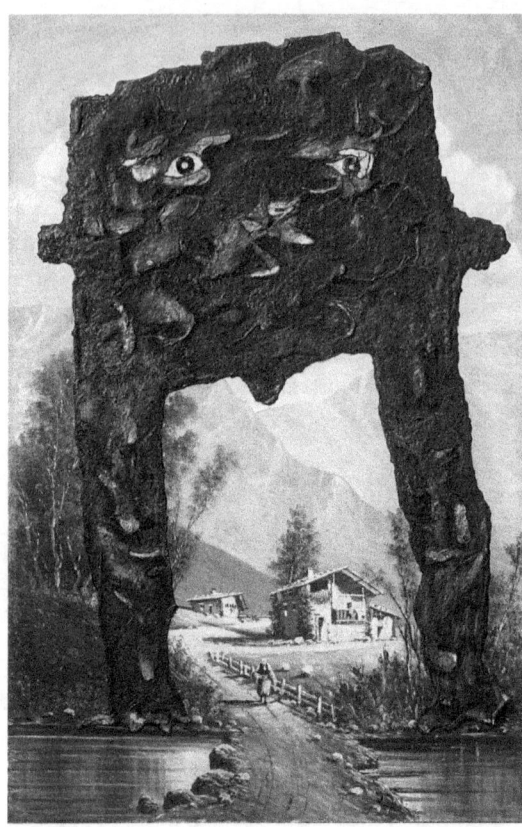

FIGURE 15.6 Enrico Baj,
Ultracorpo in Svizzera
(*Ultrabody in Switzerland* or
*Bodysnatcher in Switzer-
land*), 1959. Oil and collage
on canvas. Courtesy of the
Estate of Enrico Baj.

not been the hub of such avant-garde activity since the Futurists and, like the
Futurists, Fontana and Baj reinvigorated the avant-garde optimism toward
technology.[24] Lucio Fontana, Manzoni's family acquaintance and eventual
colleague, first advocated an art liberated by the potentiality of technology in
his "Manifesto Bianco" of 1947.[25] Fontana's Spatialist manifestos of the 1950s
mobilized technologies such as television to develop the idea of "an art in
and of space."[26] At this moment of synthesis between art and science, Fontana proclaimed: "Man's true conquest of space is his detachment from the
earth, from the horizon line, which for thousands of years was the basis of
his aesthetics and proportions. Thus the fourth dimension is born, volume is
now truly contained in space in all its dimensions."[27] Although the immate-
riality and conceptualism evoked through the broadcast media of television
sought new alternatives for artistic production, Fontana ultimately retained
the canvas as his site of avant-garde interrogations. His radical works of the

early 1950s were produced by piercing the canvas and, in 1958, he infamously began to slash the canvas support.[28] Enrico Baj began to organize intellectual gatherings in the jazz cellars of Milan in 1951 in response to Fontana's transcendent goals for art.[29] It was in this milieu that Baj composed the "Manifeste de la peinture nucléaire" (Manifesto of nuclear painting) with Sergio Dangelo in 1952.[30] For the Nuclearists, the fear of the atom bomb was transformed into a potential for reconceiving humanity and art whereby the specter of total annihilation was appropriated to serve a desire for constant self-annihilation and the refusal of stylistic convention. Like Fontana, the Nuclearist movement remained committed to the medium of painting; through constant experimentation the artist could "reinvent painting."[31] In their material experimentations, nuclear artists produced dark, quasi-pictorial figurations in a variety of traditional and novel materials on canvas and other supports in which "all forms disintegrate: the new forms of man are those of the atomic universe."[32]

During the late 1950s Manzoni began working with the Nuclearists and in 1957 signed their manifesto "Contro lo stile" (Against style).[33] Fontana and Manzoni exhibited with Baj during this period, seeking out new artistic solutions to the radical upheavals facing the contemporary free man.[34] Together, the three artists participated in a renewed interest in the Dadaist strategies of Picabia and Duchamp in Milan.[35] Manzoni's work from this period was diverse and included his *Achromes,* paintings of Ominidi-like figures, and canvases that were repetitively imprinted with objects dipped in tar and other materials. The Dadaist strategy provided a way of working between the apolitical materiality of the Art Informel and the explicit political painting of the Social Realists.[36] As the decade drew to a close and the elder two artists retained their engagement to painting, however, their collaborations slowed until Manzoni ultimately broke from the Nuclearist group in 1959.

Every invasion requires an arrival, and in the case of Manzoni and Baj's respective series of *Ultracorpi* and *Ominidi* this arrival took place in a 1958 collaborative work by the two artists. *Arrivano Gli Ultracorpi* (The Ultracorpi are arriving) depicts an Ultracorpo on a horizontally applied kaolin ground that evokes a bleak landscape. Upon the white clay used by Manzoni in many of his *Achromes,* the Ultracorpo lumbers clumsily over the horizon line. *Arrivano Gli Ultracorpi* signals Manzoni and Baj's shared engagement with popular American science fiction film just prior to Manzoni's split from the Nuclearists: the term *Ultracorpi* comes from the American sci-fi film *Invasion of the Body Snatchers,* which was released in Italy in 1957 as *L'invasione degli Ultracorpi.*[37] Whereas mankind was threatened by the military might of Martian ray guns in *The War of the Worlds*, in *Invasion of the Body Snatchers* mankind's enemy is far more insidious. The protagonist Miles and his ill-fated high school sweetheart Becky struggle to escape their hometown as it is overrun with alien pod people. Vegetal pods containing a blank alien body would take on the physical likeness of the nearest townsperson, down to the detail of his or her fingerprints. Once the transformation was complete, the alien double was physically indistinguishable from the original person, lacking only his or her emotions. The invasion culminates in the penultimate scene when Miles, having narrowly escaped the fate of Becky and all his fellow townsfolk, runs to warn the neighboring suburbs and mankind is saved.

Through parody, Baj's *Ultracorpi* externalize the Cold War hysteria that inspired films like *The Invasion of the Body Snatchers* and, indeed, Baj's works from this period mobilize similar strategies. In one such series, Baj superimposed UFOs over paintings of ocean scenes. In another series, he painted crude alien figures over paintings of titillating nude figures so that they appear to grope and ogle the naked bodies. The importance of humor to his subversion of invasion narratives is made evident by Baj's absurd and comedic titles.[38] In this way, Baj enacts the reconceived purpose of painting as it was described in the manifesto "Contro lo stile." This manifesto revisited the original Nuclearist goals of 1952 but, unlike the earlier Nuclearist manifesto, it focused more on the movement's successful overthrow stylistic tropes than employing an overtly optimistic nuclear rhetoric.[39] Reasserting its goals, the manifesto ends with the following passage: "Painters of an ever new and inimitable vision, for whom the canvas is each time the changeable stage of an unforeseeable 'Commedia dell'Arte.' We assert the inimitability of the work of art: and that its essence should be a 'modifying presence' in a world that no longer needs celebrative representations but presences."[40] Although both Baj and Manzoni were among those who signed "Contro Lo stile" in September 1957, by 1959 their different paths spoke to the depth to which they responded to their "world that no longer needs celebrative representations." Referencing the Commedia dell'Arte, a traditional form of Italian popular theater, Baj revivifies strategies of comedic parody and exaggeration. By contrast, the antipictorialism of Manzoni's silhouetted figures tends toward the kind of iconoclastic interrogation that gave the Dadaist movement its original force. Whereas Baj remains devoted to the potential of representation as a committed artist, Manzoni's work signals his commitment to the experience of modern life. Baj's *Ultracorpi* are visible, nameable, and therefore (at least psychically) less threatening. The threat of the *Ominidi*, by contrast, was silent and nearly impossible to identify or inextricable from the body, thus bringing them closer in kind to Don Siegel's body snatchers than the *Ultracorpi* that were named after the pod people. Manzoni's *Ominidi* are not made of externalized, naturalized stuff that has been safely expelled and remains outside of the subject. Rather, they are rendered in a shadow-like silhouette that was used so frequently in science fiction films to indicate the threat of an ominous presence or the charred remains of a victim of alien ray guns.[41] For Manzoni, the threat to modern man is not superimposed or clearly visible. It is integrated with the surface and stuff of life.

Hope, anguish, utopia, and dystopia are all at play in Manzoni's space-age invasion. The *Ominidi* drawings point toward Manzoni's "atopic" attitude. Like the rejection of color in the *Achromes*, Manzoni denies simplistic binary positions, adopting a more nihilistic stance as the somber silhouettes veer toward the dystopic yet ultimately resist facile moralizing. The *Ominidi* do not succumb to either the base matter of Baj's excrement-like *Ultracorpi* or the transcendent pretensions of Lucio Fontana's slashed canvases. Instead, they hover between the ground and the sky in a state of invasion endured from the outside in, and the inside out. In the difficult space between two positions, these hybrid humanoids announce the presence of an emergent neocapitalist subject. The paradoxus of 1960 is simultaneously threatened from above via the silent surveillance of a new global order, while forced to internalize and reproduce social control from within.

Up-and-Down (Lines)

The fact that the *Ominidi* series was not exhibited during Manzoni's lifetime should not preclude their consideration in relationship to Manzoni's publicly exhibited works of the same period: the *Linee* that opened the gallery Azimut in 1959 and the performance-event *Consumazione dell'arte dinamica del pubblico divorare l'arte* (*The Consumption of Art Devoured by an Art Consuming Public*) that closed its doors in 1960.[42] Rather than considering the *Ominidi* series to be marginal to Manzoni's more conceptual works, sci-fi references and the controlled existence of the neoliberal subject manifest themselves in these two bodies of work. Manzoni opened the Galerie Azimut with Enrico Castellani and Agostino Bonalumi in December 1959 with an exhibition of twelve *Linee*. This new work had been produced in printing factories during the autumn of 1959.[43] Working with the machinery and laborers of that industry, Manzoni would press an ink-filled sponge to the surface of a large roll of paper as it spun from one reel to another beneath his stationary hand (see figure 15.7). The "lined" paper was cut at various lengths, individually rolled, and contained within labeled black cardboard tubes to be priced and sold according to their length. When visitors descended into the subterranean Galerie Azimut they saw eleven *Linee* placed on small shelves and dramatically lit from above, and a single *Linea* removed from its tube and displayed horizontally along one wall.

In contrast to Manzoni's newfound antipictorialism, Enrico Baj continued to produce the *Ultracorpi* in 1959.[44] His first generals were produced in this year, parodying masculinist militarism by depicting cookie-cutter figures costumed using wallpaper, yarn, and sequins. A few years later, Baj planted similar characters firmly on a clearly delineated and densely materialized horizon.[45] Whether depicting Ultracorpi or generals, Baj's interests remained situated firmly on the ground with a clear view to the future. By this account of Manzoni and Baj's work circa 1959, the dominant historiographic characterization of Manzoni's definitive break with the Nuclearists appears accurate. Indeed, Manzoni did eventually split with the Nuclearists by the end of that year. Manzoni worked on an edition of Fontana's Nuclearist publication *Il Gesto* in early 1959 but he did not involve himself in its last volume. More importantly, Manzoni did not sign the interplanetary manifesto that was published in that edition. Whereas "Contro lo stile" largely eschewed atomic rhetoric, the "Interplanetary Manifesto" relocated such strategies up into the cosmic skies of the post-Sputnik era, adopting a tone that was almost parodic of the optimism of the founding Nuclearist manifesto of 1952. In the end, however, a sincere proclamation is made in its final lines: "in spite of this, a new hope guides our sensitivity toward the interplanetary aspect of artistic pursuits."[46] Thus, the new hope felt by the Nuclearists in 1959 lay in the intellectual and aesthetic travels of the liberated artist as articulated in the "Interplanetary Manifesto." Lucio Fontana, although he did not sign this Nuclearist document, voiced his continued investment in man's detachment from the earth's surface in an interview from 1968: "Today we are still too firmly glued to the earth."[47] Having not signed the "Interplanetary Manifesto," Manzoni's new hope rejected strategies of painterly pictorialism and cosmic optimism. But this did not result in Manzoni's complete rejection of his previous engagement with Cold War technologies and emerging mechanisms of biopolitical control. References to his specifically space-age historical context are implicit in many aspects of Manzoni's work following the split from the Nuclearists, as the case of the *Linee* will show.

A defining moment for Manzoni's shifting interests and allegiances occurred when he cofounded the gallery Azimut and journal *Azimuth*. The term *azimuth* (from the Arabic word for "direction") is a calculation that determines the position of an object in space relative to the observer. This measurement relies on the division of the earth's horizon into 360 degrees to fix the angle that lies between the observer and an entity in the sky. The azimuth calculation is used in land surveying, military operations, and space exploration; when the first meteorite Martian spaceship fell from the sky in the beginning of *The War of the Worlds,* the operators at Pine Ridge called in the sighting using the azimuth and altitude to locate its point of arrival. Thus, Manzoni's title *Azimuth* and its French translation *Azimut* allude to the control of space rather than its free exploration. These ideas are registered in the design of the cover of *Azimuth* in which the circle and intersecting lines evoke a state in which man is reduced to a fixed, relational, and calculated position between the earth and the sky (see figure 15.8). The name *Azimuth* explicitly rejects the romanticized possibility for endless discovery described in the "Interplanetary Manifesto," the freedom of the human gesture evoked by the title of the journal *Il Gesto,* and the interests expressed by *Il Gesto*'s founder in 1951. Whereas Lucio Fontana's "new fantasies of art" posited man's necessary separation from the earth's surface, Piero Manzoni's new project imposed the same kind of precision and control that mapping technologies imposed upon earth-bound subjects.

The art critic Lorenzo Borghese's review of Manzoni's inaugural exhibition in *La Corriere della Sera* demonstrates the resonance of the titular reference to space-age calculation.[48] Borghese begins the article by explaining the meaning of the term *azimuth* and then describes his initial impression of the gallery as a kind of underground laboratory. He describes the gallery as "fantascientifica" filled with the black tubes that are "fantatechnica."[49] Reflecting on the single *Linea* that was horizontally unfurled in the subterranean space, Borghese considers the invisibility of the remaining eleven lines within their containers: "But after all, you all, without recurring to the X-rays without even seeing them, the tubes could flash a little with the brain and see with the mind all the other eleven sublime lines, sublime lines, rather maybe of space to one to two to three to four dimensions etc. Of the horizon, of azimut, maybe of an interplanetary voyage, of artificial satellites, of time, maybe, of

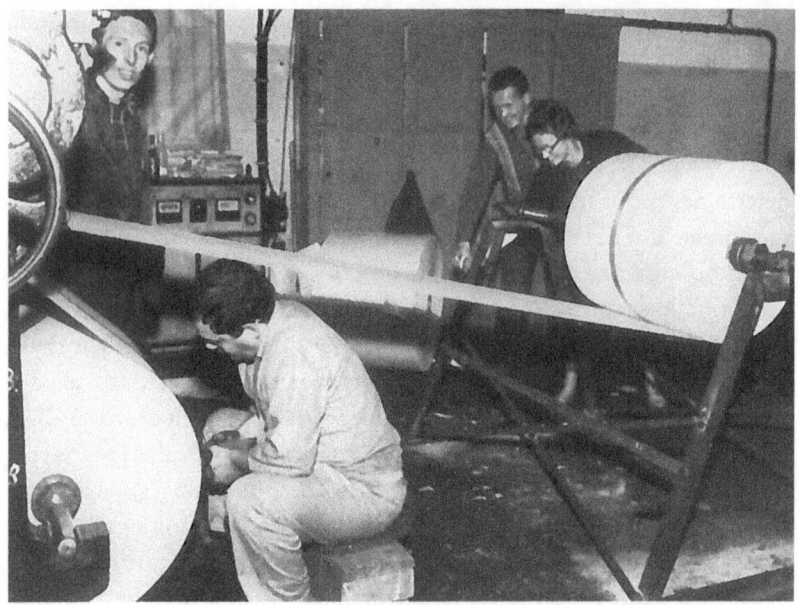

FIGURE 15.7 Piero Manzoni executing *Line, 7200 m*, in Herning, Denmark, 1960. Gelatin silver print. © DACS 2015. Photo by Eva Sorenson.

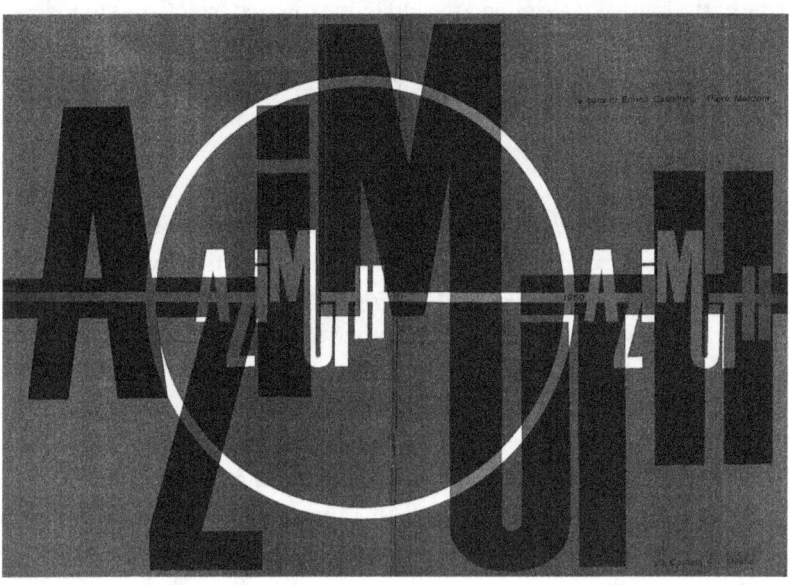

FIGURE 15.8 *Azimuth* 1, December 1959.

infinity, infinity according to the ancient Greeks, of infinity finished according to the philosophers, and modern scientists."[50] Conflating sublimity and
satellites, Borghese's reflections shift our understanding of the *Linee,* and the
discursive specificity of their radical conceptualism.[51] Through the storage
of the *Linee* in small black tubes that Borghese describes as "fantatechnica,"
Manzoni withholds them from the viewer's visual comprehension. Thus, the
invisibility of the contained lines was tied to the in-finitude of their conceptualization. Freedom, if any is to be found at the exhibition of the *Linee,*
could only be realized in the mind.

In his review, Borghese also describes his desire to turn the contained
Linee vertically and unroll them in a gallery fifty meters high. Borghese thus
conceives of an imagined voyage that would occur along the impossible axis
of a vertical horizon.[52] If, by contrast, Borghese had literally enacted his grand
gesture, the vertical unfurling would only partially expose the *Linee*: from
the embodied position of an earth-bound viewer standing on the subterranean floor of the Galerie Azimut, the reoriented display would fulfill vision
(through the removal of the work from its canister) only to deny it again (by
unfurling it upward into space). Overcoming this final denial of vision could
only occur by overthrowing gravity, through the circumambulation of the
earth, or by the ability to fly. Following Borghese's formulation, the similar
treatment of Manzoni's *Infinite Line* of 1960 would have proven the ultimate
sublime: the entirety of an unfurled line of infinite length could never be
known by rising along its vertical axis.

Manzoni's space-age sublime counters the rhetoric of cosmic travel employed by Fontana and Baj, a strategy that was not the exclusive domain of
the Nuclearists. Giuseppe Pinot Gallizio's 1959 "Manifesto della pittura industriale: Per un arte unitaria applicabile" (Manifesto of industrial painting:
For a unitary applied art) offers a critical counterpoint.[53] Pinot Gallizio lived
and worked in the northern Italian town of Alba west of Milan, just north
of the small seaside town of Albissola Marina.[54] In the 1959 manifesto, Pinot
Gallizio explains the impetus behind the newly invented "Industrial Painting" that he had been practicing since 1957, a process in which long rolls of
canvas were painted using simple machines created from printing apparatuses that were affixed with rollers.[55] Working alongside these rudimentary
contraptions, artists intervened in a process of collaboration that would produce unique works of gestural abstraction that were sold by the meter during
dynamic events that took place in galleries and at the market in Alba.[56] At
these events the long paintings were cut, draped, staged, and photographed

with the artist, models, and the purchasing public. Industrial Painting was thus conceived as a liberating form of revolutionary praxis, and as a founding member of the Situationist International, Pinot Gallizio's interests and aesthetics reflect the group's leftist activism.[57]

The utopic goals of Industrial Painting did not exclude the rhetoric of cosmic travel. In the "Manifesto della pittura industriale," Pinot Gallizio renewed Fontana's notion of the fourth dimension of space, writing that man must rise into the skies in order to found new myths. The skies are to be inhabited by this new man as the bleachers for the spectacle of freedom: "The world will be the stage and backstage of a continuous performance; the earth will turn into a vast amusement park, creating new emotions and new passions. The cosmic spectacle presented by humanity will manage to become in effect universal and visible in its all-together from a telescopic distance, forcing man to climb up to take in the entire spectacle: the front seats will be reserved in Heaven."[58] Although Pinot Gallizio maintains a tone of space-age optimism, his utopian aims and aspirations were distinct from those of Fontana and Baj. The Situationist's goal was explicitly Marxist, insofar as he sought to instigate a popular revolution that overturned the mechanization, banalization, and alienation of (post)industrial life: "Today man is part of the machine that he created, the machine now denied him, by which he is dominated. This nonsense must be reversed, or there will be no more creation; we must now dominate the machine and force it to make the single useless, anti-economic, artistic gesture, to create a new anti-economic society that is poetic, magical, artistic."[59]

Thus, machines are at the heart of Pinot Gallizio's revolution and, accordingly, the 1959 manifesto conjoins the rhetoric of space-age ascension with the potentiality of earth-bound industry. By contrast, Manzoni's work does not participate in the pleasurable and performative anticapitalism that is enacted by Pinot-Gallizio's kilometers of painted canvas.[60] Whereas Pinot Gallizio and his human collaborators regularly intervened and superseded the machinic forces at play in the process of Industrial Painting, Manzoni's rejection of the artistic gesture in his *Linee* demonstrates the artist's submission to the machine and its linear movement.[61] Moreover, Manzoni measured the lengths of the *Linee* according to an ostensibly arbitrary logic rather than the needs or desires of the consumers of a revolutionary art. Most importantly, whereas the canvases of Pinot Gallizio were displayed and utilized in spectacular participatory events, Manzoni's *Linee* were denied any use value and withheld from the sight and touch of the gallery visitor or consumer.

Imagined voyages into space may have been frustrated by Manzoni's *Linee*, but the artist evoked flight as a metaphor in his manifesto "Libera dimensione" ("Free Dimension"). Published in the second and final edition of the *Azimuth* journal in 1960, Manzoni writes in this manifesto: "The emergence of new conditions and the appearance of new problems bring with them new methods, plus a need for new solutions. You can't take off from the ground simply by running and jumping: you need wings."[62] For Manzoni, flight spoke to the urgent need for a completely new set of artistic tools in the contemporary moment and, indeed, one new method with which Manzoni sought to replace traditional painting was his *Linee*. Manzoni asks, "Why should one worry about how to arrange a line in space? . . . A long line stretching to infinity can only be drawn beyond the concerns of composition and dimension: in total space dimensions do not exist."[63] In total space, we can assume, the space calculated by the azimuth does not exist. The possibility of total space is intimately bound to the brief cerebral flash that occurs before the *Linee*. The sealed tubes contain and withhold each *Linea*, offering it to the imagination only as a sublime possibility of a fanta-senza-scienza. Thus, Manzoni's *Linee* are neither utopic nor dystopic, but offer the atopic possibility of a flash of conceptual freedom created by the impossibility of their visual comprehension. A similarly atopic aspect is manifest in Manzoni's plans for unrealized (and deliberately unrealizable) *Linee*. Manzoni proposed that he create a series of *Linee* at different locations around the globe that would, if unfurled, reach around the circumference of the earth.[64] A similar interest in the mapping of the earth's surface is found in Manzoni's proclaimed desire to draw "a white line around the entire Greenwich meridian!"[65] This irreverent invocation destabilizes the grand gestures of utopic avant-gardism.[66] Both these projects combine the tropes of historic avant-garde strategies with the mapping of the earth's surface that disallows cosmic escape to the skies.

Although the exhibited *Linee* of 1959 did not stake any heroic claims, they did not fall into pure negativity either. Germano Celant characterizes Manzoni's oeuvre in overly nihilistic terms when he states: "As a member of the post-Informale generation that had left behind the ideological and liberational myths of the postwar period, Manzoni posits no future path, no utopia; any element whatsoever is a sign of loss and negation, as well as of irony and critique of the consumerist acceleration of life."[67] For his part, Lorenzo Borghese deliberately contrasts the temper of Manzoni's work to what he calls the "lively optimism" of Michel Tapié's Art Informel. Borghese writes that when faced with the *Linee,* "nobody feels like laughing" and "all this makes me sad." The word Borghese used in this passage also translates as "heavy" and carries the association of a weight and a burden. Of this burden, Borghese writes that the tubes are "symbols, maybe, of anxiety and new anguish, and also of security and of joy, who knows, and maybe of a protest, of a rebellion again."[68] Unlike Pinot-Gallizio, Manzoni's rejection does not take him into despair but closer to anguish. Manzoni's work cannot be reduced to an entirely negative or nihilistic response to modern life, having succumbed neither to the moralizing despair of the dystopic nor to the unfettered flight of utopic pretension. In the gallery, each *Linea* sits on a shelf that is nearly invisible, creating an illusion that they are floating or hovering in space like the Ominidi, unable to move freely. Thusly situated, Manzoni's *Linee* tenuously tremble in a position that posits a future path, albeit a difficult one.

Manzoni's difficult path between utopic and dystopic positions in art runs parallel to postwar philosophical debates in Milan.[69] Italian philosophy after 1943 "hungered for bodily and . . . human experience" and sought a new objective order of "life as it was lived."[70] Italian theorists sought a new metaphysics of the eternal and the infinite that could avoid the transcendental effect of traditional metaphysical projects as well as the logical reductions of Croce's Idealist Historicism.[71] The Milanese philosopher Antonio Banfi worked through these ideas at the University of Milan until his death in 1957, and Banfi's project was continued by his student Enzo Paci in the late 1950s. Paci sought to reconcile the transcendentalism of Edmund Husserl's phenomenology with a Marxist critique of modern alienated existence and published a literary and philosophic journal titled *Aut Aut* in Milan that dealt with these philosophic interests.[72] Paci's work did not stake any transcendent claim but was instead a "metaphysics of relation, historical and naturalistic . . . a metaphysics of substance."[73] He thus articulated a philosophy of naturalism and organicism in order to work against the hypostatization and abstraction of modern man, producing a Marxist phenomenology that positioned "being" as an antidote to alienated modern existence.

Manzoni's manifestos evince his interest in substance, matter, and being.[74] His later use of the body as medium was anticipated in the 1957 "Manifesto di Albissola Marina," in which he writes that "the canvas will no longer be an arid invention devoid of meaning, the utopia of an aesthetic order . . . the folly of pure idealism without concrete, human origin. . . . Rather it will be living flesh, a direct, scalding, unaltered version of the innermost dynamics of the artist and his most secret emotions," and "all this induces us to believe that our experiences, despite their many different directions, herald the possibility of a new moral organism."[75] Through human experience Manzoni reconceives the art object as living matter, undoing its objectification. The artist thus constructs an alternate ethics for the Cartesian dualism of subject and object. This is Manzoni's "new moral organism." Life and being were discussed three years later in "Libera dimensione where Manzoni argues that value is situated in embodied being, which cannot be commodified or objectified. The lines that artists impose onto a canvas are antithetical to the needs of the modern age: "A surface with limitless possibilities has been reduced to a sort of receptacle. . . . Why not empty the receptacle, liberate this surface? Why not try to make the limitless sense of total space, of a pure and absolute light, appear instead? To suggest, to express, to represent: these are not problems today."[76] For Manzoni, the artist's freedom is guaranteed by rejecting the pictorial crutches that contain and control space. Attending to life and being in a process of becoming is shown to be the ultimate goal of art. There is, as he ends "Libera dimensione," "only to be, to live."[77] Atopic until the end, the utopic possibilities opened up by Manzoni's moral economy of embodied being are tempered by the controlled nature of his production of the *Linee*. Whereas artists such as Pinot-Gallizio appropriated the machine in art in order to transcend modernism's mechanization of life, Manzoni is present with the machine and physically located under it. Manzoni's artistic gesture is effectively annulled when he positions himself as a part of the machine, and approximates a hybridized existence closely linked to the one that is depicted in the *Ominidi* series.[78] Manzoni's mechanized production of the *Linee* echoes the narrative of disembodied reproduction in the *Ominidi* series. In both cases, the state of the subject has been reduced to a role of puritan efficiency and a state of utter alienation.

Aesthetically and philosophically, Manzoni walks a fine line between utopic and dystopic pretensions in order to open a total space between the horizontal and the vertical. This is not the free space of the Spatialists.[79] Manzoni's *Linee* do not create a liberating space that rises up infinitely into the sky, nor are they located on solid ground to be laid out like paths to follow or horizons into the future.[80] Instead, the *Linee* destabilize the viewer, posit multiple horizons, and create a psychic space where life is "tout-azimut!"[81] Hovering above the ground between the earth and sky, the modern subject is suspended in a controlled existence of the azimuth-man. Contending with these lines, Manzoni balances between hope and despair in a state of restrained anguish. This balancing along and between the lines—in and out and up and down—was, as we will see, a most difficult burden to bear.

Up-and-Down, In-and-Out (Eggs)

Many of Manzoni's works from 1959 to 1963 were documented using dramatic points of view that replicate the act of rising and falling. The viewpoint from above a *Linea* and the viewpoint from below a *Linea* mimic Borghese's fantastic act of psychic travel up and down an imagined vertical installation. The view from below a *Magic Base* and the view from above a *Magic Base* reassert the potentially endless mounting and dismounting of those who aspire to be art. Up and down like a nauseating ocean crossing or the passionate irregularities of human intercourse that was emptied from the series of drawings with which we began. Sexual overtones in the *Ominidi* series are perhaps most explicitly developed in the drawing *Avanti* in which the command "forward" is invoked at the moment just prior to contact. Indeed, both the disembodied sex act and repressive domesticity are countered in Manzoni's self-portraits. In *Io e il mio gatto* Manzoni stands stoic and alone beside his cat, rejecting the domestic role depicted in *Giovanni Smith e Signora*. Manzoni's miming of the domestic relationship contrasts his self-portrait in *P. è scoppiato*. Here Manzoni is bursting in a rapturous moment of sexual release that counters the bourgeois repression of desire, an ecstatic liberation of jouissance tempered by the memory of the ray-gun explosions depicted in *Paradoxus 60*.

If Manzoni's "atopic atomic" project is imbricated in the subject matter and rhythms of sex, it is equally pressed up against the domestic norms that were delivered throughout Italy in print and electronic media in the 1950s.[82] One such source was the American dystopic film *On the Beach* (in Italian, *L'ultima spiaggia*), released simultaneously in eighteen capitals around the world on December 17, 1959.[83] The Hollywood adaptation tracks the oscillation of hope and despair following nuclear war as radiation spreads and eventually extinguishes the human race. With plodding pacing and trite character development, *On the Beach* relies on the familial unit and romantic love to symbolize the health of the social order prior to the atomic strike. Conversely, the tragic fate of society after the war is signaled by the destruction of these relationships, articulating the dissolution of the natural order of mankind. In a particularly charged scene, a young father is forced to purchase suicide pills for his wife and infant and watch them die. In another scene, the same young man recalls seeing his future bride for the first time at the beach. In this way, the beach comes to stand for a better time of innocent love and possibility that is used to reinforce the moralistic message of this dystopian film. The shoreline, however, is also the site of the tragic good-bye between two lovers near the end of the film. Standing on a grassy bluff, a woman watches as her lover's submarine disappears under the surface of the water for the last time. There is a remarkable similarity between the grassy dune at the end of *On the Beach* and the grassy seashore on which the *Ominidi* incubate. These grassy bluffs are echoed in the isolated grass-like tuft that sits just below the uomonido Giovanni in *Giovanni Smith e Signora*, an addition that establishes narrative continuity between the domestic portrait and the scene of gestation. Ultimately, the titles *L'ultima spiaggia* and *Domani al mare* reveal a crucial distinction between the mobilization of the beach in these two works. The Italian translation of *On the Beach* suggests the finality of an end ("ultima" translates to "last") that suits the purpose of this dystopic film. By contrast, *Domani al mare* points toward a future tomorrow that takes place on the shore. The beach is no longer a site of bourgeois leisure, new love, or final good-byes. Rather, it is a desolate space where the human race is transformed into the *Paradoxus 60*.[84]

A far cry from Hollywood's moralistic eschatologies, Federico Fellini's controversial 1960 film *La dolce vita* critically examined the state of modern man as it had emerged in Italy during the peace of the postwar period and the affluence and Americanization that took place during the economic miracle.[85] The film takes place over seven days, charting the existential struggle of the protagonist Marcello in a world in which "alcohol and sex are the only values and suicide the only escape."[86] Marcello is a celebrity columnist in Rome who resists the domestic aspirations of his girlfriend Emma in order to work in the shallow celebrity scene and pursue a number of liaisons with other women. In the final scene set on the beach, Marcello turns away from the hope embodied by a young girl toward a life of debauchery and mediocrity as an agent for a second-rate actor. Thus, for Fellini, the beach is a site where Marcello rejects the choice to live an authentic existence. On the beach, Marcello transforms from an existentialist character to a purely modern subject.

Manzoni's Giovanni Smith seems more closely aligned to the character of Marcello in *La dolce vita* than any of the emotionally laden patriarchs in *On the Beach*. However, whereas Giovanni Smith does not struggle to find value and meaning in life, Marcello's struggle, though by no means melodramatic, shakes his character to the core. The faceless, silhouetted Giovanni Smith appears as calm and emotionless as the pod people in *Invasion of the Body Snatchers;* emotion is a definitive signifier of what is human in this science fiction film. Describing the alien double of her uncle, one character states that "there's no emotion. None. Just the pretense of it. The rejection of emotion that Manzoni invokes in *Giovanni Smith e Signora* is also found in a hypothetical sculpture described as follows: "In '59–'60 I studied the idea of a moving, autonomous sculpture for outdoors. This mechanical animal would be independent because it would draw its nourishment from nature (solar energy). At night it would shut down and close in on itself. In the day it would move and emit sounds, rays and antennae in order to seek energy and avoid obstacles. It would also have the ability to reproduce itself."[87] Manzoni's autonomous sculpture recalls both the morphology and the alienated reproduction of the Ominidi. Pinot Gallizio shared Manzoni's interest in the self-reproduction of machines. The inventor of Industrial Painting appropriated the biological term *parthenogenesis* in order to convey the productive role that machines could play in the creative processes of life. *Parthenogenesis* refers to the asexual reproduction of a biological organism, and by appropriating this term Pinot Gallizio subordinates the reproductive capacity of the machine to that of biological life. By contrast, Manzoni's Ominidi reproduce through a purely mechanical process that submits life to the force of the machine.[88]

Manzoni describes his autonomous sculpture without emotion, using self-consciously neutered language; the life of the mechanical animal itself abjures emotionalism. Such an existence is eerily akin to that of the joyless pod people in the *Invasion of the Body Snatchers.* This rejection of emotion in the film signifies the lack of humanity of the alien doubles who claim that "love, desire, ambition, faith—without them, life's so simple, believe me." The rejection of emotion is of a different order in *La dolce vita,* where emotion does not stand at the center of what is human but at the center of the control of modern man. In a monologue against bourgeois love, Marcello shouts at his girlfriend Emma: "A man who agrees to live like this is a finished man, he's nothing but a worm! I don't believe in your aggressive, sticky, maternal love! I don't want it, I have no use for it! This isn't love, it's brutalization!" For his part, Manzoni shows a similar interest in the coercive nature of emotion when he considered naming his gallery Pragma rather than Azimut.[89] *Pragma* refers to a practical or pragmatic love that is characterized by an efficacious paucity of emotionalism. Similarly, the lack of affect registered in Manzoni's description of the autonomous sculpture evacuates superfluous emotions from art and life and whittles existence down to the ethical state of being that is put to task against the manipulative coercion that normatively controls the modern subject.

Themes of reproduction, birth, and life are increasingly present in Manzoni's work after 1959 and reflect the imperative "to be, to live" in "Libera dimensione." Unable to do anything but be and live, the egg is a powerful metaphor in *Consumazione dell'arte dinamica del pubblico divorare l'arte*, a seventy-minute event in which Manzoni boiled seventy eggs, printed each egg with his inked thumbprint, carefully placed each in a small wooden box, and handed these out to attendees who were asked to consume the art during the event (see figure 15.9). An egg is a body yet unformed, a pure body as it were, or the potential for a future body that is more innocent than a child. In this way, Manzoni enacts a kind of filicide upon his art-egg-children (see figure 15.10). There are no grand gestures here. There is only the up and down of ink-stained digits and, through the dissipated multiplicity of an audience's digestion, the in and out of ingestion and excrement.

The fragility of life that is embodied by the eggs is registered in the shattered shells that could not stand the pressure of Manzoni's thumbprint (see figure 15.11). This pressure stands in contrast to the emancipatory gesture that Lucio Fontana used to produce his cut canvases. If Fontana's gesture indexically signifies the agency of the artist's body and the artist's ability to transcend matter and to "free space,"[90] Manzoni's act of fingerprinting subverts any heroic ideals of individuality or agency.[91] This gesture can only occur through the objectification and mechanization of Manzoni's own body as a mere stamp. Referencing a specific set of cultural practices that regulated social bodies, the controlled stamping of Manzoni's digit calls attention to the fragility of life that is subject to conditions of bodily discipline, social control, and instrumentalization.[92] Thus, the art-murderer Manzoni criminalizes himself.[93] But the performance *Consumazione dell'arte* raises not only the issue of the subjugation of the "free" subject but also the threat to the freedom of thought. In *Invasion of the Body Snatchers,* the completion of the cloning process was made visible by looking at the fingertips: once the fingerprints had been imprinted onto the pod person, the townsperson was impossible to retrieve from his or her mindless existence, and once this bodily transformation of the pod person was complete, the mindless alien clone was fully formed.[94] Intriguingly, in 1958 the term *egg-head* was translated into Italian as "testa

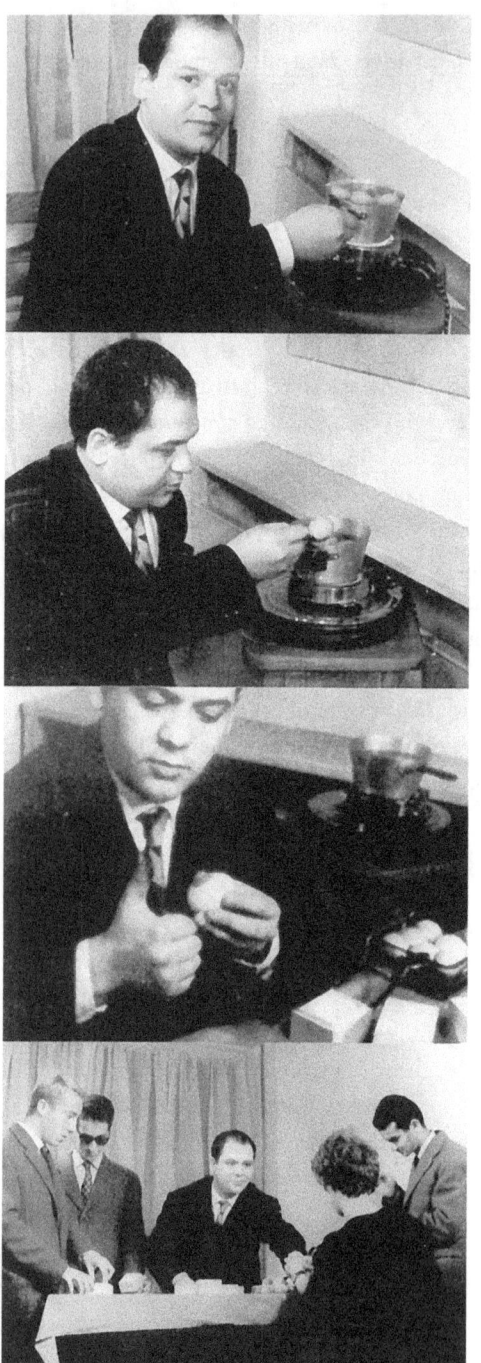

FIGURE 15.9 Giuseppe Bellone, Piero Manzoni boiling, printing, and distributing eggs during *Consumazione dell'arte dinamica del pubblico divorare l'arte* (*The Consumption of Art Devoured by an Art Consuming Public*), Milan, 1960. Gelatin silver print. © DACS 2015.

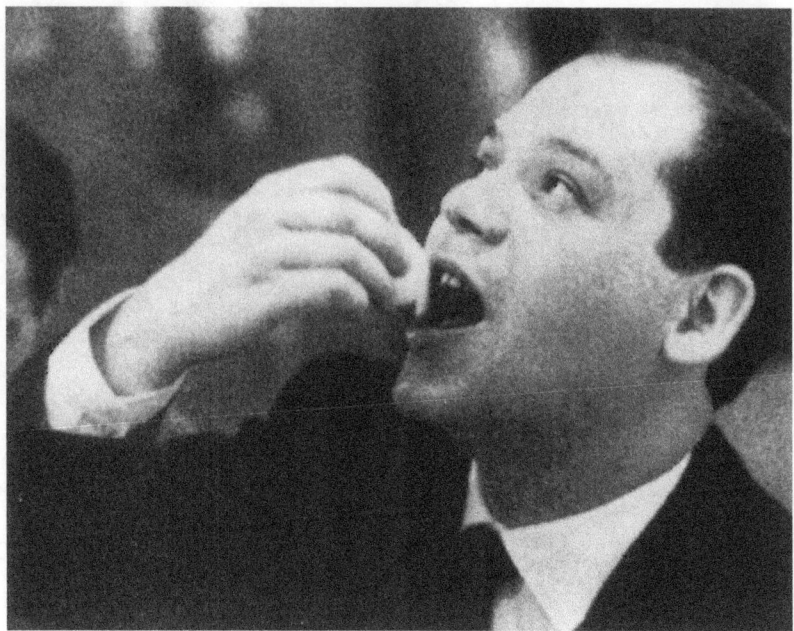

FIGURE 15.10 Installation shot. Piero Manzoni in the act of devouring art, Copenhagen, June 1960. Gelatin silver print. © DACS 2015.

d'uovo": the pure intellectual, an intellectual of the left, an American Cold War intellectual, or simply a person who thinks in theoretical terms.[95] With this in mind, the eggs in *Consumazione dell'arte* could stand for the artist-intellectual Manzoni. In this way Manzoni's thumbprints register not only the instrumentalization of the artist's body as a mere stamp but, simultaneously, the pressure of a body turned against itself. As a kind of self-portrait of the artist, Manzoni's artistic act in this performance is also one of suicide, ostensibly the only agency available to the subject who is under biopolitical control.

When Manzoni died in February 1963 it was not suicide, and yet some have implied that there is a connection between Manzoni's death and his work.[96] Marcel Broodthaers asked, "Is there a connection between his untimely death and the attitude that he took in the context of art?"[97] Enrico Baj suggested that Manzoni's early death was the result of his cerebral approach to art: "Manzoni moved into inventions that became increasingly more esoteric and conceptual. . . . He continued to protest against the artistic and critical establishment, which was then (and is perhaps also now) especially burdensome. . . .

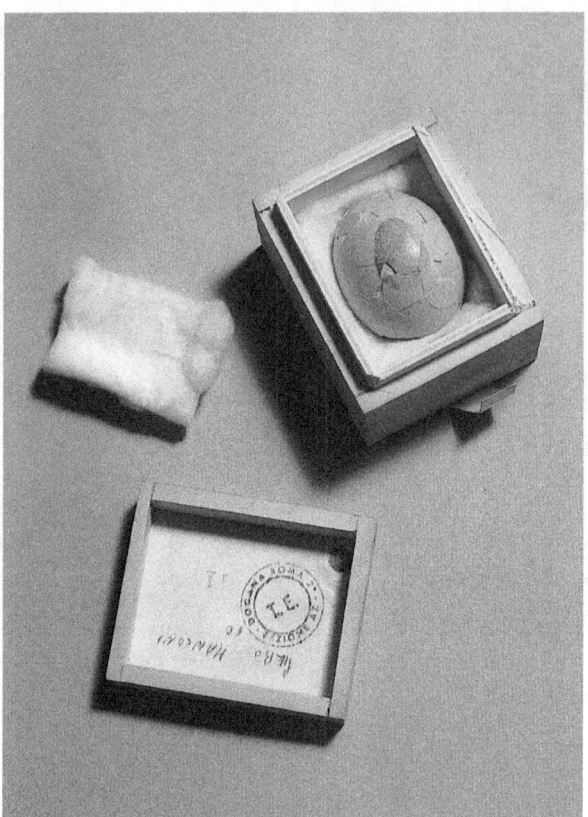

FIGURE 15.11 Piero Manzoni, *Uova n. 11* (*Egg no. 11*), 1960. Egg, ink, wood. Collection of Archivio Opera Piero Manzoni. © DACS 2015.

His rabid involvement in the polemics of art and the art world finally pushed him to the brink of psychological collapse. . . . He became increasingly restless; he started to travel and to drink heavily. By the age of thirty he had drunk himself to death."[98] Perhaps most explicitly, the art historian Alberto Abruzzese argues that Manzoni's death was his final work: a disappearing act that was a "warning for the future."[99]

Manzoni's implied filicide-suicide in *Consumazione dell'arte* and the term *testa d'uova* are intimately connected to the fate of the modern intellectual. This fate is powerfully allegorized in *La dolce vita* by Marcello's mentor, Steiner, a wealthy intellectual who is married with two young children. Only days after Marcello witnesses Steiner tucking his children into bed, Steiner murders them both in their sleep and then turns his gun on himself. This scene was a highly controversial sequence in the film but unlike Don Siegel, who acquiesced to demands for a more comforting ending to *Invasion of the Body Snatchers,* Fellini ultimately retained the scene of Steiner's death.[100] It is Marcello who receives the call from the police regarding Steiner's death. Rushing to the crime scene, he runs past the curious onlookers and paparazzi that line the long flights of stairs to Steiner's upper-floor apartment in yet another act of rising upward.[101] Inside, the police photograph the dead infants in their beds and call out measurements of the distances between the bullet holes. The scene contrasts Lucio Fontana's claim in 1969: "Nowadays in space measurement no longer exists . . . and that means that you are nothing, that man is reduced to nothing."[102] Whereas Fontana maintains that there is a freedom to be found in space, Fellini and Manzoni reassert the control of space, the body, and the subject. The measurements recall Manzoni's arbitrary lengths of *Linee* and the calculated positioning enabled by the azimuth: an existence where not only is life regimented and controlled but "everything is bureaucratized, even death."[103] Each number punctuates Marcello's response to the scene and suggests a critique of the social order that attempts to understand life and death quantitatively.

Steiner "epitomizes the fate of the modernist intellectual," according to the film historian Alessia Ricciardi, who notes the devastating postwar transformations to the life of "free" man.[104] The threat of "peace" experienced by the neocapitalist subject is directly referenced in a monologue made by Steiner in *La dolce vita*:

> Sometimes at night this darkness, this silence, weighs on me. Peace frightens me. I'm afraid of peace more than anything else. To me it seems that it's only an outer shell and that hell is hiding behind it. I think of what my children will see tomorrow. "The world will be wonderful," they tell us. From what point of view? When a phone call can announce the end of the world. One should live outside of passions, beyond emotions, in that harmony you find in completed artworks. We should learn to love each other so much, to live outside time, detached . . . detached.

Steiner's imperative to love through detachment recalls the kind of pragmatic love that interested Manzoni in the abandoned journal title *Pragma*. This mode of being and living proves too difficult for Steiner, who ultimately succumbs to the weight that accompanies modern existence. The phone call that "can announce the end of the world" in Steiner's monologue foreshadows the police call that announces the end of Marcello's world following Steiner's

death. When Marcello descends Steiner's upper-floor apartment, his character is never the same. The police cannot see what Marcello does as they call
out measurements: that if he wishes to survive he must accept the regimented
banality that surrounds him. It is this scene that can explain Marcello's choice
(made on the beach) to live inauthentically, the choice that was rejected by
Steiner and Manzoni.[105]

Ultimately, Federico Fellini's *La dolce vita* and the oeuvre of the ill-fated
artist Piero Manzoni reveal two choices available to the "liberated" neocap-
tialist subject: to live life as a kind of living death shown by Marcello's empty
existence at the end of Fellini's film; or to try to live an engaged life, which
resulted in the death of Steiner and perhaps even the tragic death of "the last
of the avant-garde," Piero Manzoni. This is the real invasion that Manzoni's
alien drawings have pointed us toward: a crisis of the subject whereby power
is reproduced by body, in a manifold invasion that moves with nauseating
regularity in-out, in-out, in-out, and in.

Notes

I would like to thank Serge Guilbaut for his perceptive comments and timely provoca-
tions, without which this chapter would not be what it is today.

1. Enrico Baj, "Scatalogical White," in *Piero Manzoni* (New York: Hirschl and Adler
Modern, 1990), 5. Baj claims this is what he thought upon first meeting Manzoni at the
Bar Giamaica in Milan.

2. See Stella Santacatterina, "Piero Manzoni: Art as Reflection on Art," *Third Text*
13, no. 45 (winter 1998–99): 23–28; Jaleh Mansoor, "We Want to Organize Disintegration," *October* 95 (winter 2001): 28–53. Of all the work on Manzoni's commodity critique, Briony Fer's *Infinite Line* stands apart. Fer argues that Manzoni's work
should be understood as a complex series of repetitions that constitute his critical
response to the conditions of modern life. The current chapter extends and expands
upon Fer's interpretive work by examining Manzoni's historical and cultural context,
the critical response to his work, and his own writings and affiliations. See Briony
Fer, *Infinite Line: Re-making Art after Modernism* (New Haven, CT: Yale University
Press, 2004).

3. My translations of the writing inserted into the *Ominidi* drawings are not those
of a native Italian speaker, let alone someone embedded in Manzoni's historical and
cultural moment. Additional nuances certainly exist within each inscription as acro-
nyms, historically specific terminology, or personal jokes. Unless otherwise noted, all
translations in this chapter are mine.

4. *The War of the Worlds,* directed by Byron Haskin (Hollywood: Paramount Pictures, 1953), DVD.

5. Sheldon Ungar, "Sputnik and the Challenge to America's Destiny," in *The Rise and Fall of Nuclearism: Fear and Faith as Determinants of the Arms Race* (University Park: Pennsylvania State University Press, 1992), 112.

6. Stephen Petersen, *Space-Age Aesthetics: Lucio Fontana, Yves Klein, and the Postwar European Avant-Garde* (University Park: Pennsylvania State University Press, 2009), 14–15.

7. Michelangelo De Maria, Lucia Orlando, and Filippo Pigliacelli, "Italy in Space, 1946–1988," European Space Agency, accessed November 22, 2008, www.esa.int/esapub /hsr/HSR_30.pdf. Italy actively participated in the space race throughout the period, including the cosmic-ray research of Edoardo Amaldi between 1947 and 1952; the rocket testing of Luigi Broglio between 1952 and 1957; the International Geophysical Year, 1957–58; and the development of a national Italian space program between 1959 and 1961.

8. Christopher Wagstaff, "Italy in the Post-War International Cinema Market," in *Italy in the Cold War: Politics, Culture, and Society, 1948–1958*, ed. Christopher Duggan and Christopher Wagstaff (Washington, DC: Berg, 1995), 89–115.

9. Luigi Cozzi, *Space Men: Il cinema italiano di fantascienza* (Rome: Profondo Rosso, 2008); Diego Zancari, "Anglo-American Linguistic Borrowings, 1947–1958," in *Italy in the Cold War: Politics, Culture, and Society, 1948–1958*, ed. Christopher Duggan and Christopher Wagstaff, 180 (Washington, DC: Berg, 1995).

10. UFO Sightings 1870–2008, Listing of Sightings and Images, accessed January 1, 2009, This site listed the following UFO sightings in Italy between 1950 and 1960: December 10, 1954, in Sicily; October 19, 1954, in Monte Carlo, Rome; October 1957, in Pescara.

11. Anthony White, "Lucio Fontana: Between Utopia and Kitsch," *Grey Room,* no. 5 (autumn 2001): 63.

12. Christopher Duggan, "Italy in the Cold War Years and the History of Fascism," in *Italy in the Cold War: Politics, Culture, and Society, 1948–1958*, ed. Christopher Duggan and Christopher Wagstaff, 1–24 (Washington, DC: Berg, 1995).

13. A painting from 1957, *Paradoxus Smith*, signals the continuity between the *Ominidi* drawings and Manzoni's previous work.

14. Duggan, "Italy in the Cold War Years," 1–24. The Italian Communist party—which had been suppressed in Mussolini's unpopular Fascist dictatorship—played a large part in liberating the North from German occupation during the Resistance period. Heroized by the majority of Italians after the war, the PCI quickly returned to their previous strength before Fascist rule. Although the PCI could never aspire to election in the climate of Allied control, the party continued to influence the course of Italian politics and culture in the postwar period before, and even after, the Soviet suppression of the Hungarian uprising in 1956.

15. Phillip Nash, *The Other Missiles of October: Eisenhower, Kennedy, and the Jupiters, 1957–1963* (Chapel Hill: University of North Carolina Press, 1997).

16. Alessandro Brogi, *A Question of Esteem: The United States and the Cold War Choices in France and Italy, 1944–1958* (Westport, CT: Praeger, 2002), 19–46. The centrist DC government sought to raise its international profile through strategical acceptance of

Americanization. Unlike the French, who resisted American interference and control on the basis of their perceived prior cultural and political superiority, the Italians saw an opportunity to build their national strength and international presence where one was previously lacking.

17. Adam Arvidsson, "The Economic Miracle: Mass Consumption and Modernization," in *Marketing Modernity: Italian Advertising from Fascism to Postmodernity* (London: Routledge, 2003), 68–89; Roberto M. Dainotto, "The Gubbio Papers: Historic Centres in the Age of the Economic Miracle," *Journal of Modern Italian Studies* 8, no. 1 (2003): 71; Stephen Gundle, "What's Good for Fiat Is Good for Italy: Television, Consumerism, and Party Identity," in *Between Hollywood and Moscow: The Italian Communists and the Challenge of Mass Culture, 1943–1991* (Durham, NC: Duke University Press, 2000), 75–105.

18. Hugh R. Slotten, "Satellite Communications, Globalization, and the Cold War," *Technology and Culture* 43 (April 2002): 315–60.

19. Zancari, "Anglo-American Linguistic Borrowings," 183.

20. Michel Foucault, "17 March 1976," in *Society Must Be Defended: Lectures at the College de France 1975–1976*, ed. Mauro Bertani and Alessandro Fontana, trans. David Macey (London: Penguin, 2003), 239–64.

21. Manzoni's narrative is interesting in relation to Pier Paolo Pasolini's description of the effect of the economic miracle as a true "anthropological mutation." See Dainotto, "The Gubbio Papers," 68.

22. While he was affiliated with the Nuclearists, Manzoni also produced paintings of rudimentary mechanical tools such as scissors, pliers, and tongs. Each canvas evoked a methodical mass of functionality by imprinting the surface with the paint- or tar-dipped objects. The low-tech tools stand in contrast to the increasing alienation developing in the postindustrial West.

23. Petersen, *Space-Age Aesthetics*, 1–4.

24. The mobilization of space-age rhetoric by avant-garde artists of the early 1950s has received increased attention in recent years. Stephen Petersen, in *Space-Age Aesthetics*, thoroughly considers this thematic in the work of Fontana, Baj, and Yves Klein. For a consideration of Fontana's Television Manifesto specifically, see Jaleh Mansoor, "Fontana's Atomic Age Abstraction: The Spatial Concepts and the Television Manifesto," *October* 124 (spring 2008): 137–56; Anthony White, "Industrial Painting's Utopias: Lucio Fontana's 'Expectations,'" *October* 124 (spring 2008): 98–124. Further references to this thematic are included in the following sources: Germano Celant, "Reasons for a Metamorphosis," in *The Italian Metamorphosis, 1943–1968*, ed. Germano Celant (New York: Guggenheim Museum Publications, 1994), xviii; Jan Van der Marck, "Milan in the 1950s: An Authentic Avant Garde," in *Baj, Fontana, Manzoni: September–October 1989* (New York: Marisa del Re Gallery, 1989), n.p.; Marcia E. Vetrocq, "Painting and Beyond: Recovery and Regeneration, 1943–1952," in *The Italian Metamorphosis, 1943–1968*, ed. Germano Celant (New York: Guggenheim Museum Publications, 1994), 27.

25. Mansoor considers Fontana's contradictory invocation of technology in her piece "Fontana's Atomic Age Abstraction." Although Fontana retained an optimistic and tran-

scendent potentiality for technology and art, his complex invocations fundamentally differed from his predecessors.

26. Petersen, *Space-Age Aesthetics,* 6.

27. Lucio Fontana, "Manifesto tecnico dello spazialismo (Technical manifesto of Spazialismo)," in *The Italian Metamorphosis, 1943–1968,* ed. Germano Celant (New York: Guggenheim Museum Publications, 1994), 714–15.

28. For more on Fontana and his later views on space-age themes, see Sarah Whitfield, *Lucio Fontana* (London: Hayward Gallery in association with Hayward Publishing, 1999), 44–47. Whitfield discusses his shift from the 1940s to the 1960s as a movement from the innocence to the harshness of man in space.

29. Fontana's Spatialist movement was open ended and did not preclude his participation in other movements. For more on the beginnings of the Nuclearist movement, see Van der Marck, "Milan in the 1950s," n.p.; Martina Corgnati, "Armaments of Imagination or Hypothesis of Resistance: From the Movimento Nucleare to Pataphysics," in *Vanished Paths: Crisis of Representation and Destruction in the Arts from the 1950s to the End of the Century* (Milan: Edizion Charta, 2000), 109; Baj, "Scatalogical White," 5.

30. Eugenia Paulicelli, "Art in Modern Italy: From the Macchiaioli to the Transvanguardia," in *Cambridge Companion to Modern Italian Culture,* ed. Zygmunt G. Barnkjo and Rebecca J. West (Cambridge: Cambridge University Press, 2001), 256.

31. Enrico Baj and Sergio Dangelo, "Manifeste de la peinture nucléaire (Manifesto of nuclear painting)," in *The Italian Metamorphosis, 1943–1968,* ed. Germano Celant (New York: Guggenheim Museum Publications, 1994), 716.

32. Baj and Dangelo, "Manifeste de la peinture nucléaire," 716.

33. Van der Marck, "Milan in the 1950s," n.p.

34. Van der Marck, "Milan in the 1950s," n.p.

35. Van der Marck, "Milan in the 1950s," n.p. Arturo Schwartz was regularly showing works of Duchamp in his gallery and Francis Picabia's writing would be featured in Manzoni's 1960 edition of the journal *Azimuth.* Picabia and Duchamp's works were also featured in the Nuclearist publication *Il Gesto.*

36. Germano Celant, "In Total Freedom: Italian Art, 1943–1968," in *The Italian Metamorphosis, 1943–1968,* ed. Germano Celant (New York: Guggenheim Museum Publications, 1994), 2–19; Carolyn Christof-Barkaglev, "Thrust into the Whirlwind: Italian Art before Arte Povera," in *Zero to Infinity: Arte Povera, 1962–1972* (Minneapolis: Walker Art Centre; New York: Distributed Art Pub, 2001), 21–40; Nancy Jachec, *Politics and Painting at the Venice Biennale, 1946–1964* (Manchester, UK: Manchester University Press, 2007), 96–116.

37. *Invasion of the Body Snatchers,* directed by Don Siegel (Los Angeles: Allied Artists, 1956). Although I argue that the collaboration signals Manzoni and Baj's shared investment in this sci-fi subject matter, the Ultracorpo in *Arrivano Gli Ultracorpi* was quite clearly Baj's unique contribution to the work. In a similar collaboration between Fontana and Baj in 1959, the horizon line for the Ultracorpo was Fontana's characteristic slash in the canvas while the Ultracorpo again seems to have been Baj's own addition.

38. Examples of this series of works include *Vieni Qua Bella Bionda* (*Come Here Blondie*) and *Esseri provenienti da altri pianeti molestano le nostre donne* (*Beings from Another Planet Molest Our Women*). Both were completed in 1959.

39. Enrico Baj et al., "Contro lo stile (Against style)," in *The Italian Metamorphosis, 1943–1968*, ed. Germano Celant (New York: Guggenheim Museum Publications, 1994), 719. The manifesto was signed by Baj and Dangelo along with international artists and critics that included Manzoni, Yves Klein, Mimo Rotelli, Pierre Restany, and Arman. On this shift, see Corgnati, "Armaments of Imagination," 111.

40. Enrico Baj et al., "Contro lo stile," 719.

41. Here I am referring to *The War of the Worlds*.

42. It appears that the drawings were produced privately for someone close to Manzoni, most probably for a cousin or friend of the artist who supported his practice. This is indicated by the large inscription on *Paradoxus 60*, "Al Cuginetto," or "to my cousin." The suffix "etto" attached to the noun *cugino* connotes a familiar or personal relationship. To my knowledge, the series was only publically exhibited once in a small exhibition of Manzoni's works on paper. Flaminio Gualdoni and Rocca Sforzesca, *Le carte di Piero Manzoni* (Milan: Charta, 1995).

43. Fer, *Infinite Line*, 35.

44. Baj exhibited a number of earlier *Ultracorpi* and other works in Paris at the Galerie Rive Gauche in the spring. See Enrico Baj and Martina Corgnati, *Enrico Baj* (Paris: Galerie Rive Gauche, 1959).

45. See, for example, Baj's *Parta a sei* (*Departure of Six*), completed in 1964. This work depicts six generals in profile marching enthusiastically uphill.

46. Enrico Baj et al., "Arte Interplanetaria (Interplanetary Art)," in *The Italian Metamorphosis, 1943–1968*, ed. Germano Celant (New York: Guggenheim Museum Publications, 1994), 724. The place of signing of this manifesto is listed as "Planet Earth."

47. Lucio Fontana, interview with Tommaso Trini, in *Declaring Space: Mark Rothko, Barnett Newman, Lucio Fontana, Yves Klein* (Fort Worth, TX: Modern Art Museum of Fort Worth in association with Prestel, 2007), 52.

48. Lorenzo Borghese, "Il Pittore che 'Crea' Linee a Metratura," *La Corriere della Sera*, December 16, 1959.

49. Borghese, "Il Pittore che 'Crea' Linee a Metratura."

50. Borghese, "Il Pittore che 'Crea' Linee a Metratura." Borghese's invocation of a fourth dimension may refer explicitly to the earlier writing of Lucio Fontana, who posited space as the fourth unifying dimension. Borghese's review may seek to situate the work of the young Piero Manzoni within a longer trajectory of avant-garde thought, and his reflections deserve further consideration in relationship to other artists' writings.

51. My interest in Manzoni's conceptualism runs parallel to the analysis of Fontana's latent conceptualism the TV Manifesto in Mansoor, "Fontana's Atomic Age Abstraction." See also Fer, *Infinite Line*, 35–37.

52. Petersen's introduction lays out the many discourses surrounding the imagined voyage into space during the postwar period. Petersen, *Space-Age Aesthetics*, 10–11. Regarding similar strategies in the historic avant-garde, see Petersen, *Space-Age Aesthetics*, 21.

53. Giuseppe Pinot Gallizio, "Manifesto della pittura industrial: Per un arte unitaria applicabile (Manifesto of industrial painting: For a unitary applied art)," in *The Italian Metamorphosis, 1943–1968*, ed. Germano Celant (New York: Guggenheim Museum Publications, 1994), 720–23.

54. In 1955 Alba was the site for the formation of the International Movement for an Imaginist Bauhaus (IMIB) between Baj, Dangelo, Askar Jorn, Piero Simondo, and Pinot Gallizio. The 1956 First World Congress of Free Artists took place in Alba, allowing members of the Lettrist International to connect with a number of art collectives, such as the IMIB. This meeting facilitated the formation of the Situationist International in the following year. Alba is relatively close to Albissola Marina, a small Ligurian resort town frequently visited by Manzoni and other members of the Milanese avant-garde. Artists who lived, worked, or visited Albissola Marina include Lucio Fontana and Enrico Baj as well as Sergio Dangelo, Askar Jorn, and several older Futurist painters and sculptors. Manzoni began visiting Albissola as a child with his family and it was there that he first met Lucio Fontana.

55. For a fuller description of this process, see Frances Stracey, "Pinot-Gallizio's 'Industrial Painting': Towards a Surplus of Life," *Oxford Art Journal* 28, no. 3 (October 2005): 396–97.

56. The exhibitions of Industrial Painting in Milan make it likely that Manzoni was familiar with this movement. Exhibitions took place in Alba, Turin, and Milan between 1957 and 1959. See Giorgina Bertolino and Francesca Comisso, eds., *Pinot Gallizio: Catalogo generale delle opere, 1953–1964* (Milan: Mazzotta, 2001), 101, 113, 129, 157. These exhibitions culminated in their display as a total environment titled "Cavern of Anti-Matter" in the Rene Drouin Galerie in Paris in May 1959. See Giorgina Bertolino and Francesca Comisso, *Pinot Gallizio*, 129; Frances Stracey, "The Caves of Gallizio and Hirschhorn: Excavations of the Present," *October* 116 (spring 2006): 88.

57. In a letter to the artist, Guy Debord called Industrial Painting "the final blow." See Bertolino and Comisso, *Pinot Gallizio*, 178.

58. Pinot Gallizio, "Manifesto della pittura industrial," 723.

59. Pinot Gallizio, "Manifesto della pittura industrial," 721.

60. On Pinot Gallizio's early development from chemist to artist (among other roles), see Nicola Pezolet, "The Cavern of Anti-Matter: Giuseppe 'Pinot' Gallizio and the Technological Imaginary of the Early Situationist International," *Grey Room* 38 (winter 2010): 64–67. Pinot-Gallizio's Experimental Laboratory of these years is interesting in relation to Lorenzo Borghese's description of the Galerie Azimut as an underground laboratory. Both Manzoni and Pinot Gallizio draw on the associations of secret science (and the atomic bunker) in their respective 1959 exhibitions. While Manzoni's Galerie Azimut is literally underground, Pinot Gallizio's Cavern of Anti-Matter evokes a subterranean space. For an analysis of this aspect of the antimatter, see Stracey, "The Caves of Gallizio and Hirschhorn," 89, 87–100.

61. Coterminous with the emergence of Industrial Painting, Manzoni was producing the dark imprints of tools (see note 22). These works indexically signified the presence of the objects. The mechanical role of scissors and other tools is underscored by the

mechanical gesture of artistic creation. This work predates the *Linee* and demonstrates Manzoni's early investment in the quasi-machinic antigesture.

62. Piero Manzoni, "Free Dimension," in *Piero Manzoni—Paintings, Reliefs and Objects* (London: Tate Gallery Publications, 1974), 46.

63. Manzoni, "Free Dimension," 46.

64. Germano Celant, "In the Territory of Piero Manzoni," in *Piero Manzoni*, ed. Germano Celant (Naples: Museo d'Arte Contemporanea Donnaregina in association with Electa, 2007), 43.

65. Fer, *Infinite Line,* 29.

66. For more on this topic and the avant-garde interest in vertical ascension, see Petersen, *Space-Age Aesthetics.*

67. Celant, "In Total Freedom," 13.

68. Borghese, "Il Pittore che 'Crea' Linee a Metratura."

69. Relatively little scholarship has explored Manzoni's writings in relation to the philosophy of the period. For a discussion of Manzoni's metaphysics, see Alberto Abruzzese, "Manzoni Incarnate," in *Piero Manzoni*, ed. Germano Celant (Naples: Museo d'Arte Contemporanea Donnaregina in association with Electa, 2007), 78–88.

70. Stephano Zecchi, "Enzo Paci: The Life World from an Empirical Approach," in *Phenomenology World Wide: Foundations, Expanding Dynamisms, Life-Engagements*, ed. Anna-Theresa Tymieniecka (Dordrecht: Klewer Academic, 2002), 479–81.

71. Nicola Abbagnano, "Philosophy in Italy," *Philosophy* 30, no. 112 (January 1955): 60–61.

72. Zecchi, "Enzo Paci," 479, 481. See also Giovanni Anceschi, "Introduction to Enzo Paci's Presentation at the 10th Triennal," *Design Issues* 18, no. 4 (autumn 2002): 50.

73. Abbagnano, "Philosophy in Italy," 61.

74. It is likely that Manzoni was aware of the philosophic discourses circulating in Milan in the 1950s, as he was a student of philosophy before he devoted himself to art. In addition, Milanese philosophical circles frequented the same bars as avant-garde artists in Milan, and it was in this milieu that Antonio Banfi became an acquaintance of Fontana in the mid-1950s. The likely contact between Manzoni and the ideas of the Milanese philosophers would be increased by Paci's journal *Aut Aut*, which translated philosophical texts and literary and cultural reviews and would have made Paci's views more widely known. I have not been able to locate any scholarship that considers this fascinating source or the connection between philosophical and artistic circles in Milan.

75. Piero Manzoni et al., "Manifesto di Albissola Marina," in *The Italian Metamorphosis, 1943–1968*, ed. Germano Celant (New York: Guggenheim Museum Publications, 1994), 718.

76. Piero Manzoni, "Free Dimension," in *Art in Theory: 1900–1990,* ed. Charles Harrison and Paul Wood (Oxford: Blackwell, 1992), 723.

77. Manzoni, "Free Dimension" (1974), 47. In the translation in Wood and Harrison's *Art in Theory: 1900–1990*, the final phrase of the manifesto is translated as: "nothing to explain: just be, and live."

78. Manzoni's practices of documentation are a fascinating and important adjunct to his artworks. His insertion into many of these photographs speaks to a self-consciousness that alternates between narcissism and an ironic spoof of the artist celebrity. See Fer, *Infinite Line*, 27.

79. Whitfield, *Lucio Fontana*, 14.

80. Manzoni explicitly states that lines are not horizon lines in "Free Dimension."

81. My thanks to Serge Guilbaut for pointing out this turn of phrase and its translation. In French, "tout-azimut" translates to "in all directions" and suggests a situation where there is no rhyme or reason (or alternatively that everything is fucked up). The postwar sense of having no solid ground to rest on is well expressed in a Disney cartoon of that period that is discussed by Petersen in *Space-Age Aesthetics*, 17.

82. Adam Arvidsson, "The New Ethic of Consumption I: The New Housewife," in *Marketing Modernity: Italian Advertising from Fascism to Postmodernity* (London: Routledge, 2003), 90–108.

83. This unprecedented film marketing event was chronicled in "San Francisco atomizzata in un apocalittico film: Proettato contempraneamente in 18 capitali," *La Corriere della Sera*, December 18, 1959.

84. Manzoni's interests are clearly different from those of a standard leftist critique of the beach. Such a critique is exemplified in Renato Guttuso's Social Realist painting *La spiaggia* (*The Beach*) of 1955–56. Nevertheless, Guttuso's painting signals the discursive purchase of this social space in the 1950s.

85. *La dolce vita* premiered in Milan in February 1960. *La dolce vita*, directed by Federico Fellini (Rome: Koch Lober Films, 1960), DVD.

86. Louise Jury and Chris Bunting, "British Cinema-Goers Fall in Love with Fellini's 'La Dolce Vita' All over Again," *Independent*, October 24, 2004.

87. Piero Manzoni, "Some Realizations, Some Experiments, Some Projects," in *Piero Manzoni—Paintings, Reliefs and Objects* (London: Tate Gallery Publications, 1974), 84.

88. A related body of work is Fontana's *Naturae* of the same period. The *Naturae* recall the vegetal pods of the *Invasion of the Body Snatchers* and evoke the sex organs of both male and female. On the asexual features of Fontana's *Naturae*, see Whitfield, *Lucio Fontana*, 34–35, 48.

89. Santacatterina, "Piero Manzoni," 24.

90. On Fontana's slash as signature, see Whitfield, *Lucio Fontana*, 19–20. His piercing and slashing was meant to open up beyond the canvas to "free space." Elio Grazioli discusses the imprint as index and the link between this indexicality and Fontana's conceptualism. Elio Grazioli, *Piero Manzoni* (Turin: Bollati Boringhieri, 2007), 90.

91. Manzoni continued to produce and sell his thumbprints after this period. The thumb is an unsettling symbol of human potentiality. The opposable thumb signals a unique human capacity for manipulation of matter. However, it is of little use without dexterous manipulations of the fingers, leading to the (admittedly anachronistic) description of being all thumbs.

92. Anthony Walsh, "The Holy Trinity and the Legacy of the Italian School of Criminal Anthropology," *Human Nature Review* 3 (2003): 1–11.

93. There is a photograph of Manzoni with a *Linea* that is not taken with either a bird's-eye or worm's-eye view but facing the artist head-on. I would argue that this photograph has the effect of a deadpan mock mug shot in which both Manzoni and his antipictorial artwork are indicted.

94. The role of the fingerprint is underscored even in the posters of the movie, which often included a palm print of a hand. This is, of course, a commentary on the blind devotion demanded not only by Communism but by American capitalism as well. See Don Siegel, interview by Stuart M. Kaminsky, "Don Siegel on the Pod Society," in *Invasion of the Body Snatchers*, ed. Al LaValley (New Brunswick, NJ: Rutgers University Press, 1989), 153.

95. Zancari, "Anglo-American Linguistic Borrowings," 168–69.

96. Most scholarship avoids a specific explanation of the nature of Manzoni's death. Among the many unsubstantiated explanations, the most consistent is that Manzoni died of alcohol poisoning or an alcohol-related liver disease such as cirrhosis. Alternatively it is believed that he died of a coronary attack. See Abruzzese, "Manzoni Incarnate," 78.

97. Mansoor, "Fontana's Atomic Age Abstraction," 53.

98. Baj, "Scatalogical White," 5.

99. Abruzzese, "Manzoni Incarnate," 78. The argument I make here is neither entirely biographical nor exactly fictional. Suggesting that Manzoni's death functions like a suicide is a deliberate interpretive strategy positioned against the historiography. My argument is deployed specifically to press upon the less committed invocations to Manzoni's death. In response, I push art history's fascination with this tragic demise to the extreme. By forcing the issue of Manzoni's death I hope to get at something at the core of his life.

100. Alessia Ricciardi, "The Spleen of Rome: Mourning Modernism in Fellini's *La dolce vita*," *Modernism/Modernity* 7, no. 2 (April 2000): 206. Don Siegel describes his alternate ending of the film in Don Siegel, "Don Siegel on the Pod Society," 153. Ernesto Laura describes the difference between the book and filmic ending in his 1957 Italian-language review of *Invasione degli Ultracorpi*. See Ernesto G. Laura, "Invasion of the Body Snatchers," in *Invasion of the Body Snatchers,* ed. Al LaValley (New Brunswick, NJ: Rutgers University Press, 1989), 182–83.

101. Significantly, this scene follows Marcello's violent monologue against love to his girlfriend Emma and defeated return to their domestic union. After receiving this call, he never returns to domestic life.

102. Lucio Fontana, interview with Carla Lonzi, in *Declaring Space: Mark Rothko, Barnett Newman, Lucio Fontana, Yves Klein* (Fort Worth, TX: Modern Art Museum of Fort Worth in association with Prestel, 2007), 41.

103. This is a line from *On the Beach* when a doctor responds to a young father's request for suicide pills for his wife and infant. *On the Beach,* directed by Stanley Kramer (Santa Monica: MGM Home Entertainment, 1959), DVD.

104. Dainotto, "The Gubbio Papers," 67–68; Ricciardi, "The Spleen of Rome," 202.

105. Steiner himself warned Marcello: "Don't be like me. Salvation doesn't lie within four walls. I'm too serious to be a dilettante and too much a dabbler to be a professional. Even the most miserable life is better than a sheltered existence in an organized society where everything is calculated and perfected."

SELECTED BIBLIOGRAPHY

Agamben, Giorgio. *The Signature of All Things: On Method*. New York: Zone Books, 2009.

Aguila, Jésus. *Le Domaine musical: Pierre Boulez et vingt ans de création contemporaine*. Paris: Fayard, 1992.

Appadurai, Arjun. *Modernity at Large: Cultural Dimensions of Globalization*. Minneapolis: University of Minnesota Press, 1996.

Arman. *Mémoires accumulés: Entretiens avec Otto Hahn*. Paris: Belfond, 1992.

Artaud, Antonin. *The Theatre and Its Double*. Translated by Victor Corti. London: Calder and Boyars, 1970.

Arvidsson, Adam. "The Economic Miracle: Mass Consumption and Modernization." In *Marketing Modernity: Italian Advertising from Fascism to Postmodernity*, 68–89. London: Routledge, 2003.

Baj, Enrico, and Sergio Dangelo. "Manifeste de la peinture nucléaire" [Manifesto of nuclear painting]. In *The Italian Metamorphosis, 1943–1968*, edited by Germano Celant. New York: Guggenheim Museum Publications, 1994.

Baker, George. *The Artwork Caught by the Tail*. Cambridge, MA: MIT Press, 2007.

Bakhtin, Mikhail. *Rabelais and His World*. Bloomington: Indiana University Press, 1984.

Barjot, Dominique, and Christophe Reveillard, eds. *L'américanisation de l'Europe occidentale au XXe siècle: Mythes et réalités*. Paris: Presses de l'université de Paris-Sorbonne, 2002.

Bataille, Georges. *The Tears of Eros*. Translated by Peter Connor. San Francisco: City Lights Books, 1989.

———. *Visions of Excess: Selected Writings, 1927–1939*. Edited and translated by Allan Stoekl. Minneapolis: University of Minnesota Press, 1985.

Belton, John. *Widescreen Cinema*. Cambridge, MA: Harvard University Press, 1992.

Bonnefoy, Françoise, ed. *Restaurant Spoerri*. Paris: Éditions du Jeu de Paume, 2002.

Bordwell, David. "Widescreen Processes and Stereophonic Sound." In *The Classical Hollywood Cinema: Film Style and Mode of Production to 1960,* edited by David Bordwell, Janet Staiger, and Kristin Thompson, 358–64. London: Routledge, 1985.

Bourdet, Claude. Preface to *La génération des blousons noirs: Problèmes de la jeunesse française,* by Émile Copfermann. Paris: Maspéro, 1962.

Bourgeois, Louise. *Destruction of the Father/Reconstruction of the Father: Writings and Interviews, 1923–1997.* Cambridge, MA: MIT Press, 1998.

Breuning, Margaret. "Pots, Pranks and Paintings," *Art Digest* 28, no. 6 (December 15, 1953): 14.

Brogi, Alessandro. *A Question of Esteem: The United States and the Cold War Choices in France and Italy, 1944–1958.* Westport, CT: Praeger, 2002.

Brottman, Mikita. "Ritual, Tension, and Relief: The Terror of *The Tingler.*" In *Planks of Reason: Essays on the Horror Film,* edited by Barry Keith Grant and Christopher Sharrett, 265–82. Rev. ed. Lanham, MD: Scarecrow, 2004.

Buchloh, Benjamin. "Figures of Authority, Ciphers of Regression." In *Art after Modernism: Rethinking Representation,* edited by Brian Wallis, 107–34. New York: New Museum of Contemporary Art; Boston: David R. Godine, 1984.

———. "Plenty or Nothing: From Yves Klein's *Le Vide* to Arman's *Le Plein.*" In *Premises: Invested Spaces in Visual Arts, Architecture, and Design from France, 1958–1998,* edited by Bernard Blistène, Alison M. Gingeras, and Alain Guiheux, 96–98. New York: Guggenheim Museum, 1998.

Burroughs, William S. *Junky.* New York: Penguin, 1977.

———. *Naked Lunch: The Restored Text.* Edited by James Grauerholz and Barry Miles. New York: Grove, 2001.

Butor, Michel. *La modification.* Paris: Éditions de Minuit, 1957.

Camfield, William A. *Francis Picabia.* Princeton, NJ: Princeton University Press, 1979.

Canaday, John. "Odd Kind of Art: Thoughts on Destruction and Creation after a Suicide in a Garden." *New York Times,* March 27, 1960.

Carrick, Jill. *Nouveau Réalisme, 1960s France, and the Neo-Avant-Garde: Topographies of Chance and Return.* Burlington, VT: Ashgate, 2010.

Caruth, Cathy. *Unclaimed Experience: Trauma, Narrative, and History.* Baltimore: Johns Hopkins University Press, 1996.

Celant, Germano, ed. *The Italian Metamorphosis, 1943–1968.* New York: Guggenheim Museum Publications, 1994.

———, ed. *Piero Manzoni.* Naples: Museo d'Arte Contemporanea Donnaregina in association with Electa, 2007.

Centre Georges Pompidou. *Paris-Paris: 1937–1957.* Paris: Éditions du Centre Pompidou; Gallimard, 1992.

Cogniat, Raymond. "L'âge de la jeunesse." *Perspectives, Bulletin d'informations et d'études critiques publié par la Biennale de Paris,* no. 1 (August 1959).

Corman, Roger, and Jim Jerome. *How I Made a Hundred Movies in Hollywood and Never Lost a Dime.* New York: Delta, 1990.

Davis, Blair. *Battle for the Bs: 1950s Hollywood and the Rebirth of Low-Budget Cinema.* New Brunswick, NJ: Rutgers University Press, 2012.

de Baecque, Antoine. *La Nouvelle Vague: Portrait d'une jeunesse.* Paris: Flammarion, 1998.

Debord, Guy. *The Society of the Spectacle.* Translated by Donald Nicholson-Smith. New York: Zone Books, 1994.

Debray, Cécile, et al. *Le Nouveau Réalisme.* Paris: Galeries Nationales du Grand Palais, Éditions de la réunion des musées nationaux/Centre Pompidou, 2007.

de Duve, Thierry. *Pictorial Nominalism: On Marcel Duchamp's Passage from Painting to the Readymade.* Translated by Dana Polan and Thierry de Duve. Minneapolis: University of Minnesota Press, 1991.

De Kesel, Marc. *Eros and Ethics: Reading Jacques Lacan's Seminar VII.* Translated by Sigi Jöttkandt. Albany: State University of New York Press, 2009.

Deleuze, Gilles. *Cinema 2: The Time Image.* London: Athlone, 1989.

Deleuze, Gilles, and Félix Guattari. *A Thousand Plateaus: Capitalism and Schizophrenia.* Translated by Brian Massumi. Minneapolis: University of Minnesota Press, 1987.

Derrida, Jacques. *Signéponge/Signsponge.* Translated by Richard Rand. New York: Columbia University Press, 1984.

Doherty, Thomas. *Teenagers and Teenpics: The Juvenilization of American Movies in the 1950s.* Philadelphia: Temple University Press, 2002.

Duchamp, Marcel. *Notes.* Paris: Flammarion, 2008.

Duggan, Christopher, and Christopher Wagstaff, eds. *Italy in the Cold War: Politics, Culture, and Society, 1948–1958.* Washington, DC: Berg, 1995.

Dutton, Jacqueline, and Colin Nettelbeck, eds. "Jazz Adventures in French Culture." Special issue, *Nottingham French Studies* 43, no. 1 (spring 2004).

Eburne, Jonathan. "Trafficking in the Void: Burroughs, Kerouac, and the Consumption of Otherness." *Modern Fiction Studies* 43, no. 1 (1997): 53–92.

Flynn, Charles, and Todd McCarthy. "The Economic Imperative: Why Was the B Movie Necessary?" In *Kings of the Bs: Working within the Hollywood System: An Anthology of Film History and Criticism,* edited by Charles Flynn and Todd McCarthy, 13–43. New York: Dutton, 1975.

Foster, Hal. *The Return of the Real.* Cambridge, MA: MIT Press, 1996.

Fraenkel, Beatrice. *La signature: Genèse d'un signe.* Paris: Gallimard, 1992.

Freud, Sigmund. *Civilization and Its Discontents.* In *The Standard Edition of the Complete Psychological Works of Sigmund Freud,* vol. 21. London: Hogarth, 1953–74.

———. *The Origins of Psychoanalysis: Letters to Wilhelm Fliess, Drafts and Notes, 1887–1902.* New York: Basic, 1954.

Gell, Alfred. *L'art et ses agents.* Brussels: Les presses du réel, 2009.

Giroud, Françoise. *La Nouvelle Vague: Portraits de la jeunesse.* Paris: Gallimard, 1958.

Greenberg, Clement. *Clement Greenberg: The Collected Essays and Criticism.* Edited by John O'Brian. 4 vols. Chicago: University of Chicago Press, 1986–93.

Guilbaut, Serge, ed. *Be-Bomb: The Transatlantic War of Images and All That Jazz, 1946–1956.* Barcelona: Barcelona Museum of Contemporary Art; Madrid: Museo Nacional Centro de Arte Reina Sofía, 2007.

————. *How New York Stole the Idea of Modern Art: Abstract Expressionism, Freedom, and the Cold War*. Chicago: University of Chicago Press, 1983.

Gundle, Stephen. "What's Good for Fiat Is Good for Italy: Television, Consumerism, and Party Identity in the 1950s." In *Between Hollywood and Moscow: The Italian Communists and the Challenge of Mass Culture, 1943–1991*, 75–105. Durham, NC: Duke University Press, 2000.

Gunning, Tom. "The Cinema of Attraction[s]: Early Film, Its Spectator and the Avant-Garde." In *The Cinema of Attractions Reloaded*, edited by Wanda Strauven, 381–88. Amsterdam: Amsterdam University Press, 2006.

Heffernan, Kevin. *Ghouls, Gimmicks, and Gold: Horror Films and the American Movie Business, 1953–1968*. Durham, NC: Duke University Press, 2004.

Holston, James. *The Modernist City: An Anthropological Critique of Brasília*. Chicago: University of Chicago Press, 1989.

Jachec, Nancy. *Politics and Painting at the Venice Biennale, 1946–1964*. Manchester, UK: Manchester University Press, 2007.

Jackson, Jeffrey. *Making Jazz French: Music and Modern Life in Interwar Paris*. Durham, NC: Duke University Press, 2003.

Jones, Amelia. *Postmodernism and the En-Gendering of Marcel Duchamp*. Cambridge: Cambridge University Press, 1995.

Jouffroy, Alain. "Les Objecteurs" (1965). In *Les pré-voyants*. Brussels: La Connaissance, 1974.

————. *Une révolution du regard: À propos de quelques peintres et sculpteurs contemporains*. Paris: Gallimard, 1964.

Klocker, Hubert, Dieter Schwarz, and Veit Loers. *Viennese Actionism*. Vol. 1, *From Action Painting to Actionism, Vienna 1960–1965*. Klagenfurt: Ritter, 1988.

————. *Viennese Actionism*. Vol. 2, *Vienna 1966–1971: The Shattered Mirror*. Klagenfurt: Ritter, 1988.

Kopjec, Joan. *Read My Desire: Lacan against the Historicists*. Cambridge, MA: MIT Press, 1994.

Krauss, Rosalind. *The Picasso Papers*. New York: Farrar, Straus and Giroux, 1998.

Kroes, Rob, Robert W. Rydell, D. F. J. Bosscher, et al. *Cultural Transmissions and Receptions: American Mass Culture in Europe*. Amsterdam: VU University Press, 1993.

Kuisel, Richard. *Seducing the French: The Dilemma of Americanization*. Berkeley: University of California Press, 1993.

LaValley, Al, ed. *Invasion of the Body Snatchers*. New Brunswick, NJ: Rutgers University Press, 1989.

Lebel, Robert. *Marcel Duchamp*. Translated by George Heard Hamilton. New York: Grove, 1959.

Malbert, Marylène. "Les relations artistiques internationales à la Biennale de Venise, 1948–1969." PhD diss., Université Paris I Panthéon-Sorbonne, 2006.

Mansoor, Jaleh. "Fontana's Atomic Age Abstraction: The Spatial Concepts and the Television Manifesto." *October* 124 (spring 2008): 137–56.

Marcadé, Bernard. *Marcel Duchamp: La vie à crédit*. Paris: Flammarion, 2007.

Michelson, Annette. "About the Biennale." *New York Herald Tribune*, October 7, 1959.

Myers, John Bernard. *Tracking the Marvelous: A Life in the New York Art World*. New York: Random House, 1983.

Nettelbeck, Colin. *Dancing with de Beauvoir: Jazz and the French*. Melbourne: Melbourne University Press, 2004.

O'Brian, John, ed. *The Flat Side of the Landscape: The Emma Lake Artists' Workshops*. Saskatoon: Mendel Art Gallery, 1989.

———. *Roy Kiyooka: The Hoarfrost Paintings*. Vancouver: UBC Fine Arts Gallery, 1992.

Payne, Carol, and Andrea Kunnard, eds. *The Cultural Work of Photography in Canada*. Montreal: McGill-Queen's University Press, 2011.

Pells, Richard. *Not Like Us: How Europeans Have Loved, Hated, and Transformed American Culture since World War II*. New York: Basic, 1997.

Petersen, Stephen. *Space-Age Aesthetics: Lucio Fontana, Yves Klein, and the Postwar European Avant-Garde*. University Park: Pennsylvania State University Press, 2009.

Ragon, Michel. *La peinture actuelle*. Paris: Fayard, 1959.

———. *L'aventure de l'art abstrait*. Paris: Robert Laffont, 1956.

Rebello, Stephen. *Alfred Hitchcock and the Making of "Psycho."* New York: Dembner Books, 1990.

Restany, Pierre. "Les Nouveaux Réalistes." In *1960: Les Nouveaux Réalistes,* Paris: MAM/Musée d'Art Moderne de la Ville de Paris, 1986.

———. "The Nouveaux Réalistes Declaration of Intention." Translated by Martha Nichols. In *Theories and Documents of Contemporary Art: A Sourcebook of Artists' Writings*, edited by Kristine Stiles and Peter Selz. Berkeley: University of California Press, 1996.

———. "U.S. Go Home and Come Back Later." *Cimaise*, series 6, no. 3 (January–February–March 1959): 36–37.

Robbe-Grillet, Alain. *Jealousy*. Translated by Richard Howard. New York: Grove, 1959.

Ross, Kristin. *Fast Cars, Clean Bodies: Decolonization and the Reordering of French Culture*. Cambridge, MA: MIT Press, 1995.

Rothberg, Michael. *Traumatic Realism: The Demands of Holocaust Representation*. Minneapolis: University of Minnesota Press, 2000.

Roueff, Olivier. *Jazz, les échelles du plaisir: Intermédiaires et culture lettrée en France au XXe siècle*. Paris: Éditions la dispute, 2013.

Schaefer, Eric. *"Bold! Daring! Shocking! True!": A History of Exploitation Films, 1919–1959*. Durham, NC: Duke University Press, 1999.

Schatz, Thomas. *The Genius of the System: Hollywood Filmmaking in the Studio Era*. New York: Pantheon, 1988.

Seitz, William Chapin. *The Art of Assemblage*. New York: Museum of Modern Art, 1961.

Shannon, Joshua. *The Disappearance of Objects: New York and the Rise of the Postmodern City*. New Haven, CT: Yale University Press, 2009.

Silverman, Max. "Horror and the Everyday in Post-Holocaust France: *Nuit et brouillard* and Concentrationary Art." *French Cultural Studies* 17, no. 1 (2006): 5–18.

Spoerri, Daniel. *Topographie anécdotée du hasard*. Paris: Éditions du Centre Pompidou, 1990.

Stracey, Frances. "Pinot-Gallizio's 'Industrial Painting': Towards a Surplus of Life." *Oxford Art Journal* 28, no. 3 (October 2005): 391–405.

Strasser, Susan. *Waste and Want: A Social History of Trash*. New York: Metropolitan Books, 1991.

Sylvester, David, ed. *Katz: Twenty-Five Years of Painting in the Saatchi Collection*. London: Saatchi Gallery, 1997.

Taylor, Michael R., ed. *Marcel Duchamp: Étant donnés*. New Haven, CT: Yale University Press, 2009.

Tinguely, Jean, and K. G. Pontus Hultén. *"Meta."* Boston: New York Graphic Society, 1975.

Tomkins, Calvin. *Duchamp: A Biography*. New York: Holt, 1998.

———. *Off the Wall: Robert Rauschenberg and the Art World of Our Time*. Garden City, NY: Doubleday, 1980.

Tournès, Ludovic. *New Orleans sur Seine: Histoire du jazz en France*. Paris: Fayard, 1999.

———. *Sciences de l'homme et politique: Les fondations philanthropiques américaines en France au XXe siècle*. Paris: Éditions des Classiques Garnier, 2011.

Truffaut, François. *Hitchcock*. New York: Simon and Schuster, 1966.

Wagnleitner, Reinhold. *Coca-Colonization and the Cold War: The Cultural Mission of the United States in Austria after the Second World War*. Chapel Hill: University of North Carolina Press, 1994.

Waldby, Catherine, and Robert Mitchell. *Tissue Economies: Blood, Organs, and Cell Lines in Late Capitalism*. Durham, NC: Duke University Press, 2006.

White, Anthony. "Lucio Fontana: Between Utopia and Kitsch." *Grey Room,* no. 5 (autumn 2001): 54–77.

Whitelaw, Anne, Brian Foss, and Sandra Paikowsky, eds. *The Visual Arts in Canada: The Twentieth Century*. Toronto: Oxford University Press, 2010.

Williams, Linda. "Discipline and Fun: Psycho and Postmodern Cinema." In *Reinventing Film Studies*, edited by Christine Gledhill and Linda Williams, 351–78. London: Arnold, 2000.

Zayas, Manuel. "Un baile de fantasmas: Entrevista a Orlando Jiménez Leal." *Encuentro de la Cultura Cubana* 50 (October 2008).

Žižek, Slavoj. *Organs without Bodies: On Deleuze and Consequences*. New York: Routledge, 2004.

CONTRIBUTORS

Carla Benzan completed her PhD dissertation at University College London and has since been a Teaching Fellow at the University College London and a Visiting Scholar and Lecturer at the University of Essex. Spanning early modern, modern, and contemporary art, her research reexamines the relationship between vision and thought by attending to the role of the body and materiality in representation. Her new project, "Suspending Disbelief: visual images and the art of falling (1570/1970)," has been awarded a Mellon Postdoctoral Fellowship at McGill University, Montreal.

Clint Burnham's most recent book is *Fredric Jameson and the Wolf of Wall Street*. He teaches at Simon Fraser University and is a member of the Vancouver Lacan Salon.

Jill Carrick (PhD Bryn Mawr College) teaches art history and cultural theory at Carleton University, Ottawa. She is the author of *Nouveau Réalisme, 1960s France, and the Neo-avant-garde: Topographies of Chance and Return* and articles on "Nouveau Réalisme" in journals such as *Oxford Art Journal* and exhibition catalogues such as *Nouveau Réalisme*, Centre Pompidou, Paris. In 2010, she was a Chercheur Invité in Paris at the Institut national d'histoire de l'art (INHA).

Éric de Chassey has been professor of Contemporary Art at François Rabelais University in Tours and Director of the French Academy at the Villa Medici in Rome. He has published extensively on French and American Art: *La violence décorative: Matisse aux États-Unis*; *La peinture efficace: Une histoire de l'abstraction aux États-Unis, 1910–1960* (2001); *Made in USA, l'art américain, 1908–1947* (2001); and *Platitudes, une histoire de la platitude dans la photographie* (2007). He has also curated several exhibitions, including *La Force de l'Art*, Grand Palais, Paris (2006) and *Repartir à Zéro: Comme si la Peinture n'avait jamais existé: 1945–1949*, Musée des Beaux-Arts de Lyon (2008).

Mari Dumett is an arts writer, art historian, and curator. She teaches at the Fashion Institute of Technology, SUNY and at the Institute for Curatorial Practice in Performance at Wesleyan University, with a focus on contemporary art in a global context. Her writing on art and culture appears in journals and exhibition catalogues, and her book *Corporate Imaginations: Fluxus Strategies for Living* will be published in 2017. She won a 2015 Meiss/Mellon Author's Book Award.

Serge Guilbaut is Professor of Art History Emeritus at the University of British Columbia in Vancouver. He has published *How New York Stole the Idea of Modern Art: Abstract Expressionism, Freedom and the Cold War* (1983); *Voir, Ne pas Voir, Faut Voir: Essais sur la perception et la non-perception des oeuvres* (1994); and *Los espejismos de la imagen* (2009). In 2013, he edited *Chatting with Henri Matisse: The Lost 1941 Interview*. He has also curated the exhibition *Be-Bomb: The Transatlantic War of Images and All That Jazz, 1946–1956* (Barcelona: MACBA, 2007).

Luc Lang is a novelist who teaches aesthetics at the Ecole Nationale Supérieure d'Art de Paris at Cergy-Pontoise. His novel *Voyage sur la ligne d'horizon* (1988) received several awards, including Le Prix Jean-Freustié in 1988 and Le Prix Charles Oulmont in 1989. He has written ten novels and several books on theory and art, including *Les Invisibles: 12 récits sur l'art contemporain* (2002) and *Délit de fiction: la littérature, pourquoi?* (2011).

Hadrien Laroche was born in Paris and he is a former student of the École Normale Supérieure. He completed his doctorate in philosophy under Jacques Derrida at the École des Hautes Etudes en Sciences Sociales (EHESS). He is the author of fictions (*Les Orphelins; La Restitution; Qui va là!*) as well as essays (*Le Dernier Genet; Duchamp Déchets: les hommes, les objets, la catastrophe*).

Aleca Le Blanc is a scholar of modernism, specializing in Brazilian art and architecture of the twentieth century. She teaches at the University of California, Riverside. She is currently developing a multi-year research project entitled "The Material of Form: Industrialism and the Latin American Avant-Garde." Her publications include: "Traveling through Time and Space: Calder in Brazil," in *Calder and Abstraction: From Avant-Garde to Iconic* (Los Angeles County Museum of Art and Prestel Publishing, 2013), and "*Palmeiras* and *Pilotis:* Promoting Brazil with Modern Architecture," *Third Text: Brazil Special Issue* (February 2012).

Richard Leeman teaches art history at the Université de Bordeaux. He has published *Cy Twombly, Peindre, Dessiner, Ecrire* (2004) and has edited several books about art criticism in postwar France, including *Pierre Restany* (INHA 2009) and *Michel Ragon* (2013).

Tom McDonough is a writer and critic based in central New York and Toronto whose work addresses the intersections of art and political struggle in the postwar era, with a special emphasis on France. He has taught at University of California, Berkeley, and at Harvard, and currently is Associate Professor of Art History at

Binghamton University, State University of New York. He has published extensively on Situationism, including *"The Beautiful Language of My Century": Reinventing the Language of Contestation in Postwar France, 1945–1968* (2007).

Régis Michel is a guest professor in various universities around the world, from the USP in São Paulo to the Humboldt University in Berlin or the University of Italian Switzerland (USI), where he is currently teaching. He has curated large exhibitions and published critical studies on video art, body art, Viennese Actionism, avant-garde theater and independent or experimental cinema.

John O'Brian is an art historian, writer, and curator. He has organized exhibitions on photography and the nuclear era—*The Nuclear Machine* (Copenhagen, 2016), *Camera Atomica* (Toronto, 2015), *After the Flash* (London, 2014), *Strangelove's Weegee* (Vancouver, 2013)—and published more than a dozen books, including *Ruthless Hedonism: The American Reception of Matisse* and *Clement Greenberg: The Collected Essays and Criticism*, which he edited. He lives in Vancouver and is Professor of Art History at the University of British Columbia.

Kjetil Rødje is a postdoctoral fellow at the Department of Media, Cognition and Communication, University of Copenhagen. He is the author of *Images of Blood in American Cinema: The Tingler to The Wild Bunch* (2015) and coeditor (with Casper Bruun Jensen) of *Deleuzian Intersections: Science, Technology, Anthropology* (2010).

Tonel is an artist, critic, and curator who shares his time between Canada and Cuba. He has worked extensively in Cuba, Latin America, Europe, Canada, and the United States. His essay *Loss and Recovery of the City (in the Cinema)* was published in 2010. More recently, he has published "A Local Story in the Global Narrative: The Imagined History of Cuban Art Between Two Centuries," in *Cuba: Ficción y fantasia* (2015).

Ludovic Tournès is professor of international history at the University of Geneva. A specialist of cultural and scientific transnational circulations, cultural diplomacy and U.S.-Europe relations, he has published numerous books and articles, including *New Orleans Sur Seine: Histoire du Jazz en France* (1999); *Sciences de l'homme et politiques: Les fondations philanthropiques américaines en France au XXe siècle* (2011); *Les Etats-Unis et la Société des Nations (1914–1946): Le système international face à l'émergence d'une superpuissance* (2015).

INDEX

Page numbers followed by *f* indicate figures.

improvisation, Godard on, 23–27
Independent Group (London), 161, 174n20
Independents of Paris, 46
Industrial Painting, 291–92, 309n56
Institute of Contemporary Art (ICA),
  London, 166
Instituto Cubano del Arte e Industria
  Cinematográficos (ICAIC), 226
International Association of Art Critics
  (AICA), 234–38, 250n1
International Movement for an Imaginist
  Bauhaus (IMIB), 309n54
"Interplanetary Manifesto," 288–89
Invasion of the Body Snatchers (film),
  285–86, 298, 299, 303, 311n88
Italy, 280–83

*Jackson Pollock et la nouvelle peinture
  américaine* exhibition, 72–73
Jardim, Reynaldo, 245, 254n34
Jarzyna, Grzegorz, 200–201
jazz in France: avant-garde festivals and,
  94–96; avant-garde music and, 92;
  baroque music and, 90–91; cinema and,
  94, 95f; classical composers and, 89–90;
  cultural integration and coproduction,
  84–86; high vs. low culture and, 87–88,
  96–97; history of, 83–84; jazz critic,
  construction of, 92–93; jazzman, image
  of, 93; legitimization process, 86–87;
  popular song and, 88; Saint-Germain-
  des-prés phenomenon and, 93; Sartre on,
  82, 86–87
the Jazz Messengers, 91f, 94, 95f
Jiménez Leal, Orlando, 211, 224–28
Johns, Jasper, 73–76; *Target with Four
  Faces*, 75
Jolivet, André, 90
Jorn, Asger, 123, 309n54
Jouffroy, Alain, 16, 60–61, 129, 137–38
Joyce, James: *Finnegans Wake*, 34, 92;
  Ulysses, 205
junk culture, 160–62, 174n18, 174n22

Kafka, Franz, 199, 205
Kandinsky, Vassily, 67, 96, 118

Kane, Sarah: *4.48 Psychosis*, 200–201
Kantor, Tadeusz: *The Dead Class*, 199–200
Kaplan, Fred, 2–3
Kassel, second Documenta at, 71
Katz, Alex: *Ada*, 104; *Ada Ada*, 103f, 106–7,
  110; *Ada, Right Eye, Blue Series*, 104; *The
  Black Dress*, 106, 107f; *Blackie Walking*,
  105, 106, 108–9; circulation, 110; *Double
  Portrait of Robert Rauschenberg*, 108, 109f;
  *Double Portrait with Frames (Double
  Ada)*, 109; figuration and abstraction of
  images, 100–102; framing, 102–4; *George's
  Basketball*, 100–101; *Incident*, 111n4; *Joe
  and Jane*, 101, 110; man-made/non-man-
  made binary and, 99–100; *Marcia*, 101;
  Maxine, 106; migration of images and,
  100; Montage, 104–6; *Old Photo*, 101;
  One Flight Up, 105; positioning of, 99; *Red
  Sails*, 105; *The Red Smile*, 104; reproduc-
  tion and reduplicative portraits, 106–9;
  Vincent and Ada at Ducktrap, 105
Kennedy, John F., 229
Kerouac, Jack: *On the Road*, 13
Khrushchev, Nikita, 5, 5f
Kingsbury, Paul, 182, 185
Klein, Yves: Actionism and, 191–96, 201;
  Bos's *Homage to Yves Klein (Coming In)*,
  xf; Bos's *Homage to Yves Klein (Leaving)*,
  21f; "Contro lo stile" manifesto and,
  308n39; *Leap into the Void*, 192–95;
  living paintbrushes, 49; youth and, 65
Klüver, Billy, 154, 155, 162, 169
Kramer, Hilton, 72, 75
Krauss, Rosalind E., 115
Kubitschek, Juscelino, 234, 235, 239–41,
  249, 251n15, 251n17, 252n18

Lacan: *Seminar VII (The Ethics of Psycho-
  analysis)*, 177–83, 185
Lang, Fritz, 27
Lassaigne, Jacques, 68
Leap into the Void (Unknown), 194f
Lebel, Jean-Jacques: *Mon coeur ne bat que
  pour Picabia*, 112–14, 113f; Picabia and,
  112, 114, 119; *Wife of Caudillo Looking at
  Avida Dollars*, 122

Le *Mouvement* show (Galerie Denise René, Paris), 164
movement v. motion, 164
Muehl, Otto, 191
Musée Cantini, Marseille, 112–15
Musée National d'Art Moderne, Paris, 60
Museu de Arte Moderna, Rio de Janeiro, 234–37, 237*f*, 246
Muybridge, Eadweard, 108

negation in Nouveau Réalisme, 142, 150n48
"Neighbors and Other Monsters" (Žižek), 181–83
neighbors and the Thing in the Other: Burrough's *Naked Lunch* and, 177–78, 183–88; Freud on, 178–80, 182; Lacan's *Seminar VII* and, 177–83; Žižek on, 178, 181–82, 188–89; Zolf's *The Neighbor Procedure*, 188
neo-avant-garde: Foster on futures, pasts, and, 142; Manzoni and, 275, 308n50; Nouveau Réalisme and, 140; Picabia and, 116, 123
Neoconcretism, 244, 246–49
Neo-Dada, 158–59, 168
The New American Painting exhibit, 72
"The New City—A Synthesis of the Arts" (AICA, 1959), 234–38
Newman, Barnett, 104
Newport Folk Festival, 6
New Wave (Nouvelle Vague), 6, 23, 64
New York: Dadaists, Surrealists, and, 160; Tinguely on, 160, 162–63. *See also* MoMA
New York School, second generation of, 74–75
Ngai, Sianne: *Ugly Feelings*, 184
Niemeyer, Oscar, 234, 238–41, 249, 251n11, 251n17, 252n20, 252n25
nihilism, 167, 201, 287, 293–94
Nixon, Richard, 5, 5*f*
Nouveau Réalisme (New Realism): archaeology of the present in, 129, 137–38, 146; Arman, 129, 138–43, 141*f*; "artistic baptism" of the everyday in, 132; context

of, 140; founding of, 61; Holocaust effect and, 140–42; launching of, 129–30; memory in, 129, 139–44; negation in, 142, 150n48; Restany on, 130–31, 132; Spoerri, 129, 130*f*, 131–38, 133*f*, 134*f*, 143–46; Tinguely and, 131; traumatic realism and, 142–43, 145
nouveau roman, 16, 205–10
Nouveaux Réalistes, 167–68
Nouvelle Vague (New Wave), 6, 23, 64
nuclear confrontation, specter of, 9–13
Nuclearist movement, 122–23, 278, 285–88, 291, 307n35
Nuit et Brouillard (Renais), 149n39, 150n54

L'Oeil magazine, 134–35, 136*f*
L'Œuvre du vingtième siècle festival, 96
O'Hara, Frank, 110n3
Oiticica, Hélio, 247–49; *Monocromático vermelho*, 248*f*
Oldenburg, Claes, 174n18
On the Beach (Kramer), 296–97, 312n103
the Other, the Thing in. *See* neighbors and the Thing in the Other

Paci, Enzo, 294, 310n74
Padilla, Heberto, 226
Palacio de Bellas Artes de La Habana, 211, 212, 223–25
Panassié, Hugues, 83, 87, 92–93
Pape, Lygia, 246–47, 254n34
Paris: Biennale de Paris (1959), 16, 60–61, 63–71, 156–57; commonplaces in, 69–70; international preeminence and, 70. *See also specific artists*
Parker, Charlie, 93
parthogenesis, 298
Partido Comunista Italiano (PCI), 280–81, 283, 305n14
Pasolini, Pier Paolo, 306n21
Pearlstein, Philip, 117–18
Pedrosa, Mário, 234, 235
La peinture actuelle (Ragon), 66–67
Peña, Umberto, 215, 219, 223; *Con el rayo hay que insistir*, 224*f*; *El puf! De los*

264; later films compared to, 269–71; participatory format, 262; prologue, 255–56; *Psycho* compared to, 264–66, 271; publicity stills, 12*f*, 256*f*, 257*f*, 263*f*; story, 255; studio-era A films, B films, and exploitations films and, 257–60; Waters on, 274n42

Tinguely, Jean: as anarchist, 174n17; "Art, machines and motion" lecture (ICA, London), 166; Biennale de Paris (1959) and, 60, 156; Duchamp and, 157; "Für Statik," 131, 165–66; as "Meta-Dadaist" or "Neo-Dadaist," 158–59; *Meta-matics*, 131, 156, 159–60; Rauschenberg and, 155; Spoerri and, 132; youth and, 65. See also *Homage to New York*

Tobey, Mark, 63, 73

trap pictures (*tableaux pièges*). *See* Spoerri, Daniel

traumatic realism, 142–43, 145

Truffaut, François: *The 400 Blows*, 1

Twelve Americans exhibit, 72

Tzanck, Daniel, 53–54

Urrutia, Manuel, 212

Venancio Filho, Paulo, 244

Venice Biennale, 61–63

Vian, Boris, 6

Vienna Actionism. *See* Actionism

Villeglé, Jacques, 60, 65

Wallace, Ian, 53

Warhol, Andy: *Edith Scull Thirty-Six Times*, 109

War of the Worlds (film), 278–80, 289

Waters, John, 274n42

Weissmann, Franz, 246–47

Wells, H. G., 279

Whitfield, Sarah, 307n28

Wilen, Barney, 94, 95*f*

Williams, Linda, 264–65, 266

Wittgenstein, Ludwig, 197

Wright, Frank Lloyd, 7

Youngblood, Gene, 269

youth: Biennale de Paris (1959) and, 63–68; MoMA and, 73–76; old country vs. young nation, 76–77; as problem in the 1950s, 65

Zahar, Marcel, 67

Žižek, Slavoj, 181–82, 188–89

Zolf, Rachel: *The Neighbour Procedure*, 188

www.ingramcontent.com/pod-product-compliance
Lightning Source LLC
Chambersburg PA
CBHW072130170526

45158CB00004BA/1312